21789

McCook Community College

WITHDRAWN

D1534789

# VIRGINIA WOOLF

# VIRGINIA WOOLF
## Sources of Madness and Art

JEAN O. LOVE

UNIVERSITY OF CALIFORNIA PRESS

BERKELEY    LOS ANGELES    LONDON

McCook Community College

21789

University of California Press
Berkeley and Los Angeles, California

University of California Press, Ltd.
London, England

Copyright © 1977 by The Regents of the University of California
ISBN: 0-520-03358-2
Library of Congress Catalog Card Number: 76-48004

Printed in the United States of America

*For W. W. and P. M.*
*in appreciation*

# Contents

*Contents*

Contents

# Contents

# Acknowledgments

Many people have assisted and encouraged me as I carried out the research and wrote *Virginia Woolf: Sources of Madness and Art.* Professor and Mrs. Quentin Bell answered my frequent letters of inquiry and permitted me to quote from Stephen family papers. I am in their debt, as I think all contemporary scholars of Virginia Woolf are, for their basic work on her life and for their cataloging of materials which has made subsequent research far less difficult than it would have been otherwise. Angelica Bell Garnett was most cordial and informative in answering my questions and agreed to my publishing quotations from family documents. Ann Stephen Synge, Alan Bell, and Trekkie Parsons also approved my use of excerpts from certain unpublished materials. I had helpful discussions with Nigel Nicolson to whom I extend my thanks. I express sincere gratitude to the staffs of the several research libraries in which I worked, especially to Dr. Lola Szladits, curator of the Berg Collection of the New York Library; Penelope Bulloch and the late Professor A. N. L. Munby of the Kings College Library, Cambridge, England, and the staff of the Cambridge University Library; Adrian Peasgood of the Sussex University Library; and the staff of the Manuscript Room, The British Museum. These people provided me almost instantly with the materials I requested and I had informative discussions about Virginia Woolf with several of them, particularly with Dr.

xi

## Acknowledgments

Szladits. I am most appreciative of the assistance given me by the editors and staff of the University of California Press, Los Angeles, especially Robert Y. Zachary, Nettie Lipton, Shirley Warren, and Cheryl F. Giuliano. I had the support of my colleagues at Lebanon Valley College and the staff of the Gossard Memorial Library there. I thank the College for giving me a year's sabbatical leave while I worked on the manuscript.

My friends have helped me far more than they know and I am happy to express publicly, as I have tried to do privately, my particular gratitude to some of them. Walter N. Wells and Mrs. John R. Albert assisted me in editing the manuscript and prevented a worse confusion of commas than finally reached my editors of record at the University of California Press. They also served well and ruthlessly as critics. What they lacked in tact they made up in brute sincerity; the book is better for it. Joanne Trautmann read the manuscript critically and made many valuable suggestions. She saved me from several errors of fact; those that remain are on my own head. She gave me access to her Virginia Woolf files and library, and she and Richard Kirby helped to compose the title for the book. The late Margaret Clark read and discussed in detail an early draft of the manuscript, as she did the manuscript of my first book. She was familiar with my work on Virginia Woolf for a longer period than anyone else and I am saddened that she can no longer follow its progress and see the changes that reflect her comments. Tom Heiry, Richard Kirby, Helen Ross Russell, Mrs. Herbert Levy, Astrith Deyrup, and Julie Cherry read and commented on either the entire manuscript or on selected chapters from it. I shall always be grateful to these friends and to others whose friendship continued through my years-long preoccupation with this work and my not infrequent thoughtlessness while I underwent the exigencies of writing the book. I thank Lillian Goodman for her assistance in the final typing and proofreading of the manuscript and Grace Garrett for typing the index.

## Acknowledgments

Credit is hereby given to The Henry W. and Albert A. Berg
Collection, The New York Public Library, Astor, Lenox and
Tilden Foundations, for use of Virginia Woolf's letters, diaries,
and other documents it holds.

I express my gratitude also to the authors, and/or authors'
literary estates, editors, and publishers of the following refer-
ences from which I have been given permission to quote brief
passages: *Virginia Woolf: A Biography*, vols. 1 and 2, by
Quentin Bell, The Hogarth Press, 1972; *The Flight of the
Mind*, vol. 1 of the *Letters of Virginia Woolf*, edited by Nigel
Nicolson and Joanne Trautmann, The Hogarth Press, 1975; *A
Room of One's Own*, by Virginia Woolf, The Hogarth Press,
1929; *A Writer's Diary*, by Virginia Woolf, edited by Leonard
Woolf, The Hogarth Press, 1953, 1954; *To the Lighthouse*, by
Virginia Woolf, The Hogarth Press, 1927, "Leslie Stephen," in
*The Captain's Death Bed*, by Virginia Woolf, The Hogarth
Press, 1950; *The Voyage Out*, by Virginia Woolf, The Hogarth
Press, 1915, 1957; *Beginning Again*, by Leonard Woolf, The
Hogarth Press, 1963, 1964; *Moments in Being*, by Virginia
Woolf, edited by Jeanne Schulkind, The Hogarth Press, 1976;
*Leslie Stephen: His Thought and Character in Relation to His
Time*, by Noel Annan, Harvard University Press, 1952, and
MacGibbon and Kee, Publishers, 1951; *Henry James Letters*,
vol. 1, edited by Leon Edel, Harvard University Press, 1974;
*Julia Margaret Cameron: A Victorian Family Portrait*, by
Brian Hill, St. Martin's Press, Inc., 1973; *The Life and Letters
of Sir Leslie Stephen*, by Frederic W. Maitland, Gerald Duck-
worth & Co., Ltd., 1906; *Thackeray's Daughter*, by Hester
Ritchie Fuller and Violet Hammersley, W. J. Pollack and Co.,
Ltd., 1951. Excerpts from *Virginia Woolf: A Biography*, by
Quentin Bell, *The Letters of Virginia Woolf*, vol. 1, edited by
Nigel Nicolson and Joanne Trautmann, *Beginning Again* by
Leonard Woolf and Virginia Woolf's *A Room of One's Own*,
*A Writer's Diary*, *The Captain's Death Bed*, *Moments of
Being*, *The Voyage Out*, and *To the Lighthouse* are also

*Acknowledgments*

reprinted by permission of Harcourt Brace Jovanovich, Inc.; copyright © 1972 by Quentin Bell; copyright © 1975, 1976 by Quentin Bell and Angelica Garnett; copyright © 1953, 1954, 1963, 1964, by Leonard Woolf; copyright © 1929, by Harcourt Brace Jovanich, Inc.

Finally, my appreciation (and love) go to W. W. and P. M., to whom this book is dedicated, for reasons I know best.

# 1
# Visions and Reality

*Virginia Woolf: Sources of Madness and Art* is the first of a two-part study of the more personal side of the artist's life. In the first part, I develop the history of her family as mileu and context of her early years, and her history until she was about twenty-five. By that point, her family and early experiences had made their ineradicable imprint and had determined the paradoxical tendencies of her personality and therefore of her remaining years. In the second part of the study, I will show how she realized those tendencies and lived out the paradox, as long as she was able to convince herself to live at all.

My study is not comprehensive; an excellent general biography has already been written by Quentin Bell, Virginia Woolf's nephew.[1] I have chosen to concentrate on several topics that have remained relatively enigmatic and therefore intriguing. Some of these concern the emergence of her unhappy, even tragic tendencies: her so-called madness, her physical health difficulties, her atypical sexuality, and her preoccupation with death which led finally to suicide. Other topics concern her more fortunate tendencies: her characteristic patterns of thought and her obsessive need to write and to create that eventuated in her particular form of literary art. Another topic addressed is the most profound enigma of all — the relationship between her madness and her art. I have taken seriously, though not literally, Virginia Woolf's own statements

1

about the matter. For example, she once said that madness as an experience is not entirely to be disdained and that she had found in the residue — the "lava" — of her madness most of the things she wrote about.[2] She would have been more accurate had she said only that she found many of the themes and some of the impetus for her writing in the same complexities, contradictions, and attitudes toward life that were sources of her more serious personal difficulties. In short, her madness and her art emerged from common ground, and although they were complexly interrelated, neither gave rise to the other.

Many of the facts about Virginia Woolf's life have been made public through her letters already issued,[3] through the writings of Leonard Woolf[4] and Quentin Bell, and through Nigel Nicolson's account[5] of his parents' marriage and his mother's friendships and love affairs with women, one of whom was Virginia Woolf. From these and related sources, one is able to reconstruct the general history of her madness. She had at least four serious and several minor emotional and mental breakdowns. She tried several times to take her own life and in 1941 succeeded in doing so when she became aware that she was going mad again. Her first breakdown, occurring in 1895 when she was thirteen years old, was brought on in part by her mother's death, but more specifically by her father's elaborate and half-crazed mourning. Her stage of development and her vulnerability also contributed to it. Reputedly, she made her first attempt to kill herself during that breakdown. Her second breakdown came in 1904, after her father died, when she was twenty-two. In 1910, at twenty-eight and early in 1912 at thirty, she had two minor episodes, which nevertheless were serious enough each time to require her to go into a "rest home." Her longest and most acute emotional and mental illness lasted from 1913 through 1915, her thirty-first through her thirty-third year. It began soon after her marriage to Leonard Woolf and as she finished her first novel and continued for nearly three years with one remission of several months' duration. During this time she tried at least once to kill herself and almost succeeded. Between 1916 and 1941, she had many periods of anxiety, depression, and exhilaration, and a number of close brushes with more serious emotional and mental illness. She approached madness when she completed a novel, a time when one might have expected her to be most secure and triumphant. Other breakdowns were apparently averted by her determination not to be overwhelmed and by Leonard Woolf's support and judicious care. She also had many physical problems that were usually accompanied by psychological symptoms and sometimes appeared to take the place of what otherwise would have been another period of madness.

Many acknowledged and putative facts about Virginia Woolf's sexuality have also been discussed in the references cited above. These include her emotional attraction to women, her limited sexual responsiveness to both men and women, her intimate friendships with several women, and her love affair with Vita Sackville-West. They include also her persistent but possibly inaccurate claims that her half brothers made incestuous advances.

But Virginia Woolf's tragic personal problems are only part of her story and a minor part at that. Her life history reveals many other things that must be kept in mind as one tries to understand the unhappy side of her personality. It is most important to note that her madness comprised relatively limited intervals of an extraordinarily productive and creative life. The sheer quantity of her writing establishes that she could not often have been incapacitated. Rather, she was in control of herself most of the time, although rarely if ever secure from the threat of mental and emotional disturbance.

Above all else, her life was paradoxical. Although sometimes mad, usually she was exceptionally astute and in many respects wise, though never conventionally so. She was brave and tough, one must conclude, in spite of often being frightened, depressed, and fragile. She was as fascinated with life as she was preoccupied with death, although that preoccupation was intense and lifelong. She was a practical woman as well as a gifted artist, helping her husband establish and operate Hogarth Press, a printing and publishing firm still in operation as an affiliate of Chatto and Windus. She was capable of doing manual labor for Hogarth Press and of walking long distances over rough terrain, even though she suffered from intermittent physical problems. Regardless of Virginia's sexuality, she was in love with Leonard Woolf and he with her, and they were married for nearly thirty years, apparently without regrets on either side.

Thus, the more significant aspects of Virginia Woolf's life were its variability, discrepancies, ambivalences, vacillations, and contradictions—hence its paradoxicality. She was well aware of these qualities, referring to them in her journals and letters, structuring many of her novels around dialectical themes, and universalizing her experience of life. Her novels make it most evident that the world was mediated to her and that she interpreted it as a place quite insane, where dissolution, chaos, meaninglessness, nothingness, and death were constant threats. They also show that she was able to create sense and sanity, and to reconcile some of the contradictions and to live with others, for her novels were her primary means for doing just those things.

Information from other books about Virginia Woolf has been invaluable in my study but I have relied more extensively on personal documents. Some of the more important of these for my purposes are the memoirs she wrote about her family, and her childhood and adult years; her letters, especially the several long series to people to whom she was particularly close; and her diaries. When I began my research for this book and the second part of my study, few of Virginia Woolf's personal papers had been issued. Thus much of my writing in these two books is based on materials I first studied in their original form. Since then, some of the documents have been published and others are soon to be issued. Several of the memoirs have been edited and published by Jeanne Schulkind.[6] Two volumes of the letters, edited by Nigel Nicolson and Joanne Trautmann,[7] have also been published, and four more volumes are anticipated. Most of her diaries remain unpublished, although Leonard Woolf had abstracted and published some of them.[8] Mrs. Quentin Bell is presently preparing the more than thirty remaining notebooks[9] for publication.

Virginia Woolf's novels are, in a sense, personal documents about her life. One novel, *To the Lighthouse,* is a poetic, fictionalized story about her family and herself.[10] Many of her other novels were drawn in part from her own experience. All of them are intensely personal.

Thus there is an enormous amount of personal information from the artist herself. But more important than the quantity of material is the extent of her openness and honesty and therefore of her self revelation as she wrote, whether in her diaries and letters, or in her novels. But she was able to be open only within the limits of her understanding of self and consequently dealt with many topics in a muted, diffused fashion. For example, her writing about sexuality was less than explicit and may have been the optimum expression of her own relatively diffuse, unfocussed sensuousness.

Her ability to be personal and open in her writing—indeed, her inability *not* to be candid on most topics—is related to another paradox of her life and to another source of its tragedy. Her serious problems came, in significant degree, not from repressions, although certainly there were repressions, but from her being too involved with the realities of her life and situation. She understood much about herself, yet was never able to achieve and maintain the perspective and detachment that might have put some of her problems to rest. As she suggested in *To the Lighthouse* (pp. 192-193), it was as if briefly and repeatedly she could see her world plain and whole, but was condemned always to have her understanding broken and confused again. "It seemed now as if, touched by human penitence and all its toil, divine goodness had parted the curtain and displayed behind it, single, distinct, the hare erect; the wave falling; the boat rocking, which, did we deserve them, should be ours always. But alas, divine goodness, twitching the cord, draws the curtain; it does not please him; he covers his treasures in a drench of hail, and so breaks them, so confuses them that it seems impossible that their calm should ever return or that we should ever compose from their fragments a perfect whole or read in the littered pieces the clear words of truth." But Virginia Woolf's curse, or tragedy, is good fortune for those who study her and who admire her as an artist, for she repeatedly described her moments of truth and understanding, and, like Bernard in *The Waves*,[11] she tried much of her adult life, by means of her writing, to compose the perfect whole of her own experience.

Although the subjective documents are of course fundamental for understanding Virginia Woolf's personality and problems, care is necessary in interpreting some of them in relationship to persons and events in her life. She did not always deal in "the facts," and sometimes gave inaccurate information, though less often than might be expected from someone who was periodically disturbed. The inaccurate information seems to have come less from her inability to know the facts than from her approaching so many things artistically, using metaphor, myth, and hyperbole rather than recording objective data. But anyone as involved as Virginia with her own consciousness does not always distinguish the facts about persons and events, from her experience and interpretation, her imaginative reconstructions of them. The probability that one will not make such distinctions is increased when the person is capable, as Virginia was, of thinking and remembering in highly vivid sense imagery. Sometimes she experienced memory images as vividly as sense impressions of things she was actually seeing about her at the time. Therefore, one of my tasks has been to try to make some of the distinctions that Virginia Woolf did not always choose to make or was not always able to make. Obviously the task arose only in reference to factual matters. Virginia was entitled to her opinions and other subjective reactions; her artistic interpretations have a validity of their own, apart from questions of "truth" and "reality."

Virginia was aware even in childhood that she did not always distinguish between inner and outer events, and was always alert to the fusion of subjective and objective experience, judging from the number of references she made to that phenomenon in her various writings. In her times of madness, it became more difficult, sometimes impossible, for her to make the distinctions and to a large degree her madness consisted of this problem. At other times, she achieved truly astonishing mental feats. For example, by her own report, Virginia kept her mother, Julia Stephen, "alive" through fantasy for more than thirty years after her death, and she rarely forgot that the image or phantom was a product of her imagination.[12] Although fusions of inner and outer worlds were sometimes an indication of disturbance, Virginia did not try to avoid them. Instead, she enjoyed them. Like many artists she was fascinated and exhilarated by the union of subjective and objective realms and, therefore, sometimes courted the experience.

The "portraits" Virginia Woolf liked to do of family members and friends illustrate her manner of fusing, or simply not separating, the subjective and the objective. They also exemplify the problems that arise when one tries to discover the facts

7

about her life from her private and public writings. Some of her portraits were published; the prominent examples are those of her mother and father as Mr. and Mrs. Ramsay in *To the Lighthouse,* and Vita Sackville-West in *Orlando.*[13] Virginia called[14] Katharine Hilbery in *Night and Day*[15] a portrait of her sister, Vanessa, although much of Virginia too is present in the character. Mrs. Hilbery, in the same novel, is a caricature of Anny Ritchie, W. M. Thackeray's daughter and sister-in-law of Virginia's father, Sir Leslie Stephen. Other such portraits were left among her personal papers. Studies of her mother, her brother Thoby, her sister Vanessa, and her half sister, Stella Duckworth, comprise much of Virginia's 1908 memoir.[16] "Friendships Gallery" contains her life or portrait of Violet Dickinson.[17]

Virginia did not pretend that her portraits were realistic. But neither did she construct them in the manner attributed to Lily Briscoe, Virginia's counterpart in *To the Lighthouse,* who struggles to paint the portrait of Mrs. Ramsey and James. When Lily explains her approach to portraiture to Mr. Bankes, a scientist, he is puzzled. He questions her: "What did she wish to indicate by the triangular purple shape, 'just there'? . . . It was Mrs. Ramsay reading to James, she said. She knew his objection — that no one could tell it for a human shape. But she had made no attempt at likeness, she said. For what reason had she introduced them then? he asked. Why indeed? — except that if there, in that corner, it was bright, here, in this, she felt the need of darkness. . . . Mother and child then — objects of universal veneration, and in this case the mother was famous for her beauty — might be reduced . . . to a purple shadow without irreverence. But the picture was not of them, she said. Or, not in his sense. There were other senses too in which one might reverence them. By a shadow here and a light there, for instance. Her tribute took that form if, as she vaguely supposed, a picture must be a tribute."[18]

Except for aspects of *Orlando* and for the second half of the unpublished "Friendships Gallery," Virginia was seldom as radical in her departure from the facts about people as she permitted Lily Briscoe to be. The credo she attributed to the literary character was not one that Virginia usually followed. Her portrait of her mother as Mrs. Ramsay is a case in point. Far from being a triangular purple shadow, Virginia's picture of Julia Stephen is complex and multilayered. It is at least three portraits, superimposed as if panels of a tryptich formed a montage. In one of the pictures, Virginia brought out less than complimentary, information about her mother as no one else has done. In the other pictures of Julia Stephen in the novel, Virginia gave her imagination more rein and became more mythic in constructing her tribute. However, she never reduced her mother to the image of a purple shadow—rather, she tended to exaggerate her mother's qualities as she experienced or imagined them.

Virginia's tendency to merge the subjective and objective realms in her writing is not the only problem in interpreting the personal documents. Another is Virginia's fondness for whimsy, teasing, and joking, especially in her letters. A more serious problem involves Virginia's memories of her early childhood, principally given in documents referred to here as her 1908 and her 1939-1940 memoirs.[19] Her "memories" no doubt are mixtures of true memories—impressions made at the time of the recalled events—and of Virginia's imaginative reconstructions of such events. However, her early memories were recalled with eidetic vividness that is very convincing, and most of them contain internal signs of their own validity. For example, one finds in her early memories dramatic instances of synesthetic and egocentric thought, typical of young children's thinking, which must have derived from some memory of her early years. Whether or not she was actually recalling *what* she felt and thought during those years, as she believed she was, the evidence is conclusive that she was remembering *how* to feel and think in the manner of children hardly out of infancy. In that respect, her memoirs of childhood, especially the 1939-1940 memoir, exemplify a quality pervading and distinguishing her novels—a combination of the most sophisticated, mature use of language and an almost infantile naïveté and directness of perception.

I have tried to determine the relative accuracy of Virginia Woolf's subjective accounts of various persons and events by comparing what she said with other reports of the same matters, found in letters and other primary sources. I was assisted also by other persons' comments on Virginia's accuracy. For example, Virginia's sister corroborated her portraits of their parents as Mr. and Mrs. Ramsay.[20] Her sister also said that Virginia's 1908 memoir was relatively accurate, both in respect to Virginia's portraying of the several family members, and as an interpretation of the family situation during Virginia's disturbed early adolescence.[21] Accuracy of Virginia's reports has been checked further by comparing her several versions of given persons and events one with another, by comparing them with presumably more objective information, and, wherever possible, with other accounts, written at the time an event took place. Many times when using secondary sources, I checked related passages against primary sources and so indicate either in the text or by means of multiple documentation in my notes. Occasionally, I have had to disagree with points of alleged fact provided by others who have written about Virginia Woolf. There have been other instances, though not many, when my interpretation of primary materials has lead me to conclusions contrary to those of others.

There is an enormous body of information by which to check Virginia's and others' accounts of the Stephen family— information about her parents (Sir Leslie and Julia Jackson Duckworth Stephen), their courtship and marriage, their conduct as parents. Records and reports about Virginia's father go back to his troubled early childhood with difficult parents. There is also much information about Virginia's sister and brothers (Vanessa, Thoby, and Adrian), and about her half sister and brothers (Stella, George, and Gerald) from her mother's first marriage to Herbert Duckworth. I have been able to discover more details of the story of Laura Stephen, Virginia's psychotic half sister from her father's first marriage to Harriet (Minny) Thackeray. From all this information, it is possible to deduce a great deal about the inner dynamics of the Stephen family and of the personalities of its individual members, as well as to clarify Virginia's references to persons and events.

One of the more important items for my study of the Stephen family is the long "letter" that Sir Leslie wrote to his children about Julia Stephen, his marriage to her, and other family matters. The Stephen children called this lugubrious "letter" the "Mausoleum Book," because of their father's preoccupation with necrology and their own sense of his absurdity. Most of it was written shortly after Julia's death in 1895 but Sir Leslie added to it from time to time until he neared his death nine years later. Accompanying it is the notebook he called his "Calendar of Correspondence," which contains portions that he chose to preserve from Julia's letters to him and some of his letters to her.[22]

The "Mausoleum Book" has influenced and, I think to some extent, misled previous interpretations of the Stephen family, including Virginia's *To the Lighthouse*. It is an astonishingly revealing psychological document, a fact the Stephen children perhaps recognized but could not fully appreciate. It is most interesting and revealing when compared with correspondence between Virginia's parents. It becomes clear from such a comparison that not all of the "Mausoleum Book" is to be believed. Though not as fanciful a portrait as those Virginia created, it

11

is fanciful, for Sir Leslie was not always willing or able to record events consistently. Although he was a man who prided himself on his logic and an objective approach to "the truth," in the "Mausoleum Book," he sometimes shaped "the truth" to his own ends. He probably did some of the shaping knowingly, for he studied and abstracted the correspondence between himself and his wife — at the time he wrote the "Mausoleum Book." Therefore the discrepancies in it cannot be attributed solely to nonreflective memory distortion.

Ostensibly written for all of Julia's children, the "Mausoleum Book" is directed principally to the Duckworth children, or so one may infer from the fact that they are mentioned lovingly and repeatedly by name. The Stephen children are addressed obliquely and Virginia is hardly mentioned. Although Leslie's avowed purpose in writing the "Mausoleum Book" was to eulogize his wife and fix her memory in her children's minds, he succeeded principally in memorializing his own love for Julia and his grief for her, a grief he believed (or wanted others to believe) to be almost infinite. Rather than preserving Julia's memory for her children, the "Mausoleum Book" could only have distorted it. Moreover, the "Mausoleum Book" represents Sir Leslie's attempt to justify himself and his conduct toward his wife and to elicit forgiveness and absolution from the Duckworth children whom he suspected (with reason) of blaming him for making their mother unhappy and contributing to her death by his exorbitant demands. Other important information about the Stephen family comes from the unpublished letters Virginia's parents wrote during their courtship and the many times they were apart after they married.[23] There is extant a series of approximately five hundred fifty letters from Sir Leslie to Julia Stephen, most of them long, for he was almost as addicted to letter writing as was his daughter. This series is in addition to the portions of their letters abstracted and preserved in the "Calendar of Correspondence" accompanying the "Mausoleum Book." The series of letters from Leslie Stephen to Julia Stephen was lost for several decades and therefore was not available to Quentin Bell, despite his diligent efforts to locate it when he compiled his biography of Virginia Woolf.[24] The series was among the letters Virginia studied and abstracted in 1904 when she assisted Frederic Maitland with his book, *The Life and Letters of Sir Leslie Stephen,* although that book makes only minor references to the Stephens's correspondence. Apparently, the series of letters has not been used in any other major study of the Stephen family or of Virginia Woolf. Consequently, I make extensive use of the information given in these letters, especially when there are references to Virginia and when their content extends previous accounts of what life must have been for her growing up within the Stephen household.

Virginia's novel *To the Lighthouse* is, as I have indicated, another rich source of information. However, I have limited my use of it. Virginia was determinedly honest when writing it, as she was with all of her novels. But because she adopted poetic fiction as a framework for biography and employed metaphor, myth, and hyperbole freely, it cannot be treated as fact. Therefore, I use the novel more to clarify information compiled from other sources than to establish fact. In general, my approach has been to occasionally use biographical material, to indicate the factual validity of certain passages of *To the Lighthouse* and other novels. I make less use of the novels to establish the history of Virginia and her family. However, I have found that one would be justified in making even greater use of *To the Lighthouse* and her other novels to inform the biography and in using the biography to inform the novels than I have chosen to do. Virginia told the story of the family in *To the Lighthouse* better than it can be told by other means. She deviated from historical fact, of course, and one major deviation is her interpretation of her parent's marriage. Her

13

parents' love for each other was not as unshakable or as un-shaken by the vicissitudes of their marriage as Virginia indi-cated in the novel. One suspects, after studying the family his-tory, that she was somewhat beguiled by her father's claims of a happy marriage and of the great love existing between him-self and Julia, and by her own wish to believe him.

Although my concern is with the family as milieu and con-text of Virginia's early years, its history is inherently interest-ing, with much drama, tragedy, and pathos; not a little comic absurdity; and some elements of mystery. Most of all, the family history is the story of personalities — often dominant and complex, and always intriguing. Virginia excepted, the most fascinating members of the family were her parents, to whose personalities her own was inextricably bound. She was bound to Sir Leslie by the strongest and most conflicting of emotions ("passionate love" and "passionate hatred"), and to her mother because she had so little immediate relationship with her. She was bound to both of them because the nature of their rela-tionship to each other perpetually intrigued her and perpetu-ally eluded her comprehension. She was also bound by choice, for in many respects she did not want to be free of them.

Many of Virginia's problems and strengths derived from her father and the nature of her ties to him. He was maddeningly complex and variable, a man Virginia called both "an old wretch" and "the dearest of creatures." He was also an emo-tionally damaged man, but nevertheless, from the present viewpoint and distance, he also appears comically absurd. On occasions, he could publicly acknowledge his absurdity, as Noel Annan established.[25] But all too commonly in his private life, he took himself with dead seriousness and greatly pitied himself which only added to his absurdity. Worse, he tried to get his family, especially his wife, to take him just as seriously and to pity him as much as he pitied himself. Apparently Julia usually succumbed to his entreaties and seems not to have comprehended his or anyone else's absurdity, for life was often grimly serious to her. Fortunately the Stephen children recognized his absurdity, hence their sobriquet, the "Mausoleum Book," for his memoir. Virginia's portrait of her father as Mr. Ramsay in *To the Lighthouse* also acknowledges his absurdity. However, it was many years after his death before she managed sufficient emotional detachment to appreciate how very comical and absurd he was, or to achieve any consistent view of him.

Leslie Stephen had so many opportunities to make an impression on Virginia through their daily association that one hardly need look for other ways he may have influenced her. Nevertheless, the possibility of his having passed on to her some genetic predisposition to emotional problems must be acknowledged for Virginia's temperament and health resembled those not only of her father, but of her father's father as well. She blamed heredity for some of her difficulties, although she may not have understood the matter well. Jokingly, but with more than an element of seriousness, she said that she had inherited her "secondhand" nervous system from her father and her grandfather, and that if they had not each abused it, she would not have had so many health problems.[26]

Virginia's father provided the comic absurdity and some of the tragedy in the family history, while her mother supplied legend, pathos, and additional tragedy. Many people, including Sir Leslie and Virginia have found Julia Stephen heroic and have created legends about her. And she was in many ways heroic. But for Virginia, her mother's heroism was a complicated issue and a source of much confusion. Evidently she found her mother elusive and paradoxical, for she called her a "large, austere presence," a "commanding empress," and a "wise Fate," in attempts to say what she had been like.[27] Because Julia Stephen was difficult to understand and has been obscured by legends, a certain mystery still pervades accounts of her. Other, more sinister, mystery has been introduced about Julia's son from her first marriage, George Duckworth, who Virginia said made sexual advances to her. Since Quentin Bell published his plausible and believable reconstruction of the events surrounding Virginia's allegations, he has modified some of his statements,[28] and questions must be asked and, if possible, answered about the charges. Which Duckworth was involved, George or Gerald? Were both involved? Or neither? Did the alleged events take place at all? Was Virginia only building another portrait, and if so, why did she give it such ugly proportions?

Despite Julia Stephen's elusiveness, Virginia adored her, or perhaps she adored her imaginative constructions — legends, fantasies, and myths of her mother — rather than the real woman. Her relationship with her mother — or more accurately, her lack of relationship — was one of Virginia's deepest and most persistent hurts. It left her unprepared for an independent existence and endowed her with a lifelong need for a mother-daughter relationship that, next after her needs to be a writer and artist and to fight against madness, was the strongest motive in her life. Moreover, Virginia's belief that life would almost inevitably betray and was most likely to do so when it seemed to promise greater happiness, was, in part, a legacy from her mother, reinforced by both important and minor events within the Stephen family. Virginia's preoccupation with death may also have been derived from Julia Stephen, who was often melancholy and spoke many times of wanting to die. Her father's attitudes toward death and his tendency to ruminate about it also affected Virginia. Moreover, unexpected and tragic deaths recurred with horrifying frequency in the family, reminding all its members and convincing some of them, that life indeed did betray and was least to be trusted when it seemed most promising. This attitude is central to Virginia Woolf's tragic vision and is a source of both her madness and her art.

# 2

# That Old Wretch . . . the Dearest
# of Creatures: Sir Leslie Stephen

Leslie Stephen was born in London in 1832, the third and youngest son of Sir James and Jane Venn Stephen. Presumably he was born in his parents' house in Kensington Gore, later known as Hyde Park Gate, the street where he spent most of his adult life, and where he died in 1904. He is remembered now chiefly as Virginia Woolf's father and the personality upon which Mr. Ramsay in *To the Lighthouse* was based. Ironically, her life and work have overshadowed him and his achievements, making him seem the footnote to literary history he feared he might become. However, during the Victorian period he was, and deserved to be, far more than a footnote even though he was given to mournful deprecation of his accomplishments. The record of his work and the studies of him by Noel Annan, Desmond MacCarthy, Frederic Maitland, and David Zink, as well as the first volume of Quentin Bell's biography of Virginia Woolf show that he was an influential public figure, justly honored and admired.[1] As a child Virginia Woolf was vaguely aware of her father's reputation, although as she grew older she found it difficult to reconcile that knowledge with her experience of him as a father. That was one of many reasons she could never decide what she felt and thought about him. He was in at least the second, perhaps the first, rank of what one of his biographers, Noel Annan (pp. 1-2), has called the intellectual aristocracy of nineteenth-century England. Annan generously placed Leslie Stephen at

17

the top of the first rank, for he (p. 91) believed Stephen to have been the foremost man in English letters following Matthew Arnold's death, a belief seconded by David Zink (pp. 109-110).

Whatever Stephen's rank and status, he was an exceedingly complex, deeply divided man. The division between his public and private personalities has often been noted. The way he appeared professionally and with other men, did not correspond with the private personality Virginia Woolf knew as a child. Beneath that division was a more dangerous schism. On one side was the tough-minded, determinedly rational image that Leslie Stephen tended to equate with masculinity. Virginia Woolf believed he always assumed that stance before men. The other Leslie Stephen was irrational, sometimes angry, sometimes sentimental, always excessively sensitive and self-pitying. He tended to equate some elements of this side of his personality with feminity, but let it dominate him at home. The division in his personality made him an almost perpetual problem to his family and to himself, for he was less able than anyone to gain perspective of and reconcile the varying, contradictory sides of himself.

So incongruous were the two Leslie Stephens that even his closest friends doubted the full measure of the private man — when they knew of it. John Morley insisted that Leslie was the " 'most considerate and faithful of men,' " conceding only that those who didn't know him might think him "unceremonious" and grim.[2] When Henry James came to London, he found Leslie Stephen more than cordial when they first became friends and said that he was an "excellent fellow" who would make James "adore him prostrate" if he kept up his cordiality and offers of assistance.[3] But later James found him so silent and morose that he had to conclude that Stephen was "mortally untalkative" in spite of his good nature.[4] Many thought of him much as did Charles Eliot Norton, the American scholar, whose description of Stephen contrasts markedly with Virginia

Woolf's Mr. Ramsay. In Norton's estimate, Leslie was a most affectionate, honest-minded, and modest man, who could maintain "equipoise of sense" and "imaginative sympathy" under all adversity. He was "muscular physically and mentally" but never brutal; he did not hope for or fear much in life.[5]

Frederic Maitland—who married Julia Stephen's niece, spent time as a guest in Leslie's home, and was asked by him to be his official biographer—refused to listen to the more onerous facts[6] about Leslie Stephen when Virginia and Vanessa hinted about them. As a result, Maitland's study reveals little of Leslie's private character, making him seem more consistent, sanguine, and two-dimensional than he ever managed to be in life. Noel Annan achieved a relatively balanced view and concluded (p. 73) that there were two Leslie Stephens: "staunch friend," " 'most lovable of men' " and the extremely "vexing pater familias." Annan said further, "Friends dimly apprehended part of the truth, his family saw all" (p. 97).

The Public Man

In his public life Leslie legitimately earned so many titles that one doesn't know just how to refer to him. He was all of the following and more: a critic of literature and religion; a philosopher and historian of British thought; a biographer; a Cambridge tutor and Anglican clergyman; an alpinist and mountaineer; and an editor and author. Virginia called him a professor and metaphysician in her letters to Dame Ethel Smyth to twit her for being "only" a general's daughter and to remind her that daughters of professors and metaphysicians might be incompatible with generals' daughters.[7] Leslie called himself a jack-of-all-trades[8] in times of self-deprecation, and a "logician"[9] in his more satisfied moments, but neither of these appellations is wholly accurate. He also came to take satisfaction in being known as an agnostic, cynic and controversialist.

Leslie Stephen's career began at Trinity Hall College, Cambridge where he first became a fellow, then a junior tutor and rowing coach after studying mathematics. He chose mathematics, he said, because in mathematics one can give "palpable proof" of the superiority of his knowledge.[10] Holy orders were required of both fellows and tutors, and since he had not yet developed strong feelings against religion, he became an Anglican clergyman. Later he explained and excused his having taken holy orders by saying that he had wanted to relieve his father, Sir James Stephen, of the necessity to support him. According to Maitland (pp. 130-131), Leslie was gently but firmly directed into the clergy by his father.

By the time of his appointment at Cambridge, Leslie already came to identify himself with scientific humanism and with the tough-minded, empirical approach to truth that he later espoused so determinedly and absurdly, though never consistently. It was not surprising, therefore, that while acting nominally as a clergyman, he became increasingly uncomfortable with religion. According to the explanation he gave his children in the "Mausoleum Book," he began to move away from religion because he could not take the biblical stories of Noah and Jonah seriously. He indicated that his doubts began before he was fourteen.[11] Unlike Virginia, he was never able to see value or truth in myth, and, equating myth and falsehood, he decided eventually that lying and religiosity must go together.[12] But evidently in telling his children about it, Leslie simplified the explanation of his apostasy. His decision to leave religion was the result of a difficult intellectual process and reasons more complex than he told them. His faith was shaken most by the problem of evil and his inability to reconcile evil with doctrines of a beneficent God. He was also influenced by the study of Mill, Comte, Kant, and German criticism of the Bible. Charles Darwin's theories and Charles Lyell's work in geology have also been cited as influences.[13] Furthermore, Leslie tended to blame the church, possibly with his father in mind, for having deprived him of his important, productive years — an accusation Zink considered inexplicable (p. 32). Still, his views about mythology remained significant in his refusal to participate any longer in religious services. Having to read the stories of the Flood, of Joshua's making the sun stand still, and other biblical myths as authentic, historical narratives offended him.

But finally, the major problem of his faith, Leslie Stephen insisted, again simplifying the matter, was that religion had really only occupied a "superficial stratum" of his thoughts and had not been a "fundamental conviction."[14]

When Leslie's changing attitude toward religion began to emerge in 1862, he refused to continue taking part in religious services and resigned from his tutorship at Trinity Hall. He was permitted to retain his fellowship, but after two years in that position, Leslie left Cambridge. Subsequently he wrote many times about his agnosticism, enjoying the consternation it caused among his contemporaries. He wore the label, agnostic proudly and belligerently for the remainder of his life and brought up his children to disdain religion. He reaffiliated himself for one year (1883-1884) with Cambridge University when elected lecturer at Trinity College. Thus Virginia Woolf's occasional references to herself as a professor's daughter contained an element of truth.

Noel Annan suggested (p. 47) that it was more than coincidence that Leslie's change of faith surfaced at the time of his father's death. After his father died, Leslie had an independent income and could live comfortably and at little cost in his mother's house in London. He no longer needed the modest "living" afforded by the Cambridge post. Also, with the death of Sir James, there was less opposition to Leslie's change in religious beliefs. Based on his reading of the "Mausoleum Book," Quentin Bell (p. 9) suggested another possible reason for Leslie's leaving Cambridge and recanting his religious vows —his delayed realization that he wanted to marry and that "the celibacy and religion of Cambridge" were not right for him. But Bell called his speculation "guess work."

Many others knew what to think and feel about Leslie Stephen even though his daughter did not. He was widely acclaimed in his lifetime but was never able to believe in his renown. He was awarded honorary degrees from four major universities: Edinburgh, Harvard, Cambridge and Oxford. When Edward VII became King in 1902, Leslie was made Knight Commander of the Bath, an honor he claimed not to want, saying that he would accept knighthood only because his children wanted him to do so.[15]

Leslie Stephen traveled to the United States on three occasions. The first trip was during the American Civil War. He went to Washington and was received by President Lincoln, who was familiar with the reputation of Leslie's father as an opponent of slavery. Leslie also openly espoused the side of the North in the Civil War, although popular sentiment in England favored the South.[16] His second trip was made in 1868, and his third, when he was awarded the honorary doctorate by Harvard University, in 1890.

As a public figure, Leslie Stephen was the admired and loved friend of other prominent people of his day, on both sides of the Atlantic. Many of his well-known friends visited him and were known to Virginia. Some were members of his hiking club, the "Sunday Tramps." James Russell Lowell was a special friend, to Julia Stephen as well as Leslie. Bell has noted (p. 25) that the Stephen children liked to think Lowell had been in love with their mother. Leslie also spoke in the "Maussoleum Book" of the "mutual affection" between Lowell and

Julia. Lowell was asked to be Virginia's godfather, or in the words of Leslie, who by the time of Virginia's birth was too self-consciously agnostic to use that term, Lowell was asked to stand in "quasi-sponsorial relationship" to her.[17] Other friends of Leslie Stephen were Oliver Wendell Holmes (the younger), Charles Eliot Norton, John Morley, Henry Fawcett, John Ruskin (whom Leslie never liked), and Henry James. He made his first ascent of the Alps with Francis Galton. George Smith, the founder of the *Dictionary of National Biography,* and Sidney Lee, the assistant editor, were friends as well as professional colleagues. George Meredith was still another friend, and, like Lowell, a staunch and awed admirer of Julia Stephen. He said that he never reverenced a woman more than Julia, a sentiment that Leslie also voiced about Julia[18] and that Virginia had Mr. Bankes express about Mrs. Ramsay in *To the Lighthouse* (pp. 46-48, 75). Meredith, like Virginia, saw literary possibilities in Leslie Stephen and modeled Vernon Whitford, a character in *The Egoist,* after him.[19]

Many facts about Leslie Stephen's private life are well known. He married Harriet (Minny) Thackeray, the younger daughter of William Makepeace Thackeray, a man Leslie never met. With Minny and Anny, Thackeray's other daughter, he set up a tense, often stormy household, for Leslie and Anny had little in common other than Minny and a desire by each of them to dominate her. Leslie and Minny had a daughter, Laura, in 1860 and were expecting their second child in 1865 when Minny died. Leslie's mother died during the same year. She was the most important woman in his life, Minny not excepted, before he met Virginia's mother, and Leslie was unable for a long time to cope with his grief. His sadness increased as he slowly became aware that his young daughter was not developing normally. Three years after Minny died, Leslie married Julia Jackson Duckworth, a widow nearly fifteen years his junior, and the mother of three children. Within the next five years, they became the parents of four children. Adeline Virginia (Virginia Woolf), their third child, was born in 1882. The marriage of Leslie and Julia lasted and indeed was fiendishly strong in spite of strains and frictions and in spite of times when Julia's passion for nursing and other charitable work, and Leslie's for tramping and mountain climbing took them apart. Julia's death, in 1895, bewildered Leslie and precipitated orgiastic grief, guilt, and self-commiseration from which he never fully recovered. He developed cancer of the bowel in 1902, and, as Quentin Bell has observed (pp. 82-86), he declined slowly and painfully, but with surprising grace and, even more surprisingly, with very little self-pity. He died in 1904.[20]

### The Private Personality

Virginia Woolf was impressed by what she knew of her father's public and professional life, and was probably somewhat influenced to become a writer because writing had been one of his major public activities. However, she was affected to a greater extent, and more unhappily, by the private man, for in his relationships with his family, the more difficult side of his personality was unleashed. To understand his private personality, and therefore the way he affected Virginia, one must study his parents, for Leslie, like Virginia later, was very much bound to and affected by his mother and father.

Leslie's erratic temperament and unstable health — his complex nature and his tendency to vacillate from being lovable to being odious — appeared in him when he was very young. In many of these respects, he resembled his father. Quentin Bell, the great grandson of Sir James, has written (p. 5) that he was a shy, gloomy, pessimistic, self-mortifying man who had a fanatic commitment to duty and hard work, who abjured pleasure and praise, and who was "terrified of being comfortable." Except for the self-mortification and fear of comfort, those terms apply also to Leslie. But he was less given to self-mortification than to self-deprecation and that came from sources other than his father. His self-deprecation often was a gambit intended to serve Leslie's much stronger wishes for self-gratification, self-indulgence and self-pity.

Sir James, like his son, was said to have a restless and fiery temperament. Leslie and others have said that Sir James was inordinately "thin-skinned" or sensitive[21] — a quality Leslie claimed as if it were a mark of honor. He firmly believed he had inherited his sensitivity from his father and therefore could do nothing to change it.[22] Most important, both men were exceedingly complex. Maitland has written (p. 11) that Leslie's father was such a "mosaic" of "scarcely compatible" qualities that it was almost impossible to make him seem a composite whole when writing about him — a problem that must have been encountered by everyone who has tried to describe Leslie, and a problem compounded tenfold for those who try to describe his daughter.

The two men also had positive traits in common, many of which were to emerge in Virginia also. Some of these arose because of their difficult temperaments and some in spite of them. Their stubbornness was translated, in certain kinds of enterprises, into self-determination and boldness, and prevented them from capitulating completely to their shyness and vulnerability. Both men were bright, and each was entitled, in his own way, to a reputation for intellectual genius. Both used words well and were talented writers. Sir James published many articles in the *Edinburgh Review.* Each respected literary art presented in conventional, staid forms, and each was unfamiliar with, and to a degree suspicious of, other arts and artists. Sir James used his facility for words in law and public administration and held a professorship at Cambridge for a time. He had wanted to be a "true man of letters" he said. Leslie thought his father should have been a writer.[23]

While the similarities between father and son can be noted, they cannot be explained. Possibly some hereditary quirk accounted for their temperament. But it is more likely that Leslie learned to be like his father through association with him, especially since he was told repeatedly that he, like his father, was an irascible genius. Moreover, both men were responding to similar cultural values and pressures, and were under similar duress to make their own fortunes, and to get ahead, intellectually, financially, and socially. For as Bell said (pp. 20-21), the Stephen family at that time was on the rise, or in today's terminology, it was upwardly mobile, moving from lower middle to upper middle class. As with so many in early Victorian times, the Stephen family advanced through the accomplishments of its individual members, in whatever calling they elected. For both father and son, being recognized as intellectuals was significant.

Either in spite of, or because of their likenesses, their relationship was not amicable. Little is known about Sir James's feelings for Leslie, but Leslie disliked and disdained his father.[24] Ironically, he criticized Sir James for some of the very tendencies and petty habits they had in common — for example, his practice of forcing Leslie to walk with him, only to treat him to dull conversation and "lugubrious silence."[25] Leslie also ridiculed his father for traits they did not share, such as Sir James's religious faith.

Like his parents and most of their friends, Sir James was a member of the Clapham sect, a middle-class, hard-working, and relatively prosperous group. Remaining within the Anglican church, the Claphams became known for their evangelism and for an impressive political sophistication which aided them in achieving social goals. Sometimes called the "conscience of the British middle classes," their *cause célèbre* was

the elimination of slavery, a profitable institution still practiced in the early nineteenth century in some of the British
colonies, and approved by many in England itself.[26]

According to Leslie, Sir James justified his self-denial, his
abjuration of pleasure and praise, his unremitting dedication
to hard work and duty, and indeed almost everything, on the
basis of his religion. Leslie said that his father saw the "gracious will of God" everywhere manifest.[27] But one presumes he
did not see it in quite everything, for he tried assiduously to
avoid whatever pleasure and satisfactions God may have intended for him.[28] Leslie also thought his father much too narrow, a view he expressed after converting to the agnosticism he
practiced as narrowly and rigidly, though not as evangelically,
as his father practiced his Christianity. Leslie was evidently
wrong in his accusation. Sir James's hard work, self-mortification, and rejection of pleasure must have arisen from something more morbid in him than his religion, if one judges his
religion from the relatively liberal tenets of the Clapham group
and from Sir James's other religious practices. That he chose a
straight path for himself is true, but if he had thought such rigidity a basic religious obligation, it is likely he would have expected others to follow a similar course. But he did not. Not
even his own children were required to be like him, and he was
never the "living categorical imperative" that Leslie accused
him of being.[29] Annan's opinion (pp. 13-14) was that far from
advocating narrowness, Sir James worried about that trait in
his children, especially about the priggishness he noticed in
young Leslie. In some ways, Leslie was more narrow and rigid
in bringing up his own children than his father had been with
him. Also, Virginia and others believed Leslie was tyrannical,
a charge that cannot be fairly placed against Sir James.

Sir James followed avidly the Clapham sect's tenet that one's
first obligation to religion is to practice it in the social and political arena, not to preach it. He relinquished his prosperous

law practice to take up his father's work opposing slavery and assuring protection to Negroes in the British Colonies. Choosing the Colonial Office as his arena, he became a diligent and capable administrator, first as Assistant Under Secretary and then as Under Secretary of State for Colonial Affairs. His self-will and stubbornness served him admirably and he was determined, implacable, and uncompromising in the antislavery cause. Despite strong political opposition from proslavery colonials and their London cohorts, Sir James Stephen contributed a great deal to the successful outcome of the antislavery campaign. He deserves to be remembered, along with his father and his father's friend and relative, William Wilberforce, as a hero of the antislavery movement in England.[30]

No matter how admirable others thought Sir James's manner of carrying out his religious beliefs, Leslie could not accept his father's religion. Consequently, when he espoused any religion at all, it was of the "Broad Church," middle-of-the-road, Anglican variety. Leslie's eventual rejection of religion was obviously a rejection of what was most central to his father's life and what gave his father's personality coherence in spite of its diversity, a fact Leslie was never able to appreciate.

Leslie Stephen's mother influenced him as much as his father, for Leslie was unmistakably his "mother's darling," and she was his, until he fell in love with Virginia's mother.[31] Jane Venn Stephen shared her husband's religious commitments, but apparently none of his moroseness and few of his morbid traits. Her personality was the complement and reciprocal of his, as Julia Stephen later was to be in relationship to Leslie. Jane Venn Stephen protected her nervous, sensitive husband and supported him emotionally, making much of his work possible. Thereby she caused Leslie to form certain expectations concerning the role and attributes of wives of irascible, thin-skinned husbands, expectations that were responsible in part for his exhorbitant demands upon Virginia Woolf's mother.

But if she tried, Jane Venn Stephen was unable to keep her husband from neurotically overworking himself. The tendency to work too hard was present also in Leslie, who suffered several emotional and physical crises because he was overdiligent while editing the *Dictionary of National Biography*. Virginia's inclination to overwork herself continued the family trend, and was fostered, perhaps, by her mother as well as her father.

Jane Venn Stephen may have failed to keep her husband from working too hard, but many thought that otherwise she was an ideal wife and mother. In a letter to John Morley, Leslie said that she was the "healthiest minded person" he had ever known.[32] Quentin Bell concluded (p. 6) from his research that she was strong, amiable, given to optimism, and "as sane a woman as ever breathed." Her strength was apparently physical as well as mental. Leslie said in a letter to Oliver Wendell Holmes that his robust elder brother Fitzjames had inherited their mother's good health, a trait Leslie said he had not inherited. Leslie then added, either in defense of his mother's femininity or possibly his brother's masculinity, and with his chronic, keen concern for sex roles and differences, that his mother's health and strength "combined with a womanly tenderness always sweet and affectionate."[33]

Jane Venn Stephen has had at least one detractor, however. In a letter to Vanessa Bell in 1947, Adrian Stephen, Virginia and Vanessa's younger brother, said that his grandfather had been hagridden all his life, presumably by Jane Venn Stephen for much of the time.[34] And Jane's diaries, quoted at length by Maitland, indicate that she was not unerring in raising her children, although one cannot doubt that she compensated for many of their father's limitations. At least she was not without faults in bringing up Leslie, and seems to have been at least as responsible for Leslie's emotional problems as his father. Her preoccupation with him and his health caused him to take himself with absurd and preposterous seriousness, to worry

McCook Community College

21789

excessively about signs of ill health, and to feel that he was a creature greatly deserving pity.

Initially Leslie's mother had good reason to worry about his health, for early in life he was frail and had a gangling, almost emaciated, asthenic physique like his father and his sickly brother, Herbert.[35] Moreover, she concluded quite early that Leslie was exceptionally nervous and sensitive, like his father. As a result, Leslie came to think of himself as a nervous weakling, "thin-skinned" like Sir James, believing it so thoroughly that, as an adult, he often referred to himself in the same language his mother had used about him when he was young.[36] Although he learned to be deeply ashamed to let anyone outside the home know about his "weaknesses," within the family he accepted the ascribed traits as inevitable, pitying himself for them, and demanding special attention and privilege. Whenever it suited his purposes, he pleaded his physical frailty, long after there was justification for it. He was only wiry and had never become strong, he explained to his children in the "Mausoleum Book." Inconsistently, when it suited his purposes to appear physically well, he argued his good health, citing his prowess and stamina in mountain climbing and long-distance hiking. In defense of his temperament and irritability he would say, "I am I," that his "nerves, humours and vagaries" were part of his character, or that many men were better than he but that he could not change himself into one of them.[37]

Noel Annan was correct when he said that a key to Leslie's character was his attempt to change himself,[38] as he professed to be unable to do. However, the effort to change or to appear changed, was true only of Leslie's public life; the inability to change or even to see the possibility of changing continued true of the private man. Moreover, his attempts to change publically redounded upon his personal life and his family. Trying to change required great effort and strain, leaving him increasingly in need of reassurance and sympathy at home. For that reason, as Zink has said (p. 110), Leslie Stephen's children "paid a dear price for [his] lifelong efforts to overcome his introverted, hypersensitive nature."

Leslie's reputation for sensitivity and nervousness was not without foundation. By the time he was two years of age, his mother was making diligent note of his emotional problems and temperamental disposition, and even at that early age, signs of Leslie's divided nature were evident. His problems were complicated and reinforced by his mother, who began his lessons when he was only three years old, and by a crisis in his eighth year. Most of the problems continued throughout his life.

When he was two, according to Maitland's report (pp. 23 ff.), his mother said that he was turbulent, impetuous, self-willed, and passionate, but able to quickly become kind and affectionate. She described him further as extremely sensitive, "most sensible of a balk," unable to bear reproof, and so shy that he was scarcely able to ask for what he wanted. As an adult, these tendencies, slightly attenuated, became hallmarks of Leslie Stephen. He never learned to tolerate "balks" and became proficient in a kind of game-playing, often trying to get what he wanted without admitting that he wanted it, sometimes specifically denying that he did want it.

Other characteristics of the two-year-old which worried his mother were his violent temper and his loud crying when displeased. The fact that he never learned to control his temper fully is evident in the descriptions by Quentin Bell (pp. 62-64) and Annan (p. 71) of Leslie's open rage against his wife, his stepdaughter Stella Duckworth, and his daughter Vanessa, who each in turn was luckless enough to have to keep the household accounts. Virginia Woolf also spoke about her father's explosions over the accounts, although she never had to keep them. Her explanation for his temper, and much else, was that Leslie had been indulged since an incident during his childhood when he broke a piece of pottery and threw the pieces at his mother.[39] As an adult Leslie's anger appeared as irritability, sulkiness, and what he called his "peeves" and "tantarums" as well as in his fits of rage over the accounts. The loud crying of the two-year-old was attenuated but nonetheless retained in a new form, for in his letters to Julia he habitually complained, bewailed his lot, and pitied himself. Symbolically — or in times of bereavement, actually and openly — he tended always to weep for himself and did all he could to get his family to join him in the ritual.

Apparently Leslie's mother found in him more worrisome than optimistic traits, but did allude to a few early signs of the lovable, admirable Leslie Stephen. For example, when he was two, as Maitland noted, she said that he was "'a most independent-spirited little fellow, very bold and very persevering. He climbs up chairs and sofas and seems to have no fear at all when he's trying to do anything. He will persevere for a very long time and seem to be quite delighted when he succeeds.'" But even the more optimistic signs were not free of problems, for when Leslie failed, he "'cried most loudly.'" Also, his endearing qualities, even as a child, were manifest not so much in extending affection to others, as in efforts to get others to express affection to him. His mother said that when he was three he was very responsive to affection and attention, quickly turning off his obstreperousness when he got them. When he was four, his mother noted that encouragement was good for him and that "every notice taken" seemed to draw him out. When he was five, she observed that the "feeling of being loved gives him a peculiar pleasure."

"Nervousness" and excessive "sensitivity" were recurrent and prophetic themes in Jane Venn Stephen's diary entries about Leslie throughout his early years. When he was "naughty," she said, his behavior seemed to result from nervous irritability and was not true "naughtiness." He reacted emotionally to accounts of "naughtiness" in others, even to accounts of "naughty" animals in make-believe stories. Evidently there was a bit of the moralist in him even as a young child. He also reacted emotionally to accounts of "suffering and sorrow,"[40] a tendency still present later in his life, which combined with an active imagination to produce almost hallucinatory effects. For example, during his adult years he was so upset by accounts of the Boer War, that he imagined he could hear the gunfire from South Africa to England.[41]

Jane Venn Stephen's diaries, as reported by Maitland, show that she was concerned about Leslie's intellect as well as his temperament. Apparently she tried to make a prodigy out of a bright child who was maturing at no more than an average rate, possibly at a rate slower than normal. Beginning her teaching efforts when he was only three years old, she got results that further convinced her of his frailty and nervousness, but did not acknowledge her own part in making him nervous. She said that at lessons "a sort of nervous feeling seems to come upon him and really to prevent him from doing what" she told him to do. When Leslie was six she described more serious signs: he soon "wearied of application in study"; after ten minutes he turned pale and yawned; he could hardly think when fatigued; he had "languor of body" when studying. She was forced to conclude that he was not an intellectual prodigy, though bright and quick, and so imitative that his brothers called him "the mocking bird."

When Leslie was seven, his mother began to be more hopeful about his intellectual development, not anticipating the serious crisis just a year ahead. She recorded that he expressed a preference for books that were steady and regular, as he described them, rather than a book of anecdotes that seemed to him to "wiggle" from one subject to another. He wanted "a great deal on one subject," and wanted it in "regular order." Latin was his favorite subject because he thought it more "boyish" than other subjects.[42] He seemed to be developing into a more normal pupil, better able to learn, with standards in intellectual matters similar to those of the later public Leslie Stephen, though not the private one whose letters to Julia Stephen sometimes did "wiggle" in tortured perplexity from one subject to another. He was also showing an interest in being masculine, a forerunner of his tendency in later years to stereotype even intellectual matters according to conventions about sex roles.

Whatever else his mother's early instruction may have accomplished, it taught Leslie one of the overriding values of his life, that is, the importance of intellect and learning. Regrettably, she also caused him to be insecure in intellectual matters. Most likely it was her influence as well as his need to feel secure in the intellectual aristocracy of the Victorian period that made Leslie work so hard for intellectual success and left him always doubting the worth of his own achievements. His mother's early teaching also left him dependent upon her for reassurance that he was succeeding. Eventually he transferred the dependence to his second wife, Virginia Woolf's mother, asking her so often to reassure him that eventually she lost patience with his pleas. He also played his games to get reassurance, and usually rejected it when it was extended to him, adding further strain to his marriage.

When Leslie was working on the biography of his brother Fitzjames in 1894, he was bemused by some of the things his mother had said about him in her diaries and in family correspondence. What interested him, he said in a letter to Julia, was how one could say exactly the same thing with and without religious explanations. "I can be just as morbid and sensitive and overrefining as [my father] was, without bothering about the gracious will of etc. My mother was as sensible and kind as you and believed as much as her children. I find that before I was two, I rather scandalized her—no, I don't think she was scandalized—by suggesting that the donkey should say his prayers. She says at the same period that I was the most troublesome and rampageous of the lot. Sir J. says afterwards that I was the cleverest; but I cannot make out why I did not do better at school."[43]

## To Crush a Poet . . .

A startling continuity exists between the personality of Leslie Stephen, the child, and the man Virginia Woolf knew as her father. However, his mother made one comment about Leslie in childhood that did not describe the person he became, namely, that he had a "passion for beautiful things."[44] Except for his love of nature, particularly rugged mountain scenery— anticipated with strange precision in childhood by his fondness for a pictorial scene of the Alps—as a man he showed very little appreciation for beauty and was generally insecure about aesthetic questions. True, he definitely had an eye for beauty in women, but not for reasons of aesthetics. He married Julia Jackson Duckworth, reputedly one of the most beautiful women in England. However, his letters to Julia and his life with her show that it was not her beauty as much as her maternal and domestic virtues that attracted him. In the "Mausoleum Book" he praised her beauty chiefly by saying it was expressive of the qualities of her character, which he avowed had been "absolutely" without flaw. But while she was alive he had sometimes refused to tell Julia what he thought of her looks, saying he believed it wrong and insulting to tell a woman she was beautiful. Whatever he thought of her appearance, he said, he loved it as he did everything else about her, adding cautiously that there might be a possible exception or two he couldn't think of at the moment.[45] When Julia wrote to question him about the exceptions, he replied that he still couldn't think of them, but thought there must be some and would try to tell her when he saw her.[46] He admitted having reservations about her beauty at times, not finding the shape of her nose to his liking and thinking it a little "obstinate."[47] These remarks were manifestations of his often absurd and pedantic faithfulness to "truth." However, it was irascibility that led him to write her that he was glad that nine-year-old Virginia's beauty was unmarred by a nose "like someone else in the family."[48]

Leslie's problems with beauty and aesthetics stemmed from the crisis that occurred when he was eight which involved both his unusually vivid memory and his love of poetry. The crisis clearly indicated a serious emotional illness and helped to confirm and deepen the divisions in his personality.

From all accounts, Leslie had a truly remarkable visual memory as a child, one typified by the eidetic imagery that Virginia was later to experience. He had the ability, in childhood and in his adult life, to call up scenes, particularly faces, with great fidelity. He used this to comfort himself while away from his family, calling up his wife's or children's faces in memory. His capacity for vivid imagery may also explain his talent and passion for drawing.[49] His eidetic imagery sometimes failed him. His inability to visualize the shape of Julia's nose and his reference to it as obstinate gave the clue to his disapproval of it, a clue that Julia saw immediately for what it was.[50]

Leslie's auditory memory was likewise very acute and was best illustrated by his ease and facility in learning verse by rote. Possibly this explains why his brothers called him "the mocking bird." Desmond MacCarthy said (p. 28) that Leslie "did not need to learn" verse that pleased him. Evidently to read it or hear it once was enough to imprint it in memory. But his ability to memorize verse overshadowed taste and discrimination, for "most poetry was the same to him." Virginia Woolf wrote in her essay about him that verse of all kinds, from what he called utter trash to the best of Milton and Wordsworth, stuck in his memory and emerged in a "strange rhythmical chant" whenever it suited his mood, especially when he was walking or climbing.[51] She included his tendency to recite poetry at odd moments in her characterization of him as Mr. Ramsay, who strides back and forth on the terrace, sometimes forgetting himself and shouting poetry. Virginia Woolf was amused by and admired this eccentricity of her father. In *To the Lighthouse* (pp. 41-42), she indicated that she appreciated what it meant to him. Desmond MacCarthy recalled (p. 28) that Leslie Stephen as an old man would mumble verse while on his solitary walks in London parks and that his mumbling and his gaunt, abstruse appearance startled passersby. In *To the Lighthouse* (p. 107), Virginia Woolf joked about how others reacted to her father's behavior: Mr. Ramsay frightens an elderly lady by unexpectedly shouting in her presence, "Brightest and best, come away."

Even as a child, Leslie Stephen startled people and eventually alarmed his parents by reciting poetry and occasionally shouting it in public places. His mother said that as a boy of eight, Leslie became so absorbed in poetry while traveling in a coach that he recited it "' . . . so loud that the passengers turned round in astonishment. He hardly hears if he is spoken to and seems to observe nothing that is going on.' "[52] He recited the poems with great expressiveness and excitement, sometimes humming lines, which he called "playing the band."[53] Clearly, his involvement in poetry was part of a fantasy strong enough to make him oblivious to his surroundings.

Jane Venn Stephen's first comments about Leslie's interest in poetry and his feats of memory show her unmistakable approbation. Much of the verse he knew, he learned from listening to her, for she had a great store of poetry in her memory. Later, however, both Leslie's parents began to be frightened by his preoccupation with poetry and his tendency to lose contact with himself and his surroundings, as well they might. They consulted a doctor who attached the label "disordered circulation" to a condition that sounds like an incipient psychosis, and duly prescribed "school, fresh-air, 'hum-drum lessons,' and a rigorous abstinence from poetry. . . ."[54] Among other benefits, school was to get Leslie away from "injudicious stimulation at home."[55] Maitland related (p. 26-28) that the boy could hardly be kept from crying when he learned that he was to be deprived of poetry. He suggested also that the doctor crushed a poet to make a critic, although Leslie's attitudes resulting from the incident eventually modified his effectiveness as a critic as well.

When Leslie wrote the biography of his brother, he studied his mother's accounts of this crisis and, very much the urbane, slightly humorous, public man, made comments about it which show that he and his family were impressed with the seriousness of his condition. He said that in 1840 his mother observed in him certain peculiarities that she took at first to be signs of precocious genius. However, the doctor concluded that it was not genius he suffered from, but disordered circulation, and that he was in danger of becoming feeble in mind and deformed in body. The doctor advised a school where Leslie's brain would be less in jeopardy of overstimulation than at home. His very life was at stake. His father decided not to trust such a delicate child away from home and arranged to move the family from London to Brighton where Leslie could both live at home and attend school. Because the move caused great hardship for his father (whose work was in London), it showed how serious his father thought Leslie's condition to be.[56]

The doctor's prescription, and the Stephen family's application of it, did not destroy Leslie's love of poetry, although they did check some of his excesses. Rather, the result was to leave him at best ambivalent about himself, and at worst, guilty and ashamed. As Maitland said (pp. 28-29), after ups and downs in behavior and health in school, " 'healthy flesh and blood' habits of reserve and self-control" were formed, and although Leslie continued to feel keenly and deeply, he would let no one see this outside the home. His love of poetry became a sign of his weakness, and to Leslie, who was already too concerned with sex roles, weakness equaled feminity. Later he would engage in defensive, airy definitions of certain poetry as effeminate and other poetry as masculine, but that was too fine a distinction, mentally and emotionally, for a boy of eight.

For similar reasons, Leslie was also ambivalent about his drawing. Virginia Woolf reported that he would absent-mindedly cover margins of books with sketches and would entertain his children with his rapidly penned drawings. But he refused at a social gathering to acknowledge his drawings as his own even though they were being admired at the time.[57]

Leslie's "disordered circulation" made him afraid that he was weak and feminine — irrationally afraid, for there is no evidence to question his masculinity. His worries were increased because his puny, asthenic build as a boy resembled that of his sickly brother Herbert. Perhaps worse, Leslie lacked the masculine physique and athletic interests of his brother, Fitzjames.[58] The anxieties about weakness and feminity were exacerbated still further when Herbert died at the age of twenty-four, when Leslie was fourteen.[59] Leslie's serious illness at the age of fifteen or sixteen added to his and the family's conviction that he was weak and frail and would always have to protect his health. He recalled this illness as his "most sickly time," for it required him to spend most of the summer of 1848 in bed and to be treated with leeches. The memory, years later, could still make him "shiver in his bones."[60]

## Eton and Cambridge

Leslie attended Eton as a "day boy" for four years until his father removed him due to dissatisfaction with the headmaster's attitude toward his son. In general, Leslie's experience at that school was harmful.[61] His anxieties and shame about possible weakness and femininity increased when his stronger and stereotypically masculine brother Fitzjames, also at Eton, had to protect him from the cruelty of the other boys. Guilt and repression were possibly operating in later years when Leslie was peculiarly unable to recall, or at least to admit in public, his bad experience at Eton. Maitland (pp. 30-31) said that Leslie had been bullied and unjustly flogged at Eton, but that he covered it up out of humiliation at being delicate. Leslie admitted that both his mother and Fitzjames had said that both brothers were bullied tyrannically. He reported other horrors as well, but went to some length to deny that it was as bad as people alleged. Very much the public man again, he said that he recalled no particular tyranny, that there was occasional bullying, but none that impressed him. He was, of course, less able than Fitzjames to protect himself. Consequently he learned to evade the kind of assaults that his brother would meet with open defiance. Leslie stated specifically that he did not believe he could have forgotten serious torment. He admitted recalling an instance of being so bullied that Fitzjames had come to his rescue "with the toe of his boots between the coat tails of the bully," thus uncharacteristically using a sexually suggestive description. Rather than his own experiences at Eton, Fitzjames's memories of their days there impressed Leslie. Fitzjames said that he had felt shame and contempt for his boyish weakness and that he had been shy, timid, and cowardly.[62] It is interesting that in a family where many things were labeled in terms of sex roles and where Fitzjames was called masculine, that Fitzjames himself recalled feeling like a sensible, grown-up woman among a crowd of rough boys at Eton. It thus seems likely that Leslie felt like a frail defenseless girl in the same crowd.

Leslie's days at Eton had other effects. As "day boys" he and his brother were treated as despised outsiders, a fact that Leslie never forgot.[63] He made not even one friend at Eton. As a consequence, when he went to Trinity Hall College at Cambridge, four years after leaving Eton, Leslie was much in need of acceptance, especially acceptance as a man among other men. All his life friendship was important to him. After initial disappointments, such as not being admitted to "The Apostles," the intellectually elite group in which his brother was prominent, he did find ways of fulfilling the need for friendship at Cambridge, some that were quite healthy emotionally, and some that complicated things further for him. He gained some satisfaction by developing his athletic ability through rowing, and subsequently through tramping and mountain climbing. Each of these sports gave him the sense of winning over great odds that had exhilarated him since infancy. They also made him feel like a successful member of a group. A significant accomplishment grew out of his rowing: because Leslie was too tall to row well, he became an excellent coach. His coaching yielded the satisfaction that other men looked up to him and had confidence in him.[64] Respect and admiration always remained important to him. Throughout his life he was respected and trusted, although strangely enough, he never really believed it true. His athletic interests also contributed to his professional development, for his first published articles were about mountain climbing.[65]

A less healthy result of Leslie's Cambridge days, according to Noel Annan (p. 32), was that he learned to sacrifice intellectual values—one of the things most important to him—in order to gain comradeship and to become a leader. Virginia also blamed Cambridge for what she considered her father's narrow intellectual attitudes.[66] There is some basis for these allegations, but apparently Leslie was only extending at Cambridge the compromise forced upon him when he was taught to be ashamed of poetry. He compromised his values even further when he took holy orders to become a tutor. As a tutor, he identified with the interests of the athletic undergraduates, aligned himself too closely with them and shared much of their scorn for dons who opposed their interests. Among the intellectual undergraduates he admired most was "the hard-headed man who stood for no nonsense — a type too often blind to the subtler kinds of sense,"[67] and, no doubt, also blind to poetry, literature, and art. Quentin Bell said (p. 8) that Leslie may have been imitating Fitzjames's "more robust habits of thought" and therefore became "half a Philistine, almost anti-intellectual."

Leslie felt that he had to justify his participation in athletics while a tutor and did so on the basis that sports kept the undergraduates out of mischief. This excuse may have been close to one of his true motives. His strong, often ridiculous moral standards, expressed as a child in his overreaction to stories of "naughtiness" in others, were ingrained in him by the time he got the post at Cambridge. His wish to prevent "mischief" also influenced his tutoring of undergraduates, according to Annan (p. 38). Leslie was suspicious of the "atmosphere of the mind" that literature and learning in general might generate in the young. What the undergraduates needed was an adult mind — *his* adult mind — to tell them what to accept and what to reject.

The accounts of Leslie's worries about the effect of literature on young, impressionable minds raise questions concerning Virginia Woolf's description of her father as a man who let her read all manner of books in his library.[68] There may not have been all types of books in his library. Many books alarmed him. For example, he was "angry" when Anny Thackeray's husband, Richmond Ritchie, let her read a book Leslie considered more scandalous, brutal, cynical, and indecent (his adjectives) than "French novels even," but assuaged his conscience and outrage by telling Anny that because she was married her morals were no longer his problem.[69] Annan (pp. 57-58) and Zink (p. 31) have noted also that Stephen's friendship with Lowell was strengthened by their shared attitude that sex was a topic unsuited for treatment in literature. No doubt Virginia was free to read whatever she liked in the library, but in the library Leslie censored as he compiled it.

Leslie Stephen's prudery and his tendency to compromise intellectually marred his professional life, especially, it seems, as editor of *Cornhill Magazine*. He believed that the editorship required him to be a slave to "popular stupidity," and to cater to readers' tastes and moral prejudices. Noel Annan writes (pp. 66-67) that Leslie seemed to think that *Cornhill* was read mostly by parsons' daughters—which, incidentally, Leslie's mother had been. Annan said also that in actuality Leslie's tastes often coincided with what he supposed the audience's to be. That seems likely in view of his exaggerated concern with what he termed "verbal shock."[70] In several instances he required writers to make changes that were indeed overrefined. For example, although he was one of the first to recognize Thomas Hardy's talent and sponsor him, he also censored him.[71] He once had Hardy delete the word "amorous" from a story and substitute "sentimental," thereby sacrificing Hardy's meaning to Leslie's prudery and concern with "verbal shock." On another occasion, he said that he might be somewhat "over-particular," but he didn't like the reference to a "close embrace in the London churchyard."[72]

Leslie's attempts to serve public taste and his failure to realize that tastes were changing accounted in some measure for the magazine's decline under his direction. Circulation dropped, *Cornhill* went into debt, and Leslie resigned as editor.[73]

Leslie Stephen was not entirely to blame for *Cornhill*'s decline in popularity, and, according to Zink (pp. 71-75), he defended his part in the magazine's difficulties. Circulation was already dropping when he assumed the editorship. After all, he said, he had inherited policy in matters of taste from William Makepeace Thackeray, the previous editor, and only applied it honestly. Also, Leslie accomplished a number of changes that improved the magazine's literary quality. But unfortunately his changes made *Cornhill*'s literary policy appear erratic, for he published in serial form several excellent novels by Thomas Hardy and others of similar stature, as well as the poorer, maundering, sentimental novels of his sister-in-law, Anny Thackeray, and of Margaret Oliphant.

## The Divided Man

From childhood Leslie Stephen progressed inevitably toward the divided condition of his adult years, the ultimate reality about him. Prone, virtually from infancy, to vacillations in temperament, to inordinate shyness, self-distrust, and dependency on others, his dividedness was increased and given form and substance by the crisis over poetry when he was eight as well as by his experiences at Eton and Cambridge. He was left, therefore, with a major division between what he desperately wanted to be and pretended to be in public — the tough-minded rationalist that symbolized manliness — and the regressive, infantile self he felt justified in being at home. His staunch rationalism was both a pose and a partially effective self-deception. Although he could deceive himself at times, his overconcern with projecting that image was responsible in part for the intellectual compromises we have noted and also earned him a reputation as pedant.

His determinedly tough-minded public stance fed his belief that he could never "measure up" intellectually, the belief prompted initially by his mother's premature efforts to make a scholar of him then reinforced by the crisis over poetry and his experiences at Eton and Cambridge. His need to appear tough-minded, and therefore masculine, led him to evaluate his work in one way while his reading public evaluated it in another. Perversely, or so it must have seemed to him, the public liked his literary criticism, his least tough-minded work, the work he could never trust himself to like.

Virginia was cognizant of her father's tendency to value his work differently than others did. In a letter to Dame Ethel Smyth in 1932, she commented about the irony of her father's having discredited his literary criticism when people continued to read it at the centennial of his birth.[74] Desmond MacCarthy spoke to the same point (p. 7), saying that Leslie Stephen thought it of little value if he brought some reader to understand Fielding and DeQuincey or if he gave a "true" account of someone's life. It was more important, Leslie thought, to help men to a "truer conception of the nature of things," or to be a man of science.

Another unfortunate consequence of Leslie's trying too hard to project a stern masculinity was his rather rigid approach to literary criticism. He believed that intuition had no place in such criticism; conclusions must be based on "facts" and on clear reasoning. Desmond MacCarthy pointed out (pp. 11, 17) that Leslie Stephen did not, or thought he should not, trust himself to tell a good coin by its ring. He believed that the critic should proceed cautiously in such "delicate matters," instead of leaping to truth rapidly and intuitively, as his daughter was later to do in her literary criticism. Because of these beliefs, Leslie Stephen was considered by many to be the "least aesthetic" of the noteworthy critics of his time. Quentin Bell (p. 10) was more complimentary of Leslie Stephen. He cited the delicacy, humor, and fantasy in all of Leslie's writing, implying that elements of the poet and artist survived in him, in spite of himself.

As later chapters will show, Leslie Stephen's dividedness disturbed his private life far more than his public life. Some of the complications and unpleasantness he caused at home are directly attributable to his exaggerated pose of tough-mindedness. According to Virginia Woolf's estimate in *To the Lighthouse,* he expected his children and other members of the family to emulate his pedantic adherence to "the facts" and to view the world, therefore, as "realistically" as he liked to think he did. She suggested that he blamed women's minds, especially his wife's, for their "folly" and irrationality. In his view, women were inevitably less faithful to empirical truth than were men.[75]

Illustrating the silly lengths to which Leslie carried his demands for factual accuracy is a letter he wrote to Julia telling her he couldn't understand when he was to meet her at Victoria Station. She said she was coming at 1:45 and he only knew of a train arriving at 1:44.[76] Had his family adhered to his demands for factuality life would have been unnecessarily gloomy for them. In effect, they were forbidden to hope for anything unless firm evidence existed that they would get it, as Virginia indicated in *To the Lighthouse.* That proscription was one of the qualities his children found tyrannical. It was also puzzling in light of so much else they knew about him. To Virginia his demands emphasized the discrepancies between different views of the world and the unfairness of being asked to relinquish her unique perspective for that of someone else. But her father's attitudes and rigidity also provided her with one of the major concerns of her fiction. In many of her novels, especially in *Night and Day* and *To the Lighthouse,* she developed the theme of contrary views of the world and the conflicts both within oneself and with others which often arise from them. Her father's demanding personality was also a source of conflict, discrepancies and vacillations in her personal life.

Leslie's demand for facts caused problems for Virginia's mother as well, for he tended to disparage her as illogical and unrealistic, even though she was more practical and had more common sense than he.[77] His rigid insistence on fact also brought on many conflicts with his sister-in-law, Anny Thackeray Ritchie (Mrs. Hilberry in *Night and Day*), who was vague, wandering, whimsical, and often unabashedly disorganized in her thought and speech. Others could find poetic charm and much amusement in Anny; Leslie only thought her illogical and given to optimism not supported by "the facts."[78]

Within the family, however, Leslie tended to turn loose the overly emotional, often irrational, regressive parts of his personality which wholly preempted his concern for "facts" and "truth." An infuriating aspect of his character was that he made little pretense of squaring his emotional temperament with his vaunted tough-mindedness or with his careful watch for inconsistency in others. His regressiveness was often burdensome, but it was not always unpleasant. Sometimes it evinced itself as boyish charm. Virginia said in her 1939-1940 memoir that she found her father most lovable when he was open and as direct as a child. Evidently a large measure of his regressiveness was benign; for example when he relaxed and played happily with his children during their infancy, he was very childlike in a harmless way. There was something enormously appealing about Leslie when he forgot himself and became, in effect, a small boy who unselfconsciously shouted or chanted verse. His helplessness, dependency and ineptitude in practical matters appealed to women and brought out their maternal feelings, making them want to care for and protect him. He was sufficiently cognizant of this appeal to turn it to his advantage. His helplessness assisted him to win and hold Julia's affection, although in the end it made him a burden to her. When Julia, with her propensity to assume responsibility for others, encountered Leslie, with his need to be nurtured and mothered, she was beguiled into dedicating herself to his welfare. That led, in turn, to their marriage and subsequently to her pushing herself beyond her physical limits, in major part by futilely trying to keep him comfortable, well, and happy.

# 3

# A Large and Austere Presence: Julia Stephen

Much less information is extant about Virginia Woolf's mother than her father. Quentin Bell (p. 17) has observed that Julia Stephen was relatively elusive to researchers, and Virginia Woolf indicated that there was something elusive about her as a person. Since Julia was often the subject of legendary stories, much of the information which remains about her is questionable. Except for what she revealed in the letters to Leslie Stephen during his courtship, which I will discuss in subsequent chapters, Julia appears to have been an opaque personality. Her inner motives often must be surmised from the pattern of her life, for she rarely revealed information about herself. During the courtship she said that she thought it "stupid and selfish" to talk about oneself,[1] and Virginia suggested in *To the Lighthouse* (p. 46) that her mother made it almost a policy not to do so.

There is sufficient information to establish that Julia and Julia's family were in many respects unlike Leslie and the Stephens. Much of the information has been brought together in Brian Hill's book on Julia Margaret Cameron, Julia's aunt, and Virginia's great aunt.[2] The maternal branch of Julia's family was the most important in her life, and within that branch, the Pattles — Julia's mother and her six sisters — set significant styles and family traditions. Apparently they partly shaped Julia's personality, though they influenced it less than did the traumatic death of her first husband, Herbert Duckworth. The Duckworth family—three of whose scions Julia brought into the Stephen family and other members of which frequented the household as relatives-by-courtesy to the Stephen children —was also unlike the Stephen family. As Quentin Bell said (p. 18), the differences between her maternal and paternal relatives led Virginia to say that two contradictory blood streams clashed in her veins, creating conflicts and polarities in her. Certainly two very different traditions met and, in some measure, clashed in her parents' marriage.

Julia's relatives were better off financially than the Stephens, and they spent more money on travel and dress. They kept more servants and their children were often given over to the care of governesses, rather than having the intimate contact that Leslie had with his mother. Bell said (pp. 20-21) that Julia's family had a higher social position than Leslie's, and was well established in the upper-middle class before the Stephen family entered it. Perhaps the Pattles were not entirely satisfied with their status. A remarkable number of them and their descendants, including George Duckworth, found it desirable to marry titles. By contrast, the Stephen family had their titles awarded for merit. The Pattles also liked to recall that they were descended from French "nobility." In *To the Lighthouse* (p. 17), French nobility became that "very noble, if slightly mythical Italian house, whose daughters, scattered about English drawing-rooms in the nineteenth century, had lisped to charmingly and stormed so wildly . . . ," and to which Mrs. Ramsay's wit, bearing and temper are attributed.

The women among Julia's relatives were reputedly blessed with more beautiful faces than were the Stephen women. The Pattle sisters gained their reputations primarily for their beauty, and Julia Stephen was considered one of the most beautiful of the clan. Bell said (pp. 19-20) that the Pattle women tended to be "grave, noble, majestic but neither vivacious nor very approachable." Leonard Woolf thought that the admixture of Stephen blood made Virginia lovelier than if she had been "pure" Pattle.[3]

The Pattle sisters also became known for allegedly marrying docile husbands — a tradition Julia clearly did not follow in marrying Leslie Stephen.

Little evidence has been found to suggest that Julia's relatives were ever concerned with political causes on as large a scale as the Stephens. They were thought to be less intellectual.[4] Most of them were less gifted with language; Julia believed that she was inept with words[5] although her essay, "Notes from the Sickroom," belies her estimate. As Annan has noted, (pp. 100-101) Julia's essay anticipated something of Virginia's verve and style with language. Whether gifted with words or not, the Pattles were interested in literary art, especially poetry. They were interested in other kinds of art as well. Mostly they were interested in artists and poets, the principal "causes" they sponsored, and they lauded and bestowed their favors on the near great as generously as the great.[6]

At the point of merging, the Stephen and Pattle families were not totally unlike each other in values and traditions. One significant factor they had in common was a great interest in health. For example, Hill said (p. 86) that Julia's aunt, Julia Margaret Cameron, went immediately into action when friends became ill, accusing the patient's doctor of carelessness and ignorance, and "spending hours in doctors' waiting-rooms so that she could describe the patient's symptoms and extort a diagnosis and advice from some leading Harley Street authority who had never so much as set eyes on the sufferer." Another aunt, Virginia Pattle, who became Lady Somers, was given to even greater concern and more dramatic action in questions of health. After one of her children died from diphtheria, she became obsessed with the health of her two remaining daughters. A cold, a stomach upset, or some other minor condition was cause enough for her to pack up the children, their governess, servants, and sometimes their piano, and rush them to Brighton or some other health spa. Hill quotes (pp. 164-165) one of Lady Somers's many letters to her children. " 'Do you feel *very well?* Are you sensible of feeling much stronger for Brighton air? Does your throat look better? Do you or Addy ever have backache? Or pains or aches anywhere? Is your appetite good?' " Lady Somers's exaggerated concern with health is also made evident by advice to her daughter that she might sing if she didn't go higher than E and thereby strain her throat.

Perhaps Julia Stephen was following a family interest when she became a "nurse," but evidently that had more to do with her mother, Maria Pattle Jackson, who was also very much concerned with health, including her own. On the Stephen side, Leslie and his mother were unduly interested in health — mainly Leslie's. Also significant at the time of their union were the strong ties both Leslie and Julia had with their mothers.

### "Pattledom"

Four members of Julia Stephen's family were especially colorful, interesting, and of some significance in her life and background. They were her great grandfather, the "noble" French ancestor; her grandfather, James Pattle; and her aunts, Julia Margaret Cameron and Sarah Prinsep. From Hill (pp. 19-22) we learn that Julia's "noble" French ancestor was Chevalier Ambroise Pierre Antoine de l'Etang, an officer of the Gard du Corps to Louis XVI, and superintendent of the royal stud farm. For obscure reasons, but allegedly because Queen Marie Antoinette was too openly devoted to him, Chevalier de l'Etang was exiled to India. He was fortunate because he was exiled before the French Revolution for, as a reputed favorite of the hated Austrian Queen, he would likely have been put to death had he remained in France. In India he ran a riding school, managed stud farms, traded in horses, and acted as a veterinarian. He married a French woman who had been born and brought up in India and fathered two sons and three daughters. One of the daughters married James Pattle, and from the marriage the seven Pattle sisters were born and "Pattledom" — to borrow Thackeray's term — was founded. Chevalier de l'Etang perhaps did not have the highest credentials as a noble ancestor, but he did give the family a vaguely romantic aura that pleased the Pattles and Virginia Woolf.

If Chevalier de l'Etang added the romantic touch, James Pattle contributed to the family history something of the roguish and macabre, or so family legend indicates. James was the subject of many family stories of doubtful truth.[7] He was said to have been one of the most wicked men in India, to have earned the nickname, "King of Liars," and, contradictorily, to have been an important and reliable figure in the East India Company for fifty three years. Nevertheless the persisting legend was that he was almost perpetually drunk, and that eventually he drank himself to death. Even then, the story goes, he managed to drive his wife out of her wits, as perhaps he had almost done while he was alive. The keg of rum in which his body was embalmed to be transported to England for burial (some say, thus embalmed at his deathbed request) allegedly exploded and ejected his corpse before his unfortunate wife's eyes. Some accounts have it that the experience drove her insane, others, that she died of fright. Virginia got the latter version in 1917 from a conversation with Lady Strachey, Lytton Strachey's mother, whose family had known the Pattles in India. In recording the story in her diary in 1918, Virginia said, possibly adding a fillip of her own, that the sailors aboard the ship "drained the tank" long before the reencased body of Great-Grandfather Pattle reached England.[8]

Julia Margaret Cameron, James Pattle's daughter, is the next of Julia Stephen's family to merit attention, and in this study she merits far more consideration than either Chevalier de l'Etang or James Pattle. Mrs. Cameron earned a reputation — which has long outlived her — as a photographer and an eccentric. Though some of her photographs were eccentric, their artistic merit continues to be acknowledged. Her eccentricity in her personal life derived from an imbalance that many of the Pattle women evinced, Virginia's mother included — the tendency to give themselves too wholeheartedly to certain of their interests. Mrs. Cameron pursued photography with that kind of devotion, although she brought a real talent to it as well. She and several other Pattle sisters pursued friendship in a similar manner, and were benevolent and generous as friends — whether or not the recipient needed or felt he could tolerate the benevolence and generosity of the moment.[9] Julia Stephen practiced benevolence in a typically Pattle fashion, and followed family tradition in her obsession with health.

Two of Julia Margaret Cameron's many friends were Alfred Tennyson and the minor poet Henry Taylor, whose work seemed to her to be as meritorious as that of Tennyson, or of anyone — an opinion not generally shared.[10] Maria Pattle Jackson (Julia's mother and Virginia Woolf's grandmother) befriended Coventry Patmore, another minor poet considered by Mrs. Jackson to be equal to the best.[11] Sarah Prinsep, another Pattle sister, cultivated friendships with artists, literary figures, and learned men, in grand and generous style. She and her husband, Thoby Prinsep, were friends and patrons of the painter George Frederick Watts, providing him with living quarters and a studio for many years. Around Watts, Sarah Prinsep built a salon of impressive proportions and constituency at Little Holland House, the Prinsep home in the Kensington section of London, and later in Freshwater, Isle of Wight. Holman Hunt, Edward Burne-Jones, John Everett

Millais, and Dante Gabriel Rossetti were among the painters attracted to the salon by the presence of Watts and also by the beauty of the Pattle sisters, of whom they made many drawings and finished portraits. Other persons sometimes present were the actress, Ellen Terry, briefly the wife of Watts; the poets Tennyson, Aubrey de Vere, and Henry Taylor; the novelists Thackeray, George Eliot and Thomas Hughes.[12] After Thackeray's death, Mrs. Cameron took his young daughters under her care, making them part of the Prinsep circle, and she duly recorded the girls' grief for their father by photographing them in mourning.[13] John Ruskin, Benjamin Jowett and Thomas Carlyle represented the "learned men" in the Prinsep group. The Prince of Wales was reputedly in attendance at times and was said to have danced with Julia Stephen.[14] Disraeli and Gladstone were said by Quentin Bell (p. 15) to have been *habitués*. The Brownings came at least once to the Prinseps' salon, but Mrs. Browning disapproved of the "class" represented by Mrs. Prinsep and of the "noisiness" of the group she met there.[15]

Virginia Woolf was fascinated by stories of Julia Margaret Cameron's friends and by Sarah Prinsep's artistic and literary salon, as her play, *Freshwater,* shows. The Prinsep salon was one that even "Bloomsbury" might have envied, and was brought together more self-consciously and deliberately than "Bloomsbury" was. It contributed to Mrs. Prinsep's equivocal reputation, for in many minds during the middle and late nineteenth century in England, art was associated with immortality. Hill recounted (p. 57) that Edward Lear, an occasional member of Sarah Prinsep's salon, overheard the following comment: " 'I've just found out that chap we were talking to last night is nothing but a beastly landscape painter.' " Inevitably, there was gossip about Mrs. Prinsep's establishment, though no reason for scandal. But apparently the Prinseps were oblivious to malicious reports about themselves, as members of the Bloomsbury group were to be in Virginia's day.[16]

Julia Stephen, as a girl, often visited at Little Holland House and looked back upon her times there with great nostalgia.[17] Virginia Woolf thought that her mother's associations at Little Holland House provided much of Julia's education. Perhaps her visits accounted for Julia's being less narrow and judgmental than Leslie Stephen and her belief that she was less concerned with proprieties than he was,[18] although certainly her aunts set ample precedence for propriety whatever their reputations.

Parentage and Early Life

Julia's early life remains particularly obscure. She was born in 1846, nearly fifteen years later than Leslie. Possibly she was born in India, where her father, John Jackson, was a physician from 1830 to 1855, or possibly in England where Mrs. Jackson sometimes made trips for reasons of health.[19] Virginia thought her mother had been born in India, in 1848.[20] The scant knowledge of Julia's childhood thus begins with a fact that allegedly was one of the least important in her life—her having been the daughter of Dr. Jackson. It was Leslie's opinion, expressed in the "Mausoleum Book" (pp. 54, 57), that fathers counted much less in Julia's family than fathers should count. If, in fact, Dr. Jackson "did not count," it may have been because he married Maria who, like other Pattle women, was said to dominate her husband.[21] Concerning Dr. Jackson, Leslie said further that Julia's love for her father had not been among her stronger affections, and that her love for her mother had been the dominant force in her life. Leslie hinted that Dr. Jackson had not merited her love, saying that he had had only "commonplace understanding" and had "worshipped respectability" too much. Moreover, according to Leslie, Dr. Jackson was unresponsive to "loftier moods," to his wife's "high morality," and to the "poetical and lofty in life."[22]

A Large and Austere Presence

However accurately he may have expressed family attitudes and Julia's feeling for her father, Leslie was speaking from, or pretending, a strangely limited knowledge of Dr. Jackson, and perhaps was satirizing Mrs. Jackson, whom Leslie often resented. Dr. Jackson was an eminent physician and leading medical consultant during his twenty-five years in India. Although he retired to England in 1855 and died in 1887, his name was venerated in Calcutta, the site of most of his work, well into the twentieth century. He was the first professor of medicine at the Calcutta Medical College, and the author of a book on varieties of tetanus in India. After returning to England, he practiced medicine in West London, then set up an office in Sussex because of his wife's wish to be near her idol, Coventry Patmore.[23] In later year, Dr. and Mrs. Jackson resided in Brighton, where the Stephen children were frequently taken for visits when they were very small.

Julia's beauty is one of the more reliable facts recovered from her early life. But here, as in so many instances, the facts are entangled with and obscured by doubtful stories. A silly and improbable story, cited with approval by Leslie in the "Mausoleum Book" (p. 24) and recalled by Virginia Woolf in her 1939-1940 memoir, recounts how Julia was saved from consciousness of her beauty by Mrs. Jackson's careful handling of her as a child. Leslie said that Mrs. Jackson customarily had a less beautiful sister accompany Julia to protect her from the adulatory attentions of men — by what means he did not say. It may be true that a sister acted as her chaperone, but the procedure did not prevent Julia from knowing she was beautiful, a realization upon which Leslie Stephen and Mrs. Jackson frowned. Another of the reliable facts about Julia's early life shows that if Maria Jackson did send Julia's sister as a chaperone, her precautions were inconsistent and, therefore, destined to fail. With her mother's approbation, Julia was among the many members of the Pattle family to model for the artists who

56

stayed at Little Holland House. Watts sketched her as a child and painted her on two later occasions. When she was ten, the sculptor, Marachetti, elected her to model for the statue of Princess Elizabeth, daughter of Charles I, which was part of his monument at Carisbrook. Julia's most famous sitting was for the madonna in Edward Burne-Jones's painting, *The Annunciation.* Her aunt, Mrs. Cameron, made many photographs of her, including some of her in mourning.[24] The frequent requests that she sit as a model must have made Julia aware that others thought her beautiful. Quentin Bell (p. 18) believed her to be quite aware of her beauty. Virginia Woolf agreed. She might be bored by it and regret it, Virginia said in *To the Lighthouse,* but carried it with her like a torch and could not help knowing it.[25] Julia also became aware from modeling that her beauty was "flawed"; when Leslie wrote that her nose was obstinate, she replied that it had "aggravated" everyone who had drawn her.[26]

Julia became more than a favorite model to the artists whom she met at Little Holland House. As she grew up, several of them fell in love with her, and at least two wanted to marry her —Holman Hunt, the painter, and Thomas Woolner, the sculptor. Watts was said also to have been in love with her. Noel Annan reported that Hunt and Woolner later married sisters, but that both were in love with a third sister, their mutual sister-in-law, who had a great physical resemblance to Julia. When Hunt's first wife died, he incurred Woolner's lasting displeasure by marrying the third sister. The marriage had to take place abroad because British law then forbade marriage to a deceased wife's sister.[27]

Another reliable fact about Julia's early life is that she and her mother had an extraordinarily close relationship that became even closer in later years. Quentin Bell said (pp. 16-18) that Julia was the best loved of Maria Jackson's three daughters and that Mrs. Jackson required almost constant reassurance of

Julia's affection. At the very least, Julia was almost constantly in her thoughts, for when they were apart, Mrs. Jackson wrote her three or four letters a day and sometimes wired her as well. Bell described Mrs. Jackson (pp. 16-18) as a silly, sentimental woman, and she manifested some of her silliness in writing to her daughter. She had other sides; while mawkish with those she loved, she was given to strong dislike of others. As one acquaintance put it, she was very fond of some persons and equally averse to others. The same acquaintance called her "a great invalid" and commented also on her beauty and stateliness.[28] Hill credited her (p. 159) with inner serenity — a misleading impression, for she had "nervous" as well as physical complaints.

Leslie Stephen said in the "Mausoleum Book" (pp. 56-57) that neither Julia nor her mother ever said a word to displease the other and that they loved each other so well that it seemed as if they were alone together in the universe. But once again Leslie is not to be taken literally; he was writing, to some extent, out of his jealousy and resentment over the closeness between his wife and her mother. Moreover, Leslie must have known of and applauded at least one instance when Julia hurt her mother deeply. During her widowhood, Julia gave up religion, which distressed Mrs. Jackson, a devout, though sentimentally religious, woman.[29]

The emotional bond between Julia and her mother reputedly developed due to Mrs. Jackson's "great invalidism," and began when Julia, as a young child, was called upon to nurse her mother through a serious illness. This experience gave Julia her "training" as a nurse, and led her to think of nursing as a kind of calling. What began then was to continue. Nursing her mother was a duty, or perhaps a pleasure, which recurred many times, for Mrs. Jackson's physical and "nervous" complaints, whether valid or contrived — to gain her daughter's company — often brought Julia to her side. Julia almost never ignored a summons from her mother no matter what the state of her family, her household, or even her health.

When Julia's first husband died, her deep unhappiness increased her bonds with her mother. Her use of nursing to divert her grief also increased the bonds. Following a Pattle tradition, Mrs. Jackson emerged as a kind of medical seer and soothsayer, although hardly a "wise Fate." Julia talked over her cases with her mother, and, sight unseen and with little medical knowledge, Mrs. Jackson made diagnoses and prescribed treatment.[30] Dr. Jackson might have been a better ally if he had been asked, but no evidence has been found to suggest that he was consulted.

By present day, post-Freudian standards, the relationship between Julia and her mother seems much too stultifying to have been healthy for either of them, even allowing for exaggerations in reports about Julia. It was also inverted, with the daughter, even as a child, acting more nearly the traditional role of mother. In her own day, however, the age of Florence Nightingale, it established Julia's reputation among family and friends as an ideal daughter and as an ideal woman. She was following a sufficient number of the Pattle traditions to be looked upon with great approval.


Education

Julia's "training" as a nurse was a significant part of her education. In general, she was not well educated, although probably as well educated as most women of her class in that period of English history. In her 1939-1940 memoir, Virginia Woolf said that Little Holland House, and all it entailed, had "educated" her mother; that Julia had been taught by a governess to speak French with a good accent; that she was musical and learned to play the piano; but that, all in all, her mind was less trained than instinctive. Virginia believed also that her mother had a passion for literature. Her favorite books, according to Virginia, were *Confessions of an Opium-Eater* which Julia kept at her bedside, and the works of Sir Walter Scott, which she had once requested of Dr. Jackson as a birthday present.

Julia deplored her limited formal education, much as Virginia in turn was to regret her own, although Julia had more justification. During their courtship she asked Leslie to expound his ideas about education for women. He replied that both women and men should be better educated than men were at that time in history; that women should be educated in whatever directions their talents and preferences might indicate; and that they should be well enough educated that they could earn a living, or be authorities, in freely chosen areas.[31] Julia was upset — "depressed utterly" — because he described an ideal so unlike her actual education, and she accused him of making her feel all the more inferior to him. With the bitter incisiveness she exhibited at times, she added that if one did show a particular bent, no doubt she would be forced into some other calling.[32] With exchanges like these, Leslie and Julia may have taught Virginia some of her feminist attitudes. However, Leslie Stephen in practice was the antithesis of the Leslie Stephen in his mind. In bringing up his children he did little to promulgate his avowed ideals in the matter of women's education. And as Virginia knew, her mother once took a stand against feminist causes.[33] Moreover, the record shows that Julia Stephen was more concerned with her sons' than her daughters' education.

First Marriage

Reliable facts about Julia Stephen are more easily recovered from the period of her life starting with her first marriage. She met Herbert Duckworth in Venice, and they fell immediately and idyllically in love.[34] They were soon married. Evidently it was a marriage of equals, and one of the few important relationships in Julia's life that did not require her to be the stronger partner emotionally. Duckworth was a young barrister of the landed gentry class and a man of independent means. He was handsome, poised, and socially adept, but not brilliant. He seems to have been well suited to the social life of the Pattles, and most acceptable to Julia's mother.

Leslie Stephen had known Herbert slightly at Cambridge, long before either man became interested in Julia. He had been envious enough of Herbert to remember him and record his envy in the "Mausoleum Book" (pp. 26-27) in 1895, long after Herbert's death. Leslie said that he envied Herbert's ability to form friendships, a capacity he lacked when he went to Cambridge. He also envied Herbert's fashionable way of dressing, which he called an "outward and visible sign of breeding." Leslie thought that fashionable dress rather than inherent merit had enabled Herbert to acquire friends. Leslie felt slovenly in comparison and blamed his scanty wardrobe for his lack of friends.

After Julia's death, Leslie read the correspondence between his wife and her first husband, noting in the "Mausoleum Book" (pp. 27-29) that he was "driven" by "a kind of fascination" to "glance through" their letters. After doing so, he described Herbert Duckworth as a modest, sweet-tempered man and concluded that Julia had had her "purest happiness" with her first husband. He said that in keeping with her personality, she had surrendered herself completely to Herbert and that the surrender was mutual. It was Leslie's opinion that such a lack of reserve was personally "dangerous" and, in most cases, a prelude to disaster. However, he believed that Julia's faith in her young husband had been fulfilled because it was based both on "thorough insight" and "strong passion." But Leslie was describing Herbert Duckworth for the sake of the Duckworth children, and the opinions of Herbert that he stated may have been affected for that reason.

Leslie's references in the "Mausoleum Book" (pp. 27-29, 65) to Julia's first marriage reveal more about her two husbands than they do about her. However, he did unveil one important facet of his wife's personality during her first marriage — her tendency to be extremely anxious, especially when separated from Herbert. Leslie and his first wife had witnessed Julia's distress when Herbert missed a train and left her waiting. Julia's sister told Leslie that Julia was commonly in a state of near panic when separated from Herbert. Leslie felt that Julia's anxious temperament also caused her to be overly concerned about her childrens' illnesses. However, extant information contradicts that conclusion; her desire to nurse sick adults sometimes took her away from home when the children were ill.

Virginia Woolf wrote briefly on two occasions about her mother's first husband and her marriage to him. The first time was in her 1908 memoir when she expressed the belief that Herbert Duckworth had been inferior to her mother, but that her mother's great gifts, her "superabundance," had compensated for his shortcomings to make a happy marriage. Virginia said that the marriage would not have continued to be happy if Herbert had lived, contending that her mother had found her ideal mate in Leslie Stephen, not Herbert Duckworth. Not even Leslie professed this belief. Virginia wrote again of Julia's first husband in her 1939-1940 memoir and was less defensive about her father. She said that she regretted knowing so little about Herbert Duckworth, for if she could have known more of him, she would have found her mother less elusive. She believed that Herbert Duckworth must have been simple, genial, normal, and ordinary — because it would have been natural for her mother to love a man like that. Presumably, Virginia concluded that it was less natural for her mother to love and marry her father. She said also that one of the outstanding things about her mother's life was that she had married two persons who differed as widely as Herbert Duckworth and Leslie Stephen. Julia had married Leslie, Virginia concluded, because she pitied him and admired his intellect.

Widowhood

Julia married Herbert Duckworth when she was about twenty-one. They had been married less than four years, had two children (George and Stella) and were expecting a third (Gerald), when suddenly Herbert died. The account of his death reads like a Victorian melodrama. He reached up to the topmost branch of a tree to pick a fig for Julia; an abscess burst in his brain; he fell unconscious at his wife's feet and died within twenty-four hours. It was of course no melodrama, but an existentially absurd and painful event, no doubt made all the more painful by Julia's earlier anxieties about her husband. His death changed Julia's life and character insofar as one can determine from the scant information about her earlier life. It was to have far reaching influence upon her children as well, especially Virginia, for Herbert Duckworth's death was one of the many instances in the family history when expectations were dramatically and tragically reversed and life seemed to betray by promising happiness and providing calamity instead.

Julia spoke of her reactions to Herbert's death in a number of her letters to Leslie, and was uncharacteristically self-revelatory. Her life, she said, had become "entirely a shipwreck" when she was only twenty-four. (In the "Mausoleum Book" Leslie translated her words into his own terms and described Julia as he sometimes described himself: life for Julia became a futile procession of shadows without "life" and without meaning.) It would have been easier for her if she could have mourned openly, she said, and if she could have "broken down more." However, she had to think of her unborn child and everyone around her kept urging her not to give in to her grief.[35] And it was hardly in her character to break down and express feelings, for Julia was "not demonstrative."[36] Apparently, by the time of her widowhood she was already trying to live out the expectations of others that she was strong and could bear up, no matter what, and that her role was to extend comfort and consolation, not to need them herself—qualities that later made her so attractive to Leslie.

According to a letter from Julia to Leslie quoted in the "Mausoleum Book" (pp. 31-32), the person who seems to have comforted Julia most was not, as one might have supposed, her mother to whom she was so close, but Anny Thackeray, Julia's close friend and Leslie's sister-in-law. Quite unlike Julia, Anny was not only able to express her emotions, but believed it a social obligation to do so in times of grief. The friendship of the two young women was a complementary one, for they had few traits in common. In this respect it was like most of the important relationships in Julia's life, with the exception of her first marriage.

During Julia's immediate bereavement, Anny Thackeray visited her almost daily, and although Julia could not "pour out" her grief, Anny would talk with her about it. She got Julia to take an interest in Anny's social life and work, which was writing or trying to write novels. Despite her gift for language and her whimsical, fanciful imagination, Anny was much too disorganized for the occupation. It was Julia's part to supply some of the order that Anny lacked by copying and arranging her manuscripts—as Virginia Woolf showed Katharine Hilbery doing for Mrs. Hilbery in *Night and Day* (pp. 134 ff.). Perhaps Anny was trying to repay, through Julia, some of the kindness the Pattle sisters had shown her and Minny when their father died. Later, Julia was able to return Anny's kindness by assisting her after the death of Minny.

Julia's grief was uncommonly strong, in part no doubt, because of her inability to mourn, as she later realized. She was left with persisting melancholia and suicidal ideas that turned her into a "chronic" mourner. She told Leslie that the major horror she experienced when Herbert died was knowing that she had to continue to live on and on without him, and that for a long time she had wanted nothing so much as to die.[37] Mrs. Cameron recalled that five years after Herbert's death Julia had asked her, with tears in her eyes, to pray that she (Julia) might die.[38] Julia continued to talk to Leslie Stephen of longing to die throughout his courtship of her, using that as an argument not to marry him. Thus the vague suicide wish that Virginia Woolf attributed to her mother in *To the Lighthouse* (p. 127) was actually present in her, and was both stronger and more lasting than Virginia indicated in the novel.

During her marriage to Leslie, which took place about eight years after Herbert's death, Julia manifested a strain of morbid sadness so strong and persistent that Leslie tried painstakingly in the "Mausoleum Book" (pp. 45-47, 30-31), often contradicting himself, to argue that the sadness had only been an "illusion." Julia had been happy, had busied herself spreading love and happiness during their marriage, he claimed, in spite of the theme of unhappiness that recurred in her letters, and the "clouds" that sometimes passed over her mind. He blamed the illusion of Julia's melancholia after their marriage on her excessive concern with the sick and the dying. But Leslie also quoted Julia in the "Mausoleum Book" (p. 30) as saying that her nursing was a way of fighting her melancholia, not the root of it. One of his most contradictory statements was that although Julia's care of her children, her mother, and friends brought her much deep, quiet happiness, she hardly rose to anything more than cheerfulness.

Julia's melancholia and preoccupation with dying did not
incapacitate her, even during the immediate shock of Herbert's death. She showed admirable strength of character and
determination, and eventually adjusted to her grief. She
learned to live with it, she said, by being as cheerful as possible, by doing as much as she could, and by trying not to
think. To Leslie she expressed the opinion that when she got
over the worst of the shock, she was happier and more cheerful
than most people.[39] However, her claim must be understood in
the context of her other belief that few people are happy, that
the world is filled with pain and unhappiness, and that one
must combat these problems, as she did by means of her
charity.[40] Evidently, she was never very cheerful, and Virginia
said that she could not imagine her mother happy.

Whether or not Julia ever overcame her unhappiness, she
fought hard to do so, as she said she would, by keeping herself
as busy as possible. Eventually she damaged her health, speed-
ing her own death by her busyness. Her interest in charity was
well established before her second marriage and partly accounted for her friendship and eventual marriage to Leslie.
After she married Leslie and had four more children, other
duties kept her busy. Much of her time was spent keeping Leslie minimally content and tractable. But she also did more
nursing and charitable work after her second marriage, seemingly grateful for reasons to be out of the household. As Virginia said, her second marriage more than her widowhood
caused her to give herself to others.[41]

In the "Mausoleum Book" (pp. 31, 49, 63-64), Leslie described his wife's charities, admitting resentment that she gave
so much attention to others and at the same time insisting that
he admired her for doing so. He acknowledged that she felt
better and "more content" when she busied herself with these
activities, saying that thoughts of dying came to her when she
turned away from such work. Leslie professed to see a philoso-

phy and something analogous to a religious calling in her activities. He said further that there was a system, a calculated
plan, in the way Julia bestowed upon others both what they
wanted and what she thought they needed.[42] Leslie's description made Julia seem somewhat in the tradition of her aunt,
Julia Margaret Cameron although less eccentric in her charities. Mrs. Cameron had a penchant for giving presents according to her own whims and sometimes startled the recipients.[43]
For example, Hill said (pp. 87-88) that Mrs. Cameron once
stayed up all night to redecorate a room in order to surprise
her host, and (p. 133) that she sent Tennyson's ailing son, Hal-
lam, a pair of loose, purple and gold Oriental trousers, Japa-
nese tea cups and a teapot, and a roll of flannel. There were
important differences: Mrs. Cameron gave gifts that the Stephen household would not have been able to afford and that
would have angered Leslie.

Leslie said in the "Mausoleum Book" (pp. 49, 63-64) that
Julia tried to make her kindnesses appear as a repayment for
some kindness done her. He believed Julia's charities were a
manifestation both of her anxiety and of a "spontaneous over-
flowing" of compassion so great that she constantly had to seek
outlets for it. His analysis, the multiple and contradictory
explanations he cited for Julia's good will may indicate his
reluctance to face one of her most probable reasons, namely,
her need to have respites from him. They also indicate his own
bewilderment, for her perpetual giving of herself to others was
so antithetical to Leslie's own inclinations, that he could
hardly have comprehended it. He was, nevertheless, correct in
suggesting that she had more than one motive, for her benevo-
lences were definitely overdetermined.

Much that has been said about Julia's almost obsessive bene-
ficence, including Virginia's account in *To the Lighthouse,*
make her appear, at least potentially, a dangerous meddler.
She would have been especially dangerous in her charity if she

ever played the role of commanding Empress as Virginia thought she did at times in arranging marriages.[44] However, Virginia also said in her 1908 memoir that Julia was less dangerous than she intimated in the novel. Certainly others seem not to have thought her dangerous since so many people asked for her assistance. Quentin Bell (p. 38) referred to these requests in telling of the letters Virginia found in Julia's traveling desk when she died.[45] "There was a letter from a woman whose daughter had been betrayed, . . . one from a nurse who was out of work; there were begging letters, there were many pages from a girl who had quarreled with her parents. Everyone demanded some kind of help or sympathy, everyone knew that, from her, they would get it."

Julia may have been saved from greater error because she was truly compassionate (though probably less so than Leslie thought), and also because she could identify with people in difficulty. Julia's essay, "Notes from the Sickroom," quoted in part and discussed by Annan (pp. 100-101), shows that she carried out her nursing with a sincere wish to help others and usually with a judiciousness made possible by sensitivity. Her reserve, detachment, and emotional distance were qualities that many persons must have appreciated in the sickroom, with the noticeable exception of Anny Thackeray. As Noel Annan stated, Julia reacted to others' feelings instinctively, but delicately and remotely. Thus she seems to have avoided some of the pitfalls one expects of those who are helpful more for reasons of their own than because of the needs of those they try to help. Nevertheless, Julia did cause damage, much of it to Virginia. She undertook to help many people, and recognized so few practical limits to her responsibilities to them that she had little time and energy for her children. Why she did so comprises on of the paradoxes of her life.

The reports of Julia's widowhood leave no doubt that, for the most part, she adapted constructively to her grief and that her manner of doing so was determined by complex motives. Her compassion, strength, and courage were admirable, and all that happened to her elicits pity, the kind of pity she gave little evidence of feeling for herself. Her contemporaries, possibly her children as well, were led to admire and pity her, and these feelings encouraged the legends about her. Julia's story was turned into both legend and melodrama in Leslie Stephen's telling of it. In the "Mausoleum Book" (pp. 74, 80) he cast her as a grief-stricken young woman whose life is shattered by the sudden death of her beloved husband, but who summons the strength to behave nobly and turn her grief to the benefit of mankind. Leslie also wrote and lectured about the utilitarian application of sorrow and about hidden benefactors. He admitted privately that he had Julia in mind, as no doubt everyone knew. But perhaps because he was uncomfortable about what he regarded as unmanly feelings, he said he was reluctant to admit publicly that he was referring to his wife.

However, if one is to understand Julia and her influence on her daughter, it is necessary to follow Virginia's and Julia's leads, not Leslie Stephen's, and to avoid seeing her as the heroine of a melodrama. One must turn a blind eye to the real tragedy of the situation, as Virginia said in *To the Lighthouse* (p. 294) one must with respect to her beauty, and keep in mind that there was something overdone and a-tilt, and probably something neurotic in Julia's perpetual charities. Possibly there was also something incipiently suicidal in the extent of her self-sacrifice.

Betrayal by Life

Julia's effect on Virginia can be attributed to her style of life, which was greatly influenced by her inverted, overly close relationship with her own mother, by the death of her first husband, and by her manner of adjusting to her grief. It was her style of life that led her to her involvement and complex relationship with Virginia's father, the subject of the next two chapters of my study. In addition, Virginia was influenced by Julia's sudden bereavement, a stark and horrifying example of the tragic theme and pattern of the Stephen family history, that life is likely to betray one just when it seems to promise great happiness. Julia's loss of her first husband was only one of many instances of this phenomenon. Leslie's first wife died suddenly when they were expecting their second child. Leslie's daughter by his first marriage was tragically psychotic from an early age. His nephew, James K. Stephen, a young poet of some merit, incurred a head injury, went insane and died when he was only thirty-three. Julia herself was to die as her young family approached maturity. Her daughter, Stella Duckworth, died several months after her wedding day and while expecting a child. Julia's son Thoby died at the beginning of what everyone expected to be a distinguished career. The pattern followed the family into the next generation, for the promising scholar and poet, Julian Bell, Vanessa's son, died as a young man fighting in the Spanish civil War.[46]

Julia Stephen would not know about most of the tragedies in the family. However, they made their impression on Virginia, giving her a major theme for her writing and accounting in part for the serious problems in her personal life. For example, some episodes of her madness were precipitated in part by the seeming betrayal of promise. Although Julia did not know about most of the tragedies, there is evidence that she taught Virginia to be on guard against life's hideous trickery. *To the Lighthouse* (p. 92) shows that Virginia was aware of her mother's expectation that life would betray her and that she thought it quick to "pounce" on one. Also, in one of the remaining letters from Julia Stephen to Virginia, Julia tells of a woman who years earlier had killed her child unintentionally by "waltzing" it around the room until all its breath was gone. Mrs. Stephen ended her brief, macabre account with the chilling admonition that Virginia must be careful never to waltz children around the room.[47]

# 4

# Winning a Great Prize
# over Insurmountable Odds

Virginia Woolf implied that Leslie and Julia Stephen and their family backgrounds were very different from one another when she said that two contrary bloodstreams clashed in her veins. They were so unlike that it is not surprising that during most of the couple's courtship, it appeared that they would never marry. For a long time, Julia could not even think of marrying Leslie, though more because of her own problems than because of admitted objections to him. And it seemed to him improbable that she would ever consider the marriage. But that may have been an attraction, for since childhood he had liked winning over great odds.

At their first meeting, Julia made Leslie feel shy, and he went away without even trying to attract her. Their first encounter occurred before either was married the first time. Leslie had been told by the novelist Thomas Hughes, a mutual friend, that Julia Jackson was a woman in whom he might well be interested.[1] Since Leslie in his early thirties was coming rather belatedly to realize that he wanted to be married, he made a tentative move in Julia's direction. He visited Little Holland House where she was staying with her aunt and uncle, the Prinseps, met her and her artistic friends, looked them over and went away. He said in the "Mausoleum Book" (p. 22) that his shyness had made him go away and that he was uncomfortable with artistic people, whose world was so unfamiliar to him. As Leslie himself implied, his feelings of insecurity about aesthetic concerns, dating from the crisis over poetry in his childhood, made him give up. The equivocal reputation of the Prinsep salon may also have aroused a degree of uneasiness in Leslie's overly puritanical mind. He was not unattracted to Julia, for he reported that he was jealous when he heard she had married Herbert Duckworth. In addition to their brief meeting at Little Holland House, they wrote several formal letters to each other, as Leslie noted in his "Calendar of Correspondence." In 1866 Leslie wrote Julia to commiserate on the death of her friend, the wife of Holman Hunt. Julia wrote to congratulate him when he became engaged to Minny Thackeray.

## A Period of Mourning

A friendship between Leslie and Julia finally began in 1875, at the time of the death of Leslie's first wife and five years after the death of Herbert Duckworth. Julia was twenty-nine and Leslie was forty-three. Julia had already become better acquainted with Leslie through reading some of his articles and through her friendship with Minny, Leslie's wife, and Anny, his sister-in-law. Julia had known Leslie and Minny well enough to call on them the evening before Minny's sudden death. But she soon went home again because, Bell said (pp. 11-13), she thought her continued melancholia over Herbert's death might shadow the contented domestic scene of Leslie and Minny happily anticipating the birth of their second child. Soon after Julia went home, Leslie and Minny retired for the night. Minny was apparently feeling only slightly ill, but before morning, she went into convulsions and died the next day. The shock was terrible for Leslie and for Anny who had gone away overnight, leaving her sister comparatively well and had returned the next day to find her dead.[2] Leslie's grief was intensified when his mother died during the same year. His mother's death may explain why Leslie's attitudes toward and expectations of his second wife differed from those of his first, and why he expected, and when necessary extorted, a kind of mothering from Julia when reputedly he had been willing to protect and cosset Minny.[3] In effect, now that Jane Venn Stephen was dead, Leslie's new wife would have to be both mother and wife to him.

Following Minny's death, both Leslie's situation and his grief were complicated by Anny Thackeray. She and Leslie had been incompatible throughout his marriage to Minny. As Leslie said in the "Mausoleum Book" (pp. 17-18), Anny was shut up with a surly beast (himself) that she persisted in rubbing the wrong way. Her remaining in Leslie's household after Minny's death caused serious problems, for both of them. Leslie, the chief mourner, had to share with Anny the spotlight as well as the consolations of family and friends, which he desperately needed and wanted for himself. He offended Anny by his agnosticism, for even during Anny's grief he could not tolerate, or keep quiet about, her belief in the immortality of the soul. They argued about the topic, Leslie storming and raging until Anny broke down.[4]

Leslie and Anny had a vacillating relationship from first to last. Leslie's relationships with women were often uneven because of his own divisions and complexities and his relationship with Anny was especially so, for she brought out a great many of his complicated and contradictory feelings. He had resented Anny's customary domination of Minny and had struggled with her to see which of them would control Minny and the household.[5] He admitted in the "Mausoleum Book" (p. 15) that Anny had been the "most conspicuous figure" in the household. Leslie claimed, nevertheless, that he and Minny had lived in "unbroken harmony" in spite of Anny, which is hardly credible in view of the varying personalities of the three.

Leslie found Anny exceedingly unlike himself, or more precisely, unlike his tough-minded side. He said he had had an almost religious zeal to stamp out her optimism, of which her belief in immortality may have been an example, and to correct what he regarded as her erratic and illogical thinking. He called it his "pedantic mania" for correcting Anny's flights of imagination and checking her "exuberant" manner. Their natural antipathy began to get out of hand even while Minny was alive, and, as Leslie said, without Minny there to keep the peace between them, the situation grew much worse.[6]

But the relationship was complicated by more than Leslie's disapproval of Anny, or she would have been less of a problem to him. Despite his antipathy, Leslie was attracted to Anny personally and probably sexually, as his later, persistent jealousy of Anny's love for Richmond Ritchie suggests. Other problems arose because Leslie looked to Anny for assistance in running his household, thinking it her duty to help him. She not only denied him the assistance he thought his by right, but also added to his financial difficulties, which always brought out Leslie's most irrational behavior. He said in the "Mausoleum Book" (p. 18) that she didn't carry her share of the household expenses and often presented him with unexpected bills, causing him to adopt a number of tactics to get her to pay a fair share of the expenses as well as the bills she incurred. His tactics inevitably failed. Before Minny died, Anny sometimes spent Minny's allowance as well as her own. Finally Leslie gave up and paid "the largest share of the expenses" himself. He wrote to Julia, who sometimes had to intervene in his quarrels with Anny, that he knew he was irrational about money but couldn't help being "fidgeted" about it, especially when in a "nervous state." It was his "stupid nervous feeling," not reason, he said, that made him fret so about money.[7] His feelings about Anny and finances were only slightly assuaged when Anny gave him part of the proceeds she derived from her writing based on Thackeray's letters.[8]

Leslie had problems enough without Anny, Annan has noted (p. 73). He cherished and nourished his sorrows after he lost his first wife as he would do later, after Julia's death. He was, Annan said, "in love with his sorrow" and became a "self-tortured misanthrope." There was more to the picture than self-pity, however. During his mourning, many of his childhood emotional problems recurred, and in his letters to Julia he complained of these as well as others not previously attributed to him. The complaints included helplessness, dependency, the inability to plan for the future or to accept responsibility,[9] unrealistic worrying over finances,[10] and anger over comparative trifles, often expressed in his letters as though the trifles were planned to make him personally uncomfortable.[11] Perhaps his most serious complaints were of disorientation and confusion. For example, he said that he could not explain a queer feeling that often came over him, as if life were a jumbled phantasmagoria of things without meaning. It would not surprise him, he said, if he awoke to discover everything a dream, "a confused and purposeless mess of odds and ends."[12] He said too that there were times when he wanted to die, when his housekeeper would weep over him and beg him to live, for his daughter Laura's sake, if not for his own.[13] Another problem he mentioned, specifically in reference to his rages at Anny Thackeray, was a lack of self-control. It was almost impossible for him to "act rightly," he said, and he was "a brute" to act wrongly. He was "really frightened," and he begged Julia to take responsibility and force him to do what was right.[14]

### Friendship

As already noted, the friendship of Leslie and Julia which led to their marriage grew out of their separate ties with Anny Thackeray. Julia's talent for nursing the sick and her desire to assist relatives and friends struck by disaster, as well as her concern for Anny, led her to do what she could to comfort Anny after Minny died. She was in and out of the grieving household almost constantly, and she took lodgings near Leslie and Anny when they went to Brighton to try to recover from their grief. Because Anny required actual nursing care, Julia was able to repay her for her kindness and help during her own mourning for Herbert Duckworth.[15] But Julia's friendship was not wholly satisfactory to Anny who said that she would have preferred a greater outpouring of grief from Julia. Anny told Leslie that Julia seemed "stern" during the mourning, citing a quality that many persons, including Virginia, attributed to her.[16] With Julia's assistance, Leslie and Anny moved their household to 11 Hyde Park Gate in order to live next door to Julia whose residence was 13 Hyde Park Gate. Julia's house later was renumbered and became 22 Hyde Park Gate, the house the Stephens occupied during their marriage and thus Virginia Woolf's childhood home.[17] At first Leslie fell subject to Julia's ministrations because he was living in the household with her friend Anny and despite the fact that Julia was somewhat intimidated by him.[18] He found her attentions very much to his liking—indeed, he found in Julia just the antidote, a substitute mother, that he needed. What Julia had found, other than someone who needed her help quite badly, she apparently didn't quite understand, then or ever.

Gradually Leslie became as much an object of Julia's kindly attentions as Anny. Leslie expressed his gratitude in a letter to Julia's mother,[19] which disguised as much as it revealed, for it was written at approximately the time that Leslie told Julia he loved her, a fact that he and Julia were careful for some time to hide from everyone, including Mrs. Jackson. In the letter, he thanked Mrs. Jackson for a toy she had sent to Laura and went on to say that Julia had taken Anny in hand and was worth more to her than "all the doctors." Then, disarmingly and with seeming frankness, he said that Julia had been the saving of

Anny by protecting her when his (Leslie's) low spirits, bad temper, and general fussiness might have caused all manner of havoc. He concluded with the gross understatement that he was almost equally grateful to Julia on his own account. He did not mention in the letter what motivated it in part—that his serious courtship of Julia had begun.

A "Special Friendship"

According to Julia, it was February 2, 1877, the date of Leslie's letter to her mother, and according to Leslie, it was February 5, 1877, when he made his first open move to court her. He wrote her a letter telling her that he loved her "as a man loves a woman he wants to marry."[20] But he said also that he knew she did not and could not love him as he loved her and that "upon his honour" he would never speak of love again to her. Instead of love and marriage, all he wanted, according to his letter, was a special friendship.

The letter was an instance of his old childhood tendencies and of his vacillating nature: it was both a proposal and not a proposal. If Julia accepted it as a proposal, well and good; if not, he might gain something without having risked a great deal. He was aware that he appeared inconsistent in telling Julia he loved her and that he didn't want anything more than friendship, and tried to explain that in his letter. He said he was telling her that he loved her because she was unsuspecting and had to be warned to be on her guard against him for her own sake, and to help him be a friend instead of a lover. It was not the most peculiar love letter ever written, but it was a strange one for a man who prided himself on logic. In the "Mausoleum Book," Leslie equivocated about his reasons for writing the letter, making no reference to the warning. However, the letter as he copied it into his "Calendar of Correspondence" included the warning.

He said in the letter that he felt half mad and half wicked, and that he would not give her the letter until they had one more evening on familiar terms. Therefore, as Julia was leaving a dinner party at his house, Leslie slipped the letter into her hand. She went home, read the letter, and returned, surprising Leslie and his guests. Her return was less than conventional in 1877, and she was afraid it had shocked Leslie's guests. She stayed on after the party ended and talked with Leslie in his study, patting him fondly on the shoulder. He recalled this gesture in the "Mausoleum Book" (p. 37) as a seal on the occasion. The outcome of the conversation was that Julia accepted the terms of "closest friendship," but no more. Marriage and love were out of the question, but she would be "what she could to him," and they need "move no farther apart" because he was in love with her. It was understood also that no one, not even Julia's mother, was to know of their agreement.[21]

Judging from subsequent letters between them, their special friendship resembled an engagement without marriage plans, and later in the relationship Julia referred to it as an engagement.[22] These letters also indicate that Leslie seemed to expect the relationship to provide him with many of the benefits of marriage although not sexual ones. He would have someone committed to him in a special way, listening to his complaints, sympathizing with him, understanding him, and making him feel less lonely—in brief, someone providing the care and consolation so necessary to him. He also gained an advantage over other competitors for Julia's hand, of whom there may have been at least one with powerful backing. Julia Margaret Cameron was trying to match Julia with Charles Norman, her deceased daughter's wealthy husband.[23] Leslie said in the "Mausoleum Book" (p. 50) that Julia had been afraid she would be influenced to marry Norman when she didn't want to marry anyone.

Remaining documents do not disclose Julia's reasons for

entering into such an agreement with Leslie, nor do they explain what she thought the relationship entailed other than their seeing each other often and confiding in each other. She said in her next letter to him that she was grateful that he loved her, and that she would consider his love a "blessing to her always," although she could not return it.[24] She admired him as a scholar although she was still a little in awe of him.[25] Later in the friendship Leslie suggested that Julia was flattered that a person who terrified everyone else so much was mild and tractable in her hands,[26] but there is little to indicate that Julia felt this way, or that she found him in the least mild. Whatever her reasons, in her letters Julia expressed many doubts and reservations about the commitment.

One of Julia's reservations about their special friendship grew out of her belief that she was inferior to Leslie. She stated her feelings of inferiority immediately after they made the commitment to each other,[27] when Leslie asked for her advice and help with his financial accounts.[28] His request evidently alarmed Julia, for the tone of her reply suggested that she did not realize that a commitment to special friendship would involve so much. She avoided the assignment, replying that she could be of no use in finances since Leslie knew far more about business matters than she. She said also that she felt frightened to think how she differed in every way from his conception of her: she was much more inferior than he realized, and fell short even of her own standards which were less demanding than his. If he really knew her, she said, he could not love her.[29] She returned repeatedly to the theme of her inferiority, saying among other things that she felt "like a fool" when she conversed in his presence, and she insisted that he thought her one.[30]

Leslie was hardly comforting or reassuring when Julia expressed her belief that she was inferior and he did little to disabuse her of the idea. Obviously he did not disagree with her.

His pedantic and torturous statements to her on the matter conveyed the illogical message that, although he was in some ways superior, she was not necessarily inferior. When he upset her with his ideas on the education of women, he tried to smooth over ill feelings by saying that her ways of feeling about things were congenial, even when he disagreed with her, apparently unaware of his inconsistency. He also said that even if she had been able to reason "ever so logically" and bring "ever so much information to bear" upon problems, it would not matter to him, because it was Julia he loved and not "accidents" about her.[31] On another occasion when she referred to her inferiority, he said that he had no illusions, that he was apt to think anything belonging to him inferior in some way. He continued to say that of course he had certain advantages over her; he knew things she didn't know, and he had certain merits as a logician—merits seldom in evidence in his letters to her. He concluded, with double-edged magnanimity, that his advantages over her had little to do with real personal value— it was her character he loved, not her intellect.[32]

Another of Julia's reservations about her relationship with Leslie was her fear that "so much closeness" would do him "injury," as she put it, by making him "restless" and less content with his books and writing. She had apparently expressed this concern when she agreed to be his special friend[33] and returned to the theme often. She said each time that it was reason to terminate their friendship, or that it would be "wholesomer" for him if they parted.[34] In the "Mausoleum Book" (pp. 39-40) Leslie named Julia's concern over his restlessness as the most serious problem in their courtship. Although Julia did not use the word "sex" in regard to his restlessness, she was nevertheless quite forthright and sophisticated in her references to and her understanding of the problem, leaving little doubt that she had sexual matters in mind. She sounded bitter as well, for she said that the feelings of women in such relation-

ships didn't matter since women were more or less slaves anyway. But she had a special dislike for women who kept men
bound to them, "taking all" and "giving nothing." She had a
feeling that she could only hurt people, and that he should be
careful she didn't hurt him.[35]

Julia's strongest reservation about the commitment came
from her own emotional state—her melancholia and dread of
the future. She correctly recognized that her continuing grief
was reason enough not to marry anyone, particularly Leslie,
who would demand far more of her than would most men. She
knew him well enough by that time to realize that marrying
him would be an enormous emotional and physical under-
taking. On one hand she was not as "wounded" and "broken"
as he, she said, but had less life. On the other hand, because
she identified with Leslie's emotional state, she found it difficult to break with him. As she said, she had known, and felt
for him, "all the sadness and dreariness."[36]

Julia spoke of her sadness many times, warning Leslie not to
think of marriage because she could not even contemplate it.
She said that she continued to feel that death would be the
"greatest boon" that could be given to her, and that, therefore,
it would be wrong for her to take up a new life.[37] It was not,
she said, that she was especially unhappy or to be pitied, but
that she was tired and cowardly about the future.[38] Still later,
after she had said that she loved Leslie, she said that she had
had so many different kinds of pain and was left with so many
terrible memories, that she felt bruised all over as if from
actual blows, so that every touch hurt her.[39] Again, she explained that so many things were always happening to her that
she never got to be "anything to herself." She felt sheltered and
protected by him, she said, but even when he was nearest, she
had no courage for life. Yes, she loved him with all her heart,
but it was a "poor, dead heart." If she could be close to him
and feel him holding her, she would be content to die.[40] Julia

said also at one point that she felt as if she had some disease for which there was no cure, and that Leslie wanted to marry her in spite of it.[41]

A kind of morbid guilt showed through Julia's melancholia, expressed in references to her deserving unhappiness[42] and her selfishness at being melancholy.[43] Her guilt was also present in her beliefs that Leslie would dislike the "real Julia" if he knew her,[44] and that she could only hurt people.[45] Leslie said in the "Mausoleum Book" (p. 39) that Julia had believed that she could wound but could not heal.

Although Julia gave up her religion after her first husband died, during Leslie's courtship she talked of going into a convent.[46] She may not have been serious, but her talk of convents alarmed and angered Leslie who wrote, ironically, that the "happiness" of convent life was "suicide or semi-suicide." She could give up her children and friends, he said, read her prayerbook, and continue to live at 13 Hyde Park Gate.[47] Julia responded that reading a prayerbook was not her concept of convent life. Rather, such a life meant the "spirit of submission" and the faith to give one's life entirely over to superiors and "think no more" about the matter. But she was too obstinate to do that she concluded.[48]

Leslie too was sometimes reluctant about marriage, although generally he was impatient in his love for Julia and often said that he wanted to marry her. In professing reluctance to take up a new life, he said that he, like Julia, was a "crippled person," who shrank instinctively from responsibility. And although he did not cite the fact in his letters, he knew that marriage to Julia meant a significant increment in responsibility: she had an income, but she also had three children. He said also that he still felt too damaged by Minny's death to have much courage for the future.[49] Talk of the future aroused Leslie's conflicting attitudes about time. For example, he vacillated from saying on one day that the sense of rapidly passing time frightened him,[50] to saying on the next that the slowness of passing time bored and distressed him.[51] Mostly he had a special dislike for arranging his life and planning ahead, he told Julia.[52]

Looking back to the period of his courtship, when writing the "Mausoleum Book" (p. 36), Leslie attributed his reluctance to think about remarrying to his continued pain over Minny's death. He thought his condition resembled Julia's, he said, but also that it was different from hers. Then, generalizing loosely, he said that their different reactions to loss represented characteristic differences between the sexes. The loss of Minny, he said, had damaged him, but had not injured him "organically." It had not destroyed his capacity for happiness, he said, although it had deprived him of "sustenance" for a time. By contrast, Herbert Duckworth's death had "numbed" and "petrified" Julia, and she had never regained her confidence in life. The contrast showed, Leslie said, the difference between the masculine and feminine ways of taking life.


### A Secret Marriage?

Not only was Leslie wrong in his generalization about the sexes, but he failed to appreciate the depth and essential nature of Julia's reservations. When their special friendship was about two months old, almost on impulse, he proposed a secret marriage. He may have been emboldened by Mrs. Jackson's semi-official blessing on his friendship with her daughter. When Julia finally summoned the courage to tell her mother about the friendship, Mrs. Jackson said that she "understood" and had known all along, but thought the relationship hard on Leslie.[53]

The terms of the proposal, made in a letter of April 7, 1877, written while Leslie was in Brighton with Laura, were that

Leslie and Julia would enter into a secret, legal marriage with neither of them changing their present residences and modes of life. He was fretted, he said, because "proprieties" kept them from being alone with each other as much as he would have liked. He argued unrealistically that if they married secretly, he would have to worry less about propriety and could see her as often as he liked. Leslie equivocated about his proposal in the "Mausoleum Book" (p. 39), saying that he had meant only to state his complaints in an exaggerated way, and that he hadn't been serious. Whether or not he meant it, Julia thought he did, and turned down his suggestion by return post, calling it impracticable.[54] She said she believed that the relationship he described might make some people happier, but that it was not possible for them because it would increase rather than solve the problem of propriety. After all, the "world" talked so much anyway, and people would be even more scandalized if an already close friendship became closer. If she loved him less than she did, she might agree to such an arrangement, for talk and scandal, she said, did not for a moment weigh with her. She went on to say once again that it worried her that she made him "restless," and that perhaps they should break off their friendship. As for herself—now that her mother knew about their commitment, Julia was "perfectly comfortable" and didn't care what anyone else thought.

Leslie was openly angered by Julia's reply, which suggests that he meant the proposal seriously. He was angry because she rejected him and also because of her independence. Most of all, he was angry because she had again cited his restlessness and suggested that they terminate their relationship. His letter in response to hers was indignant and illustrates the adult Leslie Stephen in one of his tantrums, being "sensible of a balk."[55] He could not, he said, affect her opinions in the least. "You treat me like a baby; don't 'cry dear,' or I shall take your toy away altogether and that will be much worse. . . . Well I am

85

not or have been [sic] a baby and you were perfectly right and a very kind nurse, though you have not been able to make your medicine altogether sweet, I have no doubt it was healthy. And now, my dear, you will have no more conflicts from me of any kind." Then he proceeded both to insult Julia and to show that she had struck a sensitive point by citing his restlessness. "So for now lay aside your pigheadedness and believe me... I am not a person to whine for what I can't get; or to let my life become fretful and peevish and unsettled. I have more courage than that could imply." He knew now what she wanted, he said, and didn't expect her to change any more "than the monument." Then, becoming milder, he said that she mustn't leave him, that she must not cut off his bread and water because he had asked for cake and wine. If she did, he threatened, his only refuge would be hard work and that would ruin his physical and, ultimately, his mental health.

After his initial anger, Leslie took Julia's rejection with better temper and tried hard to adjust to the terms of the friendship. He said in the "Mausoleum Book" (p. 40) that he had been made to realize that he had almost lost her because of the very fretfulness he had denied at the time. He was also relieved that his angry letter had not, when it was written, caused a more serious quarrel between them. Moreover, if he had not gained cake and wine, at least he had gained a more open admission from Julia that she loved him, and for some time following, they were less constrained in talking of their love. Also, after Mrs. Jackson had been told about their commitment, Leslie and Julia were able to see more of each other. There was still a problem about that, however; it continued to be necessary to "put their minds to it," as Leslie said, to find some uninterrupted time alone with each other every day.[56]

Leslie's morbidity and his thoughts of death were stated in a startling and revealing fashion in his letter expressing relief that Julia was not more angry at his rudeness when she turned down his proposal.[57] Perhaps in response to something she said, since she often spoke of wanting to die, he ruminated about what would happen to him if she did die. He might reconcile himself to his fate and find someone else, but he doubted it and thought he would probably be permanently sad and gloomy — his chief argument that she should go on living.

There were no more proposals of secret marriage, and in subsequent letters Leslie restated his reservations about marriage, usually as a way of agreeing with Julia that neither was ready to remarry. But he did not in the least lessen his efforts to edge Julia toward marriage, and almost everything he did gave the lie to his expressed reluctance to marry. To influence her in favor of marriage he often talked about love and marriage in his letters. He contradicted this fact in the "Mausoleum Book" (p. 41) where he said that he had wished Julia to be guided only by her own feelings. He stated further in the "Mausoleum Book" that he had kept his promise never to speak of love again and had abstained from appealing to his feelings. Both claims were patently untrue. Perhaps without intending to do so, Julia encouraged his talk of love and marriage by her frank references to his restlessness and by urging him to tell her everything he thought and felt. In addition to the frequent references to love and marriage, Leslie tried to move her toward marriage by talking her out of what he called her "morbid shrinking from happiness." He said that he had a "half-fancy" that if she didn't "exactly encourage" her sadness, she didn't consciously try to get the best of it either. Rather, she accepted it because it had become so familiar to her.[58] On the whole, this described Leslie as well as Julia.

## Getting What One Wants Without Asking

Leslie's most effective maneuver to get Julia to marry him was acting helpless and convincing her that he would be in a desperate state without her. He may not have plotted such a course deliberately, but rather may have acted only on the basis of his need to be dependent. He had Julia continue to mediate his difficulties with Anny, and he took it well when Julia consistently supported Anny's position. He gave Julia some of the responsibility for Laura, who was becoming an increasingly serious problem to him, making him feel especially helpless. On July 5, 1877, with Julia's concurrence, he drew up a document to make her Laura's personal guardian in case of his death.[59] His brother, Fitzjames, and Anny Thackeray's husband, Richmond Ritchie, were to be legal guardians. Leslie's plan may have been incited in part by his anger with Anny. He said that Anny's approaching marriage disqualified her from being Laura's personal guardian, but that she could see Laura as much as she liked. As Laura's nearest relative, Anny would have been the logical choice as guardian if Leslie died, and a more dispassionate appraisal might have seen her marriage as increasing her qualifications.

Leslie's biggest ploy and the one Julia, ever the nurse, could not resist, was his asking for sympathy and assistance in solving his persisting physical and emotional problems. Virginia Woolf suggested in *To the Lighthouse* (pp. 57-58, 100) that all her father needed to do to get her mother's attention and sympathy was look mournful. He did a great deal of that during the courtship, as Julia Margaret Cameron observed in a letter to her niece when she learned of their engagement.[60] Since she wanted Julia to marry her son-in-law, Mrs. Cameron could not quite understand Leslie's appeal to her niece. Perhaps drawing her metaphor from photography, Mrs. Cameron described Leslie as "the shadow" that sat and waited for Julia. Mrs. Cameron said that she had observed Leslie's "mournful manner" and felt that by his sitting close to Julia, "tall, wrapt in gloom, companionless and silent," Leslie would eventually make a powerful impression on Julia. However, still finding it difficult to explain the attraction, Mrs. Cameron concluded that the appeal was the "vastness" of Leslie's intellect, not his sadness.

Leslie did more than sit and wait for Julia to notice his problems. He still defined himself as a puny weakling, as his mother had taught him to do, and was ever alert to report symptoms of ill health to Julia. He had neuralgia and, in several letters, explicitly described his every twinge, trying to be humorous by personifying his pain as the devil who should go away to his own place.[61] He detailed his health and hygiene measures, telling Julia how much or how little he smoked, what he ate, and how well he slept.[62] When they were apart after their marriage, he continued to write such details to her. However, he then included reports about his problems with constipation and diarrhea, topics much too indelicate to mention during courtship.[63]

Consonant with her interest in nursing, Julia may have encouraged Leslie to talk about his health. At least, she tolerated a small-boy-to-mother attitude on his part, which was evinced as a concern for obeying her or confessing when he had not. For example, he wrote that he'd climbed a mountain against her orders[64] and asked if she were angry that he had walked eleven hours in one day.[65] He said that he had half a mind to disobey her and write an article.[66] At a minimum, if Julia did not tell him to bring his physical problems to her for guidance, she encouraged him by too readily acting as if his health was her responsibility.

When Leslie had no physical complaints, he offered Julia, his mental and emotional problems. He felt better in body, he wrote, but queer in mind. Always divided, his "queerness in mind" consisted in an improbable combination of depression, peace, and improved happiness.[67] He was always hypersensitive to reproach, and when his housekeeper "looked and spoke unpleasantly" to him, "not insulting him exactly," he complained to Julia piteously, telling her how much it depressed him. He was also depressed at the time about a famine in India and told Julia that the little woe, the housekeeper's rudeness, and the large woe, the famine, worried him equally.[68] He wrote frequently about his feeling that everything, including himself, was ghostly, meaningless, and unreal, usually repeating his belief that if Julia were with him he would not feel that way—thereby implying that the problem was her fault.

A letter of August 18, 1877, reveals one of Leslie's mental states and what he did to comfort himself. It also illustrates the games he played with Julia and was, therefore, a confession and a warning. "I read your letters and know that you must have written them; and yet you seem to me like a good angel who vanishes into space as soon as I disappear. I cannot think of you as walking and talking and looking after the children or giving orders for dinner. But it is equally true that I don't seem quite real to myself. I have not indeed felt that for a long time. Life has been a queer sort of dream to me. But still when you are by, the dream has substance in it. I can really enjoy something and am not a mere formless ghost—or a mere literary machine grinding out imbecile articles." He went on to say that he wished Julia were coming into the world of realities sooner, for it was not good for people "to live altogether among phantoms." The liveliest emotion he had, he said, was to wonder whether he would choose fish or soup for dinner. "Everything is of a dingy, idiotic whity brown, with no vivid colour in it," but at least he could comfort himself by visualizing mental pictures when half asleep. He could not picture Julia in daily routines, he said, but in his fantasies, he could see himself somewhere on a beach or lawn sitting alone with Julia. She would look affectionately at him and he would "abuse Anny" to her with certainty that she would agree with him. He would threaten to overexert himself so that Julia would show concern for him. He would praise John Morley's writings so that Julia would compliment his own and he would pretend to be ill and tired so that she would caress him.

Leslie ran repeated risks of defeating his efforts to get Julia to marry him by his persistence in telling her everything he thought and felt. She seemed never to express impatience when he complained of ill health, but often when he complained of other things, Julia was unsympathetic and upbraided him bluntly. She showed relatively little concern about offending him, despite his plaints that he was such a skinless, sensitive man. She chided him for grumbling when he had to stay alone in lodgings while traveling. She had stayed alone in lodgings for many years, she said, and didn't find it as trying as he said it was. Moreover, she knew full well that if he could not count on four or five hours of solitude daily, he would become desperate.[69] It was illogical for him to say that tourists were loathsome when he himself was a tourist.[70] He was unreasonable to complain about Laura and foolish to mind the chil's "contradictoriness"; after all, Laura was his daughter and couldn't help being contradictory.[71] He was also wrong to say that Laura was unlike him; Laura's disposition was ridiculously like his.[72] She said that George and Gerald were not afraid of Leslie because, as a rule, "very frightening people" aren't alarming to children.[73] She was sorry he had had a scene with Anny, but thought it absurd of him to swear about it.[74] When he complained that Anny could not manage the housekeeper, Julia observed correctly that Leslie created the problem because he wouldn't give Anny authority over the housekeeper.[75] Julia was blunt with him again when he grumbled that he couldn't talk to or get along with his sister, Caroline Emilia, when she was a member of the household, and when he complained that she shrank from responsibility. He could talk with his sister if he really tried, Julia said, and even if Caroline Emilia did dislike responsibility, at least she had "sentiment."[76] Caroline Emilia might be alarming in her silences, but so was he. His sister was not as alarming as he "in speech." He "scorned and shriveled one up" after having sat in silent judgment.[77] She argued with Leslie about religion when he put forth his idea that calling Christ "divine" denigrated mankind, saying that she didn't agree with him about Christ any more than Caroline Emilia did.[78] Applying the term "divine" to Christ did not imply that there were no "divine" qualities in human beings, she said.[79]

Perhaps the biggest chance Leslie took during their courtship was to tangle ungraciously and brashly with Julia's mother. Mrs. Jackson had sent him, as a gift, a book of poetry by Coventry Patmore, her special friend and protégé. Given Leslie's old insecurities about poetry and effeminacy, the gift may have offended him, in and of itself. But the offence was related more to his opinion that Coventry Patmore's poetry was "effeminate" and religious. He explained his ideas in a letter to Mrs. Jackson. He equivocated in order to avoid thanking her, saying that he *should* thank her but could not admire her gift. His making a distinction between masculine and effeminate poetry is interesting in view of his old shame about poetry and his continued, lifelong love of it. His explanations of the differences are even more interesting. Masculine poetry, the poetry that he liked, was hot, strong, written in plain English, and had no aura of religion about it. Men should have feminine feelings, that is, quick and delicate feelings, he said further, but no man or poet should let such feelings overcome his intellect. When that happened, he and his poetry were *effeminate.*[80]

When Mrs. Jackson wrote to object, Leslie stood his ground, squirming mightily in place and only half apologizing.[81] After another, "more forgiving" letter from Mrs. Jackson, he did apologize, gallantly but insincerely, assuming all the blame, saying that he'd had a short but acute fit of temporary insanity, a "Berkserker fit in literary form." He added, with good humor and some insight into the situation, that it was not wise for Elijah to quarrel with his ravens.[82]

It is not known whether Julia was aware of the exchange between Leslie and her mother, but if aware she apparently left

Leslie to work out the matter by himself. However, Julia did speak to him on a later occasion about his attitude toward conventional religion, the beliefs Mrs. Jackson espoused. Personally, Julia said, she did not think him irreverent in his books and speech, but sometimes he did "tear down veils rather ruthlessly." She was sorry when he did that, for she did not want him to shock her mother.[83]

Mrs. Jackson and Leslie would continue to have their problems after his marriage to Julia, and Leslie would continue to let his irritation and jealousy slip into his letters to his mother-in-law. He wrote sarcastically to Mrs. Jackson when she suggested that a man with his family responsibilities should not endanger his life by overwork, or by going on long hikes, or climbing mountains.[84] She suffered from a superstitution about male relatives, common to all women he said. It was a vain and groundless belief that he ever overworked. The proof was a long tramp that he had just taken and the fact that he felt better afterwards. He concluded his letter by reminding Mrs. Jackson of her own health, saying that he only wished others were as well and healthy as he.[85] This brutal jibe expressed Leslie's deep resentment over the invariable demand that Julia come when Mrs. Jackson was ill.

Household Crises

Julia first admitted that she was thinking of marrying Leslie about ten months after committing herself to the special friendship with him. Perhaps Leslie was right in saying that her feelings about him and about marriage had changed unconsciously over the months.[86] But it took still another of his household crises to bring her to consider marriage. A series of such crises had occurred since the death of his first wife. Each centered on the problem of which woman was to be in charge of the household and each was brought on by Leslie's helplessness and his inability to remain on good terms with the women who tried. Anny Thackeray had been nominally in charge after Minny's death, but Leslie had never given her authority over the housekeeper.[87] Then to the great surprise of almost everyone, Anny married Richmond Ritchie, her cousin and godson, aged twenty-four, and seventeen years her junior. Leslie was one of those surprised by the romance, but surprise was the least of his confused feelings. He had precipitated the engagement when he discovered what he called the "catastrophe" of Anny and Richmond kissing each other in the drawing room. He demanded of Anny that she make up her mind, saying that it was "plain to see" where things were leading,[88] but he could not quite bring himself to name the dire end he envisioned. Perhaps it was Richmond Ritchie who was forced to make up his mind rather than Anny, for she had been willing, if not eager, to marry him. She loved Richmond, she said to a friend, but not quite well enough to give him up.[89] However, Hester Ritchie Fuller, the daughter of Anny and Richmond, said that Richmond was a very determined, self-confident young man and had taken the initiative in announcing the engagement when Anny herself hesitated.[90] In any case, before the end of the day when Leslie confronted Anny, she and Richmond told him that they were engaged to be married. If Leslie's account in the "Mausoleum Book" (pp. 34-35) is accurate, once he got Anny and Richmond engaged, he rushed the marriage because, he said, realistically if a bit ungallantly, Anny, past her fortieth year, had had little time to waste.

Leslie said in the "Mausoleum Book" (p. 35) that he incurred the wrath of the Ritchie family for his part in the engagement and the marriage, and that they disapproved the match. But he imagined more disapproval than actually existed. According to Hester Ritchie Fuller, although friends disapproved, the

Ritchie family was accepting and Richmond's three sisters were enthusiastic. Mrs. Fuller quoted a letter from Richmond's mother welcoming Anny as a prospective daughter-in-law.[91] Nevertheless, Leslie was convinced that the Ritchies were angry and for months continued to fret and complain about Anny and her marriage in his letters to Julia.[92] He was not mollified when Julia persisted in approving a marriage Leslie thought almost perverse. Julia predicted it would be a happy marriage, and said that in a world as gloomy as this one, anything that brought a little more happiness should be welcomed.[93] (The marriage did prove to be happy in its first years, but, according to Vanessa Bell who visited the Ritchies in 1904, it became strained as Anny grew older.)[94] Leslie continued to say that he abhorred the match as much as he would have abhorred finding a gritty bug in his food—a significant analogy from one who frequently used the word "delicious" as well as metaphors about food in referring to his love for Julia. However, Leslie provided money for Anny's dowry, later congratulating himself for his generosity,[95] and attended the wedding with Julia at his side.[96]

One of Richmond's sisters was a bridesmaid for Anny. She described the wedding for Lady Tennyson, the poet's wife, whose son Lionel was Richmond Ritchie's best man. One of the things that impressed the bridesmaid most was the contrast between the wedding guests on the groom's side and the bride's side of the church. She said that Leslie "looked very deplorable" and that Julia wore a thick, black velvet dress and heavy black veil, giving "the gloomiest, most tragic aspect" to her side of the chancel. She also said that eight-year-old Stella Duckworth was present and looked as tragic as her mother.[97]

Leslie's reaction to Anny's engagement was multifaceted. His statement of relief at freedom from the responsibility for Anny[98] accords with Mrs. Fuller's view that Leslie tried to precipitate Anny's marriage to get her off his hands and to clear the way for his marriage to Julia.[99] He was not so relieved that he could be pleased when Anny started flaunting her happiness at him; he believed that she was deliberately trying to annoy him with her ecstatic letters about her happy marriage. He said that it angered him and made him "sick" to hear about Anny's happiness and that she was "making him loathe" the name Richmond.[100] Leslie said also that he was bewildered by the marriage, and could not get the whole thing in focus.[101] Finally, in the "Mausoleum Book" (p. 35), he admitted that he had been jealous, because "all men are jealous," (an idea he attributed to Julia), and that he had been put on a lower level in Anny's affections. He generalized, saying that men, at least, don't like the idea of a young man marrying an older woman.

Quentin Bell observed (p. 12) that the "quasi-maternal situation of the bride aroused feelings in [Leslie] the nature of which he may not have understood. . . ." The truth of Bell's statement is supported by Leslie's admitted bewilderment and by the varying descriptions he gave of his feelings. The nature of the feelings are easy enough to guess in a man whose love and general attitude toward his second wife were so markedly filial. Most likely he was attracted, and therefore threatened, by the Oedipal and incestual overtones of Anny's marriage to her godson, a man so much younger than herself. In Leslie's mind the concept of godson was probably much too close to that of son.

Leslie's sister, Caroline Emilia, was the next person he tried to place in charge of his household. She was given a little more authority than Anny, over Laura at least, with whom she had some success in teaching and management. Caroline Emilia loved and admired her brother, but Leslie didn't get along with her even though he viewed her as someone, like Julia, who could take charge of his life and his household. In the "Mausoleum Book" (p. 43) he indicted Caroline Emilia unfairly for identifying with him too much and for taking him too seriously. He had complained earlier to Julia that his sister accepted things too quietly and would never "blow him up." Evidently it was true that she didn't oppose him enough. If Leslie's remarks were accurate, it would appear that his games only bewildered Caroline Emilia. He said that during arguments he supported his position just to get her to disagree with him. But she took his arguments so seriously that he would begin to think there was something to them. When he was in doubt, she was completely perplexed; when he was sad, she wept. He found her friends dull and boring, and she found his friends too worldly.

To say the least, Leslie Stephen was not fair to his sister, either in his conduct or his comments about her. According to Annan, she was a talented woman, bright enough to belong to the Cambridge "Apostles," had women been eligible to join. She was the author of four books on Quakerism.[102] Her writing about religion no doubt either left her brother unimpressed or antagonized him, as her religious view invariably did. Leslie's attitudes toward Caroline Emilia and her religion were apparently adopted almost without examination by Virginia and the other Stephen children who nicknamed her "Nun" and "Quaker." She is still known to students of Virginia Woolf by these names. Leslie's reports in the "Mausoleum Book" of his difficulties with his sister may be entirely reliable, for he made contradictory assessments of his relationship with her. For example, he stated (p. 3) that he had had, and continued to have, a warm intimacy with Caroline Emilia, a claim inconsistent with other statements he made about her in the same source. The claim is also inconsistent with her reaction to living with him and being his housekeeper, for after a three-week trial as head of the household, she collapsed and, as he described it, was carried away to her own home by her nurse and doctor.[103] Leslie was left alone with Laura, without anyone to take charge of the house.

Leslie said that after his sister left him he began to think of hiring a housekeeper, but he consulted Julia first since that had become his practice with all perplexities. He talked "in sadness" with her because he believed that taking a house-keeper would "seal" his and Julia's separation.[104] The discussion brought Julia to consider, for the first time, whether she should marry Leslie. She told him what was on her mind as they separated for the Christmas holidays and in order for her to have time apart to consider the matter.[105]

## A Decision to be a Good Wife

Julia's state during the holidays was what Leslie called "painful indecision."[106] Her letters to him indicate great conflict and the renewal of many of her doubts about her readiness for marriage and her relationship with Leslie.[107] It may be significant that in the parts of her letters Leslie chose to preserve, Julia seldom spoke of love. Since it would have been out of character for him to discard any references she made to loving him, one wonders whether she did in fact love him in the romantic sense.

Julia also expressed worries about her obligations to her children even though Leslie had assured her that he liked them and that they were the only children who did not make him jealous.[108] She said that she dreaded change; that she had an instinctive dislike of new things; that she was exasperated with herself because she was so complicated;[109] and that she should have clearer and less confused ideas about what she could and should do. Perhaps it was her obstinacy, she said, that made her doubts increase rather than dissipate when she thought about marrying him.[110]

During Julia's conflict, Leslie operated in a typically contradictory manner. On one hand, he refrained from explicitly urging her to decide in his favor. He wrote saying he was so "poor a creature" that he was tempted to tell her to decide against him. He added that he wouldn't say that she should decide against him, but he wouldn't say that she should "come closer" either.[111] In fact, Leslie refrained so much that he seemed to waver in his desire to marry, as he had when considering whether to marry Minny Thackeray (Bell [p. 10] and Annan [p. 62]). He told Julia that she was right not to try to argue with her feelings, that feelings were not susceptible to logic.[112] He compared her to a person who found it painful to revive after nearly drowning. He also said that they were like two battered old hulks leaving a harbor and sailing out into a storm.[113] Julia replied with some vigor, saying that if she felt she could be his wife, she would not be setting forth into a storm, although she knew things would not be smooth. Moreover, she said, her haven at present was hardly a safe one. With hints of family disapproval she said that she was well aware of the pain she'd have to bear when she made known such a change, but that she could deal with it when the time came if she were more sure of herself.[114]

On the other hand, Leslie behaved in ways that may have influenced Julia more than his arguments for marriage could have. In his familiar pattern, he made Julia feel that she must take responsibility for him. For example, he wrote to say how sad and lonely he was without her, and how everyone neglected him in Brighton where he had gone for the holidays. He had thought that the Morleys or the Smiths would have asked Laura and himself for Christmas dinner, but they had not. He took Laura to call on the Smiths on Christmas morning, and although they were nice to them, still there was no dinner invitation. He wrote self-pityingly to Julia, asking why didn't the Smith's take notice of him?[115] Another thing Leslie did was to put the decision entirely in Julia's hands. He wrote that because he had so much confidence in her, it was as if the responsibility were no longer on his shoulders. He added that responsibility was the one thing that was "really unbearable" to him. He could take whatever came if he didn't have to decide what it was to be.[116]

Mrs. Jackson helped her daughter decide upon marriage, although, according to Leslie[117] and Julia Margaret Cameron,[118] she, too, had fears about the future. When Julia told her mother that she was finally considering marriage to Leslie, she wept as she spoke. Mrs. Jackson responded that marrying Leslie would not be such a "dreadful thing." She told Julia that her feelings would change "insensibly" as time went on, and she would feel better about the idea of marriage. Julia replied that her mother's suggestion was not true because she had felt much worse since she had started thinking of marriage; she had been secure and tranquil in her feelings until she began to wonder if marriage to Leslie might be possible.[119] She wrote to Leslie that she felt somewhat better for having talked with her mother but that she continued to feel that she should let herself sink rather than try to revive from drowning. Then quite suddenly, early in January 1878, when Leslie and Julia were back in London, she said that she would be his wife and would try her best to be a good wife to him.[120]

Immediately after agreeing to marry Leslie, Julia was called away to Freshwater to nurse her uncle, Thoby Prinsep, in his final illness, and remained there during most of her engagement. She wrote to Leslie on January 15, 1878, not as a woman in love and excited by the prospect of marrying, but as one relieved to have made a decision and who was, nevertheless, fully committed to it. She wrote that she felt commonplace and quiet about her plans; that their relationship seemed so old and well established that she could hardly believe they were not already married; and that they seemed so much a part of each other that she could not think or talk of him. Leslie reported much of the contents of this letter in the "Mausoleum Book" (p. 44). However, he omitted from his account two sig-

nificant things in the letter. But he did copy them into his
"Calendar of Correspondence." First, he omitted Julia's remark that she felt "callous" and "horribly unsentimental"
about her engagement. The second omission was Julia's response to her uncle's question whether Leslie would make a
good husband. She told Leslie that she had replied that he
would not.[121]

What of Leslie and his feelings? No doubt he was happy and
proud. Mrs. William Kingdom Clifford, the widow of one of
Leslie's close friends, said that she heard him laugh for the first
time when he spoke of his engagement.[122] Leslie wrote to other
friends somewhat diffidently, and not quite candidly, about
his engagement. He told Oliver Wendell Holmes that his
future bride was a lady who could be described as good and
beautiful since everybody agreed on that ever since Leslie had
known her.[123] To James Russell Lowell he described his feelings for Julia as pity and reverence.[124] And to Charles Eliot
Norton he said that if he could make Julia's life a little happier,
he too would be happy once more.[125]

Leslie also adopted a nickname, and seemed younger and
more boyish in his letters, signing some of them "Wowski."[126]
But apparently he was somewhat intimidated by his victory.
The man who cast himself as Julia's protector experienced an
increased sense of helplessness. His indecisiveness more accurately predicted his future with her than did his statements to
his friends. He thought that perhaps he should be with Julia at
the Prinseps', but couldn't make up his mind. He wrote that he
was "greatly perplexed," thinking both that she might like him
with her to have someone to talk to, and that she might prefer
him to stay at home and care for the children.[127] The next day
he wrote again that he was in a quandary. He thought he
might come to her, but perhaps he could tell from her next
letter if she thought he ought to do so.[128] Again, in a second
letter of the same day, he complained that he was "so driven

backward and forward" about the matter, that he didn't know what he ought or ought not to do.[129] She didn't tell him to come, and he could not decide to go. Consequently, they were separated during most of their engagement.

# 5

# Good Times, Bad Times,
# All Times Pass Over

Leslie and Julia were married on March 26, 1878, and began a
life together with their children — Laura Stephen, Leslie's
daughter from his marriage to Minny Thackeray; and George,
Stella, and Gerald Duckworth, Julia's children from her marriage to Herbert Duckworth. Within five years, four more children were born — Vanessa on May 30, 1879; Thoby on September 8, 1880; Virginia on January 25, 1882; and Adrian on
October 27, 1883. Leslie and Julia were relatively happy during their first years together. His letters to her during that time
were almost free of complaints and self-pity. Virginia Woolf
argued in her 1908 memoir, and wanted to believe, that her
parents had been happy together until their later years. But
she thought their happiness had been *in spite of*, or, perhaps
because of, "discord and incongruity," and that as years went
on, their struggles increased and their "pinnacles" of harmony
became fewer.

Apparently, however, the best years had passed by the time
Virginia was born. The year of her birth was a crucial year for
the family for several reasons. A crisis with Laura occurred,
requiring the services of a special governess.[1] It was also the
year Leslie became the editor of the *Dictionary of National
Biography,* a decision he considered his most serious professional error. There was, however, one other happy occurrence
that year, in addition to Virginia's birth. The family took

possession of Talland House in St. Ives, Cornwall, the property they had leased the previous year.[2] Some of Virginia's more pleasant times were spent there in later years, and it became the setting for *To the Lighthouse.*

The following year was also crucial, for Julia became pregnant with Adrian, against Leslie's wishes and perhaps her own. Before Virginia's birth Leslie had written that, although he didn't like to speak of such things, after "Chad" (the name planned for Virginia evidently in the hope that she would be a boy), there must be no more babies. The admonition was as much for himself as for Julia, he said, for if his "selfish indifference" ruined Julia's health, it would destroy his happiness and make his life bleak.[3]

By 1882, Leslie's letters to Julia were again full of the self-pity and complaining that had characterized his letters to her before their marriage. Apparently from that time on, happiness within the Stephen household lasted only briefly and was considerably less than profound. Even the good times, such as vacations in St. Ives, only kept the problems within bounds and did not eradicate the tensions. The good times could never be trusted to last very long, for as Virginia suggested in *To the Lighthouse* (pp. 143-145, 296-298), almost any incidental, innocent act or word might bring on one of Leslie's moods that he expected virtually the whole universe to share. It was a cosmic crisis that his beard would not grow;[4] he swore at the elements when it rained during one of his tramps;[5] he cursed when Julia postponed returning from a trip.[6] He began letters to her, "Damn this pen!"[7] and "My Beloved, Damn this stylograph."[8] True to his motto, good times, bad times, all times did, indeed, pass over.[9] Good times seemed to pass more rapidly thanks, more often than not, to his conflicts, divisions, complaints, and general irascibility. Nevertheless, there were good times as well as bad.

Virginia, who was greatly preoccupied with the transience

and ephemerality of life, recalled that her father's attitudes about time were matched by similar concerns by her mother. She said that Julia had two epigrams about time, both emphasizing ephemerality and uncertainty. The first was for good times: make the most of the present for we know nothing of the future. The second was for bad times: what does it matter? Maybe there is no future.[10] Perhaps Julia found fewer occasions for the first motto than the second, for she enjoyed few and probably only brief periods of contentment during her marriage to Leslie. The underlying reasons for her lack of contentment were her constant worries about Leslie, her mother, and other relatives, and her continuing melancholia and grief for Herbert Duckworth. In the "Mausoleum Book" (p. 31) Leslie said that her years of sorrow had left their mark. In an unwitting *double entendre,* forgetting it was he whom she had married, he said that Julia had accepted sorrow as a "life-long partner."

Increased Responsibility

Not all the tensions within the Stephen household were caused by Leslie. But a great many of them were due to him, and others were aggravated by his contradictory reactions to things, for example, to his children. Leslie loved his children. After his tragic disappointment with Laura, he was, no doubt, quite relieved that he could father healthy children. Marrying Julia and having four children, two of whom were sons, seems to have made him feel more manly than anything, except perhaps climbing mountains. But as usual with Leslie, there was at least one other side to the question, for having children meant more responsibility, and in his private life, at least, Leslie always found responsibility threatening. His worries increasingly focused on money, or whatever money symbolized to him.

Again, that was in his private life; he was never stingy with his friends and gave generously to causes he believed in.[11] His money concerns were not groundless, of course. He had financial responsibilities that might have unsettled a much more secure man. In addition to himself, there were his wife and eight children to be supported in most part literally by his wits. There was also a bevy of servants, and after 1881, two large houses, 22 Hyde Park Gate, London, and Talland House in St. Ives. Leasing Talland House elated Leslie but it also brought on an attack of the "night horrors." He feared the possibility that the furnace would blow up and injure or maim the servants, and that he would be required to provide for them for the rest of their lives.[12]

Actual responsibilities notwithstanding, Leslie was irrational about money, and he admitted it. He never lacked a good income from his writing and editing, and Julia had an income from Herbert Duckworth's estate. Leslie used some of her money, and of course her income also meant that her children were not the burden to Leslie that they might have been. Yet Leslie never felt financially secure and never entirely left off his bedeviling of his family about finances. Clearly money meant more than financial security to him. Noel Annan (p. 7) suggested that it represented love and appreciation. "This preoccupation with money in the family circle arose partly from [Leslie's] determination to make it clear that those dependent on him were really dependent and partly from his desire for gratitude and appreciation. The sub-conscious process runs: if I impress them that but for me they would be in the workhouse they will love me and appreciate my talents all the more." But money more obviously symbolized his insecurity and his anger that others should be dependent upon him, rather than he upon them, which he would have much preferred.

His treatment of his family in money matters was an expression of his "nervousness," but was nonetheless reprehensible.

After they were married, he turned the "entire responsibility" for household accounts and payment of bills over to Julia, or so he claimed in the "Mausoleum Book." Yet, he subjected her to his fits of rage at least once a week when he inspected the family account book. Virginia Woolf said that when it became Vanessa's turn to keep the accounts, after Julia and Stella died, her father could have been no more cruel if he had taken a whip to her, and that Julia and Stella had been treated in a similar manner.[13] Virginia said also that Leslie's radically different attitudes toward women and men were reflected in these tantrums, and that if a man had kept the books, he would have been treated courteously. Apparently, in keeping the accounts Julia set a pattern of conniving with the cook to deceive Leslie about how much had been spent.[14] Stella and Vanessa followed this pattern when they managed the accounts. Virginia admired Vanessa for imitating her mother's behavior, and once listed "deceiving father" among her mother's virtues.[15] She recalled that Julia had to skimp in ways that embarrassed her, such as not furnishing the upper floors of the house as she would have liked. Julia could spend very little on her own clothing, and the children, especially Virginia, were concerned that their mother seldom had new dresses.[16] When rooms were added to 22 Hyde Park Gate, Julia saved architects' fees by sketching what she wanted on a piece of paper.[17] Although Virginia had called her mother's deceiving her father a virtue, she indicated in *To the Lighthouse* (pp. 61-63) that she believed her mother had found scrimping and lying to Leslie about money especially demeaning.

Leslie interpreted the matter in the "Mausoleum Book" (p. 69) and denied that he had much to regret concerning his treatment of Julia over finances. But he did say he might have erred in giving Julia the "entire responsibility" for the accounts. His version of his fits of rage was that he would become "a little nervous without just reason" when totaling the balance sheet and that some of his worry "reflected" on Julia. He could not charge himself with more than the inevitable results of a "nervous temperament," he said, and Julia had known that his reactions to the accounts did not mean he did not love her.

Leslie Stephen thought that the burden of supporting such a large household "explained" some of his professional compromises. Family responsibilities and his unrealistic fear of poverty contributed to his decision to take the editorship of the *Dictionary of National Biography* in 1882. Although the *Dictionary* may have been his idea originally,[18] and although he fulfilled the position of editor admirably, even brilliantly, it did not suit him intellectually and temperamentally. He prided himself on his philosophical writings and seems to have found much satisfaction as an adult, as he had when a child, in working with a great deal of material on a single subject, and "that in regular order." The work for the *Dictionary* involved regular order, but otherwise fulfilled none of his preferences. Moreover, it cut down on his time so that he could never completely satisfy his intellectual interests by other endeavors. He had hoped that he might organize the operation of the *Dictionary* so that once it was under way, he could bow out from the active work and let the *Dictionary* "run itself."[19] His plan never worked, partly because Leslie Stephen could not complain to George Smith, the publisher of the *Dictionary*, or to Sidney Lee, the assistant editor, about being put upon, and partly because he could not demand the additional assistance he needed. Instead, he tried to do too much of the work himself and felt more and more frustrated and emotionally strained. Even before his second marriage, he came to feel that his productive years had slipped by him, or that he had sacrificed them (he never knew which) to making money. Once when he was called a "penny-a-liner," he complained to Julia that the charge had a horrible plausibility, only to have her tell him he was "stupid" to "mind" such remarks.[20] As years in service of the *Dictionary* passed, his complaint became that he had never found a sense of direction and had not persisted in any one direction long enough to produce the level of scholarly work of which he was capable.[21] He grumbled also that since he wasn't much good for anything else, he might as well "dictionary,"[22] when what he wanted was to break away from it and work at more serious writing. It was all his fault yet, somehow, not his fault, and he made his family feel that they were to blame, just by being.

The children added more to Julia's difficulties than to Leslie's although there is no evidence that she complained of them or even thought of them in that light. Leslie implied in the "Mausoleum Book" (p. 49) that Julia had been tired from the time she had nursed her Uncle Thoby to the end of her life. According to Leslie, Vanessa's birth was an unusually difficult one, and left Julia's health poor. She was either not well or fatigued much of the time she carried the other children. It was necessary, because of her health, to wean Virginia from the breast when the child was only about ten weeks old. Leslie wasn't sure he liked the idea but said that of course it was acceptable if it harmed Julia to breastfeed the child.[23] Although she spent little time actually caring for them, having the responsibility for eight children, one of whom was psychotic, meant that she had very little relaxation. If Julia were still trying to avoid thinking about her grief for Herbert, as seemed to be the case, her efforts must have succeeded.

But the children were only a small part of what Julia undertook as her responsibility. She apparently had a most unrealistic sense of her personal duties and what could be left for others to do. She assumed many tasks, according to Virginia, because she thought she could accomplish them better and more quickly than others.[24] She also had an unrealistic sense of her physical capacity to meet the responsibilities she assumed; or else she was almost consciously suicidal in the way she drove herself beyond her physical limits. She never deliberately neglected the children, but all too often they were low on her list of priorities. It is not quite certain whether Leslie or Julia's mother and other "patients" were first on her list of priorities (Bell [pp. 38-39] said Leslie was first), but Leslie and the others took precedence over her children, whose care was usually delegated to servants.


The Marriage

And what of the marriage itself, the relationship between Leslie and Julia? Apparently each, according to personal needs and priorities tried to make the marriage a good one. But both failed and therefore must have felt that life perpetually betrayed them. Even with her other commitments, Julia tried extremely hard to be a good wife, as she had promised, and to make it a good marriage. Leslie did not try as hard as Julia, and he always worked against himself, but he did try. Leslie's confused definition of a good marital relationship posed a serious problem. He could not feel his marriage was good unless he had Julia totally at his service, listening to him, sympathizing with his endless complaints, soothing and comforting him, and assuring him that he indeed deserved pity. When discussing Minny Thackeray, Noel Annan (p. 63) analyzed Leslie's attitudes toward love and marriage, some of which became more pronounced after Leslie's second marriage. "Love for Stephen was a simple emotion. Passion, obsession, delusion, could never steal upon him unseen, breed upon his heart and possess him; the fascinating and alluring and those attractions which are mysteriously generated by the temperament and physique, were alien to his nature and repelled him." Annan was not entirely accurate about Leslie's response to the attractions generated by the flesh. But he was correct when he said that to Leslie: "Love meant devotion: to adore and be adored. But on the level of humdrum existence he found it difficult to translate this devotion into sympathy and understanding. Stephen regarded his wife as a soothing creature who would dissipate worry, attend his needs and bend to his will, but he discovered to his surprise that marriage cannot be circumscribed by a series of rules and concepts."

Leslie's ways of showing his love for Julia were confused and confusing; at a minimum, they were neurotic. In his view, his endless complaints and self-pity were valid indications of love, for they showed how profoundly he needed her. To others, they seem more nearly to be expressions of his tyrannical, strangling dependency on her. They were also at least slightly hostile and accusatory, for they meant that Julia had never done enough for him, and that she must try to do more. In *To the Lighthouse* (pp. 225-228) Virginia revealed the egocentrism of Leslie's expectations of love: if others really loved him they would feel his woes as deeply as he did and they would fill their worlds with his sorrows.

Whether or not Leslie discovered, as Annan believed he did, that marriage cannot be defined by rules and concepts, the family letters indicate that he discovered that he could not fully control Julia. Rather, he was the one who had to be circumscribed, if she and the children were to survive emotionally. Her efforts to control him including trying to curb his more infantile demands. Contradictorily they also included mothering him, a practice elicited not only by his needs and her compassion, but also by the consequences if she left his wants untended. Thus Julia worked against herself, for mothering Leslie encouraged his more infantile behavior. And the more she gave in and treated him in terms of his filial and infantile demands, the more difficult it became to think of him as an equal and satisfy his wish that she look up to him as head of the household. Evidently she wanted to respect his wish and only added to her frustrations by giving in to his demands that she baby him.

Virginia Woolf's interpretation of her parents' marriage in *To the Lighthouse* reflects her belief that her mother wanted to lean upon Leslie as well as protect and baby him. That novel also suggests that her mother's attitudes toward men were complicated and possibly confused. However, one suspects Virginia, not Julia, was confused, and was writing about her own puzzlement about the nature of her mother's or any woman's love for a man. In the novel, Virginia said (p. 129) that Mrs. Ramsay, representing her mother, always pitied men as if they lacked something, and never pitied women, as if they had something. Again, she made the statement (p. 159) that Mrs. Ramsay "let . . . this admirable fabric of masculine intelligence" uphold and sustain her. In still another statement (p. 13), Mrs. Ramsay "had the whole of the male sex under her protection, for their chivalry and valor; for the way they negotiated treaties, ruled and controlled finance; and for their reverential, trustful, and child-like attitudes towards her." These statements pertain to a fictional character. The real woman, Virginia's mother, whatever her inclinations, was allowed to do very little leaning on her husband. Leslie's inability to let her be dependent added to his feelings of guilt and to her dissatisfaction.

## Sulking through Inevitabilities

Many of the pervasive tensions between Leslie and Julia Stephen were subterranean and were acted our rather than spoken. They were, therefore, all the more damaging to everyone concerned, as Virginia Woolf showed so well in *To the Lighthouse*. But some of their problems were discussed in Leslie's letters to Julia. Although he usually addressed their differences rather obliquely, he often said enough to reveal her dissatisfactions as well as his own. Their being apart was a problem frequently cited in his letters. Most of their separations were initiated by Julia, and since she had admirable reasons to be away — nursing the sick and dying — Leslie tried to be magnanimous and gracious. He never succeeded, and his complaints of his dire need for her and his reports of how he spent his time when she was away made his effort at graciousness seem half-hearted at best. He said that he overworked himself to avoid boredom and loneliness,[25] that life without her was ghostly and unreal,[26] and that without her he sat at home in a "comotose" state[27] or a state of suspended animation.[28] He lied to avoid accepting dinner invitations while she was away, annoyed to be asked,[29] or he accepted them and reported that he was bored and irritated to have gone out.[30] Once he refused to see his friend, James Russell Lowell, telling Julia that he was too sulky to see Lowell or anyone else, that he would "creep into a corner and snarl" until she returned.[31] On another occasion, when he did accept a dinner invitation, he was irritable for the two following days because a woman at the party had "fidgeted" him by laughing like an "imbecile poll-parrott" trying to be "ecstatically amused."[32]

Leslie might of course creep into a corner, sulk and snarl, on social occasions when Julia was with him. He said, boastfully, in the "Mausoleum Book" (p. 69) that, of all mankind, he was the most easily bored. When he and Julia entertained, he was given to "plunging into the back den," leaving Julia with friends whom he found dull. After all, he once generalized absurdly, women don't mind dullness "half so much" as men do.[33] Even if he didn't disappear from the dinner table, he might groan aloud that he wished the guests would leave, a tendency that grew worse after he became deaf.[34]

The times away from Julia were often times when Leslie seemed to feel obligated to be miserable, perhaps out of the confused notion that to be content away from her would indicate that he didn't love her. Julia was less miserable away from him, even though the tasks she undertook must have made her trips unpleasant. Leslie accused her of staying away just because she enjoyed the pain of separation, but no evidence that she was that morbid exists.[35] Julia once extended a trip of hers into a vacation, justifying it by saying it was her duty to accompany her son, George Duckworth, and a friend on a trip to Paris. Leslie was "peeved" that she had gone to Paris and "peeved" also that she called on "the Jewess" while in Paris,[36] but acknowledged that he would have made everyone miserable if he had gone with them.[37]

Leslie traveled without Julia when he lectured or went to be awarded honorary degrees. But most often he went away for vacations, to hike, or to climb in the Alps, as his custom was for one or two weeks each January. Although he never failed to express his longing for her and his dependency, typically he was more content when he went away than when she left him. The obvious reason was that he felt less rejected, when he initiated a separation than when she did. Also, because Leslie seemed to feel most whole and at peace with himself when he was hiking and mountain climbing, these activities were some compensation for separation from Julia. However, when sent away for his health, even to his beloved Alps, Leslie was most unhappy and self-pitying. His real and supposed illnesses brought back insecurities from his childhood and made him want to be dependent as almost nothing else could. When Julia said that he should stay longer than he had planned, his distress was acute.

Although Julia may sometimes have been glad for respites from Leslie, and although she could always claim laudable reasons for going away, she tried not to neglect him more than was absolutely necessary. Before going, she added appreciably to her own work by preparing his favorite foods to be left for him, arranging the work for the servants, and planning for the children.[38] As he said, she wound up the house like a clock before leaving, but he could only feel the house run down without her.[39] She was not always glad for respites from him, however, and he initiated separations at times when she needed him. For example, he decided on several occasions to hike at least part of the way between London and St. Ives when the household was being moved to Talland House for vacations, or back to London.[40] Even though the servants helped, his absence left Julia with the entire responsibility and the arduous work of moving the young children, the luggage, and the household items, and of managing the difficult train trip. Leslie's avoidance of such responsibility was consistent with the division of labor among the sexes in nineteenth-century England, but inconsistent with his repeated avowals that he wanted to protect Julia. He said that he felt embarrassed to enjoy his tramps, and on one such occasion when "everything went wrong" on Julia's trip, he said that he was "brought low" by her account of her troubles.[41] After Julia experienced a "very bad" journey, he said he was ashamed not to have helped her, but that it was well he was out of the way. Still more of his inconsistency was evident in his claims that the chief purpose of taking the house at St. Ives was to give Julia vacations.[42] He hoped she would get some rest there and would be less overrun by so many kinds of "wild beasts," that is, by relatives and friends wanting her help.[43] The truth was, however, that although Julia enjoyed St. Ives, Talland House pleased Leslie much more than it did Julia. Leslie admitted that also, saying that although he felt selfish in leasing Talland House since it was so far from Julia's mother, he knew that he could never find any other situation so curiously suited to his own tastes.[44]

In 1893 Leslie was forced to take the children to St. Ives by himself when Julia remained in London with Stella, who had the mumps. He professed to have had a very comfortable trip, but complained that he was terribly forlorn without Julia after his arrival.[45] Perhaps the trip was as comfortable as he claimed, for the children were older and required less care. But at least one unpleasant incident occurred to upset the children. Adrian recalled the incident in 1945 in a letter to Vanessa. A container of lemonade had spilled over the lunch Julia had provided and the children had been repelled by the soggy and "perfectly disgusting" sandwiches that Leslie forced them to eat nevertheless. Only Vanessa had escaped the ordeal of eating them, pretending motion sickness and burying her head in a book.[46]

After arriving at St. Ives, Leslie's customary litanies dominated his letters until Julia and Stella were able to join the family. He reported that St. Ives was terribly haunted; he could not bear to look at the cricket ground and other places where they had had so many happy times.[47] He couldn't manage the children or get them to spend time with him.[48] He complained that they avoided him by slipping off to the garden to collect bugs, and that they bickered over their game of billiards, teasing each other until he intervened.[49] He was irritated because Adrian didn't seem to have the right clothing or couldn't dress himself; the boy had appeared with his "velveteens below" and his "linen above."[50] The real problem was that Julia was not with Leslie and that she had specifically forbidden him to complain about it. But he could not restrain his need to complain and commiserate with himself. He was lopsided without her; it was more like sleeping than waking; he was so bored that he was reading a bit of German metaphysics, chiefly to be able to say that it was damned nonsense.[51] He pressed for Julia to come to him, saying it was "right" that she should do so. He said also that there was no danger that the children would get the mumps, for they stayed out of doors much of the time. There was no worry about his getting it, for he'd had it fifty years ago. Or so he then thought; nine years earlier when Julia had stayed with George at his school because he had the mumps, Leslie had worried greatly about catching the disease.[52] When Julia and Stella agreed to come to St. Ives, Leslie was disturbed about the necessity of finding a bedroom for the still ailing Stella. He was displeased that either he and Julia, or the children, would have to be moved from their rooms to make Stella comfortable.[53]

Leslie was never happy to be apart from Julia under any circumstances, and was most disgruntled when she was called to her mother. He was jealous of Mrs. Jackson and would have liked to feel that he and Julia, not Julia and her mother, were alone together in the universe. As early as 1879, the second year of the marriage, Leslie expressed skepticism about Mrs. Jackson's need of Julia. He said that Mrs. Jackson was not dangerously ill and that she needed "managing" more than she needed nursing.[54] He was correct in part for Mrs. Jackson had problems with her "nerves." Although Leslie couldn't appreciate Mrs. Jackson's psychological problems, the pressure on Julia to tend to her mother was probably greater than if her mother had been physically ill.

Much of Leslie's complaining about Julia's being away was due to jealousy and resentment. Although these emotions were no doubt his principal motives, more objective reasons to oppose Julia's trips existed. She often made the trips at great hardship to herself, as she did by going to nurse her mother before recovering from the effects of Vanessa's birth.[55] Also, there was the problem of arranging for the children when she went away. Sometimes Julia took only the youngest children with her, sometimes she took all of them, including Laura, and sometimes all of the children remained with Leslie. On several occasions when Julia was called away and Leslie was on one of his trips, he arrived home to find that she had departed, leaving the Stephen children with the servants or the older Duckworth children.

*Good Times, Bad Times*

Leslie the Protector

Leslie's wish to protect Julia was a recurring theme in his letters, cited many times in reference to their separations. His desire to protect her was often confused with the wish to keep her at his side, which even he realized was not the best protection. As he once said, he hated to see her slaving—for other people.[56] If she were to sacrifice herself, he felt that he had prior rights and, as a Victorian husband, he had custom on his side. It was most improbable that he or anyone could have managed to get Julia to submit to protection in any event, but that made him no less inconsistent in his avowed reasons for wanting to protect her. An instance already cited, which occurred when Julia was nearly six months pregnant with Virginia, typifies the self-interest that almost invariably pervaded his expressed concern for Julia's welfare. Away on one of his tramps, Leslie wrote that he was "low" about Julia because she was tired, suffering from a cold, and should be trying, he said, to summon strength for the ordeal of the next birth. He felt that she was overworked in every way and that something must be done to relieve her, for if she became an invalid, "life would be indeed bleak for him."[57] Again, he wrote that he was a "happily domestic" man whose only discomfort, at the moment, was to see her looking worn and to feel that he was to blame for not making her happier. He wished that he could see her spirits improve so that he did not feel like a "brutal wet blanket." They must retire to St. Ives for her sake, he concluded.[58] A few days later, after an argument with her, he wrote to say that she must not think that he was blaming her or complaining of "anyone's" not making him happy. He was as happy as he had the power of being. He did think of her burdens and was unhappy in part because he could do so little to help her. Thinking about how worn and tired she was almost ruined the quiet time he was having.[59] And sometimes Leslie

118

wanted to "protect" Julia from things she liked to do, such as going to a dance with Stella Duckworth.[60]

Other inconsistencies in Leslie's wish to be Julia's protector were evident in his grudging thanks when she performed exceptional duties on his behalf. For example, in 1886, after the house at 22 Hyde Park Gate was remodeled, Julia assumed the responsibility for getting the house back in order, including putting Leslie's new study in order and arranging his bookshelves. He thanked her and said that he was pleasantly surprised that she had done that for him. But he did wish that she had arranged "something" (he didn't know how to say it "delicately") for his convenience so that he would not have to walk all the way to his dressing room and back when "necessity [arose]." Also he would have to rearrange the books "a little" so that he could find the right ones when he needed them. The whole arrangement would be perfect in a short time; he really should have helped more, but he was incompetent and got into such "tantarums." Then, in an uncharacteristically explicit reference to sex, he said that "by abstaining so much" he became even more "tantarous," but would "say no more" on that. He did say more on the arrangement of his books, however, reporting, in four letters over a period of a week, that he was still having to rearrange his bookshelves.[61]

Two Climactic Separations

In 1887, Leslie and Julia had two separations that put exceptional strain on everyone concerned. The first was a result of Leslie's overwork for the *Dictionary of National Biography*. His health was so affected that it became necessary for him to go away for three weeks in the Alps. At least Julia and the family doctor thought that such a trip was necessary; Leslie was not so sure. The nature of his health problems is unclear.

Evidently he had been threatened with an emotional collapse, and, at a minimum, was showing evidence of serious stress and fatigue. There was talk of physical collapse, but since his physical complaints disappeared when he got away from work, it seems probable that they were due to emotional strain. Leslie doubted the problem was physical stress for he reported to Julia that he could eat and sleep well, and walk long distances in the snow without tiring. After walking twenty-five miles in the snow without effort in one day, only a week after his arrival in the Alps, he wrote Julia that all the talk (hers and the doctor's) about his health was "damned nonsense." The problem was his nerves; he should come home at once, for the best prescription for nerves was to be quietly with Julia. He had to be with someone who would soothe and console him, he said, not with people such as the other tourists who "rubbed his sensitive skin with sandpaper." He wanted only to be petted in her arms. If he couldn't come home soon, he'd be intolerably bored by the solitude and would have "tantarums."[62]

Julia was under great strain herself, in part because of Leslie's health, so she wrote that he should extend his trip and take a fourth week in the Alps. He replied that he could not bear it, especially could not bear being ill without "his nurse" at his side.[63] He would try, he said, to "plod through" one more day. He did remain in the Alps one more day, but he wrote to proclaim his excruciating boredom and to remind himself and Julia that good times, bad times, all times "pass over."[64]

The second separation that year came only a few weeks after Leslie's return from the Alps, when Julia went to nurse her father through what proved to be his final illness and help her mother through the difficult time. Julia tried, as usual, to arrange everything for the Stephen household in her absence. She put Stella Duckworth in charge and made occasional trips back and forth to see to family matters. Leslie pretended at first to accept Julia's being away and to sympathize with her trials. He wrote that Stella admirably assumed charge of the household, that she was quiet and businesslike, and that she treated him well.[65] However, Leslie was still concerned about his own health and was more self-pitying than usual about his being deprived of Julia. He expressed a relatively callous attitude about Dr. Jackson's imminent death, as he was inclined to do about other people's dying unless it affected him directly. Dr. Jackson's death would affect Leslie less than his continuing illness, which kept Julia away. Leslie wrote to Julia to say that he hoped her trials would soon be over.[66] When Dr. Jackson did die, Leslie wrote that he was relieved, for Julia could come home as soon as the funeral had taken place. He invited and then urged Julia to bring her mother to live at Hyde Park Gate, asking a kind of personal bonus. He hoped that Mrs. Jackson would "make a point of loving him." She had "done well" by him so far, but he wanted to do what he could for her and there was nothing like being encouraged by her loving him.[67]

Days passed and Julia continued to postpone her return. Then Leslie learned (but not from Julia) that Mrs. Jackson wanted to stay in her own home for at least six weeks to recover from her grief and that Julia planned to stay with her. He was outraged and gave up all pretense of magnanimity about sharing Julia. Then began an exchange of letters with Julia expressing his arguments for and her arguments against her immediate return. Some of Leslie's letters were angry, some badgered her to account for money she had spent, and all complained about how inadequate he felt without her. Her arrangements for him were not at all satisfactory, he said. When Julia arranged for Florence and Frederic Maitland to move in and help run the Stephen household, thereby relieving Stella, Leslie complained that the Maitlands were no substitute for Julia. Florence Maitland angered him by not sharing his "gravity" about Julia's continued absence.[68] Besides, he said, the Maitlands were a little excessive in "the dining department." Surely, he said, Julia could "impel" her mother to move "without bothering her."[69]

Leslie became more and more pitiable, saying that he felt as if he were in a nightmare; people looked on "quietly without the power of moving." Julia's absence became a moral issue; it was not "right" that she was sacrificing herself and not "right" that she wasn't giving him more consideration. He felt more and more deserted and professed more and more concern for Julia. It was all he could bear to see how worn and bothered she was and how she "calmly submitted" to torment — that being his, not Julia's, interpretation of her prolonged stay with her mother.

Julia continued to say that it was necessary for her to stay for her mother's sake. She said reasonably that her mother wanted and needed to get through her grief in her own home. Leslie replied that it would do Mrs. Jackson "good" to undergo "the pain" of getting over her "morbid feelings" and that Julia and her mother should come at once to Hyde Park Gate.[70] Finally, Leslie's persistence in attacking Julia's reasons for staying in Brighton elicited from Julia the fact that she herself was tired and needed time away from him and the family. The possibility that Julia was fatigued had not occurred to him, and the idea that Julia needed to be away from him and the family was too strange for him to comprehend it. He said that he certainly hadn't understood that staying away would be good for her, and that even though he shouldn't complain, her wanting time away from him was "upsetting" and bewildering. The only solution was for him to go to Brighton and settle the matter with her in person.[71] He went there, but returned without Julia who stayed on nearly two more weeks to help her mother sort Dr. Jackson's papers. Leslie was somewhat mollified after seeing Julia, but vowed that when he died he would leave no papers to inconvenience anyone; he rather thought he would just destroy them at once.[72]

Apparently Julia tried even harder after his visit to her in Brighton to see that Leslie should feel that she was not neglecting him. She sent him a gift from Brighton, and George Duckworth, acting for her, saw to it that Leslie's pipes were filled. Leslie wasn't quite sure they were filled to his liking, but was touched nevertheless. He continued to complain that he was lonely and he had one of his attacks of overwhelming worry about the disasters of the world — this time over rumors of crop failure and the threat of widespread starvation.[73] He said he could only overwork himself when Julia was away, and that he would be a bag of bones when she returned.[74] He worried about his writing; he expected a bad review which would put him in a "tantarum" for a week. He knew it was absurd to worry, but then, he was an absurd man.[75] If Julia postponed her return even one more day, he'd tear off all his hair.[76] He was saved from deciding whether to act on that threat, for she did not again postpone her return. She was home after an absence of twenty-eight days, seventeen days after her father's death.

Once again Leslie's recollection of matters in the "Mausoleum Book" is slightly at variance with the contemporary evidence. If he was correct in the "Mausoleum Book" (p. 56), and he may well have been in this instance, it puts a different light upon Julia's extended time with Mrs. Jackson after Dr. Jackson's death. It does not, however, make Leslie's conduct appear any more rational. He said that Mrs. Jackson's nerves had broken down completely when Dr. Jackson died, and that Julia wanted to be with her mother for that reason. He said further that Mrs. Jackson's nerves were "perpetually weak" after her husband's death, and that her "pitiable state" had always been on Julia's mind.

Julia ... Independent and Impatient

Many of the strains in the Stephen marriage were due to separations. Leslie found these extremely trying because of his childish and seemingly pathological dependency upon Julia.

He felt incomplete and "lopsided" when she was away, and the substance of his complaints indicates that he almost always underwent a drastic personality change without her. Moreover, her going away spelled out to him the fact that she needed him far less than he needed her. Not even her need to assume responsibility for others when asked, which largely accounted for their relationship and marriage, could make her submit totally to his insatiable and childish needs for nurture. Her trips away from him made it all too evident to him that even if she loved him she loved him differently than he loved her and had a very different conception of marriage. There may have been a question in his mind whether she did love him; he could never get her to say so, once they married.[77] Everyone — Leslie included — knew that she had loved Herbert Duckworth and still mourned him. But did she love Leslie Stephen? Julia would work to the point of damaging her health while providing for his welfare and comfort, but, perversely, would never say that she loved him.

After Julia died, Leslie tried to convince himself and their children that although Julia had had a more perfect union with Herbert Duckworth, she had loved Leslie Stephen also and had been happy with him. In the "Mausoleum Book" (pp. 38, 70), he protested much too much, saying that verbal expressions of love were unnecessary between husbands and wives living in intimate association. Leslie suggested that it was just one of Julia's foibles to refuse to use the words, while Virginia Woolf in *To the Lighthouse* (p. 185) attributed it to her mother's shyness with words. While Julia lived, however, Leslie acted as if expressions of love between husband and wife were extremely important, and, in at least two ways, belied his arguments in the "Mausoleum Book." First, he himself was much given to endearments and to expressing his love for Julia. His letters to her rarely failed to contain such expressions. Of course his avowals of love were in league and entangled with his expressions of resentment and his suggestions that she was failing to make him happy, but he rarely failed to say the words. Second, his arguments that expressions of love were unnecessary between husband and wife were belied by his importuning Julia to say the words to him.

Did Julia love Leslie in a romantic sense? Was she "in love with" him? In *To the Lighthouse* (p. 38), Virginia Woolf provided a strong case that her mother loved her father. Quentin Bell said that all the Stephen children believed that their parents loved each other deeply. However, that remains one of the mysteries about Julia. At a minimum, she was emotionally independent of him, which may be all that her refusal to speak words of love indicated. Such independence was abundantly evident in the pattern of her life. Her independence is something of a mystery, too. One does not know whether it was her preference or was forced by Leslie's inability to let her lean upon him. He summed up the matter with greater than usual insight and candor when he said that he should have been the stake and she the vine that clung to it, rather than the reverse, but that he would have been a "very crooked support" for her.[78]

A good guess is that Julia wanted to be independent, despite the fact that she was forever letting others take advantage of her. Even her self-sacrifice indicated a perverse kind of independence. When she decided to give of herself excessively, no one, not even Leslie, could countermand her decision. Possibly she wanted to be more independent, in all ways, than she ever succeeded in being. Leslie Stephen intimated that Julia had wanted a career and that she had looked upon her nursing and other charitable activities as a vocation.[79] Virginia Woolf expressed a similar belief, in *To the Lighthouse* (pp. 17-18), that her mother had wanted to be a professional in endeavors in which she could only be an amateur. But perhaps Leslie and Virginia were wrong: Julia joined Mrs. T. H. Huxley, Mrs. Matthew Arnold, and some one hundred other wives of Victorian intellectuals in signing "An Appeal against Female Suffrage," a petition that argued against careers for women, among other things perceived as potential vices.[80]

If Julia Stephen had indeed wished for a career and was emotionally independent of Leslie, his efforts to chain her to him and to his service, must have been all the more onerous. That may account for some of her impatient efforts to curb his more infantile demands, efforts manifested during their courtship and more prominent in their marriage. Like Virginia, Julia must have found it difficult to know what to think of Leslie, and must have been troubled by the contrast between his public and private personalities, between the intrepid mountaineer and staunch friend, and the infantile self he so often projected at home. If he could control himself with others and show so much strength and courage elsewhere, why was he so infantile and clinging with her?

Julia became especially impatient with his self-pitying and plaintive attitudes as her health became increasingly strained by her work and as both his complaints and excuses for complaints accrued. Eventually she began to forbid him to complain, which in his view just gave him another reason to do so. It was definitely not a "balk" he would tolerate. For example, when she ordered him not to complain about her being away, he objected that she was making it difficult for him to "express himself." He could not truthfully say that he did not want her with him, he grumbled, but if he said that he did want her, she would accuse him of being depressed.[81] Then, going over the matter in a second aggrieved and resentful letter, he concluded that he would say that he would be glad when she arrived; surely, he said, she couldn't object to that.[82] On another occasion he wrote to Julia from the Alps, complaining several times about her objections to his complaints. He'd be home in a week, thank goodness; he could not help saying that and had restrained himself hitherto from saying it. Nevertheless, the Alps were beautiful; they might have melted "even her hard heart." He was depressed about his work and it was safe to say so from a distance, since she was not there to "grind her teeth."[83]

Virginia Woolf said more than once that her mother was not only impatient and independent, but that she was commanding. Two incidents record Julia Stephen's ability to be imperious and to press ahead in spite of obstacles. One of them involved the marriage of Frederic Maitland to Julia's niece, Florence Fisher. As Leslie reconstructed the event in the "Mausoleum Book" (pp. 57-58), Maitland, a widower, had shown enough interest in Florence to cause the girl and the girl's mother to expect and hope for more attention. But Maitland began to show that he wanted to keep himself free from more serious involvement, and replied to an inquiry from Julia that there were "reasons" why he should not marry. Showing few signs of her legendary sensitivity, Julia then sent for Maitland, inquired into his reasons, and elicited a sad story. He told her that he had considered suicide, that "certain sensations" had convinced him he was going mad, and that when he had asked for medical advice a doctor had confirmed his fears. Julia refused to believe he was in danger of insanity and told him he should get the best medical opinion to be had in London. The eminent physician and neurologist, Hughlings Jackson, examined Maitland and decided that he was only experiencing the effects of overwork. Meanwhile, Julia and Leslie were awaiting a letter from Maitland to hear Hughling Jackson's conclusions. But Maitland had somehow managed to misaddress the letter reporting his good news. Florence's mother added further perturbation by demanding an explanation of Leslie and Julia, who could only hint obliquely and vaguely at certain obstacles to marriage. Then Leslie, probably dispatched by Julia, went to see Maitland, learned of the misaddressed letter, and brought him and his good news back. Subsequently, Maitland

127

and Florence Fisher were married. Unlike Minta and Paul Rayley in *To the Lighthouse,* whose marriage may have been suggested by the circumstances surrounding the Maitlands, their marriage was said to have been relatively happy. Leslie concluded his account by saying that perhaps the marriage would have taken place without Julia's help, but that the situation had been "critical" and that her bold handling of the matter seemed necessary. He told Julia at the time that he was not hopeful of a marriage between Maitland and Florence Fisher, and that she would have to bring it about by some "ingenious scheme" if, indeed, she could bring it about at all.[84]

Another occasion when Julia was known to be relatively imperious occurred when James Russell Lowell died. Julia decided that although Lowell was an American, he should be memorialized in Westminster Abbey. Leslie was opposed to the idea, but Julia insisted that he write a letter to the *Times* of London proposing the memorial. Julia herself took the lead, according to Leslie, in the "rather troublesome negotiations" that resulted in the memorial, a window in Westminster Abbey Chapter House.[85]

## Leslie at His Games

It did not ease the tensions of the marriage or make Julia more patient that Leslie so often played games with her. His principal game, or so he thought, consisted of exaggerating his woes in order to elicit her "delicious" sympathy and petting. Nor did his frequent confessions that he played games do much to improve the situation, for they, too, were a game. Moreover, since he did not seem to regret the games and never gave up his almost ritualistic ploys for her sympathies, the games must have signified much more than Leslie could understand or was able to acknowledge.

The meaning of Leslie's games is revealed by what he gained

from them, that is, by their usual objectives and outcomes. He acknowledged some of his objectives, for example, that he wanted to coax verbal reassurance and tactile comfort — "petting" — from Julia. But another, unacknowledged outcome, was that of placing and keeping Julia in the wrong and on the defensive. She seems to have lost out, no matter what she tried to do for him, and was duly informed that she'd not done enough or had said and done not quite the right thing. For example, when he complained that he was depressed, he then rejected the concern she expressed, saying that is depression was of no consequence. It only came by "fits and starts" and was chiefly a scheme to get a "rise out of her," for she didn't "rise as freely" as he wished.[86] He had the "hideous trick," he told her on another occasion, of pretending to be miserable in order to coax sympathy from her because he enjoyed being petted so much.[87] What he implied was that she was so niggardly with her affections that it was necessary to coax or trick her.

The fact that Leslie played these games raises the question of whether his game-playing can be laid in some measure to Julia. Did her refusal to say that she loved him, her independence, and her want of patience in her later years imply that she was unaffectionate and that she withheld herself from him? His own witness before and after her death is to the contrary. She did soothe, comfort, and pet him; for example she patted him off to sleep like a child when he awoke in the night with "the horrors."[88] Apparently it was not a withholding of affection so much as her giving of herself that made him, in his words, "greedy" for more and more of her "delicious" sympathy. No doubt, his need to place her in the wrong, if that was one of his purposes, was likewise reinforced by the ease with which he could win that game and by some kind of perverse satisfaction he took in having her redouble her already excessive efforts to please him.

The objectives of Leslie's games were not their only significance, for their focus and content tell a great deal about him. Frequently he was worried about his alleged professional failure, and although he used his concern as a ploy for sympathy and to put Julia in the wrong, his worries must not be discounted. He would complain that his writing, and he himself, had failed; that he had never done anything significant; that he had only done enough to show that he might have done something important, and so on.[89] For a long time Julia would do the obvious and logical thing, that is, she would praise and compliment him, trying to reassure him about the quality of his writing and about his success in life. She found such assurance easy to give for she had admired his writing even before she knew him. She also hoarded compliments paid to Leslie by others so she could report them to him.[90] When she praised his writing, he often replied that he complained of failure because he wanted her to pity him and be more affectionate, not because he wanted to hear he was a good writer.[91] Or, he said he complained only because something had happened to show him how little he had done, making him want a little comfort.[92] On another occasion he responded to her praise with an air that she was wrong again—how could she say that she admired his writing when she had such contempt for his practical opinions?[93] After complaining still another time that no one appreciated his work, he once again rejected Julia's attempts to solace him. He said that he was "as appreciated" as he deserved to be and that he was intrinsically contemptible. He added, with confused logic, that "nobody" was going to be permitted to deprive him of "the comfort of that."[94]

Comments made in the "Mausoleum Book" (pp. 72, 74) suggest that behind Leslie's overt reactions there was, at least, incipient contempt for Julia's ability to form a valid opinion of his writing. After her death, when he was eulogizing her, and was therefore at his most laudatory, he told their children that he could confess to occasional self-deprecation in order to extort Julia's "delicious" compliments, and that her praise was "delicious" despite the fact that he couldn't accept a judgment so biased by love. He said also that Julia was guided only by instinct, while he was guided by logic. He could and did admit, now that she was dead, that sometimes her instincts were more to be trusted than his ratiocination. But this knowledge rarely applied to his behavior toward her while she was alive. As Noel Annan commented (p. 101), "Leslie ploughed furrows of ratiocination to reach conclusions, she had intuitively reached them and acted on them before he arrived. Thus he was forever trampling upon her feelings, wounding the person who comforted him, half-conscious of his hebetude, unable to constrain it."

Leslie Stephen showed his worries about reactions to his writing in other ways than through his game-playing with Julia. Often he was truly miserable about his alleged failures in his professional life, and about much else. His misery showed itself in overreaction to criticism much as Virginia Woolf's did years later, though in a less extreme fashion. He reached a point where he could not read negative criticisms of his work because they pained him too much. Then, sounding more like his pleasure-eschewing father than his daughter, he decided to deny himself the satisfaction of reading positive comments. He explained that if he couldn't face the bad things people said, he had no right to see their flattery.[95] There were objective reasons for Leslie to be less than completely happy with his accomplishments, but had he been more balanced, he would have recognized his achievements. His misery and sense of failure derived from, and were perhaps integral with, a fundamental irrationality, and nothing at all — not Julia, not eminence and public acclaim, not honors and awards — could convince him that he had succeeded or could remove the guilt he felt for his alleged failure. Therefore he continued playing games, needing to explain and justify, needing others to try to reassure him, even if he could never let them do so.

Leslie tried to play his games with other members of his

household, especially after Julia's death. In the "Mausoleum Book" (pp. 72-74), he both confessed his games concerning professional failure and tried to play them with both the Stephen and Duckworth children. He was unsuccessful except in his manipulation of Stella Duckworth. He excited his children's ridicule rather than sympathy by saying, ludicrously and lugubriously, that he was only a footnote, in small type, to the history of nineteenth-century letters. If only he had found his direction, he might have been a paragraph, in full-sized type. But, he moaned, it was too late, and he was too broken to hope for that.

Leslie knew, even during their courtship, that Julia could not ignore complaints of ill health, and Virginia Woolf said that her father's health eventually became her mother's fetish.[96] It is not surprising, therefore, that Leslie's health was often the focus of his games. Julia's readiness to respond to problems of health seemed to increase his lifelong belief in his frailty. It was almost worth being sick to be nursed by her, he said.[97] To the extent that health was a game, it was one that Leslie could easily win, for at least two reasons. First, he had well-intrenched, well-developed skills for health games. He could easily convince himself that he was ill or well, depending on the need of the moment. Second, because Julia had learned her role early and well, from her mother, she could be relied upon to respond almost automatically.

As in Leslie's other games, Julia often seemed to do the wrong thing, despite her almost automatic efforts to help. The rules of the games did not include his accepting Julia's advice for improving his health, any more than they included his accepting her reassurance about his writing. An incident that occurred on their wedding anniversary in 1892 illustrates both his petulant rejection of her advice and the strain between them. He flew into a rage because she advised him to take a coat on one of his trips. When he left it behind, she sent it on to him. He wrote to apologize: he was sorry they had quarreled on their anniversary; he had spoken thoughtlessly and hastily. Then he spoiled the apology by adding that he didn't want the coat; he wore it at the moment only because he knew she would ask him about it so he thought he'd best wear it.[98] Noel Annan concluded that Leslie's resistance to Julia's advice on health came from his old concerns about his masculinity. Annan said (p. 99), for example, that when Julia asked Leslie to take a hot bath when he came in soaked from rain, Leslie thought his manliness impugned. He then proceeded to behave not like a man, but like a child, refusing to eat his favorite cake at tea.

Leslie and Julia both worried about his health in relation to his work habits. Here too Leslie indulged in game-playing. When cautioned about overwork, he might reply that it was a "strange fiction" that he ever overworked; he was a coward about work and only worked to make the time pass when Julia was away.[99] On one occasion he would say that it was a great comfort that there was always work to be done[100] and later would complain that overwork was making him absent-minded.[101] His estimate of the matter in the "Mausoleum Book" (p. 67) was an accurate one: he did, in fact, overwork because he could not work without nervous tension.

Possibly Leslie was not malingering or consciously inventing symptoms, but certainly he monitored himself for every possible symptom and did so increasingly as he grew older. He also watched for signs of good health when that served his purposes. In the example already cited, when Leslie was sent to the Alps to recover from his breakdown in 1887, it served his purposes to recover physically as rapidly as possible in order to return home to Julia. Perhaps he also wanted to demonstrate that she and the doctor were wrong in sending him away—in short, that their talk of his bad health was, as he said, "damned nonsense."[102] However, his more common practice was to look for signs of ill health, and he seemed always to report his findings to Julia. His findings might amount to a "slight threatening of the dazzles";[103] a "little tickling in the throat";[104] "colly-wobbling in the side";[105] or a little constipation on one day that he "made up for" on the two subsequent days.[106] Once he reported a fit of coughing in the night that he imagined to be "asthma of the heart" or "something of that kind."[107] Another night "attack" was caused by too many blankets on the bed, making him so warm that at first he thought he was dying. When he awoke enough to realize what the problem was, he removed the blankets one by one in order not to get cool too precipitously. He dutifully but also humorously reported the details to Julia.[108]

Leslie Stephen had many health problems in the late 1880s and early 1890s, which diminished but did not disappear when he finally gave up the editorship of the *Dictionary of National Biography* in 1891. He recorded the major incidents in the "Mausoleum Book" (pp. 58-59, 65-69) rather defensively, as if to establish that there were actual reasons to worry Julia about his health and that he hadn't played games about it. His descriptions confirm that many of his troubles were "nervous" in origin, as he often said they were, and suggest still other significance to Leslie's games. He recounted that he thought he was completely recovered from his 1887 breakdown, but that in 1888 he had another serious attack. Julia found him unconscious, but the experience was made almost pleasurable for him by the sight of her face when he aroused, and by her stooping and "tenderly" kissing him. In 1889 he had a slighter attack, falling on the floor of the Atheneum Library in London, just as he was explaining to a surgeon friend how completely he had recovered his health and how he'd benefited from medication. Although he'd always been a sound sleeper, for several years he was troubled in his sleep. Sometimes he awoke with "fits of the horrors," that is, "fits of nervous depression." He twitched and started in his sleep and required various narcotics. Often he was convinced that he'd not slept for hours when he'd only been awake a short time, and when he did sleep, he was not refreshed. It grieved him that he had been such a worry to Julia and that he had caused her so many broken nights. He pleaded his heredity: he didn't think he was entirely at fault; like his father, he was "skinless," oversensitive and nervously irritable.

Leslie admitted to a "nervous" disorder, which in contemporary terms was, at least, a neurosis and, possibly, something more serious. His admission suggests that his game-playing was not done entirely to gain certain ends for himself, though he did usually get what he wanted. Nor were they played merely to express his worries and miseries about his professional standing and his health. It is not possible to know what his games ultimately meant, any more than he and Julia seem to have known. But certainly they indicate that Leslie was truly hurt and miserable and that he was too confused and divided to be satisfied with anything he demanded and received, from his wife or anyone else. His fundamental problems and his very real unhappiness could not be permanently relieved, and he seemed no more able than an infant to say exactly what it was that hurt him most and what his medicine should be. Julia was by all accounts an excellent nurse, but she never found the prescription to cure Leslie. Perhaps she did succeed in preventing something worse from happening to him, for all evidence points to the probability that without Julia, or someone else, to act as mother, nurse, and wife, Leslie's emotional problems would have incapacitated him, as they almost did when Julia died.

End of the Marriage: Julia's Last Years

Leslie's preoccupation with himself and his poor health in the late 1880s and early 1890s may explain why he failed to see the signs of his wife's fatigue and declining health, or, if he did see them, why he failed to appreciate their seriousness. Leslie tended to shut himself off from painful reality, but since Julia, herself, refused to be concerned about her health, Leslie may have taken his cues from her. Whatever the reason, nothing could quite excuse his failure to realize the condition of her health, least of all in his own estimation of the situation.[109] Nor could anything excuse his not having protected Julia, although as Quentin Bell has implied (pp. 38-39) and as the pattern of Julia's life demonstrates, it would very likely have been futile to try to protect her.

Julia's health problems dated at least from the time of Vanessa's birth, in 1879. She was fatigued much of the time from then until her death in 1895 — in short, through most of her marriage to Leslie. Throughout her childhood Virginia Woolf was aware that her mother was always too busy and too tired, so much so that, as Virginia said of Julia in her 1908 memoir, she could be little more than a generalized "presence" to her children. Virginia also said that during her mother's last years, Julia had become desperately concerned for time, that her strength had decreased, and that she had fewer and fewer chances to rest until she sank like an "exhausted swimmer." In looking back, Virginia correctly associated her mother's growing impatience with her ill health and fatigue, saying further that the fatigue brought out her mother's "true personality."

Apparently Julia's failing health became more serious in 1890, for about that time, her mother, Mrs. Jackson, asked the Stephen children to be especially careful not to cause their mother anxiety.[110] Also, in the photographs from that period, Julia appears haggard, with the physical appearance of an old woman, although she was only forty-nine when she died. Julia attended Mrs. Jackson throughout her decline in health until her death in 1892, and evidently suffered a worsening of her own health as a consequence. Leslie said in the "Mausoleum Book" (pp. 56-57) that Julia had been weak from the time of her mother's death, even though he had refused to acknowledge or had been unable to appreciate the signs of her weakness until after her death.

Stella Duckworth was closely attuned to Julia and, therefore, was more aware of and more frightened by her failing health than others. Stella tried harder than anyone to help her, as she had for many years, by assuming as much of Julia's work as possible.[111] Virginia Woolf said that Stella also tried to help by speaking "sharply" to Leslie on several occasions about Julia's health, but that she could not force him to acknowledge that Julia's problems were serious.[112] Even when Julia became ill with influenza in February, 1895, and remained ill and only on the verge of recuperating for about a month, Leslie did not face up to the matter. Julia seems not to have known how sick she was either, for by early April she insisted that she was well enough to allow Stella, George, and Gerald to go to the Continent for a brief holiday. Stella went much against her own wishes for she was terribly concerned about her mother's health.[113] Julia also felt well enough to take on another of her charitable duties in the middle of April, going on still one more of what Leslie called her melancholy journeys. While she was away, Leslie wrote to her that he was worried and haunted by how tired and weak she appeared to be, but ended with his customary pleas that she give him more attention.[114]

Late in April Stella cut short her visit to the Continent, sensing that her mother was worse. According to Quentin Bell (pp. 39, 41-42), the relatives gathered, for they realized that Julia was dying. Still Leslie, according to statements he made, could not realize it. A few weeks after her death he wrote that, although there was no doubt that her unsparing labors for the family and for others had weakened her heart, "not the slightest foreboding" of the reality ever crossed his mind. He thought that she had fully recovered from the influenza, and even when the ominous words "rheumatic fever" were mentioned, he "hoped against hope." When George called him to Julia's bedside on the morning of May 5th, he was totally unprepared for the blow of seeing his "beloved angel sinking quietly into the arms of death."[115] Julia died, after seventeen years, Leslie said, of being "such a wife as no language could describe"[116] — possibly another unwitting *double entendre*.

# 6

# A Bad and Good Piece of Work
# on the Whole: The Stephen Children

The best that can be said for Leslie and Julia Stephen as parents is that they were variable, often wrong in what they did in respect to the children, and sometimes right. However, that is to judge them by present day standards and by the effects on the children. By standards of their own period they could have considered themselves good, enlightened parents. Certainly neither Leslie nor Julia gave much indication that they doubted themselves as parents. Rather, Leslie was inclined to congratulate himself about the children, as Virginia Woolf knew. Mr. Ramsay, the character who represented her father in *To the Lighthouse,* tells himself (p. 106) that his eight children were, on the whole, a good piece of work.

Leslie expressed his contentment with his and Julia's four children many times, saying that they were "well fixed in the line of children," and that "he felt silly" but did "take pleasure" in the "creatures."[1] He said also that he felt more secure for having them, and as a consequence placed heavy expectations upon them. Like Julia, the children were to be the "buffers" between his sensitive skin and the world. He said that as long as he could surround himself with the children, like "an animal in a burrow," nothing could hurt him — an inverted and frightening concept of fatherhood.[2] Although he blamed family responsibilities for his financial worries and his professional disappointments, he believed the children were somehow a salvation to his marriage, for he thought he would have been a worse husband without them. For example, he would say that at least he wasn't as bad a husband as Thomas Carlyle, a sometimes friend of Leslie's, whose treatment of Mrs. Carlyle drew Leslie's disapprobation and, evidently, reminded him of his own derelictions with Julia. Carlyle's problem, Leslie once ventured, was that he had no children, whereas he and Julia were "happily situated that way."[3] If Leslie believed himself to have been as bad a husband as Carlyle, he would "almost be tempted" to commit suicide, he avowed in the "Mausoleum Book" (p. 68).

He professed his happiness in having children at some length in the "Mausoleum Book," but, as he so often did, contradicted himself and protested too much. For example, he insisted that the children were a comfort to him in his great sorrow. At the same time he pleaded for still more comfort and sympathy from them and said that Stella Duckworth was the only one who could comfort him — by implication at least, accusing his own children of neglecting him and of having been lacking in relationship to him. In the same source, he also made a bit too much of the happiness Julia had found in her children and averred, in his contradictory fashion, that she had found great happiness with them, and that sorrow had "clouded" her life with them. He said, left-handedly, and with an implicit warning about their future conduct: since Julia had not experienced the worst pain a parent could know, that of seeing a child go wrong morally, she had had no reason to regret loving her children.[4]


Failures in Being

The worst problems Leslie and Julia gave their children came not from bad decisions, blundering, or from anything specific they did to them. Rather, the major difficulties were inherent in the children's experience of their parents' relationships with each other, their individual personalities, and their patterns of living. The undercurrent of tensions between Leslie and Julia Stephen was especially unfortunate for the unusually intelligent and emotionally sensitive Virginia who could find little in the Stephen relationship to attract her to marriage. Although she sometimes said that her parents' marriage had been perfect, she also resented and feared both her father's excessive demands on her mother, and her mother's sacrifice of herself to her father[5] — the central dynamics of the Stephen marriage. Her father's attitude toward her mother was complex and confusing. He related to her as a small, greedy, selfish boy might to his mother, as a lover to his beloved, a husband to his wife, a patient to his nurse, a worshiper to the object of his adoration, and a frustrated man to the agent of his disappointments.

Finally, much about her parents' marriage was threatening and traumatic to Virginia because it represented an unreliable world where irrational forces could break through at any moment to ruin the happiest of times. Moreover, when tensions did erupt in the Stephen marriage, they appeared illogical and irrational, for the change in mood between Leslie and Julia usually could not be explained by the actual events one might observe taking place. Thus, Virginia had almost daily reminders that life is unpredictable and unreliable, especially when it seems happiest.

The unfortunate effects their relationship had on their children were reinforced by each parent as an individual. Leslie mediated a conflicting, traitorous world at best, an insane world at the worst, or so Virginia charged in her novel about the family and in her explorations of the lighthouse as symbol. He may have done more than act out this frightening vision. If he complained in Virginia's presence, as he so often did in his letters, that the world seemed meaningless, incoherent, and chaotic, an unreal place full of phantoms, and that he himself was one of the phantoms or ghosts, he may have verbally taught her that the world is insane[6]

Julia Stephen's liabilities as a parent included her vague but persistent melancholia, her occasional longing to die, and her compulsive dedication to work and other responsibilities that took her away from her children. One cannot imagine a man of Leslie Stephen's temperament and personality being anything but an unpredictable father. But, except for Julia's melancholy, her priorities, and her chronic overextension of herself, one can easily imagine her a good mother. Certainly, Virginia imagined her that way and even characterized her, on one level in *To the Lighthouse* as a miraculous mother figure, and a kind of earth Goddess. Nevertheless, much of Virginia's unhappiness and many of her serious problems can be traced directly to her mother's own unhappiness and extreme busyness with nursing and other charities. Julia's excessive self-sacrifice made it impossible for her to fulfill her implicit promise as a mother. Because she could not be the mother Virginia imagined her to be, Virginia was left with an unassuaged longing for her or for someone who might substitute for her.

Julia Stephen was best with her children when they were infants, and it was then, evidently, that Virginia learned to expect more from her mother than she was ever to receive. Julia often found it necessary to leave the children with Leslie and the servants, and when she took them with her to Brighton, her attention was usually preempted by her mother. The many times Julia traveled without her children symbolized the betrayal of life, both because of her absence and because of Leslie's radical changes in mood and personality when he and Julia were apart. He felt abandoned and almost unable to survive without Julia, he said repeatedly, and seems to have communicated his feeling quite well to Virginia — either that or she concluded from her own experience that her mother's absence meant disaster.

Moreover, with the exception of Adrian, the last of the four, none of the Stephen children was allowed to be an infant very long, if only because their births were so close together. Vanessa's and Thoby's births were separated by fifteen months; Thoby's and Virginia's by seventeen months; and Virginia's and Adrian's by twenty-one months. Virginia seems to have had an especially short infancy, for she was weaned from the breast when she was about ten weeks old.[7] After weaning, there was less necessity for Julia to be with her. Throughout her childhood, Virginia said in her 1939-1940 memoir, she had little intimate contact with her mother and had difficulty recalling having been alone with her for more than a few minutes at a time.

## The Ragamice

Life was by no means all gloom and despair for the Stephen children, and Virginia was displeased because so many readers of *To the Lighthouse* got that impression.[8] It was not all gloom and despair even at times when their mother went away, the times when their father tended to be especially difficult. Leslie was a divided, inconsistent man, but his regrettable traits must not be permitted to overshadow his more positive side and make him seem entirely the tyrannical old wretch. The same letters that contain so much evidence of his abrasive qualities also contain evidence of a lovable and loving father who must be made to stand beside the old wretch if one is to reach any understanding of the impact of Leslie Stephen upon his daughter. If she had not loved her father, hating him would have been less a problem.

The children had some very happy times with Leslie, for as

143

Quentin Bell said, Leslie could be enchanting. He delighted the children with his animal stories and fantasies, a form of play that had far-reaching results, especially in Virginia's life. Apparently it was a perfectly ordinary form of play, but it laid powerful hold on Virginia's imagination. Through animals, Leslie related to the children and interested them in his activities. Animals represented, perhaps, his best way of communicating with his children. When away, he wrote letters and sent messages to the children about animals.[9] He drew and made paper cuttings of animals for them, talked with them about animals, and took them to zoos and to museums where they saw collections of mounted animals.[10] He took other people than the children to visit animals also. Henry James wrote to his sister, Alice, about one of his first visits with Leslie Stephen, saying, "After dinner he conducted us by the underground railway to see the beasts in Regent's Park to which as a member of the Zoological society he has admittance 'Sundays.'"[11]

Leslie pretended with the children that they were animals, which very likely was the origin of the animal nicknames one finds in Virginia's letters to Vanessa, Violet Dickinson, Vita Sackville-West, Leonard Woolf, and others. More important, her father's many references to animals seem also to have been the beginning of certain manifestations of mythopoetic thought prominent in Virginia's novels.

Thoby and Vanessa were also influenced by their father's references to animals. As a boy, Thoby invented and drew imaginary animals,[12] read about animals, and argued with his father about the taxonomy of animals—shouldn't the sloth be classified with the monkey "tribe?"[13] Although Vanessa may have picked up her interest in drawing from her father, during her career as a painter she seems not to have been extraordinarily attracted to animals as subject matter, except to use them as a motif in decorating nursery furniture for her children.[14]

Leslie borrowed from the Uncle Remus stories in playing with the children. Vanessa was "Tarbaby," Virginia "Br'er Fox," and Adrian, "Br'er Rabbit," in one recorded instance, while Thoby was referred to as the "Wild Bull."[15] Several of the children in the Stephen household were given lasting animal nicknames, though not from Uncle Remus stories. Collectively they were "the Ragamice" to Leslie.[16] The nicknames were not always kind or gentle. Stella was called "Old Cow" by her mother, a nickname to which Virginia mildly objected,[17] but which she sometimes used when annoyed with Stella.[18] Virginia did not object, apparently, when she herself was dubbed "the Goat."

When not entertaining the children, Leslie Stephen's drawing often followed an animal themes, as both Quentin Bell (p. 26) and Virginia Woolf have indicated. Virginia said in her essay about him that his drawings of animals in his books were commentaries: ". . . [T]aking a pencil, he would draw beast after beast — an art that he practised almost unconsciously as he read, so that the fly-leaves of his books swarm with owls and donkeys as if to illustrate the 'Oh, you Ass!' or 'Conceited dunce,' that he was wont to scribble impatiently in the margin."[19] As Virginia has implied, many of her father's animals were vested with properties of both animals and humans. In one such drawing, included in a letter written to Julia just after Thoby's birth, Leslie apparently depicted himself and his family. The drawing shows a pig followed by a large bear pushing a baby carriage containing two small owls, all of the animals either in human dress or behaving like people.[20]

Leslie compared people to animals in a number of his letters to Julia. He said that he was an "old rook" and a "fairly cheerful raven." He hoped that Laura was not a young raven, but would have a touch of the dove. He could think of no bird for Julia, he said; he didn't want to compare her to anything so conventional as a nightingale or a lark. Besides, birds were perhaps too unpleasant to resemble her—they were so fidgety and had such nasty eyes.[21] For a time he settled on "Dove" as a pet name for her. In another letter, he compared Julia to a sheep, in a rather bumbling attempt to be humorous. Trying to deny that he ever played games, as he did habitually with her, he said that she was too "simple-minded" for games to be a good sport. It would be like shooting a domestic sheep with a rifle.[22]

There were other instances of animal analogies. He was an owl, Leslie said, when he went away on a trip leaving his purse at home.[23] (Frequently he forgot something important when he went on his trips, having to borrow from his host[24] or from his climbing companion or guide in the Alps, as in one instance when he failed to take important climbing equipment.[25] The tendency of Vanessa, Virginia, and Adrian to be absent-minded, to forget and to lose things, had ample precedent in their father.) Leslie said also that he was Julia's "faithful dog," her "loving animal";[26] that he felt like an "over-burthened ass" in his work for the *Dictionary of National Biography*;[27] that he was a marmot in hibernation when Julia was away;[28] and that Julia wanted him to hibernate like a marmot when he objected to the vacation for his health.[29]

## Doting on the Children

The activities involving animals were by no means the only instances of Leslie's enjoying his children and they, him. Bell said (pp. 26-27), "He could tell stories of dizzy alpine adventures, sometimes he would recite poetry and in the evenings he might read aloud, often from the novels of Sir Walter Scott, and call on his children to discuss what they had heard." When he wasn't feeling "tantarous" and when the children distracted him from self-pity and pessimistic ruminations, he could be doting. He closely followed the children's development, keeping a record on one of the shutters at St. Ives of their yearly growth, and approved when Vanessa stopped growing at just the right height — her mother's.[30] Except perhaps for Adrian, Leslie had individual pet names for each of the children, as well as his collective name, "the Ragamice." Vanessa became "Nessa," the name that Virginia often used for her when she wasn't referring to her as the "Dolphin." Thoby was "To" or "Tho" to his father, and Virginia was "'Ginia" and sometimes "Ginnums" as an infant. When a little older, she was "Ginny."

Leslie sometimes bragged about his children's intelligence, but found it difficult to boast outside the family. Nevertheless, he sized up other children, jealously comparing them with his own, and was pleased if he could conclude that other children were not as intellectual as his were.[31] When another father boasted of his child, which Leslie was too diffident to do, Leslie wrote irritably to Julia that the boasting had made him feel cantankerous. He grumbled that the other man, his host at the time, wasn't impressed when Leslie "accidentally" said something about his own children. Leslie decided that his host was "unconsciously jealous" and was therefore refusing to hear anything good about Leslie's children. Having a little turn for parental jealousy himself, Leslie said, he could detect it in others.[32]

Vanessa, Thoby, and Virginia seemed to their father to be beautiful children, as Adrian did also when he was very young.[33] Later, Adrian's looks did not please his father. When James Russell Lowell described all the Stephen children as beautiful, Leslie said to Julia that he agreed, except for Adrian.[34] Leslie was pleased when Watts, the painter, admired Thoby (aged five), but said he didn't want the boy's portrait painted.[35] He thought Virginia especially lovely as did many others.[36] Vanessa Bell recalled how beautiful Virginia was as a very young child,[37] and Stella Duckworth nicknamed Virginia "Beauty" before her parents decided to name her Adeline Virginia.[38] "Chad," the name Leslie and Julia had planned for their third child obviously was not suitable.

Leslie Stephen praised his children for more than their beauty and intelligence. He seemed pleased with Vanessa's and Thoby's interest in drawing, probably acquired in imitation of himself.[39] He liked it when some of the children began to seek him out, wanting to spend time with him, but often found it necessary to send them away. Thoby was a case in point. On two different occasions, Leslie reported that Thoby, at the age of five, came to his study to talk with him, but that he "felt obliged" to turn the boy out.[40] His study was off bounds to the children much of the time when they were young. He would clear them out when he found them there, for he needed his long hours of solitude. Thoby was rebuffed at the age of four when he brought down his father's walking stick as Leslie was setting out on one of his tramps, and Leslie worried throughout the trip about hurting the boy's feelings.[41]

Leslie was pleased, and a little puzzled as well, with the children's naive conversation. When he was six, Thoby intrigued his father by arguing that there was no such thing as fifteen hundred, for after nine hundred, one left hundreds behind and got to thousands.[42] Vanessa, aged five, asked him if there were other worlds than "this one," whether Trevis (St. Ives) was another such world, and whether other worlds had their own skies.[43] Evidently, the possibility of there being other worlds was considered from time to time by the Stephen children; as a child, Virginia had many idiosyncratic ideas about other worlds and referred to some of them in drafts of several novels.

Eventually Leslie found something of himself in each of the children. In Vanessa, it was a grave, sarcastic expression he observed on her face when she was two years old.[44] Thoby's future promise when he was five reminded him of himself. "Dear little To" grew more and more like him. "To" might never be king, but someday he might be president of the British Republic.[45] The nine-year-old "Ginny" resembled him he felt, but he couldn't specify how. But he was glad to see that she was livelier than he had been at age nine.[46] When Virginia was eleven, he had more precise ideas about how she was like him, or how she should be like him. She should be a writer and should write history since he could guide her in that line.[47] Adrian's immaturity at the age of eleven reminded Leslie of himself; although bright, the boy was much too infantile for his years, in Leslie's opinion. Implying a disagreement with Julia, Leslie added that she might be hurt by the suggestion that her favorite child was like him.[48]

Like many people who take pride in being unusually sensitive about their own feelings, Leslie Stephen was not very sensitive about the feelings of others, as his relationship with Julia made evident. But sometimes he did recognize his children's moods. He reported that Vanessa, aged five, was too much like her mother in one respect—her beautiful eyes were as sad as Julia's—but he supposed that Julia had been more cheerful when she was that age.[49] Again, he wrote that the children were sad little things; they were good and happy, but didn't have much enjoyment.[50] Virginia and Adrian, aged two and one, were observed to be "low in their minds."[51] In 1894 Leslie said that he was lonely without Julia, especially because Vanessa (aged fifteen) and Virginia (aged twelve) seemed depressed.[52]

Of course Leslie reacted to the children inconsistently at best. There was a hint of his doubleness in the way he sometimes admired behavior he thought he should disapprove, as in the instance when Vanessa, aged two, referred to a "naughty" bird as "beastly," a term not polite and circumspect in his view.[53] He also showed his doubleness by praising the children for certain behavior, then later showing disapproval and scolding them for much the same activities. For example, although

149

he apparently was pleased when Vanessa and Thoby became interested in drawing, he soon became irritated with them for drawing too much and with Stella Duckworth for providing them chalks.[54] It was especially annoying of them, he felt, not to draw with strong outlines. Thoby, aged four, was singled out for specific disapprobation because he only made blotches.[55] The problem was largely that they were not drawing as Leslie did, whose forte was line drawing.

When his children were younger, and fewer, Leslie had vowed that he wanted a touch of the devil in them; even the beautiful Vanessa would not be too heavenly, he hoped.[56] Virginia recalled that when he read stories to them and questioned them about their preferences, he was annoyed when they admired the heroes rather than the more interesting villains.[57] Yet he seemed to look on the children with most favor when they were well behaved and respectful.[58] Moreover, Leslie's doting and patience tended to end abruptly when the children showed too much individuality and often when they manifested normally and desirably childish behavior.[59] He liked them to be grave and sedate and objected to their "transports," "uproariousness," and "fits of wriggles." He was always overly sensitive about noise and disorder, feeling that they were somehow designed to make him personally uncomfortable, and there were many times when the children so offended him by being noisy and disorderly that he wrote to report it to Julia.[60]

Although Leslie was pleased when his first son was born and apparently had hoped that his next child, Virginia, would be a boy also, he did not get on well with his sons and quarreled with Julia about them. For a man who was preoccupied with appearing masculine, he had little understanding and appreciation for Thoby, a "jolly rambunctious extrovert," who in temperament and physique resembled Fitzjames, Leslie's brother, stereotyped by Leslie and the family as "masculine."[61] Leslie found Thoby's noise and assertiveness irritating. He became openly angry with him at times,[62] then flatly denied that he was "ever angry" with him when Julia upbraided him for impatience.[63] Then in reverse fashion, he would defend Thoby when Julia found him rebellious and hard to manage, as she did on occasions, according to Leslie.[64] Virginia said too that sometimes Leslie had to be called to control Thoby when he became "truculent with the nurses."[65]

Still more of Leslie's inconsistency showed itself in respect to sexual stereotyping of his children, for he made fewer sexual distinctions than his preoccupation with sex roles might lead one to expect. For example, he took all the children walking with him.[66] Earlier he had taken Laura mountain climbing. He planned to arrange "proper" boots for her because he thought she would be a "first rate walker."[67] Virginia remembered walks with him which he made unpleasant for her by forgetting that she had very short legs and he very long ones, thus walking too fast for her. Sometimes he forgot that she was with him, and usually he treated her to his famed silences.[68] She said also that even before her mother's death, walking with her father became a kind of penance for her, something "Ginny" was called on to do for his sake, not because she enjoyed it.[69] It was fortunate that he did not consider tramping a masculine prerogative only, for walking became and remained one of Virginia Woolf's most pleasant and essential pastimes later in her life.

Some of Leslie's disagreements with Julia were about Thoby's and Adrian's health. He became impatient with her once when she was away and wrote to inquire about the extent of three-year-old Thoby's illness, retorting that Thoby "had not all manner of things wrong" with him. He had only the "spasmodic croup" according to the doctor.[70] A similar incident occurred when Adrian was two; Leslie's impatient reply to Julia's inquiry about Adrian was that the child was precisely the same "as to his inside" as when Julia went away.[71] Leslie complained to Julia that Thoby irritated him by coughing when he had no signs of a cold.[72] After Julia's death a hint of accusation lingered in Leslie's references to Thoby's health problems. Leslie said in the "Mausoleum Book" (p. 65) that Thoby had made his mother anxious when he "allowed" a "playful" schoolmate to puncture his (Thoby's) femoral artery with a knife, and again, when Thoby took to sleepwalking after having influenza.

Adrian was Julia Stephen's favorite child. She kept him with her a great deal and called him her "joy" and sometimes "Joydi." Leslie had very little good to say about Adrian, perhaps because he was jealous of Julia's fondness for him. He urged that Julia turn " 'I' Adrian" adrift (wean him) when the child was one year old.[73]

When the boy was four, Leslie incited Adrian to rebellion, while six-year-old Thoby, and five-year-old Virginia, enjoying the spectacle, abetted their younger brother. As Leslie recounted the experience to Julia, Adrian had become so rampageous that he had to "call him to order." Then he demanded that Adrian come to him, but Adrian refused to obey and was encouraged by the "thoughtless levity and giggling of Thoby and Virginia." Leslie then tried to be more solemn and impressive, and although Adrian became more serious, he did not cry or give in as "absolutely" as Leslie felt he should. Nor would he apologize. Leslie surmised that he "intended to apologize," and gave up, grumbling that the boy might have been more explicit.[74]

Adrian's behavior anticipated events that were to occur later in his life. As a psychoanalyst in England in the 1940s, he rebelled against symbolic "fathers" in what he thought was an important way. He challenged the hierarchy of the British Psychoanalytical Society and believed that he had started the movement that unseated an impressive and well entrenched old guard — even Ernest Jones. Adrian wrote to Vanessa that he was extremely pleased, enjoyed the whole thing immensely, and was rather surprised at himself.[75]

## Virginia

When Virginia was an infant and young child, her father's letters to her mother show that he felt special affection for her and doted on her somewhat more than the other children. He liked to think that his particular fondness for her was reciprocated, and apparently it was. Leslie's special feeling for Virginia was indicated by the fact that his affectionate references to her in his letters to Julia were more frequent than were the references to the other children. He was extremely pleased when Virginia, twenty-one months old and not yet talking very well, sat on his knee, said "kiss," and laid her cheek against his.[76] When she was about twenty-six months old, he wrote proudly to Julia that Virginia had tried to delay his departure to his study by squeezing against him and saying "Don't go, Papa."[77] Also, he grumbled less often about Virginia than the others as all the children grew older. On several occasions when he was apart from the family and lonely, it was Virginia whose face he called up in imagination to comfort himself, Virginia whom he said he wanted most.[78] For example, he wished she could be with him on his trip to America in 1890, saying that her company "would be worth anything."[79]

Leslie expected others to find Virginia very special also. When she was two years old, she visited Grandmother Jackson in Brighton with her mother and the other children. Leslie told Julia to ask Mrs. Jackson to "say honestly" which of the children she liked best. Mothers must not have preferences, he said, but he could see no reason why grandmothers should not have favorites, and he was sure that they did. Was not Mrs.

Jackson delighted with 'Ginia? But of course everyone must love Nessa, he said, and he was sure that "old To" also had plenty of admirers. Adrian apparently was not in the running.[80]

Virginia's birthday was in January, often coinciding with Leslie's visits to the Alps, and his letters home expressed his thoughts about her on her birthday. On her fifth birthday, in 1887, when he was forced to go to the Alps for his health, he sent Virginia a "billion kisses" and the message that he longed to see her again. He said also that he wanted to bring her something special for her birthday, but couldn't think what to get her; would Julia please tell him what he should bring?[81] He said that Virginia was in his thoughts all the time and complained that it was hard to be away for her birthday celebration.[82] When Julia wrote to say that the celebration had included a bonfire, he replied, probably in jest, that he hoped they hadn't burned his manuscripts in it.[83]

On Virginia's ninth birthday, Leslie was again in the Alps. It was in his letter to Julia on January 25, 1891 that he commented about Virginia's resemblance to him and his not being able to explain it. He could imagine "her little face" quite clearly, he said. Then came his jibe at Julia: he was glad that Virginia didn't remind him of "other members of the family," at least not around the nose.[84] Writing from the Alps on Virginia's twelfth birthday, Leslie discussed and rejected the possibility of buying, as a present for her, a marmot he saw for sale. And again he jibed at Julia, this time for forcing the retreat on him. He said that he had decided not to buy the marmot because it would sleep most of the time and would therefore be of no use, and when awake, it would be a nuisance. No doubt Julia would like him to play the marmot and sleep the winter away, he wrote.[85]

In her 1939-1940 memoir, Virginia recalled some times with her father, but she could not recall others she had been told about. She was puzzled that she had no memory of her father throwing her naked into the sea, an incident one of the older residents of St. Ives reported to her. She recalled with pleasure sailing her toy boat on a pond in one of the London parks. Her boat had sailed perfectly to the center of the pond, and then it sank. She stood amazed, she said, watching it sink just as her father strode up to share her astonishment. Weeks later, just as she was passing the pond, a man dredged up her boat and gave it back to her. The whole incident made a great story to tell at home, she said, and was given a lovely ending when her mother made new sails for the boat and her father rigged it, admitting to "absurd pleasure" as he worked.

## Educating the Children

Leslie and Julia undertook to educate the children at home although, as Bell has noted (p. 26), neither seems to have had the temperament for it. Certainly neither had much sensitivity about what children are able to learn at a particular age. Leslie had terrified Thoby when the child was four by "jokingly threatening" to make him read a list of names.[86] Leslie lacked patience enough to teach; Annan said (p. 101) that eventually he had to be advised to stop trying to teach the children because he was making them so miserable. Julia, too, had little patience. Virginia said in her 1908 memoir that Julia was "impatient of stupidity," and that her "natural impetuosity" made her highhanded in disposing of other's difficulties.

Mathematics was Leslie's province in teaching. He liked to give the children "sums" to do and thought they should find arithmetic entertaining as he sometimes did. But the children were not entertained and did poorly with their sums, when they did them at all.[87] Apparently they learned little mathematics and, according to Quentin Bell (pp. 26, 28), Virginia always had to resort to her fingers in counting. Julia assumed responsibility for Latin, French, and history, despite having little more than a minimum knowledge of the subjects, except possibly for French. In any case, she did no better than Leslie. Bell indicated further that the children were educated later, the boys in school, and the girls through private instruction in music, dance, drawing, riding, "graceful deportment," and other subjects. The girls also sought out their own education. Virginia seems to have learned from Thoby that certain things, such as Greek, were very important to know, and subsequently had Latin and Greek lessons from Clara Pater, Walter Pater's sister, and Greek lessons from Janet Case.[88] After Julia's death Leslie tried again, intermittently, to educate the children, and was more successful with Virginia, in literature if not mathematics.[89]

Leslie failed as a mathematics teacher with all the children except Thoby. But Thoby's success may have resulted as much from his ability and interest as from Leslie's teaching. Subsequently, however, Leslie objected to the idea of Thoby's studying mathematics at Cambridge as he himself had done.[90] Instead, he envisioned law, public administration or politics for Thoby, careers traditional in Leslie's family. Thoby eventually chose law and was reading for the bar before his untimely death at the age of twenty-six. Leslie also objected to the suggestion that Thoby become a writer because, he said, writing was a "womanly thing," more Virginia's line,[91] a statement implying that he doubted his own manliness.

Evidently Leslie had long since forgotten the ideal he had expressed to Julia before their marriage that even women should be permitted to choose freely their educational and professional fields of specialization. Also, neither he nor Julia was impressed with the remark she made at that time that if one showed a bent in some direction, no doubt one would be forced into something else. The fact is that Leslie, to say the least, was

overbearing and made many important decisions for his children. His autocratic attitude toward Thoby's future was only
one case in point. He felt inclined to decide what Stella Duckworth should and should not do, saying arbitrarily that she
should not try to write essays,[92] and that she would make an
excellent nurse.[93] If Leslie can be charged with autocracy concerning Virginia's career, at least he had an acceptable aim for
her. Vanessa resented Leslie's highhandedness, whether or not
he tried to decide what her future would be. Before the birth
of her son Julian, she asked in a letter to Virginia, "Do you
think we shall gradually fall into all the old abuses and that I
shan't have any idea what my children are like or what they
want to do?"[94]

A lengthy disagreement between Leslie and Julia developed
when she decided unilaterally that Thoby should go away to
school and persisted in arranging for his departure in the face
of Leslie's adamant and poorly reasoned objections.[95] He protested also, though less strongly, when Adrian's turn came to
go to school.[96] There are no indications in family correspondence that any consideration was given to sending the girls
away to school. Leslie and Julia apparently held conventional
social attitudes about educating daughters, despite their exchange on women's education during their courtship. Thus,
evidently there was a basis to Virginia Woolf's belief that she
had been discriminated against in the matter of education
because she was a girl. However, blaming her father for it was
not entirely fair; he didn't want even his sons to go away to
school. In respect to university education, Virginia's accusation was more just. Leslie assumed that his sons would go to
Cambridge and evidently accepted, without thought, the cultural practice of providing university educations for men and
not for women. He had no objections to public school or university education for his stepsons.

The exact nature of Leslie's objection to sending his sons to school is not clear. Quentin Bell has suggested (p. 26) that educating the children at home may have been a matter of economics. That supposition would explain Leslie's varying attitudes toward the Spehen and the Duckworth boys, since their father's estate would have paid for the Duckworths' education. Also, Leslie's renowned irrationality about money may have been involved. However, there appears to be a more humane basis for Leslie's objection; he seemed to be afraid Thoby might be treated unpleasantly as he himself had been at Eton. At least that is one inference to be drawn from Leslie's writing bitterly and melodramatically from the Alps to Julia, saying that he had seen a calf being taken, on a sled, to slaughter, and that it reminded him of her taking Thoby to school.[97] Leslie hoped that Thoby would be popular.[98] When he learned that Thoby was initially at the bottom of the school in achievement largely because of a deficiency in Greek, he began to worry that the boy would be treated like an outsider.[99]

When Leslie finally accepted Julia's plan, already in operation, that Thoby go away to school, he became more interested and took more responsibility for it. He helped arrange for Thoby's second school, occasionally visited him, and was eager to have news of him.[100] Sometimes he wrote to Thoby, but he grumbled that he wrote despite the fact that Thoby did not deserve to hear from him.[101] Leslie attended a football match to see Thoby play, and sat where his feet would not be on the wet grass, then commented wryly that his prudence was really turning to senility.[102] Although Leslie had been unhappy and an outsider at Eton and had never really approved of the place, when he had accepted that Thoby would be in school, he wanted him to get a scholarship to Eton. But he managed to damage the boy's chances, or thought he did. Thoby did not understand directions that he was supposed to meet his mother in Eton to take the examinations for the scholarship. Instead, he came to Hyde Park Gate in London, and Leslie, by his own description, flew out at him in a rage and upset him so much that he did poorly on the examination.[103]


## Madness in the Family

The case of Laura Stephen, Leslie's child from his marriage to Minny Thackeray, illustrates the lack of understanding and the consequent mismanagement of disturbed and atypical children in late nineteenth-century England — even in a family as "enlightened" as the Stephens. It also suggests some things that might have happened to Virginia had her father been aware of her early idiosyncrasies of thought. Laura was one of the many instances of promise transformed into tragedy that characterized the history of the Stephens. She was also a source of much worry and sadness to Leslie, additional work and concern for Julia, and a disturbing and frightening specter to the other children in the Stephen family. According to Quentin Bell (p. 22), Laura caused some of Virginia's fears about herself. A question remains about how much association the younger children had with her and for what period of time. Hester Ritchie Fuller, the daughter of Anny Thackeray Ritchie, said that Laura occupied the same nursery as the Duckworth children, but suggested that separate arrangements may have been made for her within the household when the four younger Stephen children were born.[104] According to Leslie, after Virginia's birth, special governesses were retained for Laura following the crisis with her that year.[105]

As a child Virginia had some contact with Laura, although no one is sure how much. Virginia said, ". . . [B]esides the three Duckworths and the four Stephens there was also Thackeray's grand-daughter, a vacant-eyed girl whose idiocy was becoming daily more obvious, who could hardly read, who would throw the scissors into the fire, who was tongue-tied and stammered and yet had to appear at table with the rest of us."[106] Laura was part of the household at least until 1887, when she was seventeen and Virginia was five. Possibly she remained in the household much of the time until 1891, when she was twenty-one and Virginia was nine. Quentin Bell said (p. 35) that Laura was with the family until 1891, while Leslie's letters to Julia suggest that Laura was sent away in 1887.[107] Apparently temporary arrangements were made whereby Laura stayed "in the country"[108] for periods of time before she was placed permanently in a home in about 1891. She was brought for visits with the family during vacation time at St. Ives, but even that had to be terminated by 1893.[109]

Laura was, evidently, mentally deranged, although she has also been called mentally retarded. One reason for uncertainty is that in the late nineteenth century little theory and even less practical knowledge existed as a basis for diagnosis. In the area of mental deficiency, Seguin had done precursory work,[110] but more definitive work was still decades in the future.[111] A similar situation existed in regard to mental derangement. Emil Kraepilin's first work on classification was published several years after Laura's problems forced themselves upon the consciousness of the family.[112] Differentiating various kinds of mental and emotional problems remains a difficult procedure, even for professionals.[113] Thus, although the work in differential diagnosis in the two problem areas was under way, there was no reason for Leslie Stephen to have been aware of early developments in what was still an obscure science. Nor did the Stephen family physicians apparently have access to the knowledge that was available.

It is not surprising, therefore, that Leslie Stephen referred to his oldest daughter in various ways, sometimes implying deficiency, sometimes derangement, and usually in uncomplimentary terms. He said that she was "backward" or "witless,"[114] that possibly she was not an "idiot," but that she had little chance of being like other children.[115] In his use, the term "idiot" meant much the same as "defective" and did not refer to low-grade deficiency. He referred to her most frequently as "perverse," and here too his terminology was uncomplimentary and imprecise. Again, he said that she was obstinate and mulish;[116] that her behavior was meant to torture him;[117] that she lacked any moral sense;[118] and that she was "vain" but had a good character.[119] He was somewhat encouraged, he said, when she became a little ashamed of herself and was "dimly conscious" of "something bad" in herself.[120] Leslie was wrong in his specifics and was again unfortunate in his choice of language when he said that Laura's problem was that she had a "small mind" and had "quenched" it by her "perversity."[121] He erred most in believing her psychosis to be a kind of willful perversity.

It is almost certain that Laura from birth was not seriously deficient in intellectual ability, and quite certain that whatever ability she did have was greatly hampered by her psychotic condition. The principal contraindication to mental deficiency was Laura's verbal fluidity. She was an exceptionally verbal child, according to Leslie. When she was seven, he remarked that her tongue was "as fast as a pack of hounds"[122] and that she talked "sixteen to a dozen."[123] Her talking and her demands that Leslie talk with her often irritated him and put him into a "great fuss and whirl."[124] But Leslie sometimes found Laura's persistent talking both amusing and irritating as the following incident indicates. John Ruskin wanted to be friends with Leslie Stephen but, Leslie disliked him and dreaded his calls. He felt inferior to Ruskin and objected when Ruskin "pawed him all over after his manner." Ruskin also had the irritating habit of always responding to Leslie's remarks with the same comment, "You don't know how much that interests me." On one particular occasion, Laura joined freely in their conversation, annoying Leslie, but also amusing him and, perhaps, convincing him that she had some intelligence, by laughing at Ruskin. Leslie said she laughed as heartily as if she had been studying some of Ruskin's essays.[125]

Laura was quite verbal, but one doesn't know the level of her ability to use language. Nor does one know the level of her reading ability, although Leslie said that when she was seven she was reading well.[126] He mentioned that at age eleven she read *Aladdin*,[127] at age fourteen *Robinson Crusoe*,[128] and at age sixteen she read *Alice in Wonderland* aloud to Thoby.[129] Leslie said he was teaching her German when she was seven and spoke optimistically of taking her to Germany so that she might improve her use of the language.[130]

It seems probable from Leslie's description of Laura that what he called her "perversity" was childhood schizophrenia. He said in the "Mausoleum Book" (p. 71) that he was first alarmed by her inarticulate ways of thinking and her "grotesque waywardness." He thought association with Anny Thackeray encouraged the latter. Leslie complained when Laura was seven years old that she made irrelevant remarks with the most provoking good temper, and would only sing nonchalantly when he tried to get and hold her attention.[131] She developed a number of strange mannerisms involving her mouth and throat, including straining and boggling over words[132] and a "lockjaw" way of talking[133] which contrasted with her verbal fluidity as a very young child. Sometimes she made what Leslie called a "spasmodic uttering," "queer squeaking" or "semi-stammering," and he said that he couldn't understand why she didn't "stammer altogether."[134] When she was about seven, she would sometimes spit meat out of her mouth at mealtimes,[135] and at age fourteen she complained of choking through meals.[136] She was given at times to wild howling and shrieking[137] and other manifestations of anger, which Leslie called fits of fiendish temper,[138] or of irritation,[139] or of passion.[140] Sometimes, too, she had what he called "superficial tantarums." But there were also times when he said that Laura "chose" to be good and virtuous, and to respond well to efforts to teach her.[141] All in all she was extremely disturbing and extremely pathetic.

The origin of Laura's difficulties also remains a question. It has been suggested that she inherited her grandmother Thackeray's madness, and it is well documented that madness was there, whether or not a predisposition to it was passed on to Laura. Isabella Shawe Thackeray had been charming, though unstable and "flighty," and for a long time her husband and friends seemed to think or tried to maintain that she only had some rather endearing though irritating, eccentricities.[142] Anny, her older daughter, seems to have resembled her although only moderately and to a benign degree. Possibly Minny, Laura's mother, had some of Mrs. Thackeray's traits also. Annan quoted (p. 62) Thackeray as saying of Minny that at twenty-one she was " 'absurdly young for her age for she still likes playing with children and kittens and hates reading and is very shy. . . .' "

A Mrs. Severn, a friend of John Ruskin, noted Mrs. Thackeray's "absent-mindedness" in one of her letters to an acquaintance. Mrs. Severn reminisced about the old days: "O what funny things happened then from her delightful absentmindedness. Once on a Saturday after the butcher had been [,] I called and found dear 'Mrs. Thackeray' much perplexed at having asked a good many people to lunch and the landlady with nothing extra got in, and no means of getting more! and the little diningroom not capable of holding more than 6 and that with the seat close to a wall — so I suggested that we, Ruskin and I, should send on the Brantwood lunch, and come and eat it there with her guests, knowing that she [Mrs. Thackeray] particularly wished us to be there, so we and our cold pigeon pie and roast leg of lamb arrived . . ." and a pleasant though impromptu picnic was held on the lawn.[143]

Presently Isabella Thackeray's eccentricities became more serious. After the birth of Minny, Mrs. Thackeray developed a condition that her granddaughter, Hester Ritchie Fuller, believed would have been diagnosed as schizophrenia at a later time. Thackeray tried to take his wife back to her native Ireland, where he hoped she would regain her health, and while crossing the channel, Isabella jumped overboard in an unsuccessful effort to drown herself. Thackeray described the incident: "... [T]he poor thing flung herself into the water and was twenty minutes in the sea before the ship's boat ever *saw* her. She was found floating on her back, paddling with her hands, and had never sunk at all." Mrs. Thackeray did not regain her health and spent the rest of her life apart from Thackeray and their two daughters, "not too unhappily," it is said.[144]

Although it cannot be discounted that Laura inherited a potential for schizophrenia from her grandmother, and certain undesirable potentials from her parents as well, there were more probable reasons for difficulty in her case, just as there were in Virginia's. For example, her fits of temper sound quite like distorted and grotesque imitations of Leslie's tantrums. Also, her difficulties must have been increased by the trauma of losing her mother, a factor that Leslie seems not to have considered. Her close association with Leslie and Anny Thackeray during the next two years when they both grieved so exaggeratedly for Minny may have been an additional problem.

The family's reluctance to believe Laura had a problem created serious hazards. It is unclear when her condition was first acknowledged, although it had become obvious by 1875, when she was five. Fuller said that after many years of denying that anything was wrong with her, it finally became evident that the child was mentally deficient and that she would never take her place in life with other people.[145] Leslie Stephen said in the "Mausoleum Book" (p. 33) that he remembered words of Minny's "too sacred to repeat" that indicated she was completely unaware that anything more serious than "slowness" was wrong with Laura. He said further that both he and Julia had maintained hopes that the child would be all right until after their marriage. However, Leslie may well have been trying to persuade the Duckworth children that since he didn't really know anything was seriously wrong with Laura, he was relatively innocent in putting the burden of Laura upon Julia. Contemporary evidence shows that he was well aware of the problems before marrying Julia, that he wrote often to her about them, and was therefore confused or dissembling in the "Mausoleum Book." Quentin Bell concluded (p. 12) that during Leslie's bereavement following Minny's death, he became more aware that the child was not only slow, that she may have "inherited" her grandmother's madness, and that Laura's mother had known of her "backwardness."

Much harm was done to Laura because her father made prodigious efforts to teach her and to "make an intelligence" for her, both before and after he admitted that she had serious problems. His attempts to teach her were definitely a bad bit of work in which he took pride; like his mother, he seemed to think that there was intrinsic merit in pressuring children intellectually, regardless of the results. Later Leslie was joined by Julia and sometimes by Stella Duckworth in teaching Laura, much of the time drilling her in reading.

There is no reason to doubt that Leslie would have tried to correct the child's incoherent ways of thinking, as he prided himself on doing for Anny Thackeray when she was a member of his household. Leslie could not keep his temper with Laura although he acknowledged that she had taught him the mischief of becoming angry with her.[146] He also employed his practice of taking a "severe" attitude with her, telling her "decidedly not to be nonsensical."[147] Possibly by way of policy, but also out of desperation, a considerable amount of punishment was used with Laura, and her father tried to devise "better" ways to punish her. He told Julia that putting Laura to bed as punishment would not work; Laura would only grow accustomed to it, and besides, an effective punishment was one that could be repeated or increased in a given instance of bad behavior. Putting Laura to bed would fit neither of these particulars. The "great thing," he speculated, would be to find a way to punish Laura without exciting her fits of whining and without her "allowing" herself to work up a fury.[148]

The only person to have any success with Laura was Caroline Emilia, Leslie's sister, who tried to teach and control her for several weeks while she stayed in Leslie's household, when Laura was seven. Caroline Emilia was firm, but she was also gentle and patient. Thus she was as different from Leslie in her approach, as she was in temperament.[149]

Starting before their marriage, Leslie gradually let Julia take more and more of the responsibility for Laura, while he took less and less, except in teaching her. At times Julia would take Laura with her on trips away from home and was sincerely and conscientiously concerned for her welfare. But Julia never had much success with Laura, partly because she had little patience, and partly because Laura respected male more than female authority, according to Leslie.[150] He was afraid that if Julia lost control of Laura, he would have more difficulty making the child obey him.[151]

Periodically Leslie and Julia talked of sending Laura to a "home," but it was one of the many unpleasant topics that Leslie could hardly endure. He didn't see how Laura could get along in a school with normal girls — in his words, with girls "not of her own kind" — yet he didn't think that being with "idiots" would be good for her.[152] He remarked that teaching her was so difficult and frustrating, that even the best they might achieve would not be sufficient. Laura would have to live apart, and he would have to arrange for her living some place.[153] George Duckworth may have helped to bring the matter to the point of decision. He remonstrated with Leslie, saying that Julia should not have such a task as the care of Laura.[154]

When Laura was finally placed in a home, she remained institutionalized for the rest of her life except for visits to the family in the early years. It was Julia who usually visited Laura after she was sent away.[155] Laura had other direct and indirect contact with the family by mail. As girls, Virginia and Vanessa corresponded with her, although according to Quentin Bell (p. 35), they pretended that Laura was a kind of joke. Bell intimated that Virginia may have been personally upset about having a mad sister, suggesting that the pretense that Laura was a joke reflected her disturbance. Bell's idea is supported by the fact that one of Virginia's most depressing childhood memories was about the time an "idiot boy" sprang out of the bushes at her.[156]

Whatever their attitude toward Laura, after Leslie Stephen's death, Virginia, her sister, and her brothers assumed some of the financial responsibility for her. The four Stephen children mortgaged 22 Hyde Park Gate in 1906 and raised £489 to provide for her expenses. These funds had increased to £1,883 by 1919.[157] However, there is little to indicate that Virginia had any sympathy for Laura or any other atypical person. In 1915 she found the sight of a group of "idiots" so horrifying that she said they should all be put to death.[158] The idea that the mad were dispensable was expressed also by Leonard Woolf in reference to Laura herself. In 1934, when George Duckworth died, Virginia wrote to Vanessa that Leonard had said that Laura was the one they could have spared.[159]

Apparently Leslie took little responsibility for visiting Laura as long as Julia lived. He commented in 1893 that Laura was less a part of his life than she had been, but that he thought they had done the best they could for her.[160] After Julia's death, Stella Duckworth visited Laura at least once. On March 30, 1896, she noted in her diary that she had been to see Laura, but that Laura "took no notice." She commented that Laura's "talk was less noisy." The next year, 1897, Leslie had Laura transferred to a new home because of bad reports about the first place he had chosen. He and other members of the family visited her in her new location, and he said that she was unable to recognize any of them clearly and that he was "terribly pained" to see her as she was.[161]

The Stephen children eventually lost touch with Laura, although for some time they remained in contact with the persons managing Laura's financial affairs. Katharine Stephen, a cousin, visited Laura in 1909 and told Vanessa, who relayed the information to Virginia, that Laura was "much the same." But she had given up "trying to knit," a backward step, Vanessa said.[162] In 1921, despite the increase in the fund set aside for Laura by the Stephen children, the question arose whether Laura's income would be sufficient to meet the costs of her upkeep, and, if not, whether the family would have to make up the deficit. Virginia was contacted about the matter; she saw Adrian and wrote Vanessa about it, but apparently the subsidization never became necessary.[163]

When Laura died in 1945 at the age of 75, the Stephen family had been out of touch with her for so long that the authorities at the home where she had been living were unaware that she had any relatives. It was months after her death before Adrian was notified, evidently by the trustees of her endowment fund. Adrian and Vanessa divided the remainder of her estate, amounting to more than seven thousand pounds after fees and death duties, between themselves. Leonard Woolf, as Virginia's heir, raised some questions about the distribution of the estate, but apparently he did not receive any of it.[164] Ironically, with the exception of Vanessa, all of Laura's half brothers and sisters died at younger ages than she. Only two of them remained alive when she died, and she was at least as well off financially as they were at the time.

# 7

## The Duckworth Children:
## Indiscriminate Affections?

George, Stella, and Gerald Duckworth, Julia Stephen's children from her first marriage, comprised a relatively separate enclave within the family, as did the Stephen children. They were significantly older than Leslie and Julia's four children; in 1882, when Virginia was born, George was fourteen, Stella was thirteen, and Gerald was twelve. At 22 Hyde Park Gate, their bedrooms were on the second floor, just above what Virginia called her mother's bedroom floor, while the Stephen children were in the nurseries on the third floor.[1] By the time Virginia was old enough to have any conception of her Duckworth half siblings, they were much more like adults than other children to her. By that time also George and Gerald were away at school, and Stella was often acting as Julia's substitute in caring for the Stephen children.

Several of Leslie Stephen's remarks suggest that he wanted the Duckworth children to be separate from his family. During his courtship of Julia, he said that he was ill at east talking with them and trying to talk with Julia about them, but that he was not jealous of them as he usually was of children.[2] After he married Julia, tension developed because the Duckworths thought he had come between them and their mother, or so he recalled after Julia died. He admitted in the "Mausoleum Book" (p. 50) that he'd always felt "sensible" of something lacking in his relationship with the Duckworths, but now, he insisted, he loved them like a father. He said in the same reference that he had not tried to be a father to them and had only "advised" them through their mother. But Leslie was dissembling; Stella at least was an exception to his professed reluctance to influence the three Duckworth children as a father might. He made a great effort to influence Stella as she was growing up, though frequently, if not always, through Julia as he claimed. After Julia died, he came to think of Stella as peculiarly his own, and although he persisted in calling himself her father, his feelings about her became other than paternal.

The Duckworth children seemed to reciprocate Leslie's reluctance to have a close relationship, and all three resented his treatment of their mother. Leslie said in the "Mausoleum Book" that they misunderstood him. Much of the "Mausoleum Book" seems to be a defense against what he feared might be the Duckworths' estimation of him and his treatment of their mother. They had many reasons to be concerned about his treatment of Julia and many reasons to resent him. At one time or another each of the Duckworths expressed resentment directly to Leslie. Gerald, at the age of seven, "assaulted" Leslie for "playfully" pulling Julia down a "small slope."[3] George remonstrated with him about saddling Julia with the difficult task of caring for Laura.[4] Stella confronted him several times about Julia's health in the months when she was dying, trying unsuccessfully to get him to be more protective toward her—chiefly by taking less advantage of her himself.[5]

In part because of their ill-defined relationships with the rest of the family, each of the Duckworths made serious and lasting impressions on Virginia Woolf. If Virginia's claims and Quentin Bell's account are accurate, that was especially true of George, whose affection for and behavior toward Virginia and Vanessa were less than discriminating. Virginia alleged one incident of misconduct by Gerald also.

Generally, Stella influenced Virginia in more positive ways

than George and Gerald did, but Virginia had serious conflicts about Stella too. Without intending it, Stella added to Virginia's confusions by arousing Leslie's rather indiscriminate affections after Julia died. However, Leslie seems to have drawn a clearer line in his behavior, if not in his affections, than George Duckworth was reputedly able to do.

Stella Duckworth's tragic end in the face of great promise also influenced Virginia Woolf. But Virginia's emotional crises after the death of each of her parents indicate that their deaths were the most traumatic for her. Thoby's and Stella's deaths most cogently dramatized the treachery of life. In *To the Lighthouse* (pp. 198-199) Virginia used Stella as a symbol of life's betrayal when she characterized her as Prue Ramsay, a young woman who marries one spring and dies in childbirth the next. Her death was also extremely traumatic to Virginia because of the place Stella assumed in the Stephen family during the two painful years after her mother's death, the years of Virginia's first madness. More than any one else, Stella was credited with maintaining some degree of order in the Stephen household. Virginia said in her 1939-1940 memoir that Stella kept the family running, though rather like a dilapidated, creaky wagon filled with young things. She became, in effect, a surrogate mother to Virginia, and her death renewed much of the confusion and pain that began for Virginia when her mother died.[6]


Angel in the House

Stella's entire life seemed incomprehensible to Virginia. More than forty years after Stella died, and less than two years before her own suicide, Virginia was still trying to figure out the meaning of Stella's life history. One of the many things that distressed her was the sadness that marked Stella's life from the outset and that, in Virginia's opinion, was never quite dispelled even when Stella appeared gay and happy. Stella was born in 1869 and was about one year old when her father died. Therefore, as Virginia said, Stella came to her first realization fo selfhood and of life during Julia's saddest years, the time when a "crape-veiled" Julia began to go about doing good.[7] Stella's identification with her mother began early and, as we have noted, when she was only eight, she wore the same tragic mien as Julia.

Stella was very much like her mother in other ways than being sad, and seemed intent upon being as much like her as possible. She was as beautiful as Julia and like Julia and others in the Pattle family, she had her turn posing for an artist. Holman Hunt had her sit for his painting, the Lady of Shalott, but did not use the study of her in the final painting. Her personality was evidently softer and more tranquil than Julia's, for she was said to be generally good-humored, docile, and dependent. If she was as sad as Virginia thought, still Stella's sadness had neither the depth nor the external manifestations of her mother's melancholia. Stella resembled her mother most by being unselfish, dutiful, and responsible, characteristics that emerged from her identification with Julia.[8]

All accounts of Stella indicate that she adored her mother and felt very close to her.[9] However, Julia did not reciprocate with equal warmth. Quentin Bell said (pp. 36, 41) that Julia loved both George and Gerald more than she loved Stella, who, if emotions were reasonable and just, deserved her mother's affection more than her brothers did. Leslie Stephen said that George was more important to Julia than her other children until the Stephen children came along and she formed an attachment to Adrian, her youngest. Leslie said that among the Duckworth children, George seemed peculiarlly Julia's property, but insisted that Julia's "more open and emphatic expressions" of love for George didn't really mean that she loved Stella and Gerald less.[10]

Julia admitted to being demanding, harsh, and critical with

Stella. When Leslie chided her about it before they were married, she defended her treatment of Stella by claiming she saw Stella as a part of herself. She only expected of Stella what she expected of herself; she scolded and criticized Stella as she might scold or criticize herself.[11] It was, of course, a questionable defense and an admission of blindness to Stella's individuality and right to a separate existence. Evidently Leslie's chiding and Julia's defense did not lead to any fundamental change, for Julia continued to expect Stella to act as she herself did and to make the same kind of sacrifice, even for Leslie, that she herself was willing to make.

Virginia Woolf remembered that Julia required Stella to make unreasonable sacrifices, saying that her mother could be quite ruthless when she felt some good could be accomplished. As Stella grew older, however, Virginia thought that Julia's severity with her decreased, and that she treated her with more affection.[12] Leslie observed the same thing, and claimed credit for softening Julia's behavior toward Stella, although there is little evidence to support his conjectures. He thought he had helped by chiding Julia, but had helped more by marrying her. Her emotions seemed to "thaw" after she married him, and she was warmer toward her children, Leslie said.[13] The closeness between Julia and Stella continued although, according to Virginia,[14] Julia tried at times to make Stella more independent, only to bring her to tears. There is nothing to indicate that she ever succeeded in making Stella want to be more independent or that she tried very persistently. Virginia did not model herself after her mother as Stella did, but may have envied Stella's special place with her mother, for Stella had the kind of intimacy with Julia that Virginia always wanted but never achieved. She also attributed to Stella a conception of Julia that was, no doubt, more her own than Stella's—one of Julia with "divine power and intelligence." However, their closeness also seemed to Virginia to be morbid, and she disdained

Stella's "doglike devotion," her passive, "suffering affection," and her unquestioning dependence upon their mother.[15] Virginia said that any thought of Julia's would pass automatically and uncritically through Stella's mind[16]—hardly a state of affairs that Virginia would have tolerated for herself, as much as she loved her mother. She used the analogy of the sun and moon to characterize Stella's early relationship with Julia, implying that Stella got her light from Julia and was only a pale reflection. She summarized the relationship, saying that Stella derived her fundamental structure and integration from her persistent concern for Julia and a desire to be little more than her mother's handmaiden.[17]

Allegedly Stella Duckworth was not unusually intelligent.[18] Clearly, she possessed little of the impetus to think for herself that Virginia had all her life. However, Stella was made to feel that she was less bright than was actually the case. Both Leslie and Julia were responsible. Leslie deprecated Stella for her childish logic and treated her intellectual efforts scornfully.[19] For example, when she wrote an essay, he announced that she should not try to write articles; that was Virginia's line, not Stella's.[20] As Virginia observed, Julia's part, in teaching Stella to feel unintelligent, was to treat Stella like a slower, less efficient part of herself.

Stella seems to have accepted her family's image of her with very little conflict, even her alleged lack of intelligence. She also accepted her ascribed role as an extension of her mother. Quentin Bell said (p. 42) that after her mother's death, Stella was "patient, reliable, uncomplaining, bowing to the inevitable yoke of her sex." Her early history shows that she had long years of practice and training for such compliance. Starting in childhood, she gradually took on more and more of her mother's duties within the Stephen household, becoming quite the "angel in the house," to borrow a Coventry Patmore phrase Virginia Woolf used to describe a feminine role she herself resisted.[21] By being so docile and responsible, Stella made it possible for Julia to take on still more of her charitable work without feeling that she was neglecting her primary family. When still a child, she was given the assignment of accompanying grandmother Jackson on trips to and from the Stephen household, acting in Julia's place. By the time she was fifteen, in 1884, she was standing in for her mother when Julia was away, watching out for Leslie and the younger children, and working with Laura.[22]

Leslie as well as Julia expected Stella to substitute for her mother. But he criticized her for being less capable than Julia and for much else. When she was fifteen, Leslie wrote to Julia in the following vein. Stella was too lenient with the children; Stella did not do the sums he assigned but spent her time with her riding and singing instead;[23] Stella could not converse with him;[24] Stella hadn't provided him with writing paper.[25] He "was very hard up" at home while Stella acted as Julia's lieutenant.[26]

The next year, when Stella was sixteen, Leslie seemed to find much less to criticize, reporting to Julia that Stella had given him his dinner and had provided paper for him like a firstrate housekeeper. He described her as calm, conscientious, judicious, quite like Julia, and concluded that she would make an excellent nurse.[27] But he complained that Stella snubbed him when he was unusually silly, without specifying what comprised the silliness.[28] Over the next few years, he continued to report to Julia his approval of Stella's dutifulness, but also objected to some things. When Stella was eighteen, he said that she was good to him, but was a little too inclined to laugh.[29] Possibly he referred to some of the family jokes about himself. He was becoming deaf by that time, and the children delighted in making fun of him in his presence, knowing that he couldn't hear what they said.[30]

Leslie thought that it was Stella's duty to please both him

and her mother, and it would have pleased him if she had been more affectionate. For example, in 1890 when Stella was twenty-one, Leslie sent a message to her from the United States. He asked Julia to tell Stella that she didn't show her feelings openly enough, but that she was a dear daughter anyway, and that he would be happier than he could say when he saw Stella and the rest of the family again.[31] Leslie used his notions of duty to get Stella to eat when she was sick and reluctant to take food. He said that eating wouldn't do any good, but that it was her duty to please her mother by eating anyway.[32]

As a result of her imitating her mother, and possibly because of Leslie's belief that she would make a good nurse, Stella became dutiful, sometimes overdutiful, about Leslie's health. When she saw him looking ill, she took it upon herself to call a doctor without telling him that she was doing so.[33] In Julia's absence, Stella tried to dose Leslie with castor oil, but he refused it and reported the incident to Julia.[34] In 1893, Stella and Gerald Duckworth accompanied Leslie on a trip to the Continent and to Switzerland, during which Stella displeased him with her excessive attention to his health. She tried to "force" a rhubarb pill on him, but he resisted the medication, saying that he feared "unpleasant consequences" when there were so few "comfort opportunities" during their train travel.[35]

## Another Period of Mourning

As Quentin Bell has said (pp. 39, 41-43), when Julia's health began to decline seriously, it was Stella who was most concerned, trying even harder to relieve her mother of some of her work. She attempted, without success, to arouse in Leslie more concern for Julia's health. She watched anxiously as Julia became more debilitated, yet when Julia appeared to rally, Stella was denied even the opportunity to try to help. She was sent to the Continent on vacation with George and Gerald, returning only about a week before her mother died, when she guessed that she was not being informed about her mother's condition. Stella felt she had failed to protect her mother and that added to her distress when Julia died. However, Stella was forced to take on many of her mother's roles which may have eased her grief at least a little. At a minimum, she was able to keep busy, in the tradition of her mother who had used work to keep her mind off her troubles.

Leslie Stephen's reactions to Julia's death were very different from Stella's, for he was a less mature person than she. His neurotic, twisted ways of expressing love for Julia, had always caused him to act desperate when he was without her, and, of course, when she died he did that as never before. Furthermore, he had to contend with more profound guilt than Stella did. No doubt Stella keenly felt her failure to save her mother. But she had little reason for guilt such as Leslie experienced because of his having overburdened Julia and having failed to recognize that her health was in serious jeopardy. He also had to contend with the feeling that the children, especially the Duckworth children, blamed him for not making Julia happy and for helping to "wear her" to death. In addition to his burden of guilt, he was frightened about how he would survive emotionally without Julia. He was suddenly deprived of all the attention and support she had given him, without which he had always pleaded helplessness and confusion. Now, without Julia or without some substitute, he was in danger of serious emotional disorder. In his disturbed condition, he behaved typically by turning his terrible greed for sympathy and support upon the most likely woman in sight, and that was, of course, the twenty-six-year-old Stella Duckworth. Quentin Bell (p. 41) summed up the matter with great understanding. "Leslie now resembled one who, through long years of infirmity, had taught his body to move with the aid of a crutch and who then, suddenly, finds his support has gone. In such an emergency stoicism, reserve, philosophy are all beside the point; you fall and, falling, clutch at whatever may save you from disaster. Leslie, snatching at the nearest support, found Stella."

According to Virginia Woolf's 1908 memoir, Stella had at best only "respect" and "formal affection" for her stepfather. She also had many reasons to dislike him. Nevertheless, Virginia said, Stella responded automatically, trying in her typically dutiful fashion to stand in for her mother and assume responsibility for Leslie. There ensued a virtual reenactment, a reprise on a minor scale, of the emotional dialogue that had characterized Leslie's relationship with Julia, although without the conjugal involvement. Leslie played the dependent child to his utmost, an easy role, since now more than ever he felt like one. Stella reciprocated by playing the overly responsible person who falls prey to others' needs to be dependent. She played her part to the best of her ability but, as Virginia noted, was conscious always of not having the best to give Leslie, that is, of not really being Julia.

As painful as the time was for Stella, she was better able to withstand Leslie's mourning than the Stephen children were. It was Virginia's opinion that Stella found resources within herself she hadn't known were there.[36] The Stephen children, especially Virginia and Adrian, were greatly distressed by the loss of their mother, and the trauma was made far worse by their father's conduct. As Quentin Bell said (p. 42) Leslie presented the children with such a ". . . state of despairing, oppressive, guilt-ridden gloom that their own sharp, uncomplicated unhappiness seemed by contrast a relief." Virginia's references, in both her 1908 and 1939-1940 memoirs, to her own reactions at the time concur with Quentin Bell's estimation that it was her father's mourning as much as her mother's death, as terrible as the death was, that destroyed her. Seeing her father completely undone, hearing him talk time and again about how his life was now ruined and how he wanted to die, having him importune for sympathy she could not give him — all these further reinforced Virginia's belief that she and her world could not possibly go on without her mother. Also, as Virginia showed in *To the Lighthouse,* she was convinced that a principal consequence of her mother's absence, now permanent, was to leave the children unprotected against the more destructive forces of Leslie's personality.

Descriptions of Leslie's mourning more than support Virginia Woolf's and Quentin Bell's belief that it was Leslie's way of grieving as much as Julia's death that disturbed the children. Leslie Stephen was so caught up in his own agony — not to be doubted, despite his exploitation of it — that he had only a dim understanding of what others in the family, especially Stella, Virginia, and Adrian, were experiencing. He had showed a similar lack of understanding years earlier when he had had no apparent awareness of the effect upon Laura of her mother's death. Or, if aware of others' grief during his second bereavement, he failed to mention it in the "Mausoleum Book" where he only discussed his own sorrows. On Stella Duckworth's wedding day in 1897, two years after Julia's death, he did observe that something was amiss with Adrian and that Virginia was "nervous" and "out of sorts." But he thought they were only growing too fast and his note in the "Mausoleum Book" on that day contained the statement that the "young ones were satisfactory."[37] That is not to say that Leslie made no effort at all to help the children. By summoning his strength, he managed once in a while to appear the delightful father the children had sometimes known him to be in previous years. It was then that Virginia felt a special love for her father. She said that he was beautiful, simple, eager as a child, and alive to affection. At such times, she was encouraged to hope that their old life would go on in a new way.

But they could trust his good moods less than ever before and the moments of promise would pass.[38]

Leslie again devoted some of his time to trying to teach the children, but as usual his teaching was unsatisfactory.[39] His greatest effort was to try to eulogize Julia and preserve the children's memory of her. Thus he wrote the document that became known as the "Mausoleum Book." It is not known whether the children read the "Mausoleum Book" during the initial period of mourning, but when they did read it, it confused rather than preserved their memories of Julia, for Leslie made her into more of a legend than she already was. Virginia said in her 1908 memoir that her father replaced her mother with an unlovable phantom, that Julia was made unreal to them, and worse, they were made unreal to themselves by being forced to act insincerely. Leslie further confused his children's feelings about himself by his elaborate defensiveness in the "Mausoleum Book." He spoke of her and acted, after her death, in ways inconsistent with his behavior toward her while she lived. He also added to his children's confusions about their half siblings since it was clear that the "Mausoleum Book" was written for the Duckworths more than for the Stephen children.

Leslie's efforts to help the children were exceptions to his conduct, as descriptions of his mourning make evident. For example, Bell has said (p. 40) that often at mealtimes during the summer after Julia died, Leslie would groan audibly and fight back his tears, then he would weep and moan that he wanted to die. The children would sit embarrassed and miserable, unable to say or do anything to help, no doubt frightened and revolted by the spectacle. Often Leslie made no effort at all to control his grief but paraded it, histrionically, to dramatize how terrible his condition was without Julia and thus how great his love for her must have been. By demeanor as well as words, he made extravagant emotional demands upon his chil-

dren. Virginia Woolf's book, *To the Lighthouse* (p. 227), reveals that Leslie's demands, even unspoken, could spread an
almost palpable cloud over everyone within range. He demanded that everyone pity him, and demanded reassurance
and absolution from his guilt.[40] He demanded also that the
children show love for their mother, but for him most of all, by
mourning as he mourned and by feeling as much pain as he
felt. According to Virginia, he thought that only he felt "properly" for Julia.[41]

Leslie established his position as chief mourner by sitting in
a darkened, cavelike room, like "the queen in Shakespeare" as
Virginia phrased it.[42] He gathered the children around him,
while he acted out his grief melodramatically. He was assisted
in his histrionics by a Greek chorus of callers, mostly female,
who would weep with him and advise Stella how to run the
household and, no doubt, how to comfort and care for Leslie.[43] Letters of condolence seemed to affirm his deep sorrow,
such as one from Henry James, expressing sympathy and advising Leslie to take comfort in the memory of his ideal marriage,
—his "perfect union."[44] But callers, letters, and weeping children were not enough. Leslie Stephen needed to be petted and
soothed. For tactile comfort, according to Virginia's 1939-1940
memoir, he looked to Stella. He would stride back and forth,
gesticulating and wailing, untruthfully, that he had never told
Julia that he loved her; Stella would clasp him and remonstrate
with him.

The period of mourning, called by Virginia Woolf a time of
Oriental gloom,[45] turned the children's grief into a hideous
parody of what they would normally have felt after their
mother's death. "They were called upon to feel, not simply
their natural grief, but a false, a melodramatic, an impossibly
histrionic emotion that they could not encompass," Quentin
Bell wrote (pp. 40-41). At the same time, the enforced mourning made it impossible for the children, with the apparent

exception of Stella, to sympathize with Leslie, even though they wanted to do so, for their embarrassment and resentment soon cancelled their sympathy.

The children reacted in various ways. Stella tried harder to be the angel in the house and to do what her mother would have done. Virginia could do little more than feel, in all aspects of her being, the horror, confusion and chaos. She was painfully aware of her own impotence to extend to her father the sympathy and love he needed and demanded. Thoby announced that the kind of mourning expected by Leslie was wrong, and that they were "silly" to be carrying on so. Virginia was shocked by Thoby's statement, but later she decided he had been right.[46] The children, as a group, tried to turn the whole situation into a joke.

## Daughter or Mother?

Stella Duckworth was the principal object and victim of Leslie's excessive demands for sympathy, absolution, and comfort and the principal donor of them. The relationship that developed between the stepfather and stepdaughter seems strange, from the vantage point of the late twentieth century. It also seems unjust. But during the late Victorian era, few among the Stephen relatives and friends thought it strange or unjust, and few thought Stella a victim at all. Virginia Woolf and John Waller Hills — Stella's suitor, fiancé and, for the last months of her life, her husband — were exceptions. To the extent that she thought about it at all, Stella must have thought that she was fulfilling a duty and doing no more than was expected of a good daughter.[47] Leslie, in turn, thought he expected from Stella no more than his rights, and what he assumed Julia would have asked of Stella.[48] And what he expected, most of all, was Stella's maternal attentions. She gave them, seeing

183

nothing strange in the idea that the way to be a good daughter was by mothering him. Nor did either see anything extraordinary in his adopting filial attitudes toward a stepdaughter less than half his age. Indeed, Leslie could not quite resist boasting a little that Stella had mothered him. Maitland (p. 431) quoted him as saying, after Stella's death, that she had been " 'as unselfish as a human being could ever be; and during the last two years has been devoted to me and watched over me, I might almost say, like a mother.' "

Stella had other duties. In the period immediately following her mother's death, she had to maintain sufficient composure, despite the loss of the person who meant the most to her, to receive the many callers and to answer letters of condolence.[49] Virginia observed that the latter task was especially painful for her half sister.[50] Stella mothered the children as well as Leslie, probably more out of love for them than from a sense of obligation. Virginia and Adrian needed a great deal of mothering. Stella was also the housekeeper, apparently a very good one. She was able to manage the inevitable household crises such as the time when Oliver Wendell Holmes came unexpectedly to lunch, and she had to send Vanessa "flying to the market for a chicken."[51] Other exigencies of Stella's daily routine were noted in her diary; Vanessa Bell read it in 1910 and called it a "gloomy and terrific" account of days spent rushing all over London, with never a pause. Vanessa said it filled her with horror to contemplate Stella's life, and the diary made her wonder how Stella ever lived to be twenty-eight.[52]

However, Stella never quite mastered the crises of Leslie's weekly, irrational rages over the family accounts. Being subjected to the same kind of brutal scenes Julia had undergone over household finances was far more difficult for Stella, because she had less courage than Julia to stand up to Leslie. For his part, Leslie's rage was not in the least restrained by pity or by gratitude for all that Stella was doing for him and the family.

Virginia was troubled by Leslie's failure to show gratitude or sympathy to Stella, or to anyone. For example, he seemed quite unaware during the early period of mourning that Stella was under great strain even though her appearance was pale and haggard.[53] Leslie was as usual relatively impervious to signs of distress in the person whom he expected to mother him. Rather than sympathizing with Stella, he tried more and more to extract from her the sympathy he needed. Many of his actions resembled the games he played to get Julia's "delicious" comforting. He stated his wish for Stella's special sympathy quite directly in the "Mausoleum Book" (p. 45). All the Duckworth children were a help to him, he said. But in grief such as his, he continued, a woman could help most, and a woman who so resembled his dear Julia as Stella did, could give him "all the sympathy" of which he was "susceptible."

Obviously Leslie Stephen expected and got a great deal from his stepdaughter, but apparently he was too confused to know exactly what he did want and expect. He knew he wanted a housekeeper, but that was a practical and relatively incidental matter as long as Stella so willingly and capably fulfilled that function. He knew also that he wanted to be mothered. In that regard things became inevitably more complex, for since childhood, Leslie Stephen's emotional reactions to those who mothered him had been confused and relatively indiscriminate. They were in Stella's case as well. Evidently, he thought of her as his exclusive possession and was jealous of her, wanting virtually everything from her except a conjugal relationship. He wanted her to tell him that she loved him. Possibly he was "in love" with her romantically, if not sexually. Possibly he thought he meant the word "love" in a fatherly, thoroughly scrubbed, antiseptic sense, for a man of his determinedly puritanical stance could hardly admit to a romantic attraction to his young stepdaughter. Nor could a man with his stringent moral attitude let himself sort out his emotions enough to know just what it was he did feel for her.

Virginia was also confused and divided within herself about the relationship between Stella and her father, and about Stella herself. At times she resented Stella, but she also loved and admired her for what she did for the family, especially for herself, but also for Leslie. Virginia said in her 1908 memoir, seemingly with admiration and, one trusts, with exaggeration, that Stella never overlooked even one of Leslie's needs during his mourning. Yet in her 1939-1940 memoir, she said resentfully that Stella had confused her father because she had behaved "indiscriminately" when she was thrown into a position of intimacy with him. No doubt Stella did add to Leslie's confusions both because of the resemblance to her mother and because of her willingness to serve him. It is probable that in her naïveté Stella was less discriminating than she might otherwise have been in her attentions to Leslie. But whatever merits Virginia's interpretations may have, there is far more reason to think Leslie the indiscriminate one rather than Stella.

Although even Leslie's mourning had to taper off eventually, he tried to assure that the benefits of his mourning period would continue indefinitely. He particularly wanted Stella's comfort, solace, and practical contributions to go on as long as he needed them, and that was, of course, as long as he lived. Most likely he did many things without thinking them through, to appeal to Stella's sense of duty to him. But at times he acted and spoke by conscious design, a fact established unmistakably in a letter to Stella on her honeymoon.[54] In it, he told her that he was still in good health, though somewhat debilitated by his sorrow, and unless there was "some accident," he would be a "burden" on her for some time to come. He was confident, he said, that Stella would fulfill her obligations to care for him, and that her husband would help her. Before the time of that letter, however, he did everything he could to delay, if not prevent, her marriage and to keep her as near him as possible.

## To Keep a Great Prize

Leslie Stephen had a great prize in Stella, won over no odds at all, and it never occurred to him that he might have to give her up, or that she would be "stolen" from him.[55] But Stella was attractive to other men than Leslie. Sometimes she was too attractive for her own comfort, as in 1890, when Leslie's deranged nephew, James K. Stephen, fell in love with her, and the Stephen children, including Virginia, had to help Julia protect her from his frantic courtship.[56] Moreover, Stella had a suitor, and one with much in his favor, since he was a man whom Julia had approved and possibly had selected for her. Her mother's approval must have counted heavily with Stella, and perhaps it had some effect eventually on Leslie. The suitor was John Waller (Jack) Hills, a young solicitor. Although shy and handicapped by a very bad stammer, Jack Hills was determined to win Stella. He had been encouraged by Julia, in whom he confided, in part through letters,[57] no doubt unaware that at least on one occasion Leslie had opened one of his letters to Julia. Leslie reported to Julia that he had read the letter "out of curiosity," and that Jack was a pathetic young man who had Leslie's pity.[58]

Virginia Woolf thought that if her mother had lived, Stella would have married Jack sooner than she did.[59] Knowing Julia's matchmaking propensities, no doubt she would have been inclined to move the courtship rapidly along. But initially Stella was not interested in Jack and turned down a first proposal that came while Julia was still living. After Julia's death, Jack resumed his courtship, and although Stella was by that time attracted to him, she turned down a second proposal, perhaps out of obligation to remain with her stepfather and her half-siblings.[60] Virginia Woolf attributed Stella's hesitation to marry Jack to attacks of fear and to her feeling that "she had had her life."[61] But after turning him down the second time,

Stella did not break off her friendship with Jack as she had previously, making it possible, in Virginia's words, for Jack to "love and reason" Stella out of her fears. When he proposed again, Stella was ready to accept. Stella recorded her acceptance in her diary with the noticeably unelaborate statement that as of that date, Saturday, August 22, 1896, she and Jack were engaged.

Stella's engagement was a time of great excitement in the Stephen household, especially for Virginia, who said that she could literally feel waves of emotion coming from the closed door of the drawing room where Jack and Stella sat and waves of rage coming from her father. She said further that it was her first vision of what love could be like between a man and a woman, a statement that casts doubt on her belief, expressed in *To the Lighthouse,* about her parents' love for each other. She made a similar comment about the earlier engagement of family friends.[62] Stella's and Jack's love seemed to Virginia so intense and rapturous that it glowed like a ruby; Stella's whole body seemed to be lit with the incandescence of love. Virginia was excited too by the beauty of Stella coming alive emotionally. However, the excitement was not pleasant for Virginia. It left her half insane, she said, with shyness and nervousness.[63]

Others in the family were excited in different ways. Adrian cried and was rebuked by Leslie who told the children that they must all be happy about something that their mother had wished to happen. Leslie's admonition did not accord with his own feelings; he reacted with ill-contained jealousy, resentment, and disapproval. His version of the matter, according to Bell (p. 48) was that "he, a lonely old widower, a man distracted and broken by grief, had been betrayed." Leslie's female supporters among the relatives agreed with him and thought that the model daughter had turned quite disgracefully selfish.

By the time of Stella's engagement, Leslie had resumed

writing in the "Mausoleum Book," using it to record important events in the family. As Leslie himself observed, important events ran heavily toward necrology, and even though he wished it weren't true, listing deaths was appropriate to his emotional state. But he added that he would publish a birthday book[64] as a kind of antidote to the predominance of obituaries in the private "Mausoleum Book."[65] He listed important events other than deaths in the "Mausoleum Book," and to him some of the most important events were his own emotional reactions to other such events. Thus both Stella's engagement and marriage and his more polite reactions to them were duly entered. He waited a full month to record the engagement, the delay symbolizing his attitude toward the matter. The actual entry of Stella's engagement was relatively restrained and considerably less than straightforward. First he stated that his "darling Stella" was engaged, that it was superfluous to say more than that since they would all remember the engagement. Superfluous or not, he could not resist continuing. He said that Julia had talked constantly to him of the romance between Stella and Jack. Knowing that she approved would have, in turn, reconciled him to the engagement, had any reconciliation been needed. They had all known Hills so long that his becoming a member of the family hardly changed their feelings for him, Leslie said further, not specifying the nature of the unchanged feelings. He avowed politely, if uncandidly, that he himself contemplated the marriage with perfect confidence and satisfaction. If anything could make him happy, this engagement "ought to" do so, but his happiness was a "matter of rapidly diminishing importance."[66]

In the face of the diminishing importance of his own happiness, Stella's happiness was hardly a matter that Leslie considered at all. He tried to retain his great prize, and his efforts made it necessary for Stella and Jack to struggle, first, with Stella's conscience, then with Leslie, for the right to marry and set up their own household. Even when he grudgingly and resentfully accepted the engagement, Leslie tried to minimize his loss by getting Stella and Jack to agree to remain with the Stephen family, to continue to run the house, supervise the children and servants, and, most of all, to continue to make his life as comfortable as possible. Stella and Jack agreed at first to live with the Stephen family at 22 Hyde Park Gate, London. But Stella in love, cognizant of what continuing to live with the Stephens would entail, no doubt eager for her own house and some relief from her obligations to Leslie, with Jack to abet her —that Stella was a more adamant person than Leslie had ever known her to be. Eventually she had it out with him, and after a painful scene, claimed her right to set up a new household with her husband. Even so, she compromised, in fact if not in intention, when she and Jack decided to live at 24 Hyde Park Gate, directly across the street from Leslie.[67]

Stella and Jack won the tug-of-war. But nearly eight months passed between the engagement and the wedding, because of negotiations with Leslie and because Jack needed minor surgery. The delay became a matter of great poignance, for Stella died four months after the wedding day. The idea that Stella and Jack lost eight months of married life together was still troubling Virginia Woolf in the last years before her own death and was one of the blocks making it impossible for her to reconcile her feelings about her father. She said that the long engagement was "wanton cruelty" to Stella and Jack and that her father was entirely to blame for the delay. Virginia condemned him in a variety of ways, saying that his grief during Stella's engagement was a pose and that he was possessive, exacting, peevish, and hurt. She said further that Leslie acted as he did because he had become increasingly tyrannical over the years and because he was jealous of Jack and of all young men.[68]

After a visit to Julia's grave the preceding day, Stella and

Jack were married on April 10, 1897, in full ceremony, with many guests and with Virginia and Vanessa acting as bridesmaids. Leslie was a little reluctant to make it such a festive occasion that he would have to buy special clothes for the ceremony, preferring his "usual costume" instead. Nevertheless, he did buy new clothes and took part in the wedding, claiming symbolic proprietory rights over Stella by insisting that he, rather than one of her brothers, give her away.[69] He expressed his feelings about the union rather obliquely in the "Mausoleum Book" on her wedding day, and less obliquely in two letters he sent Stella on her honeyman. He began the entry in the "Mausoleum Book" by saying that he would not put down, even there, the thoughts that had agitated him. There was nothing to say about the marriage except that it was in all respects thoroughly satisfactory. However, he continued, he had had a great many "selfish pangs" during the engagement but would have been a "brute" had he really complained. The household would be changed without Stella, perhaps for the better, as others insisted, but at the moment, he resented such assurance. Finally, Leslie invoked Julia's ghost, saying that it had seemed to him all day that he felt "a presence," and knew that "she" would have rejoiced.[70] His reference to the ghostly presence of Julia is interesting and possibly influenced Virginia, who often said that she could feel her mother's extracorporeal presence, and imagined her mother alive and around her for many years after her death.

The two letters Leslie sent Stella on her honeymoon reveal his emotions about Stella and her marriage more directly.[71] Both of the letters were written on the paper with heavy black borders he used during his continued mourning for Julia, paper now symbolic of his attitude toward Stella's marriage. The first was written on the day of the wedding and one of the primary matters to get his attention was his confusion. He was tired, excited, and did not know if he were "upside down or right side up." The fault was the "world's" (for which one can substitute "Stella's"), for the world had been turned topsy-turvy since that morning. His feelings were like feelings he once had when he fell; he didn't know whether he was hurt, healed of a wound, or simply "dazzled." He could be clear about only two things: he and Stella still loved each other and would continue to do so; she would do all she could for him, and her husband would help her. Continuing, he reminded Stella that she had the same "nature" as her mother, and that he had reverenced her mother. He could hardly reverence a daughter, he said, but his feeling for Stella was "more than affection." It included complete confidence and trust. He closed by asking Stella to love him still and sometimes to tell him so. In a postscript he reported the compliments he had received from Henry James and others about "Nessa and Ginia's beauty," one of his more pleasant experiences of the day.

Leslie Stephen's second letter to Stella on her honeymoon was dated three days after the wedding. One of his opening statements was that he must not express his feelings, for he had already "uttered himself too abundantly." He followed with the warning that, barring accidents, he would live for some years yet, and therefore expected to continue to be a burden to her. Although he missed Stella, he had regained some authority over the household. At least, without her in charge, they hadn't had fish for dinner; there were some advantages to freedom even from such a kind and well-meaning ruler as herself. Calling her his "dearest," he averred that he had tried to hold his tongue, but feared that something had "peeped out." He knew that she would forgive him, and wondered if he would ever be able to write a cheerful letter. He concluded by sending his love to—he couldn't think of a satisfactory name; had anyone ever called him "Waller?"[72] As Quentin Bell said (p. 48), Jack, the name that Stella's husband evidently preferred, had long since taken on unpleasant associations for Leslie, and sounded like the smack of a whip to him. Between themselves in later years, Virginia and Vanessa did sometimes refer to Jack as "Waller."[73]

In spite of Leslie's gloom and sense of rejection, the Stephen children came to feel that Stella's marriage presaged better times, at least until the honeymoon ended, and Stella returned home ill. The homecoming took place on April 28, 1897,[74] but was not recorded by Leslie in the "Mausoleum Book" until May 7, 1897, the second anniversary of Julia's death. His entry about Stella's return was followed by a kind of verbal sigh: "Two years ago!" His association of Julia's death with Stella's return from her honeymoon may have been a further indication of the gloom he felt about Stella's marriage. Or possibly the link in his mind was caused by his forebodings about Stella's health, for the other information recorded on that date referred to her illness.

The nature of Stella's illness was uncertain; at first it was called a "gastric chill," and then diagnosed peritonitis.[75] It was also called "appendicitis," but one of Stella's nurses believed the label had been used only to disguise the true nature of Stella's illness. She shared her personal opinion with another nurse who shared it many years later with Virginia's friend, Violet Dickinson. In 1942, as a very old lady, Violet Dickinson passed on the nurse's interpretation (and gossip) to Vanessa Bell, telling her that Stella had been injured by Jack on the honeymoon.[76] Evidently Vanessa demurred, for Violet went over the matter again, in more detail. The nurse had been quite definite, she insisted; Stella had had some inner malformation that made sexual intercourse difficult. Something — Violet supposed the uterus — that should have been convex was actually concave, or maybe it was vice versa. At a minimum, Violet insisted, Jack had been a "tiring lover." She said also that the difficulty was due in part to Stella's exhaustion at the time of the wedding and honeymoon.[77]

Whatever her illness, for more than two months Stella was alternately better and worse. Late in May she was found to be pregnant, and that seemed a good omen. But her health continued to alternate between improvement and deterioration, and on July 18 it was decided that she must have surgery. On July 19, 1897, Stella died, and once again there was much of the same ghastly horror the family had experienced when Julia died. Stella, the perfect "daughter," was mourned and eulogized much as Julia, the perfect wife and mother, had been. She was not mourned and eulogized in the "Mausoleum Book," however. Leslie said only that his "darling Stella" had died.[78] It was Quentin Bell's view (p. 62) that Leslie did not grieve greatly for Stella after her death since he had already lost her.

There were many postscripts to Stella's death, including Violet Dickinson's rather macabre speculations made in her letters to Vanessa Bell, forty-five years later. Many of the later comments were written by Virginia Woolf in her efforts to comprehend the meaning of Stella's life and death and to work through some of her conflicting, though not indiscriminate, emotions about her half sister. Two postscripts concerned financial matters. One of those was written by Leslie in the "Mausoleum Book," on the date of September 24, 1897. He recorded that Jack Hills had offered to share with him some of Stella's estate (her marriage settlement) and that he thought it "right" to accept. He noted that Stella had made no will, but that she would have wanted to contribute to the maintenance of his household, for the sake of her brothers and sisters. The second postscript concerning finances occurred in 1915 when Leonard and Virginia Woolf's very meager resources were depleted by Virginia's long illness and Leonard turned to Jack Hills to ask advance payment of the £100, income from her half sister's estate, that Hills "allowed" Virginia.[79]

Father, Brother, or Lover?

Virginia's rather vague, tenuous accusation against Stella Duckworth—that Stella was indiscriminate with Leslie Stephen and therefore confused him—was paralleled by her much grosser charges against Gerald and George Duckworth. Her accusation against Gerald was the most detailed and specific and, for that reason alone, seems credible: she said that when she was about six, Gerald (who would have been about eighteen at the time) had manually explored her genitalia.[80] Insofar as I have been able to determine from the study of documentary material, Virginia was relatively vague in her charges against George, but much more persistent, telling them to various people at various times. Her implication was that over a period of years, George had repeatedly made sexual advances toward her. In a memoir about him, "22 Hyde Park Gate,"[81] she said that he was a monster, a crossbreeding of God, faun, and pig in lively opposition, and that he had tried to be a multiple of things to her, principally father, brother, and lover, but also sister and mother. Virginia held to her accusations against George. She sometimes seemed to believe them and, paradoxically, sometimes seemed not to intend them as literal fact. Evidently she was corroborated by Vanessa. Quentin Bell made the accusations public and commented on them in his biography of Virginia.

If Virginia's accusations were true, her half brothers were a pair of menaces. But it cannot be determined that the alleged offenses actually took place. Nor can it be determined that they did not. Possibly they were imaginative elaborations of some innocent action and therefore exemplify Virginia's tendencies to extend and embroider actual events. On the one hand, her accusations against George, as she elaborated them in her memoirs, seem especially to resemble her portraits of other persons. Her statements about Gerald, on the other hand, appear to be of an entirely different variety. Possibly Virginia's charges were true and possibly they were symptomatic of her own confusions about her half brothers. Eventually she tried to resolve her confusions by settling down to loathe both of them, and she loathed George more than Gerald. That was not the end of the affair, however, for she was left with a residue of painful emotions and with the conviction that her half brothers were significantly responsible for her emotional and sexual problems.

Little information remains about the Duckworth brothers' early lives other than the suggestion of their limited association with the Stephen children while they were growing up and their resentment of their stepfather. Apparently they grew up superficially resembling their Pattle relatives but lacking the verve, social acumen and many other fine qualities of the Pattles. They even seem to have lacked the eccentricities that made some of the Pattles so interesting. But too little is known to explain how that came about and why they became such anathemas to Virginia. George was born in 1868 and Gerald in 1870, a short time after his father's death. No doubt both were affected by Julia's melancholia, though in different ways than their sister was. Leslie Stephen described George in the "Mausoleum Book" (pp. 64-65) as an "open-tempered" child whose constant expressions of affection were always a source of delight to Julia, a description which contrasts with the reports of Stella's sadness as a child. Gerald was sickly as an infant and a cause of anxiety to Julia, according to Leslie. When Leslie and Julia married in 1878, Leslie took over the responsibility for teaching George and Gerald until they entered Eton, and subsequently both of them went to Cambridge. Presumably their educations were paid for by money they inherited from their father, Herbert Duckworth.

Other than his contribution to their formal education, Leslie Stephen seems to have done little about George and Gerald's upbringing. As he said, he never really tried to be a father to them, and advised them only through their mother. However, one finds from Leslie's letters to Julia that certain matters about George did concern Leslie from time to time. For example, Leslie intervened and dictated a questionable resolution to a plan concocted by George, aged thirteen, and his aunt Minna Duckworth. The plan called for George to lie or at least to deceive an uncle in order to avoid attending church with him. Leslie had no interest in George's attending church, but was bothered by the deception. Drawing a line in the general vicinity of pedantic truth-telling, if not full disclosure and honesty, Leslie avowed that it was not his concern if Minna Duckworth carried out the deception involving George. But if George himself *said* anything, he was to state "the facts." In short, it was all right with Leslie if George acted out the deception, if technically he avoided lying.[82] On a later occasion, when George was eighteen and away at school, the much less equivocal advice relayed to George through Julia concerned Leslie's library and, indirectly, his finances: Julia was to tell George to buy his own books and to stop taking books from home.[83]

Virginia Woolf blamed George's education for his alleged derelictions to her and credited her mother with having held him in line. Her pronouncement reflected also her belief that public school educations harmed young men. She said, turgidly, that school and college had given a good, priggish boy (George) certain "impressions" that remained with him as a man. Those "impressions" could do nothing, she said, to contain his "violent" gusts of emotion, but the "impressions" were instead distorted by the emotions. Only Julia Stephen had been able to restrain his violent emotions, Virginia said in one of her many instances of attributing to her mother the power to keep the difficult emotions of men under control. After Julia was gone, Virginia said, nothing restrained George.[84]

George Duckworth began playing father as well as older brother to Virginia before Julia's death, by which time he acted in some ways rather like the head of the family and household. This was due in part to George's officiousness, which evidently he had in abundance, but it was due also to Leslie's persistent helplessness and dependency and to his leaving most practical matters to others. Julia delegated some things to George, although apparently fewer than she delegated to Stella. Leslie also delegated to George, and one instance involved Virginia. In 1893 Julia was away while Virginia was ill, and Leslie wrote to tell her that Dr. Seton had been to see Virginia, but that George would have to tell her what Dr. Seton had said. He himself was so deaf that he caught only about one word in three. Leslie was satisfied to leave the matter in George's hands.[85]

When Julia died and for a time afterward, the Duckworths were more nearly in charge of the household than Leslie was able to be.[86] Evidently they were with Julia as she died while Leslie was in another part of the house, possibly asleep, but at least unaware that Julia was dying. George went to get Leslie and inform him, and as Leslie himself said, he was totally unprepared for the shock of finding Julia "sinking quietly into the arms of death."[87] As Virginia recalled it in her 1939-1940 memoir, George then went to bring Virginia, Vanessa, and possibly Adrian to their mother; Thoby was at school. George gave Virginia and Vanessa brandy in warm milk, wrapped towels around them (for what reason it is not known). He then shepherded them into the bedroom where their mother's body lay, past a terribly distraught Leslie who rushed out of the room as they entered, colliding with the girls in passing. George stayed with Virginia and Vanessa as they kissed their dead mother's face, which felt warm to Virginia's lips. The kiss and the entire scene made an ineffaceable impression upon the thirteen-year-old Virginia, for whom it was so unreal that she could feel nothing at the time except an impulse to laugh, as she sometimes did when under great tension.

Another deep and lasting impression was made upon Virginia when George took her and Vanessa to Paddington Station the next day to meet Thoby as he arrived home from school. A sudden blaze of sunlight flashed against the dark girders of the station and seemed to Virginia almost hallucinatory and almost mystical in the time of spiritual darkness after her mother died. The most traumatic experience for Virginia occurred the evening after her mother died, when Stella took her and Vanessa to see and kiss their dead mother for the last time. Julia's face appeared to Virginia to be very stern in death, and kissing it was like pressing her lips against cold iron. Virginia said that forever afterward touching cold iron revived the emotions and reinstated the experience of that last visit to her mother's body. Stella was sensitive enough to notice that Virginia started back when she kissed her mother. She apologized to Virginia for having frightened her, and Virginia cried because of Stella's sympathy. Virginia's overwrought condition made her imagine that she saw the figure of a man sitting bent beside her mother. However, she said that she might have dramatized her report of that "vision," for the several days between her mother's death and funeral were so unreal and histrionic that "any hallucination" was possible. Virginia recalled too that she was bothered by an experience that she had, many times in her life, of uncontrolled "pictures" coming to her mind. She told Stella about seeing the figure of the man and Stella replied only that it was nice that their mother was not alone — a well-meant response that may have made Virginia's near hallucination seem more "real."

Gerald Duckworth's role after Julia Stephen's death is unclear except for the fact that Leslie Stephen delegated to him the responsibility of going to St. Ives and disposing of the lease to Talland House. Leslie knew that he could never again bear to see the place where he had been so happy, and so Gerald was sent off to make the arrangements.[88]


Knowing No Bounds?

As noted, Virginia alleged only one act of indiscriminate attention by Gerald, the incident that supposedly occurred when she was six and he was eighteen.[89] She accused George of much more. According to Quentin Bell's reconstruction of the matter, George began his malefactions at the time of Julia Stephen's death when he was twenty-seven and Virginia was thirteen, and when she was seriously disturbed emotionally and mentally. George's unwelcome attentions reputedly consisted of sexual groping and "fondling" which emerged from his attempts to comfort her after her mother's death. But Virginia could not always distinguish them from his innocent expressions of affection and solicitude. Supposedly, George was repeatedly offensive over a period of nearly nine years, until after her father's death, when Virginia was again disturbed. George was stopped, according to Bell, when Vanessa told Virginia's doctor, who upbraided George about his conduct. George denied having done anything wrong, saying that he had only tried to comfort Virginia first because her mother had died and then, later, because her father was dying.[90]

If George's sexual forays actually occurred, the irony is that they took place at a time when he appeared to everyone to be a model brother to his unhappy, young half sisters. In Quentin Bell's words (p. 42), Stella, the ideal daughter to Leslie Stephen, and George, the model brother to Virginia and Vanessa, seemed like two "bright luminaries" in the otherwise unrelieved spiritual gloom of the prolonged mourning for Julia. It was a part George could play well. He was handsome, a bit of a dandy, and had his own income. Whatever his faults and motives, he was generous by nature (as even Virginia admitted) and made expensive gifts to his half sisters. These included a horse for Vanessa[91] and having Virginia's room redecorated. The old night nursery was Virginia's first room of her own and became hers when Stella married and Vanessa moved into Stella's former bedroom. Virginia was given Stella's writing table which had been made by a St. Ives carpenter and decorated by Stella herself. George arranged to have Virginia's room papered, added a fireplace, and gave her a mirror to encourage her to take interest in her appearance.[92] But George's income had its disadvantages, for Virginia said that it made her feel that he had a right to authority over her.[93]

George bestowed his affections at least as liberally as his gifts. Bell wrote (p. 42) that "After their mother's death his kindness knew no bounds," that "his was an emotional, a demonstrative nature, his shoulder was there for them to weep on; his arms were open for their relief." According to Bell's account, the girls gradually discovered just which bounds were lacking. Bell said that what often began as one kind of embrace, slowly and at first indefinitely, then more and more distinctly, turned into another, more disquieting kind of caress. Bell's interpretation was based on Virginia's statements. She said that she and Vanessa had understood that George's affections, his character, his soul were "immaculate." Then, in Virginia's conception of the matter, without her mother there to control them, George's affections burst through all restraints.[94]

Hating George, Virginia said that he was too stupid to impose his own restraints; he had a natural "animal vigour" but no brain to control it. Vanessa Bell believed that George didn't quite know when his embraces went beyond the legitimate into areas considered taboo between brother and sister, so in some very important respects, she too thought George un-intelligent.[95] In later years, Vanessa concluded that George's depressing stupidity had a terrible power over other areas of the girls' lives. She said that although George and Gerald were in the minority at 22 Hyde Park Gate, they managed to "squash" everything for the girls.[96]

According to Quentin Bell's initial reconstruction of it, the problem consisted of more than what Virginia called George's stupidity and unrestrained animal vigor. Virginia and Vanessa were confused; they never knew where they stood or what his actions meant. They never knew when he was going to be the generous, kind, and loving brother, and when his kindness was a prelude to sexual caresses. And there was the problem of Virginia's and Vanessa's helplessness in the situation. As Quentin Bell said (p. 43), there was no one to whom they could turn for protection and guidance, no one who would even believe them if they reported the malefactions of their "model" brother. Virginia was too confused to know what to do and too shy to talk with anyone other than Vanessa, and Vanessa didn't know what to do either. Neither Virginia nor Vanessa seems to have said anything to anyone else until after Leslie's death in 1904, when Vanessa talked with Virginia's doctor about it.[97]

In brief, that is the story of George's alleged indiscriminate emotions and attentions to his young half sisters. But the area of mystery and the very large question remain: was the story true? Certainly Virginia Woolf believed that something had occurred, and probably something did occur. Whatever his intentions and reason, most likely George did "transgress" in a manner that could be interpreted as sexual, with both Virginia and Vanessa. But there are also reasons to believe that when Virginia told the story she exaggerated it, and that she did not intend all of her accounts to be taken literally. Yet she never seemed concerned when her story was taken literally.

Her several known references to the alleged misconduct

included the veiled statement in her 1908 memoir, which she seems to have intended seriously as an explanation of George's behavior. This reference seems also to imply that Virginia was disturbed about his behavior. She did not specify exactly what he had done, but referred to it in discrete terms, hinting at outrage in language more worthy of her father than of herself: George's excess of "animal vigour" had "burst all restraints," leading to "violent gusts of passions" and to his behaving "little better than a brute." Her more complete statement follows: "George was in truth, a stupid, good natured young man, of profuse, voluble affections, which during his mother's lifetime were kept in check. When she died however, some restraint seemed to burst; he showed himself so sad, so affectionate, so boundlessly unselfish in his plans, that the voices of all women cried aloud in his praise, and men were touched by his modest virtues, at the same time that they were puzzled. What was it that made him so different from other men? Stupid he was, and good natured; but such qualities were not simple; they were modified, confused, distorted, exalted, set swimming in a sea of racing emotions until you were completely at a loss to know where you stood. Nature, we may suppose, had supplied him with abundant animal vigour, but she had neglected to set an efficient brain in control of it. The result was that all the impressions which the priggish boy took in at school and college remained with him when he was a man; they were not extended but were liable to be expanded into enormous proportions by violent gusts of passions; and [he] proved more and more incapable of containing them. Thus, under the name of unselfishness he allowed himself to commit acts which a cleverer man would have called tyrannical; and, profoundly believing in the purity of his love, he behaved little better than a brute."[98]

Virginia's references to George's alleged offenses also included an oral account in 1911 to a friend, Janet Case, formerly her Greek teacher. In a letter to Vanessa, written immediately after the talk with Janet, Virginia reported the conversation. Janet had recalled being revolted by George's "fondling" of Virginia during her Greek lessons and that she had thought him a "nasty creature."[99] Virginia also told the story in 1922 to Elena Richmond, the wife of Bruce Richmond, the editor of the *Times Literary Supplement,* and then recounted her conversation with Elena in a letter to Vanessa. By that time Virginia had evidently begun to enjoy her story and even to think it funny. She said to Vanessa that no doubt Elena Richmond would repeat the story to Bruce who would be compelled to spit in George's face when next they encountered each other at their club.[100]

The most important and controversial references, however, were made in papers Virginia prepared for the "Memoir Club"[101] in 1921[102] and 1922,[103] one of which was rediscovered by Virginia and possibly shown to Ethel Smyth in 1932.[104] The first of these papers contains relatively specific allegations, but the context of the allegations leads one to question whether Virginia intended them literally. Rather, this memoir in particular seems an instance of Virginia's creation of a portrait — a portrait perhaps based on fact, but extended well beyond it. She described George's overly affectionate nature, quite likely one of the truths about him. She said that when one tried to argue with him — for example about his snobbery and social ambitions — he would end the argument with an excessive show of affection. ". . . [H]e would seize you in his arms and cry out that he refused to argue with those he loved. 'Kiss me, kiss me, you beloved', he would vociferate; and the argument was drowned in kisses. Everything was drowned in kisses. He lived in the thickest emotional haze, and as his passions increased and his desires became more vehement — he lived, Jack Hills assured me, in complete chastity until his marriage — one felt like an unfortunate minnow shut up in the same tank with an unwieldy and turbulant whale."[105]

Virginia described George's alleged sexual overtures after a party, one of many parties at which he tried to introduce her and Vanessa to society, and supposedly one of many followed by such advances. In her description Virginia said that she had undressed and was trying to fall asleep and forget the party. "Sleep had almost come to me. The room was dark. The house silent. Then, creaking stealthily, the door opened; treading gingerly, someone entered. 'Who?' I cried. 'Don't be frightened', George whispered. 'And don't turn on the light, oh beloved. Beloved —' and he flung himself on my bed, and took me in his arms.

"Yes, the old ladies of Kensington and Belgravia never knew that George Duckworth was not only father and mother, brother and sister to those poor Stephen girls; he was their lover also."[106]

The belief that Virginia did not intend her statements to be understood as literal fact is supported by a diary passage of May 26, 1921, in which she referred to a conversation with Maynard Keynes. "The best thing you ever did, he said, was your Memoir on George. You should pretend to write about real people and make it all up." Without denying Maynard's implication that she made it all up, Virginia continued, "I was dashed of course (and Oh dear what nonsense — for if George is my climax I'm a mere scribbler)."[107]

In the other essay for the "Memoir Club," an extension of the earlier one, Virginia modified her story slightly but did not lessen her allegations. "It was long past midnight that I got into bed and sat reading.... There would be a tap at the door; the light would be turned out and George would fling himself on my bed, cuddling and kissing and otherwise embracing me in order, as he told Dr. Savage later, to comfort me for the fatal illness of my father — who was dying three or four storeys lower down of cancer."[108]

Virginia was not the only person to pass on the story about George. Vanessa Bell, who allegedly had been subjected to

similar attentions, believed Virginia's story and evidently witnessed some of George's actions toward her sister. She thought
the matter significant enough to report to Virginia's doctor in
1904 as a probable factor in her emotional problems. However, Vanessa was either inconsistent or did not fully appreciate the significance of what she believed to be true, for when
Virginia was ill in 1913, Vanessa did not warn Leonard Woolf
or Virginia's doctors against moving her into George's household. That move was made at George's invitation at a time
when Virginia was dangerously disturbed, just after a suicide
attempt, and when an association with one of the alleged
causes of her problems could hardly have been the treatment
of choice.[109]

Quentin Bell believed Virginia's story about George Duckworth although he did not agree with Virginia about all of the
results she liked to attribute to George's conduct. He reported
the matter only after careful study. After my own investigation
of the documentary evidence, I am inclined to believe that
there was some basis in fact for Virginia's complaints about
Gerald and George, but that she extended the truth about
George appreciably when she wrote her papers for the "Memoir Club." If it is appropriate to interpret the story of George's
alleged malefactions as one of Virginia's portraits, as I do,
there remains the problem of why the portrait of George was
given its particular features. Moreover, since Bell treated the
matter publicly in 1972, doubts have been expressed about
whether there is *any* factual basis for the charges against
George. A critic has asked, for example, whether one should
believe someone as emotionally disturbed as Virginia.[110] After
all, Virginia herself said that she was virtually hallucinatory
during part of the period in reference. She admitted to a great
deal of confusion during the same period, and as noted earlier,
some of her confusion pertained to her despised half brothers.

Several logical conjectures, but no certainties, exist about the origins and results of her confusions, and therefore about the uglier features of what I believe to be one of her portraits. Only two of the more logical possibilities are discussed here. Is it not possible that Virginia was so ignorant of sex, or so frightened of it, that she could not distinguish an erotic advance from other caresses? Leslie Stephen tried and, to some extent, succeeded in maintaining within his household a facade of ignorance in reference to sexuality—ignorance that he mistook for "purity." But facades are dangerous, and ignorance rarely if ever can be maintained about topics as vital as sexuality. What one does not know about such vital matters, one tends to invent, and Virginia was, of course, a superb inventor. Not only does one tend to invent, but many times inventions embody wishes, especially if the facade of ignorance hides those wishes from self-awareness. One of the important lessons Freud learned from his early patients was that some of their putative memories of traumatic events, such as incest, were actually memories of their own imaginings rather than memories of real occurrences. Moreover, he learned that his patients' remembered imaginings often indicated their hidden wishes.

Such reasoning leads to the second speculation: Is it not possible that someone as much in need of affection as Virginia both wanted and liked affection from George, and imagined that he had made erotic advances when he was merely being kind and innocently affectionate, in short, was trying to be a brother and not a lover? As subsequent chapters will develop, Virginia was sensuous (in contradistinction to erotic), loved physical expressions of affection, and got "exquisite pleasure" from body contact.[111] When George made his so-called advances, Virginia was at an age when she may have been as confused by her own response as she was by whatever he may have done. It should be noted in this regard that when she said that George was her lover, she did not say that she resisted his advances, thus leaving the impression (if one wants to read the story as literal fact, which is not advised) that she was also his lover. In short, the accusation about the alleged incest as made in her first paper for the "Memoir Club," by implication, indicted her as well as George. If this line of reasoning is valid, and there is no way to determine whether it is or is not, it may follow that Virginia felt all the more repelled because she found it pleasant to be caressed by someone she despised.

The questions about the alleged attempts at incest by Virginia's half brothers are legitimate, and the hypothetical explanations outlined above are logical and plausible, but they cannot be verified or disproved. Other explanations are almost equally logical and plausible, including Professor Bell's first explanation, that Virginia told no more than the truth about George. Finally, the mystery remains. Whatever one accepts continues to be a matter of opinion about the truth of Virginia's accounts and of Vanessa's corroboration of the accusations.

### Comedy and Social Aspirations

That George Duckworth committed other offenses against Virginia and Vanessa seems unquestionable. They consisted of his attempts to turn his shy and resistant half sisters into his social assets as he pursued what evidently was his life's ambitions, namely, "getting ahead," exemplifying the outward, visible signs of social status, and marrying into aristocracy.[112] Although a Moliere might have made a comedy of it, and although there were comic elements in it, the story of George's social climbing is relatively dull. However, Virginia found George's attempts to bring her out socially extraordinarily painful. She experienced them as an outrage, almost as offensive as his alleged sexual fumblings, for her shyness, social ineptitude, and worries about dress were not the usual ones of inexperienced young girls. Instead, they were indications of her deep, pathological fears. George's pompous officiousness and insensitivity in pushing her into social situations she couldn't manage terrified her, and no doubt exacerbated rather than allayed both her outward insecurities and her underlying fears. And apparently she could not say enough against George. Not only was he a mixture of pig, faun, and god. In Virginia's expressed opinion,[113] he was a "flutter-brained," "hare-brained" person who could accomplish nothing significant on his own. He was therefore so insecure in his social position that he required the titles and honors of others to convince him of a self-importance that he knew full well he lacked.[114]

Some of the more comic elements in the account of George Duckworth came from his efforts to court and marry aristocracy. As Virginia wrote in her 1921 essay for the "Memoir Club," and as Quentin Bell recounted also (pp. 81-82, 87-88), Virginia contributed to the comedy in George's first and failed effort to marry an aristocrat. He became engaged to Lady Flora Russell, who seen decided to break the engagement. When the engagement was announced, Virginia, in her enthusiasm that George might marry and move away, sent off a hasty telegram. The message, "She is an angel," to be signed with Virginia's nickname, "Goat," was garbled in transmission. The telegram arrived saying, "She is an aged goat." Virginia was involved in another comic though, to her, painful incident when George took her, one of his titled friends, and another guest to see a risqué French play, so crude that the party made a hasty, embarrassed exit.

Subsequently George became engaged to and did marry Lady Margaret Herbert. After his marriage George had occasional contact with his half sisters. He and Gerald attended both their weddings. Also, as we have noted, Leonard accepted George's offer to move Virginia and her nurses to

Dalingdridge, George's residence in Sussex, during Virginia's 1913-1915 illness, where they remained for several weeks.

Gerald Duckworth played a significant part in Virginia's professional life. In 1898 he founded a publishing business, and when Virginia completed her first novel, *The Voyage Out,* he agreed to publish it.[115] He also published *Night and Day,* her second novel, but it was a relief to Virginia when she and Leonard founded the Hogarth Press and she no longer had to ask Gerald to publish her books.

In 1924 Virginia saw George and Gerald, for the first time in years, at the funeral of her cousin Katherine Stephen and wrote to Violet Dickinson that it was the "shock of her life." She said that Gerald was comparatively spry but George was aged, tottery, and according to Virginia's unflattering estimate, "far gone in senile decay." She said that he could hardly speak, and speculated that he had no teeth left.[116]

George and Lady Margaret had two sons. He was knighted for his quarter century of work as Secretary to the Royal Commission on Historical Monuments,[117] and thus eventually earned his own title. He lived out his life in a manner that Virginia despised, but one that was no doubt to his own satisfaction, and died in 1934. Virginia and Leonard learned about his death from newspapers while they were on a trip, and Leonard remarked that Laura was the one they could have spared. Virginia's feelings about George's death were not quite so forthright. She wrote to Vanessa that thirty years earlier (1904), roughly the time her doctor allegedly confronted George about his attentions to her, it would have seemed strange to take the news of George's death so calmly. She admitted feeling more affection for him than she had ten years earlier (1924), or about the time of seeing him at Katherine Stephen's funeral. She hoped that someone in the family went to the funeral services and wished that she might have been able to go. Yet she also said that Vanessa's references to George had so overwhelmed her with horror, that she could hardly be "pure-minded" on the subject.[118]

Thus at the time of his death, Virginia continued to have ambivalent, if not confused, feelings about George Duckworth, as she had about Stella when Stella died. However, her own feelings, though presumably of a different alloy, were apparently as difficult for her to sort out as she professed to having found his feelings for her to be.

# 8

# The Past that Lay on the Future:
# Virginia's First Six Years

Others have provided less factual information about Virginia Woolf's first six years, than about the same period in her father's life. Apparently Virginia's mother, unlike Jane Venn Stephen, had neither the time nor the predilection for keeping a journal about her children. Fortunately, this limited information about her early childhood is supplemented by Virginia's recollections.

When all the extant information about Virginia's early childhood is studied in relation to normative information about young children as a group, one finds that her development was anomalous in both emotional and intellectual areas. One also finds some of the reasons for the anomalies and enough information to surmise others. Since she was born into and grew up in what was, in many respects, an anomalous situation, it is not surprising to find that her unusual development was caused in part by the interaction of her personality and her environment. For instance, she had great difficulty establishing satisfying means of consistently fulfilling her needs to love and be loved. This problem began early in her life and years later manifested itself in her sexual difficulties. But, some of Virginia's qualities may have had their basis in heredity, and given that, she would have been an unusual child in any family setting.

Virginia Woolf's inability to establish effective ways to

satisfy her need for love occurred despite the fact that she tried to elicit love and reassurance from others, and formed habitual, ritualistic maneuvers to entice affection. Although one cannot conclude that they were her first words, her father's early references, in his letters, to her use of language were references to overtures for affection. His first reference was when Virginia was twenty months old; Leslie wrote Julia to say that Virginia was "most affectionate," that she sat on his knee, said "kiss" and laid her cheek against his.[1] Leslie's second such reference, previously cited, points to a time when Virginia was about two years and three months of age. She tried to keep Leslie with her, he said, by "squeezing her little self" against him and saying, "Don't go, Papa."[2] It is interesting that at the end of her life, Virginia was using the same words in a playful, affectionate bid for attention. Dr. Octavia Wilberforce, Virginia's last physician, said that it had almost become a ritual between them for Virginia to say, "Don't go yet," to prolong their meetings.[3]

In 1932, Virginia explained another affectionate and teasing ritual she had learned at some time early in life. She told Ethel Smyth that her having asked whether Ethel loved her best was a ploy that had grown out of a childhood game. As a child she would ask Vanessa whether she loved her best, pulling at Vanessa's amethyst beads. Vanessa would shake her head, and Virginia would go over the beads, one by one, naming her friends and relatives, asking the question in reference to each. Virginia explained the game to Ethel because she said she didn't want Ethel to take her question seriously. She hoped Ethel would not "search her affections"[4] — a likely occurrence since Ethel was more attached to Virginia than either of them found very comfortable. Possibly Virginia was alluding to the same game two months before her death when, in a letter of February 1, 1941, she closed by asking Ethel to tell her, "quite simply," if she still loved her.

*The Past That Lay on the Future*

Sometimes Eden

One may infer from Virginia's requests for love and assurance, and from her apparent use of ritualistic games to attain them, that her parents and family failed to give her the love she wanted. The general situational reasons are obvious. There was her mother's chronic over-extension of herself to the point that, as Virginia said, it required a crisis such as the illness of a child for Julia Stephen to become a "concentrated force" focusing upon an individual child. But, as we have seen, there were times that not even a sick child kept Julia at home. There was also the fact that Virginia was seventh in a household of eight children, one of whom was psychotic and in a crisis stage during Virginia's first years.

But it is inaccurate to suppose that Virginia was a rejected, unloved child, although perhaps she felt that she was. Certainly she received enough affection to know that she wanted more, and since she was emotionally overresponsive in many ways, she may have been overly stimulated by the affection she did receive. Later in life this was true of Virginia, except in the case of sexual love. Virginia's mother was especially loving with infants although she seemed to have time to express that love consistently and in ways that Virginia could understand only during the early months of Virginia's life. Even then, there may have been inconsistencies due to Julia's health. One reference mentions Julia's continued recuperation three weeks after Virginia was born.[5] Another calls attention to her ill health ten weeks after the child was born,[6] about the time Julia decided to wean Virginia, citing her own health as the reason.[7] Since the weaning was premature and disrupted the physical closeness of the mother and child, it affected Virginia's psychological development.

There were other problems. During the first year of Virginia's life, her parents were extremely involved with Laura

Stephen. She was constantly on their minds, judging from Leslie's references to her in almost all his letters to Julia that year. Julia continued to take trips away from home after Virginia's birth, but when she went away overnight she usually took the younger Stephen children with her until Virginia was two and a half years old. About that time Julia began occasionally to leave Virginia at home with Leslie, the older children, and the servants. After that, it was relatively common for Virginia to be apart from her mother and in the care of nursery governesses or older siblings. During Virginia's second year, Adrian was born and became Julia's most beloved child. Thus throughout Virginia's infancy and childhood her immediate world was marked with change and variation—physical variation when she was taken from place to place, or psychological variation when her mother traveled without her and when she permanently transferred her attentions from Virginia to Adrian.

Virginia was loved by her father and, as we have seen, among his children she was at least a slight favorite in his affections. But his expressions of love no doubt were intermittent and inconsistent. He was least reliable as a source of affection when Virginia needed him most. Virginia's needs were greatest when her mother was absent, and Leslie tended to be at his worst. As Quentin Bell suggested (pp. 22-23), her most reliable sources of affection and most gratifying relationships were with Vanessa and, to a lesser extent, Thoby, who were approximately three and two years older than Virginia, respectively.

Thus the problem for the infant Virginia was not rejection and a total lack of love. Rather, the problem was that the love given to her was not given constantly or consistently. The interruptions and eventual disruption of her early intimacy with her mother were also serious difficulties. Virginia was never able to fully resolve her infantile longing for her mother. Consequently, she continued to need maternal love and protection, especially needing physical and relatively infantile expressions of such love. Although she wanted these most from women, she was able to accept them from Leonard Woolf.


## Problems with Language

Vanessa Bell[8] and Quentin Bell (p. 22) have each noted Virginia's late development of language. They said she did not learn to use language well until she was about three years old — an unusually late age for a precocious child. However, she was able to use language well enough to make overtures for affection and to use both flattery and insults to control people. As a letter from Stella Duckworth to Julia shows, Virginia was speaking effectively even though imperfectly and was supporting her words with appropriate actions when she was about twenty-seven months old. Stella conveyed the following story to Julia. Virginia asked Thoby for an object in his possession. When he refused her, Virginia hugged him and called him "darling sweetheart boy," only to have him refuse her again. Next, she bit him and called him "nasty, pugwash, horrid and usgusting" and succeeded in getting what she wanted.[9] Virginia's brother Adrian thought that she continued all her life to flatter people by "pretending" interest in them and that she was never able to resist "playing up to people."[10] She also became adept at characterizing people in insulting terms, as her references to George Duckworth show. Thus the incident Stella related seems prophetic on two counts.

Virginia's delay in mastering language occurred despite, or possibly because of, her intellectual precocity and her tendency to explore perceptually whatever went on around her. There are several possible psychological reasons for delay in learning language which seem to apply to Virginia. But none of them can be fully substantiated as the "cause" of her problem by factual information about her early years. The bright child's delay in learning language is sometimes symptomatic of a disturbance in the child's relationship with its mother.[11] However, the delay may also result from the extent of the child's awareness of what is going on around it and the nature of the events that it must learn to symbolize with language. If the child must learn to apply language to unusually complex, puzzling events and to objects and events about which no one will speak directly, delays and confusions in the learning process are very likely. Also, if the child forms vivid sense images of objects and events, he may find it extremely difficult to use words to describe them and may find it easier to think in sense images than in words. Thus, the child may continue to rely on sense imagery after language is mastered. This theory seems especially likely in Virginia's case since her facility and predilection for sense imagery are well substantiated in her novels.

Virginia's memories of her early years and her comments about them strongly suggest that her general intellectual development was influenced by her extraordinarily vivid sense imagery, whether or not the sense imagery accounted for her reputed slowness in learning language.[12] For example, in 1939-1940, when she was fifty-seven or fifty-eight, she could still recall sense impressions — her earliest memories, probably from her first two years — with such vividness that the contemporary scene formed a montage with the memory. She said it appeared to her that what she saw in front of her at the moment was coming to her "through" her memory.

Statements she made late in life indicate the possibility that, as a young child, Virginia found it difficult to use words to symbolize sense impressions. She said that there were times, especially during emotional stress, when sense imagery seemed to her to take control and when her mind involuntarily created "pictures" and "perceptions" with few verbal associations[13] (see

217

Chapter 10). This apparent autonomy of sense images comprised what she came to call her "scene-making ability." Her
mind seemed automatically to sum up complex situations, not
in words, but by means of relatively simplified scenes. She believed that her scene-making ability was her "natural" way of
thinking and remembering—"marking the past."[14] She cultivated it by adopting it as a method in writing, trying to think
first in images and scenes and then to describe the scenes in
words. Virginia described the method to which she aspired to
her sister in 1908, just after Vanessa's first child was born:
". . . I have imagined precisely what it is like to have a child: I
woke up, and understood, as in a revelation, the precise nature
of the pain. Now, if I could only see my novel like that—I have
been trying to arrange a method of imagining scenes, and
writing them, and wrote rather better this morning."[15]

Virginia's periodic difficulty in bringing sense impressions
and words together was indicated also by her admission that
words sometimes seemed like meaningless sounds to her. On
occasion she would read words that made no sense to her.
Then suddenly and exhilaratingly, the words would come together with her experience of the moment, thus developing
and extending the experience. Reciprocally, the words would
then seem to become "transparent" rather than "opaque"—as
if the objects experienced shone through them.[16]

Finally, the bright child's delay in learning to talk may be
increased by family pressure for the child to progress with the
acquisition of language. That too was very likely an aspect of
Virginia's situation. Vanessa Bell,[17] and later Quentin Bell (p.
22), said that Virginia's delay in learning to talk occasioned a
certain amount of worry in the family. One might surmise and
speculate that the worry would have been particularly acute in
view of Laura Stephen's history and because Laura was in a
crisis phase during Virginia's early years. One might also speculate that her parents would exert pressure on her to get her to
talk, and the kind of pressure placed upon Laura suggests

what they might have done. Unfortunately, there is too little extant information to permit anything more than speculation here.

Virginia emerged from her early difficulties with a facility for language and an enjoyment of it that showed few negative effects from her initial lag. Her father noted when she was five that she was talking fluently and enjoyed entertaining others with storytelling. He also noted that at five she wrote in "a most lovely hand." He said that each night she told him a story that did not change much from one telling to another.[18] He described one incident when Virginia stood on the windowsill and made a speech to him, her sister, and her brothers. She declaimed a long, involved story about a crow and a book until finally her audience had to "cough her down." If they had not stopped her performance, her father said in a letter to her mother the following day, Virginia would have been at it still.[19]


Idiosyncratic Ideas

Virginia Woolf recalled a number of idiosyncratic and mythic ideas from early childhood which suggest that she was impressed with, indeed almost overpowered by, the vividness of her own sensations. Describing her memories years later and in the sophisticated language of an adult, she said that sights and sounds seemed to be the product of a peculiarly intimate union of the world and her mind, as if the world broke through and precipitated its contents into her mind. It seemed to her that her mind was a receptacle into which moments of time and segments of space actually entered. Such moments would then remain forever within her mind. They were so real and lasting that she was sometimes convinced that they were "still going on" in the external world or that they might be recovered and their former being reinstated.[20]

According to Virginia Woolf's recollections, therefore, her

preoccupation with the preservation and recovery of the moment, so much an objective during the writing of her novels, had its foundation in her early conception of the relationship between mind and the surrounding world. Her belief, that the remembered world could still be "going on" in the world of shared reality, figured in her periods of madness as well as in her novels. For example, in 1909, in a disturbed state of mind, she made a precipitous departure from London for Cornwall, making the seemingly innocent statement that "it was all still going on" in Cornwall.[21]

Virginia did not always think that her mind and the external world were intimately fused by sensory experience. There were times as a child when she felt instead that a vast empty space separated her from the objects of her perception, particularly from other persons. After she learned to use language, words occasionally seemed to echo and reverberate between herself and others across a vast emptiness that lay between them.[22]

In her 1939-1940 memoir, Virginia referred to other naive, idiosyncratic ideas about the nature of the universe, ideas resembling mythic cosmologies that have evolved in primitive cultures. She imagined physical worlds within worlds, and worlds beyond the world of immediate time and space. "World" was a word she used in many ways, for example, as a metaphor for personality: she herself was a small world within a larger, safe, happy world "created" by her mother. From other worlds, especially those apart from her mother, dangerous and cataclysmic events might come. Virginia's naive cosmology is implicit in some of her novels. Sometimes she referred to her cosmology explicitly in a manuscript, but deleted the explicit references in favor of enigmatic allusions in the published novel. For example, in the manuscript versions of *The Voyage Out,* she referred to a world other than the immediate world of space and time, a better and more spiritual world of peace and sanity, of "beautiful drowned statues," and of music whose "notes sounded high in the air."[23] In the published novel she only referred to Rachel Vinrace's unexplained longing to be flung into the sea.

Virginia's naive cosmology may have been influenced by Vanessa, who when she was five and Virginia was two, asked their father whether St. Ives and London were different worlds, each with its own separate sky.[24] The fact that Virginia retained her mythic, primitive cosmology all her life suggests that as a child she did not talk about it, at least not with her father whose extreme valuation of rational, logical thought would have led him to try to correct her. She was sufficiently impressed with his intolerance for other than strictly "factual" thought to have learned to keep her naive, mythic ideas from his notice.

Virginia had another set of idiosyncratic notions, about life and death, that would have been at least as antipathetic to her father as her naive cosmology. Nevertheless, it is probable that he was in a measure responsible for these ideas. Apparently Virginia began her efforts to understand the incomprehensible fact of death because she heard her parents talk about death and people who had died. Her preoccupation with death began very early in life. In her 1939-1940 memoir, she said it seemed to her as a child that death was a completion and an establishment, for all time, of the person's life. Where that life was established after death and where it therefore continued varied in her conception of the matter. Sometimes it was established in the immediate world of sensation, sometimes in one of the other worlds she imagined. Often the person's life was established in Virginia's mind or memory, and when that was the case, it seemed to her that the person could "continue" or remain what he had been in life only if Virginia did not imagine him still in existence. For that reason, her mother was an exception. Virginia said in her 1939-1940 memoir that after Julia Stephen's death, she kept her alive in imagination and fantasy, "seeing" and "hearing" her everyday. In that way, Virginia constantly changed her memories of her mother until after she wrote *To the Lighthouse* some thirty years later. The imaginary mother whom she kept alive through fantasy seems to have been more real to Virginia than Julia herself had been in life, for Virginia insisted in her 1939-1940 memoir that while her mother lived she was principally a diffuse, extracorporeal presence.

Wherever the "life" of the dead person was established in Virginia's childish conception of death, unless she changed it, as in the instance of her mother, the life would remain permanently what it had been, its space and time preserved as a small bubble of sensory experience might be preserved inside her mind. Like the bubble of reality, the person, as he had been in life, might somehow be recoverable. Evidently Virginia was trying, even as a small child, to work out immortality schemes like those expressed as myth and metaphor in her novels. For example, on the mythic level of *To the Lighthouse,* one manifestation of Mrs. Ramsay continues after death, walking off into Elysian fields, followed first by "her companion, a shade" (pp. 269-270) and then by Prue and Andrew when they too die (p. 299). The myth of the novel made it possible for Mrs. Ramsay to return and sit where she had been sitting in life, so that Lily Briscoe might complete the painting of her and James (p. 300). Again, on the mythic level of *Jacob's Room,* Jacob continues to exist after death in his surroundings and in the universe of things he had experienced in life, and did so because that was how he had existed before death.


Ecstasy, Fear, Gloom and Shame

The intensity and variation of Virginia's emotional reactions and the events that stimulated her emotions comprised other significant and portentous aspects of her early experience. Quentin Bell wrote about (p. 24) Virginia's occasional rages, which her sister thought she might have enjoyed, and her times of oppressive gloom, which her sister and brothers thought reflected her displeasure toward them. "Then, as always, she knew how to 'create an atmosphere,' an atmosphere of thunderous and oppressive gloom.... It was done without words; somehow her brothers and sisters were made to feel that she had raised a cloud above their heads from which...the fires of heaven might burst...." Vanessa Bell thought that in creating these seasons of gloom, Virginia was manifesting a "Stephen characteristic," and one may surmise that she meant a "Leslie Stephen" characteristic.[25]

Virginia said little about rage in her recorded memories of her early years, except in referring in her 1908 memoir to occasional "stormy passions" between herself and her sister and brothers. However, in her 1897 diary and her 1939-1940 memoir, she referred to many times of rage, beginning with the first breakdown at age thirteen. Her early recollections substantiate and provide insight into her gloomy moods which, from her viewpoint, were exceedingly more complicated than anyone could have guessed. She recalled also times of ecstasy, of paralyzing fear, and of shame. Although her emotions were strong and vacillating, her early life was not dominated by wild swings from one extreme emotion to another. Apparently she was not a "disturbed child," or at least not disturbed most of the time. Rather, her more extreme emotions seem to have been a deviation from her usual state of general contentment, if not placidity, which made the emotions all the more impressive to her and dramatic to others. In her 1939-1940 memoir she referred to some of her emotions, even pleasant ones, as "shocks," and said also that they had the power to make her feel "in being" in contrast to the less eventful times that made her feel what she called in retrospect "nonbeing."

*The Past That Lay on the Future*

Some of Virginia's earliest recollections, recounted in her 1939-1940 memoir, were not of gloom, but of ecstasy and elation which were intimately yet diffusely part of her sensory experience. The ecstatic times she recalled took place at St. Ives and, as she described them, were similar to scenes she developed and explored in early prologues and chapters of *The Waves*. She said that she was ecstatic and rapturous when she felt dominant over her world. One infers also from her descriptions that these highly pleasant emotions came with synesthetic sensation. That is, she was enormously and pleasurably excited when sights, sounds, and other sensations seemed unified with each other. She was elated when her inner sensations seemed to be fused with sensations coming from the world around her. She remembered being intensely aware of the diffusion and unity of all her sensations and emphasized that a sense of unity and wholeness was essential to her feeling of pleasure. While recounting her pleasurable memories, she associated the sense of wholeness with her writing, saying that the rapture of writing for her came from putting parts together to achieve wholeness and to take away the separateness of things in her world.

Virginia recounted three pleasurable, synesthetic memories. In the first she was lying in bed, but felt as if she were within and coextensive with the totality of her sensations and the objects that stimulated them. She said it was like lying in a grape, where she was filmed in transparent yellow light, with ryhthmic sounds of waves pervading the whole. These sensations were fused with similarly rhythmic sounds of a window blind blowing to and fro in the breeze. Birds were calling and their calls fell through the blue gummy veil of air and were not separate from the other sounds. Flowers were a part of the scene and she was aware of her mother's presence, more than she was able to see her, on the balcony outside her room. Her feelings of ecstasy seemed to pervade the entire world around her and were not localized within her own body. Other than feeling ecstatic she had no awareness of self and called it a memory "without a self."

The second such memory was also a memory "without a self," and one recalled with such vividness very late in her life that it seemed to form a montage with the scene immediately before her. It differed from the first in that it included smells as well as sights and sounds and in that her feeling was "rapture," which she made a point of distinguishing from "ecstasy." The second memory seemed to her, on the whole, to be more robust and sensual, as if the diffuse mixture of smells from apples and flowers, of sounds from bees humming, and of sights of everything around her, was so voluptuous it pressed against a membrane. Her third memory of pleasant emotion and synesthetic sensation was more fragmentary than the first two; she mentioned only her pleasant "shock" upon seeing the whole "compose itself" of earth and flower, each being a part of the other.

Information about how infants develop confirms that there was nothing odd in Virginia's synesthetic experience of the world or in the diffuse relationship between what she saw, heard, smelled, and felt. The work of Piaget and Werner shows that rather than its being unusual and strange, synesthetic experience and related phenomena are typical and probably universal in infants.[26] What seems to have set the young Virginia apart from most children was the intensity of her emotional reactions to such experiences and her ability to retain her vivid and detailed memories of them.

Virginia Woolf's recollections of paralyzing fear and of depression and gloom seem to date from a later time than her memories of ecstasy and rapture. Her fear was associated with several things. She remembered often being afraid when trying to fall asleep at bedtime.[27] Also she was extremely frightened —inexplicably so as far as she could remember—by merely seeing a puddle of water in her path. When she saw the puddle everything became "unreal" for her; paralyzed with fear, she would be unable to move until she, like Rhoda in *The Waves* (pp. 19, 46, 113), touched something. She said in her diary that seeing the puddle made her question her identity and ask ". . . what am I?"[28] Virginia said in her 1939-1940 memoir that she felt both fear and gloom when an "idiot boy" sprang up before the Stephen children, with his hand out, and was given all their candy. She was so overcome later that night in the bath, by feelings of horror, sadness, collapse, and passivity, that it was like being struck by a sledge hammer. A veritable avalanche of meaning had precipitated itself upon her, and she could only huddle in her end of the bath, unable to tell Nessa, at the other end, what was wrong.

Also in her 1939-1940 memoir are two other examples of Virginia's overwhelming gloom and depression. She was depressed when she and Thoby were fighting, and she began to think — why should she hurt anyone? She found that she could no longer hit Thoby but let him go on striking her, without resisting him. She was depressed again when she heard her father tell her mother that someone Virginia knew by sight had killed himself. Her memory of this incident inexplicably had an apple tree in it and was used in *The Waves* as part of Neville's story (pp. 17-18). Both of these memories have the common element of persons being hurt, and in both Virginia no longer felt in control of her situation. Therefore they contrast with her memories of feeling distinctly dominant at times of ecstasy and rapture.

Virginia referred to both the pleasant and unpleasant memories as "shocks" but said that the more painful shocks appeared sometimes to come from some other world. It was as if the painful experiences came from what she called "nonreality" and "nonbeing" that were hidden behind the appearance of the scene around her. She related the nonreality and nonbeing to her writing, saying that words could get at them, change them to reality and being, and take away their ability to hurt. Later she came to feel that despite her sense of annihilation, the painful shocks were the universe's way of expressing respect for her, of telling her that she was not contingent, not the result of some mere protoplasmic accident.

Evidently shame became part of Virginia Woolf's childhood experience at a time somewhat later than did the other strong emotions. She said in both her 1908 and 1939-1940 memoirs that her earliest shame was associated with looking at her reflection in a mirror and, in the later memoir, with Gerald Duckworth's exploration of her genitalia with his hand, an occurrence that she attributed to her sixth year. She thought it relatively irrational that she should have felt shame in either instance, particularly upon seeing her reflection. She conjectured that her shame in that case may have been caused by her violation of a "tomboy code" she had made with Vanessa. Or it may have been due, she said, to an "ancestral" fear of beauty "inherited" from her father who had no sense for the sounds of words, for pictures, or for music.

Virginia said that her shame, when Gerald explored her body, was irrational because no one had ever taught her to be ashamed of the sexual parts of her body. Consequently she believed that such shame was instinctual or, to borrow Jung's term, archetypal. She thought that she'd inherited these peculiarly ancestral memories, and thus that she was "centuries old." But she had to conclude that her shame might not fully be explained by any or all of her conjectures. She was sure, however, that her early shame partly explained her later sexual difficulties and her ability to enjoy only nonsexual raptures, in her words, raptures not associated with her own body.

# 9

# Imagination and Language, Private and Public: Virginia's Later Childhood

Between the ages of six and thirteen, Virginia continued to develop the kind of imagination exemplified by the idiosyncratic notions she had formed in her earlier years. The results were both ill and good. On one hand, she retained radically idiosyncratic and mythic ideas that in the future became exaggerated still further and sometimes took her dangerously far from reality. On the other hand, she developed, on a private level, the form of imagination she later utilized poetically and to some degree exorcised in writing her novels. As a child, Virginia was not shut off in an autistic world of her own thought. Although she kept many of her ideas to herself, like most children she developed both her imagination and a language to express it, mainly within the context of shared social experience. Her sharing had the effect of bringing some of her mythic constructions closer to the world of reality as others saw and understood it. Even so — again for ill and good — by expressing her imagination selectively, she was able to avoid being reined in by social conventions. Her father heard some of her stories when she was very young but as she grew older, she told her more imaginative stories chiefly to the small, private audience of her sister and brothers. As the publisher of the family newspaper, however, she was willing to share aspects of her imagination with an audience that included her parents and other adults. With the latter she had to learn to be circumspect and restrained as she grew older, while with the former she could indulge in myth and fantasy with few restrictions.

It was possible for Virginia to have two audiences within the Stephen household because the younger Stephen children were sufficiently apart from the adults and their older half-siblings to comprise a society, almost a subculture, which Virginia called " 'us four.' "[1] In this respect, Virginia's childhood resembled that of the Brontës, although the Stephen children were not nearly so detached from the family and the rest of society as the Brontës.[2] Nor did Virginia, her sister, and brothers elaborate their fantasies to the extent the Brontës did, who imagined entire legendary worlds and societies. However, one suspects from Virginia's references to "Elvedon" in *The Waves* (p. 12), that she would have liked to develop and organize her fantasies more extensively.

There was a certain deliberateness in the way Virginia developed her imagination and language in childhood — deliberateness born of the fact that as a very young child she firmly identified herself with language and its applications. Long before she was six years old, it was "settled" within her mind and accepted by her family that she would be a writer. Vanessa Bell said that she could not recall a time when it was not understood between them that Virginia would become a writer and she a painter.[3] Virginia's identification with writing was so strong by the time she was thirteen that she could seriously characterize the two disastrous years after her mother's death as years when her writing was interrupted.[4]

An impulse toward art as strong and all-consuming as Virginia's inevitably comes from a complex of factors and has roots too numerous and too deep for one to discover them. Virginia herself likened her writing to an instinct and to the way sap rises in a tree.[5] Certainly one cannot hope to explain genius such as hers. But it is possible to identify some of the conditions and events during her middle childhood, and to deduce others, that encouraged her increasing involvement with language and with her own imagination. Among these events, a "decision" to be a writer was probably secondary and almost certainly derivative of earlier experience, much of it apparently as natural to her as an "instinct." Her development of her imagination in childhood came first of all from her enjoyment of it, from her fascination with language, and from her belief that there was something literally magical about words. These attitudes and beliefs long preceded the "decision" that she would become a writer. Apparently, she became the family story-teller, not because she had set her future course in literature, but because of relatively spontaneous activity on her part. Examples of such activity were cited by her father when she was five years old; he said that she stood in the window and made a speech, or told him a story each night. Such occasions seem to have led her and her family to think that she would become a writer.

Her story-telling also gained her a sense of intimacy with others and earned their approbation and love. Thus it became for her an important way of relating to others and of expressing her affection for the people around her. Most important, her spontaneous stories and her involvement with language provided an identity. "Being a writer" became a way to think of herself, her most positive and only stable sense of self, both in childhood and later in life. All these factors combined to move her in the direction of literature as a profession.

## Imagination and First, Failed Love

One of Virginia's more private uses of her imagination during childhood came from the peculiarly limited nature of her relationship with her mother and was manifested in her strange memories of Julia Stephen. Her mother lived until Virginia was thirteen and was, of course, a major influence on her during her childhood although she was not as intimate or constant a part of her life as Virginia wished and needed. Yet Virginia persisted in saying that she remembered her mother chiefly as an atmospheric, almost spiritual force. She said repeatedly in her 1908 and 1939-1940 memoirs that her mother was an extracorporeal presence to her, that she had been elusive, unfocused, unlocalized. It is impossible that that was Virginia's only, or even her chief, experience of her mother and the entire characterization of her mother as Mrs. Ramsay in *To the Lighthouse* established that it was not, in actuality, her chief memory of her. Yet it was easier for Virginia to acknowledge as her memories the strange notions of a generalized, atmospheric presence than to acknowledge other recollections of her mother. She said, for example, that it seemed strange to her that Mrs. Ramsay was a product of her own memory. She felt that she could not have known her mother well enough to be sure she was like Mrs. Ramsay and had to be reassured by Vanessa that Julia had indeed been similar to her literary counterpart.[6]

In her 1939-1940 memoir, Virginia admitted other memories of her mother. Many of these memories indicate that when she was not thinking of her mother as an atmospheric presence, she was remembering fragmentary sense impressions of her, including many impressions of her mother in movement, expressing her attitudes through her posture. Her first memory of her mother was not a memory of her as a whole person. In the memory Virginia was sitting on her mother's lap while they rode on a train or omnibus, and her chief impression was of the red, blue, and purple flowers on her mother's dress, like anemones on a black background. The memory belies Virginia's belief that her mother "always" wore black.[7] From a later time, Virginia could recall her mother's hands; her jewelry, including the sound of bracelets given to her by James Russell Lowell; and what Virginia called her mother's exquisite and "fleeting femininities." She remembered her mother sometimes coming to her in the night, when Virginia often wished for her. But she recalled mostly a hand shading a candle and a voice telling her to think of beautiful things and to try to sleep. Virginia introduced that memory into *To the Lighthouse* (p. 171) in the scene where Mrs. Ramsay tells her youngest daughter, Cam, that she "must go to sleep and dream of lovely palaces. . . ."

Virginia said in her 1939-1940 memoir that she could not remember whether she had been sufficiently aware of her mother to see the physical beauty that everyone immediately noticed and found most characteristic of Julia. She had known that others thought her mother beautiful and had been snobbish about the fact. But she herself could not recall the beauty except simply as a part of the whole of a woman who seemed first, "a universal force" and after that, her own mother. Virginia was more aware of her mother's physical expressiveness, but could not quite isolate and analyze it. On one specific occasion she had known merely from her mother's posture and the way she turned her body that one of Julia's patients had died.

Although she could remember that instance of wordless communication, Virginia said little about conversations with her mother, and specifically recorded in her 1939-1940 memoir that when she thought about her mother, it was difficult "to put words in her mouth." She did remember an attempt to get information from her mother about how Leslie proposed to her. When she asked about her father's proposal, her mother looked surprised, turned away, and did not answer. Virginia related only a few times when her mother spoke directly to her, although there must have been countless such occasions. Most of these references were in her 1939-1940 memoir. She told of one brief exchange to show how direct Julia could be — which contrasts with Virginia's usual recollection of her as a diffuse "presence" — and to show that Julia disliked affection. When Virginia was about to go to a party, her mother told her that she couldn't go if she held her head "like that," in a manner Julia considered affected. This suggests that Julia may have contributed to her extreme shyness about social occasions. Virginia also wrote that the last time she saw her mother alive, Julia admonished her to stand up straight. Another reference to Julia's speaking to her gave Virginia "a dream of a summer's afternoon." The incident occurred when they were walking together. Passing the site of Little Holland House, Julia remarked, "here it all was," calling up in Virginia fantasies of her mother as a young woman.

Concomitant with Virginia's memories of her mother was her persistent belief that Julia's presence had miraculous power over the entire "happy world of childhood," within which the "world" of Virginia's own personality was enclosed. Specifically, Virginia believed that her mother had the power to keep the world whole and free of danger, which Virginia never felt able to do for herself. Virginia mentioned this belief in her 1939-1940 memoir, but described it best in the early scenes of *To the Lighthouse* (pp. 9-12) where she attributed the same belief to James in his relationship with Mrs. Ramsay. James feels blissful and secure when he is with his mother, until the presence of Mr. Ramsay obtrudes. When Mrs. Ramsay dies, in the second part of *To the Lighthouse,* the world falls into chaos, disunity, and meaninglessness — Virginia's poetic and mythic representation of her own emotional disturbance after her mother's death.

In her 1939-1940 memoir Virginia also said that there were times when she was nearly overcome with fear for her mother's safety. When Julia was out late, Virginia would watch in agony for her to come home, for fear some accident had killed her —

behavior reminiscent of the accounts of Julia's own anxiety when her first husband was late in arriving. Virginia said that her father would notice her fear or catch her peeping through the curtains to see whether her mother were coming, and would tell her not to be so anxious and nervous.

The explanation for Virginia Woolf's odd memories of her mother seems to lie in Virginia's poignant need to recapture memories from her earliest years when she was physically close to her mother and in a symbiotic relationship with her. Or so one may infer from the quality of her memories and from her insistence that her mother was a generalized presence who was able to keep her world safe and whole. Virginia's experience of her mother as an extracorporeal presence is strikingly parallel to the way the tiny infant knows the mother in the first months of postnatal life.[8] It is then that the child, because of its physiological and experiential immaturity, can know the mother only as an amorphous, extracorporeal presence, coextensive with the child's bodily sensations. Since the child can have no specific awareness of the boundaries of its body and self, the mother is like an atmospheric presence without any particular bodily limits. If the child's relationship with the mother is good, the child experiences the presence of the mother as bliss and ecstasy and a lengthy absence as danger and threat, or worse, as annihilation of its own being. Therefore, if my inferences are correct, Virginia's persistent memory of her mother as a generalized, atmospheric presence that kept the world whole and safe, testifies to an especially good relationship with her mother in infancy. But it also suggests that the sudden interruptions in the relationship would have made Virginia feel abandoned and endangered. Finally, it supports the belief that Virginia's relationship with her mother was disrupted permanently before she was able to develop confidence in her ability to survive without her mother.

## Second Love

Virginia's recollections of her sister Vanessa in childhood were quite unlike those of her mother, and they leave no doubt that Vanessa was, in effect, a surrogate for her mother, and thus provided Virginia's second and more successful love relationship. Moreover, her recollections of Vanessa reveal some of the reasons for the successful relationship, for on the practical day-to-day level, Vanessa was more important to Virginia than Julia. For example, Vanessa helped Virginia develop her imagination, through healthier uses of it than Virginia's fantasies about her mother. In later years, Virginia would have pleasant moments "making up" her portraits of Vanessa.[9] But in childhood, fantasies of Vanessa were not necessary, for she was there most of the time, a flesh and blood person, not an imagined, extracorporeal, spiritual presence. She was localized, an embodied person who spent most of her time with Virginia, who slept in the same room, and was bathed with her.[10] When Virginia was quite small, Vanessa loved and protected, soothed and petted her.[11] A letter Leslie wrote to Julia when Virginia was a two-year-old suggests the manner in which Vanessa comforted Virginia. He said that Virginia had become more a part of the nursery group since Vanessa and Thoby started rubbing her down with scents and putting her to bed.[12] The rubbing may well have been in imitation of Julia, whose "rubs" in her capacity as nurse were greatly favored by Leslie and by Mrs. Jackson.[13]

Vanessa took maternal responsibility for both Virginia and Thoby, insofar as that was possible considering the slight differences in their ages. In Virginia's case it was sufficiently possible that Virginia formed a deep attachment to her, quite literally a feeling that she was incomplete without her. The attachment was mutual in childhood and involved a verbal

235

agreement, at first the "tomboy pact." After the deaths of Julia and Stella, Virginia said in her 1939-1940 memoir, she felt that she and Vanessa almost comprised a common personality, a small world within and separate from the larger social world, as a nucleus is an entity within a cell. She also referred to herself and Vanessa as a "conspiracy." Her attachment to Vanessa remained in attenuated form throughout Virginia's life. Sometimes the strength and nature of the attachment made Vanessa uncomfortable. Virginia continued at least until her marriage to Leonard, to expect inordinate expressions of affection from Vanessa and to feel endangered without her emotional support. For example, expecting to see Vanessa the next day, Virginia wrote to her: "Shall you kiss me tomorrow? Yes, yes, yes! Ah, I cannot bear being without you. I was thinking today of my greatest happiness, a walk along a cliff by the sea, and you at the end of it."[14] In a letter dated a week later she recounted to Vanessa a fantasy of falling off the cliff and being killed while walking alone there, suggesting the danger she felt without Vanessa.[15]

Vanessa slept in the same room with Virginia during most of their childhood. Her presence was particularly important since Virginia was often anxious and wakeful at night and as a young child began experiencing the "night terrors" that recurred all her life. In her 1939-1940 memoir Virginia recounted a memory that parallels an event in *To the Lighthouse* (pp. 171-172) where Cam is frightened by the skull on the wall, which Mrs. Ramsay shrouds with her green shawl. In the actual memory Virginia said that she was frequently frightened of the dark in the nursery that even in daylight sometimes seemed to be a vast empty space. She was especially frightened when the fire was left burning in the grate in the nursery, its light flickering on the wall. Adrian liked the fire and the flickering light. They made a compromise whereby the fire was shaded over by a towel placed on the fender. Virginia could still see the flickering light and was terrified by it. Sometimes she would lie there and try to bring her mother to her by wishing. When her mother did not come, Vanessa was there and Virginia often awoke her, to have company and to hear the sound of a voice.

During middle childhood or perhaps earlier, Virginia began telling bedtime stories to tide herself and her sister and brothers over the difficult time of waiting to fall to sleep.[16] Virginia may have begun them in imitation of her mother; she said in *To the Lighthouse* (p. 172) that Mrs. Ramsay would sometimes tell Cam stories of beautiful things to think about while falling to sleep. More likely they were simply other instances of Virginia's spontaneous stories.

As they grew a little older, Virginia and Vanessa began to compare some of their impressions and ask each other about things that puzzled them. Leslie Stephen, who was interested in animals, would have been amused by their conversation about cats. Vanessa inquired whether black cats had tails. After a pause during which the question seemed to Virginia to reverberate through a vast and formerly silent space, she answered that they did not.[17] Leslie would have been even more interested, one may assume, in the conversation Vanessa Bell[18] and, later, Quentin Bell reported (p. 26) between the two girls when Virginia was past six. While Virginia and Vanessa were jumping around naked in the bath, Virginia asked which of their parents Vanessa preferred. Upon being told that Vanessa preferred her mother, Virginia announced that she preferred her father.

There were many times, in childhood and later, when Virginia used Vanessa as a standard for comparison and did not always accept their differences as matter-of-factly as she evidently did when they compared preferences in parents. Virginia knew that such comparisons are common in childhood as a means whereby children discover what they are and are not like. She felt also that, more than most children, she had lacked chances to make such comparisons. For example, she said in her 1939-1940 memoir, that she had never known whether she was bright or dull, intellectually; whether pretty; and whether emotionally warm or cold. She blamed this lack of self-knowledge on the fact that she had been deprived of the experience of going to school where she could have compared herself with other children.

As she indicated in her 1908 memoir, Virginia did not usually show up well when she compared herself with Vanessa. She thought Vanessa more practical and wise and that Vanessa had more common sense and greater intellectual honesty. In Virginia's estimation, Vanessa was also more closely in touch with reality; Vanessa could not see everything but, in contrast to herself, could be counted on not to see things that were not there.

Virginia found both actual and symbolic differences between herself and Vanessa. A very real difference between the two girls was in their attitudes toward themselves. This difference was revealed when they saw their reflections. As a child, Vanessa could "look steadily" in the mirror and would become "strangely excited" by her reflection. By contrast, Virginia, who was also a beautiful child, was morbidly ashamed of her reflection and could only look at herself in the mirror when she was alone. When Virginia tried in her 1939-1940 memoir to sort out the meaning of her shame, she related it to her embarrassment when being fitted for clothing, especially underclothing, and to her fears about dressing up and going to parties — fears that George Duckworth exacerbated by trying to "bring her out" socially in the years after her mother's death. Virginia was frightened as well as ashamed to look in the mirror. Sometimes, she said, when she looked in the mirror, or possibly only when she dreamed of looking in a mirror, she would see both her own reflection and a horrible, animallike face looming over her shoulder.

Stories to Go to Sleep By

Vanessa was the most important member of the relatively uncritical audience that listened to Virginia's imaginative stories. Before this audience, composed of her sister and brothers, Virginia allowed her imagination to range with few restrictions. The other Stephen children encouraged Virginia to invent fantastic, mythical stories, but in a playful, make-believe manner that reminded all of them that the fantasies were not "real." Virginia's stories entertained and amused them — though probably not as much as they entertained Virginia herself — lulled them to sleep, and, at the same time, won their admiration and approval. Best of all for Virginia, one suspects, the stories elicited their participation, for as an audience they shared in and accepted Virginia's imaginative inventions. The fact that the other children were occasionally coinventors of the fantasies probably served to heighten Virginia's sense of intimacy with them. Since Virginia often told the stories at bedtime, consistently one of her more anxious times, her storytelling gave her a feeling of closeness with others when she greatly needed it.[19]

Virginia began her bedtime stories when all four of the Stephen children slept in the same nursery, and continued them after she was ten years old, when Thoby had gone to school and she and Vanessa slept alone in the nursery. Some of her stories took on a ritualistic quality and therefore were repeated nightly only with minor modifications. A good example is a story from about Virginia's tenth year, the story was about the Dilke family who lived next door to the Stephens on Hyde Park Gate. Quentin Bell said (p. 25) the story was begun each night by an invocation from Vanessa. "'Clementé, dear child...' this said in a very affected drawl and then Virginia becoming Clementé would begin: gold would be discovered beneath the nursery floor and this treasure trove would purchase enormous meals of bacon and eggs, the favourite diet of the young at 22

Hyde Park Gate; and so it went on, a mounting fantasy becoming grander and vaguer, until Clementé slept and her audience had to wait until the following night for her next adventure." Virginia associated the stories with the comparative wealth of the Dilke family relative to the Stephen family. She said, for example, that, unlike Julia, Mrs. Dilke got many new dresses[20] — apparently as a child Virginia at least half believed her father's talk of impending penury.

Inventing stories was not left only to bedtime. Virginia, her sister, and brothers made up stories on their long, sometimes dull walks in London and while they played at St. Ives. Virginia's references to these stories in a letter to Vanessa[21] and in her 1939-1940 memoir show that they included specific elements of mythic thought, and that they tended to be pleasant, vividly imagined fantasies. Some of them included references to "familiars," apparently Virginia's version of other childrens' imaginary playmates. "Harry Hoe" and "Jim Joe" were two familiars who owned flocks of animals, a definite attraction to the Stephen children who were so interested in animals. In other stories, the familiars were more fantastic and miraculous, and some were not altogether pleasant or attractive. For example, there was a fantasy about two evil spirits who lived in a trash heap at St. Ives and came and went through the escallonia hedge. Virginia recalled that she had ventured to tell her mother and James Russell Lowell about the two evil spirits. In *To the Lighthouse* (p. 84) she adapted this memory to Cam, who tells Mrs. Ramsay about evil spirits, and suggested that it helped convince Mrs. Ramsay that Cam had a strange mind. Some of the familiars in Virginia's stories could fly, and some she evidently imagined to be almost totally "spiritual." There was, for example, the "great mother of all familiars" whose "presence," Virginia said, she could feel "behind the hill" in 1918, in a seeming extension of, or at least association with, her professed memories of her mother.[22]

Virginia imagined the familiars sometimes as if they were part of a fantasy world and sometimes as if they were within the physical world Virginia experienced daily. Virginia's fragmentary references to her stories imply that, for her, fantasy creatures and a fantasy world tended to merge with the physical world. As a result, the physical world took on mythical and miraculous qualities of the fantastic one. When she was happy, perhaps as she played under the tall ferns near St. Ives, her fantasies made the real world seem pleasant. But the fantasies could become frightening, as they did when she saw or dreamed that she saw the evil head looking over her shoulder in the mirror, and when she imagined she saw a man sitting on her dead mother's bed. Especially in times of stress, fantasy creatures seemed to come uninvited into the real world as Virginia knew it. At those times, her highly perceptualized imagination and her extremely vivid imagery made it especially difficult for her to distinguish what was really out there, in the external world beyond herself, and what came from her own mind.

## Private Language

Virginia's more fantastic stories helped her to affirm and extend her intimacy with her sister in childhood. She accentuated that sense of intimacy significantly by a kind of private language that grew up between the sisters, as Quentin Bell noted (p. 23), or more specifically, a language of private reference. "...[F]rom a very early age, [Virginia] understood something of the magic of friendship, the peculiar intimacy which comes to those who have a private language and private jokes.... She not only loved her sister but, it would seem, loved the affectionate relationship between them.... [T]he charm of sisterly love lay simply in the intimate communication with another being, the enjoyment of character."

Certainly Virginia's sister did not lack for imagination, but from all evidence Vanessa had a more rational and less mythic imagination than Virginia's. As they grew up, these differences in their manner of thinking became more pronounced. Vanessa came to consider herself the most rational of the Stephens, as perhaps she was.[23] But Virginia's need for intimacy with Vanessa did not decrease; rather, it became even more vital to her after the deaths of her mother and Stella, and still later, after those of her father and Thoby. Virginia's need to be close to Vanessa was manifest, among other ways, by her continued use of the private language with Vanessa and by her efforts to get Vanessa to share in her fantasies. Many of her extant letters to Vanessa include instances of private language and private reference. Many of them also include implicit pleas to Vanessa to share Virginia's fantasies, pleas sometimes made even as Virginia acknowledged that Vanessa probably would not comply. She was correct. Vanessa's letters to her reveal a practical, direct, and much less fantastic imagination. They also confirm Vanessa's reiterated statement that she was less capable with words than Virginia, but make it evident that she was needlessly apologetic on that score.[24]

Several letters from Virginia to Vanessa in 1908 show how Virginia's mythic imagination entered into her adult relationship with her sister. Drawing from her more mythic thought, Virginia said she believed she could "manage whole fortnights, with outspread wings, at great altitude, with no descent. Has it ever struck you that the way we take our pleasures is very unlike?"[25] She continued to say that she had tried to write more conventionally after Vanessa had said that she wrote careless letters. "But the truth is that we are too intimate for letter writing; style dissolves, as though in a furnace; all the blood and bones come through. . . ." Three days later she wrote as if she expected Vanessa to understand what sounded like mythic and private references.[26] "By this mornings post . . . I got a card, with musical hieroglyphs; halfway through breakfast, I sang my song to keep myself in spirits, and saw it, as though in a mirror before me — mocking me. I at once changed my tune, and sang the second song, which no one knows. Tell the Chipmonk [Vanessa's husband, Clive Bell] his malice is thwarted; I sang for half an hour, and all the house crouched on the step to listen."

In letters written the following year, when Virginia was in Bayreuth, her references and language continued to be private and relatively mythic. In one letter, for example, Virginia's purpose was to get Vanessa's affection and reassurance (symbolized by food) without which Virginia (the Ape) becomes demoralized, upset, and angry. ". . . [T]he quickest Ape brain always flags after dinner. It is thought that it is partly a recollection of struggle for food, when in a wild state. I should point out to you, that it is very dangerous to allow these animals to go long uncared for: they are apt to return to their savage ways."[27]


## Animals and People in Private and Public Language

Virginia's use of animal references and her association of animals with people was a fairly specific manifestation of the private language of her youth. Evidently the animal references originated in the Uncle Remus and other play of Leslie with his children when they were quite small. Whatever their source, they were prominent in the relationship between Virginia and her sister, and also in Virginia's later private and public writing. Family nicknames exemplified the animal references and Virginia's and Vanessa's practice of associating animals with people in their private language. Often Virginia was called "Goat," "Billy Goat," "Billy," or "William." She was also called "Beast," "Ape," and "My little Monkey," by Vanessa, who in turn was called "Dolphin" by Virginia and others.

Some of the nicknames were not entirely private, of course. "Goat" as a nickname for Virginia was used by people other than the sisters, including Virginia's mother, whose last words to her were the admonition to stand up straight, "my little goat."[28] Vanessa's nickname, "Dolphin," was not exclusive to her relationship with Virginia. It was used by Vanessa in correspondence with her husband, Clive Bell.

Virginia introduced animal references into her relationship with many persons other than her sister, as an aspect of a private language she developed with them. She was "Sparroy" (half bird, half other animal) and "Wallaby" to Violet Dickinson, who was "mother kangaroo." Virginia was "Mandrill" or "Mandy" to Leonard Woolf; he was "Mongoose" to her in the early days of their marriage. She was "Potto" (possibly a mouse) in her letters to Vita Sackville-West. Sometimes she called Vita "Donkey" or "Donkey West," or "the insect." Virginia did not assign a specific nickname to Dame Ethel Smyth but frequently called her such things as the "uncastrated tom cat" and the "wild boar."

The nicknames were the least private and most understandable of Virginia's animal references in her private language, although it is not always very clear just why certain names were adopted. For example, it is by no means apparent why Virginia was called "Goat." It is a puzzling and seemingly uncomplimentary nickname, just as "Cow" seems a strange, almost insulting nickname for Stella Duckworth. Quentin Bell said (p. 24) that "Goat" referred to Virginia's tendencies as a child to be "incalculable, eccentric and prone to accidents," and to fall into misadventures that caused her sister and brothers to laugh at her, and the adults in the family to laugh with her. If so, then to her sister and brothers at least, the nickname was uncomplimentary. However, there is little indication that Virginia herself resented the nickname. Rather, she often used it to sign her letters and otherwise refer to herself, which implies that she liked it or, at least, accepted it. If so, probably it was because, as an instance of private language, the nickname did indeed symbolize affection and intimacy to her.

There was usually a playful quality in Virginia's use of animal references in private communication. Apparently she and others were well aware that it was only a verbal game between them. I have found nothing to indicate that she ever confused herself into believing, even in her periods of madness, that she and other persons were in fact animals. However, Virginia did seem to sense a special kinship between persons and animals, and according to her sister felt an unusual sympathy with animals as evidently she did with all of nature.[29]

Virginia Woolf's use of animal references in her novels is much more complex and involved than her private uses. In the novels the references are an integral part of her mythic thought.[30] But there is even more evidence in the novels than in the private communication that she did not actually mistake animals for people or vice versa. Although she expressed a variety of ideas by her animal references, in the more than five hundred instances I have found in the novels, almost every one is a simile and is clearly analogical. She revealed parallels and similarities between animals and people but did not try to establish identity between them. Few of the references are metaphors, the use of which would have suggested a closer relationship, more nearly approaching a fusion of the two orders of being.


## The Power of Personality and of Love

Another persistent attribute of Virginia Woolf's childhood imagination was more mythic and unrealistic than her usually playful, analogic association of people and animals. That was her idea that certain persons — usually women — had the power to transcend the physical limitations of their bodies. Sometimes the power consisted only in knowing what the other person was thinking. She wrote to Violet Dickinson disjointedly and incoherently, "You remember there is a very fine instinct wireless telepathy nothing to it — in women — the darlings — which fizzles up pretences, and I know what you mean though you don't say it. . . ."[31] More commonly, the power was clearly miraculous and gave the person the ability to control physical objects and other persons by nonphysical means. The idea is traced to two events that Virginia attributed to her early childhood. The most fundamental of these was her experience of union and identity between the subjective and objective realms, that is, between what went on within her own body and mind and what went on outside it. The second was her memories or imaginings of her mother as a generalized, unfocused presence existing with little reference to the body.

Throughout her life Virginia seems to have "reasoned" backwards as most persons are inclined to do at times. Specifically, she "reasoned" backwards from the experience of certain charismatic personalities and of being loved, both of which she found to have extraordinary and inexplicable effects upon her mood. The effects were subjective but her naive explanation was that the effects were literally induced by a transcendent spiritual power emanating from the other persons. Usually her experiences of this sort during her childhood occurred with women, and she continued all her life to be preoccupied with the effect a woman's love had upon her. She attributed the ability to transcend the body to a number of her literary characters, most prominently to Mrs. Ramsay and Mrs. Dalloway. She said that Mrs. Ramsay could "leave her body"[32] and that Mrs. Dalloway existed "out there," in her surroundings.[33] In *Mrs. Dalloway,* she distinguished a literary, metaphoric use of the concept from its manifestation in madness by isolating literal belief in such radically mythic ideas to the mad consciousness of Septimus Smith. Although in her novels Virginia most often attributed to women the ability to transcend the body or used that as a metaphor for women, she also created Jacob who lives before and after death in the objects of his experience. And there was also Mr. Ramsay, whose destructive qualities miraculously extend into his surroundings.[34]

Virginia Woolf played with the theme of a transcendent spiritual power in work other than her published writings. For example, associated directly with her bedtime stories is "A Story to Make You Sleep," a second, but separate, part of "Friendships Gallery," written for Violet Dickinson. The first two chapters consist of Virginia's portrait or "life" of Violet. In Virginia's experience, Violet was a charismatic personality and, moreover, a person who loved Virginia and encouraged her to write. The entire "Friendships Gallery" is a whimsical, teasing mixture of myth, fantasy, and empirical fact, usually much embellished. The third chapter is much more esoteric and mythic than the first two. In "Friendships Gallery" Virginia attributed to Violet Dickinson the ability to change people by looking at them—significantly filling them with sufficient confidence to write. Virginia compared this power to bringing fire out of ashes, a comparison illustrated by her assertion that Violet's head was so "charged with thunders and lightnings, bent beneath the winds of heaven, so piercing in the shafts of its eyes that fire will kindle and flames long blunt among ashes shoot up beneath its compulsion." Virginia said further that Violet changed persons miraculously by speaking to them and that she had the magical fire within herself. Virginia continued by asking that one "imagine a mouth which, like flame again for my figure declares its need of ashes, curls and flickers and bursts here and there into a true rose of heat, deep with quivering shades of red and opal colour as the petals

247

overlap each other and melt swiftly to the heart of the naked fire within. Ashes, even, glow like the clouds of dusk when it flushes them." She also said that sparks spurted from Duchess and the kitchen maid alike when Violet's power struck them, and that they then exclaimed, " 'I too have a fire within me' 'I too sing a beautiful song' 'my God I can write!' "[35]

"Friendships Gallery" was a playful, whimsical, often silly early attempt to do what Virginia did more seriously later when she created Mrs. Ramsay, in *To the Lighthouse,* as a tribute to her mother. In one aspect of her characterization, Mrs. Ramsay, like Violet in the earlier effort, has miraculous qualities. For example, Mrs. Ramsay can control Mr. Ramsay by looking at him, can comfort him physically without touching him, can become the things she sees. By her very presence, or even by merely existing as a living person, Mrs. Ramsay can keep the world coherent and meaningful and can hold off an ever threatening chaos. But as we have noted, Mrs. Ramsay is more than one person; she is also a natural woman who eventually dies because of the physical sacrifice required by her charitable work and her demanding husband. In yet another manifestation, she is a Machiavellian woman, insensitive to the welfare of others, whose absurd valuation of the marital estate turns her into a dangerous matchmaker. Similarly in "Friendships Gallery," Violet is at least two persons, paralleling the first two manifestations of Mrs. Ramsay. Violet is the miraculous figure whose glance and words strike fire from ashes, and a woman who must work physically, digging gardens, nursing the sick, and planning and building her own house.

## Father, Public and Private

During her childhood Virginia practiced the more conventional forms of imagination by writing and "publishing" the family newspaper, the "Hyde Park Gate News," and by attempting to write essays, novels, and other forms of fiction. Her parents were her principal audience for these expressions of her imagination, or at least for the family newspaper. As persons with their own sense of convention and as mediators of society at large, simply by being in her audience, Leslie and Julia exerted pressure on Virginia to decrease her more mythic imaginings. Even so, Quentin Bell said (pp. 28-30) Virginia managed to be quite inventive, both copying and parodying the conventions of her parents, of society, and of the authors admired by her parents. Extant examples of the fiction she experimented with during her later childhood contain less fantasy and myth than her stories for her sister and brothers evidently did.[36]

Virginia enjoyed writing the "Hyde Park Gate News," but her public writing in childhood also helped her gain the love and approbation of her parents, and it moved her toward her chosen occupation. Her recollections show that, first and foremost, she wanted to please her mother.[37] Vanessa Bell confirmed this in her memoir about Virginia.[38] Virginia experienced a moment of exquisite pleasure when her mother liked something she had written, pleasure she likened to that of a violin when it is being played. Vanessa Bell implied that Julia's reaction was perfunctory and minimum, and that Virginia overresponded. She said that she and Virginia would leave the paper for their mother to find and then would eavesdrop to learn what their mother's reaction would be, Virginia "trembling with excitement." Julia would comment, " 'Rather clever, I think'...putting the paper down without apparent excitement. But it was enough to thrill her daughter; she had had approval and been called clever...."

Although her mother's approval of her relatively public exercises of imagination seemed to excite Virginia most, she also had an eye on her father and wanted his approval as well.

249

Moreover, she had espoused Leslie Stephen's most visible occupation, writing, and imitated the methods and conventions of his kind of literature in her public writing. Quentin Bell's descriptions (pp. 28-30, 37-39) indicate that she also parodied these methods and conventions when she expressed her humor and her awareness that adults and their ways are sometimes absurd.

Virginia may have gained some measure of her father's approval by means of the "Hyde Park Gate News," but at times his response was even more minimum than her mother's. For example, once when the "Hyde Park Gate News," which he called the "Hyde Park Gate Gazette," was sent to him in the Alps, he replied only that it had arrived.[39] Virginia's father knew and approved of her ambition to become a writer, but he had so little awareness or appreciation of her imagination that he assumed that she would become a very different sort of writer than she did. In 1893, when Virginia was eleven, he said that writing articles would be her line, "unless she marries somebody at 17."[40] Two days later, he made the comments to which I have alluded previously, that Virginia should be an author and that history would be a good line for her since he could guide her in that field.[41]

Leslie Stephen must have observed some instances of Virginia's imitating him. Her practice, even as a child, was to do some of the things she saw him do. For example, she would find a private corner where she could sit to read and write, especially when she was disturbed or unhappy. It is very likely that he and Virginia were less aware of the other functions he served. Some of these were constructive, and some were detrimental and confusing, for she seems to have identified with more than one side of her father. By writing in his manner and by acquainting herself with the conventions he represented — whether to imitate, to parody, or to satirize them — she was able to bring some manifestations of her imagination closer to reality. But in Quentin Bell's view (p. 37), Virginia's writing for her father and mother eventually took her too far in the direction of social convention. He said that late editions of the "Hyde Park Gate News" and other works when she was turning thirteen, showed the detrimental effect of having an adult audience. "As might be expected, the charm and fun of the earlier numbers has evaporated. Occasionally a phrase, a joke, a turn of speech anticipates her adult style; but the general impression is rather flat. She is still writing for an adult audience; but now she has reached a self-conscious age and plays for safety. She attempts a novel of manners; she writes an article describing a dream in which she was God. These are both in their way interesting, but they are also very clearly the work of a girl making a deadly serious study of English literature."

Virginia's imagination was constricted by having her father as an audience. Nevertheless, as had been noted, Virginia was well aware of and admired the father who could distractedly forget himself and loudly proclaim poetry after he had been taught to be ashamed of his love for it. Her more secret imaginings may have been encouraged by her identification with what she called, in *To the Lighthouse* (pp. 41-42), that "delicious emotion, [that] impure rhapsody of which he was ashamed, but in which he revelled...."

# 10

# Matters of Health and Art:
# The Future Begins to Show

Virginia's first or, at least, her first verified emotional and
mental breakdown came between her thirteenth and fifteenth
years and was brought on by her mother's death and her father's extreme and prolonged mourning. Consequently, these
two years proved to be among the most crucial in her life, for
what occurred during them made it almost inevitable that she
would encounter other disturbances. Also, the occurrences of
these two years partially determined her future in art, by helping to form her characteristic style of thought and by providing
additional and far more serious reasons for writing.

It is possible that Virginia's breakdown between her thirteenth and fifteenth years was her second such experience. Bell
thought it her first, but there have been reports that she had
had an earlier breakdown, published in authoritative references such as Leonard Woolf's autobiography[1] and the *Dictionary of National Biography* entry on Virginia drawn up by
Lord David Cecil.

Leonard Woolf's statement that Virginia had had a breakdown in childhood suggests, of course, that Virginia herself
believed she had, for no doubt she was his source. But probably Leonard Woolf's reference to a childhood breakdown
should be discounted since his report of his wife's early illness
fails to mention her breakdown in 1904, one of her most
serious.

The family correspondence during Virginia's childhood

does not clarify the matter, although there are several vague references to Virginia's health. When she was three years old, her father referred to her as "out of sorts, dear little soul."[2] In 1893, when she was eleven, she had an illness severe enough for the family doctor to come in several times, but not so severe that Virginia's mother remained home from one of her charitable missions.[3] As noted previously, Leslie was too deaf to hear what Dr. Seton said about Virginia's illness and, therefore, did not say what was wrong with her when he wrote Julia about it. Thus one cannot know whether it was emotional, mental, or physical. On April 16, 1895, about three weeks before Julia died, she wrote to Leslie of difficulties Virginia was having while they traveled together. Leslie replied, again nonspecifically, "I am vexed with all the trouble you have had! Poor darling Ginia, it is maddening." Quentin Bell described (p. 25) Virginia's serious physical illness of 1888, when she was six. All four of the young Stephens contracted severe cases of whooping cough at one time. He believed that Virginia became a different child than she had been before the illness, more thoughtful and speculative.

Virginia was never an ordinary child, as we have seen, and both her emotional constitution and her idiosyncratic thought indicate that she was extremely vulnerable. However, extant evidence supports Quentin Bell's belief that her breakdown at the age of thirteen was her first. Apparently her earlier problems were not so severe, so constellated, or so prolonged as to be considered an emotional or mental "illness." Nor do her personal anomalies, either emotional or mental, appear to have been so extreme before her breakdown at thirteen as to make her illness at that time inevitable. Virginia's vulnerability was only one of three conditions that combined forces to bring about her first breakdown. The stress of her situation, especially Leslie's mourning, was by far the most significant of the three. Her age was also important. She was only thirteen and, in many respects, an unusually naive and immature girl.

As Virginia herself assessed it, her mother's death and her father's mourning came at the time when she was half child and half grown-up, when her two worlds — those of the child and of the adult — were mixed and unbalanced. Her idea was only partially correct, for she was evidently much more than half child.

Part of the horror and pathos of Virginia's breakdown at thirteen was that it need not have occurred. If her childhood had been managed differently by her parents, the frightening reciprocity between herself and her situation might have been avoided, and she might have been less susceptible to external stress. Even after her anomalous development, she might not have had serious emotional and mental difficulties if her mother had not died just when she did — and Virginia and perhaps others in the family believed that her mother's death need not have taken place so early. Moreover, even after her mother's death, an undoubted trauma, Virginia could have maintained control if her father had conducted himself more maturely and rationally.

But if ever character were truly destiny, it was for the Stephen family at that period in its history. Thus neither Virginia's breakdown at age thirteen, nor all that led up to it were in actuality to be avoided. Given the personalities of her parents, they could not conduct themselves very differently than they did, and so the pathetic drama resulting in Julia's early death had to work itself out. And since Leslie was as he was, there was little likelihood that the mourning for Julia could have gone other than it did. After that, Virginia's personal disturbance was as irresistible as a force of nature.

## A Severe Case of Susceptibility

There were several reasons why Virginia's development in childhood made her especially susceptible to the events transpiring after her mother's death. These included traits present from the time she was quite young, such as her propensity for idiosyncratic and mythic ideas and her sudden extremes of emotions. Just as important, however, were aspects of her personality which did not emerge, the absence of which comprised much of her vulnerability. The most crucial of these was her limited sense of self, which in childhood was lacking in several important dimensions.

In her 1939-1940 memoir, Virginia indicated a certain puzzlement that she had had so little sense of self as a child, and evidently she had been puzzled by that when younger. She had few ways to think of herself and few conceptions of the kind of person she was, but that comprised only a small part of the problem. Most fundamentally, she lacked a reliable sense of her own being. Words she later attributed to Rachel Vinrace in *The Voyage Out* (pp. 94-95), describe Virginia as well: she lacked a sense that she was "a real everlasting thing, different from anything else, unmergeable, like the sea or the wind . . . ." Virginia labeled the memories of her earliest times, already discussed, "memories without a self." It was as if she had been no more than a mind, a sealed vessel afloat upon experience, whose seal sometimes would break, permitting experience to enter and lodge. When experience did enter, that is, when she was actually sensing the world, she thought she had "being." At other times, for which she had no memory, she said there was only "nonbeing" or nothingness. As we have seen, her pleasant awareness of being came when she felt dominant over her experience, for this gave her a sense of her own strength. She described other times of being, paradoxically, as times when she felt annihilated, when her extremely tenuous sense of self had been destroyed. She also said that "self" was "whatever it was" in one that reacted to things for which there were no words, thus she associated self, in its entirety, with sensory experience.

Virginia believed also that she had not learned a sense of her own boundaries as a child, that is, had not learned the difference between psychological and physical properties. Her belief came from many aspects of her experience, chiefly from being too keenly aware intellectually and too responsive emotionally to what transpired around her. Also, her extremely vivid and lifelike sense imagery made certain inner events and ideas seem as real to her as external ones. For these and other reasons, it seemed to her as a child that the realm of the subjective self was not set apart from the objective being of the world beyond her senses. Instead, it seemed as if her inner, subjective world and the world outside could quite literally flow into each other. She never relinquished this belief, for she expressed it both explicitly and implicitly in her novels. She also stated it specifically in her 1939-1940 memoir, as "proof" that one's life is not confined to the body.

Virginia's conception that no boundaries existed between herself and the exterior world was similar to the ideas she expressed about her mother and Violet Dickinson, to both of whom—poetically at least—she attributed psychological powers with all the force of physical ones, and as a consequence, miraculous abilities. There was one major difference in Virginia's conception of her own case; she seemed to think that her own lack of boundaries gave her few of the "miraculous" powers she attributed to her mother and to Violet Dickinson. Although during her 1904 madness she had the delusion that she had killed her father by wishing him dead, she generally thought her lack of boundaries increased her own vulnerability to events beyond herself. In other words, it seemed to her a matter of what the world might do to her, not what she could do to it—on the whole, a fair though mythic summary of the truth.

It was not strange that Virginia lacked a sense of self when she was a young child or that she thought the subjective and objective realms were not separate. Infants, of necessity, begin life without the ability to be reflectively aware that they exist.[4]

Also, it seems to children in their early years that there are no boundaries to separate subjective processes from the world outside the self, and therefore that their wishes, thoughts, and other psychological events have physical force and power. They must become aware of self and self-limits over a period of years, and the kinds of awareness and limits learned will vary with the child, his culture, and his particular experience. Although it is universal that children begin life without a sense of self, if Virginia actually recognized as a young child that she was without a self, she was exceptional. Most young children are so unaware of self that they do not realize that they lack a sense of self. Her continued belief that she lacked boundaries was also out of the ordinary and anticipated her later mental and emotional difficulties. Another unusual and ominous feature of Virginia's personality was her fear, perhaps originating in childhood or during her first breakdown, that one could lose "self" and be without "self"—in the language of psychology, that one could feel depersonalized. Like so many other aspects of her early experience, fears about loss of self and depersonalization were introduced into her novels. An instance is found in the last section of *The Waves* (pp. 168 ff.) where Bernard fails in his effort to integrate experience and becomes a "man without a self."[5]

Virginia did not arrive at age thirteen totally lacking a sense of self. As a child she had made many of the ordinary efforts to discover what she was like. Some of her efforts succeeded, despite her feeling that she had been greatly deprived of opportunities to ascertain her own unique qualities. Happily, she had managed, with the help of her family, to form at least one definite and fateful conception of self that would persist with obsessive force for the rest of her life. The conception was, of course, that she was a writer. Since it was one of the few well-formed, positive ideas she had about herself, she tended to overinvest in that self concept.

She formed other, rather amorphous notions about what she

was like and not like. She came to think and feel that she resembled her father, and since he held the same belief, he may have encouraged her to think so. Although there were many radical differences — such as her ability to set and maintain a professional direction for herself — she was in fact rather like him. Some similarities were fortunate; these included her verbal ability and her capacity for vivid sense imagery. There were less happy resemblances, such as her unstable temperament, her tendency to overreact emotionally, and her emotionally based physical problems. Also, Virginia shared Leslie's profound belief that having a mother, Julia in particular, was essential to personal and emotional survival, even if Julia was accessible to her chiefly in her mythic imaginings. She may have adopted that belief from her father through identification with him. But most likely his excessive reactions during Julia's absences and his crazed mourning for her after her death only paralleled the feeling present in Virginia since infancy, that the world was exceedingly perilous without her mother.

To the extent that Virginia as a child recognized her similarities to her father, the knowledge must have been unpleasant and threatening in many respects. Since there were some things about him that she hated and feared, she could hardly have been entirely pleased to think she resembled him. Also, since he had difficulty holding himself together under stress and found it impossible at best to be other than a divided personality, he was a dubious model for his sensitive daughter. Nevertheless, she seems to have identified happily enough with some aspects of her father's personality, especially with his repressed side that occasionally surfaced in his poetry-quoting fits of abstraction and self-forgetfulness.

Virginia's sister was in many ways a better model, and in childhood Virginia both compared herself to Vanessa and tried to copy her. As we have observed, usually she failed to be like Vanessa and for that reason her comparisons told Virginia little about her own positive qualities. Instead, efforts to imitate and compare served to remind Virginia of what she lacked, since she inevitably did lack certain capabilities of a sister three years older than she and one whose temperament was somewhat more stable and placid.

Another of Virginia's serious limitations in childhood development was her failure to acquire an adequate command of rational, empirical thought. This lack was integral with and manifest in her beliefs about herself, for she had not taken what Piaget has shown to be an early and essential step towards rational thought.[6] That is, she had not come fully to understand and accept that the subjective world of self is relatively separate from the world beyond the senses. Without this fundamental idea, it was not easy for Virginia to know with any certainty what was real and what was unreal, what had physical being in the world beyond her, and what was simply a product of her own imagination. She was not totally immersed in imagination or in a subjective, autistic world, as we have seen, and was far from completely lacking in rational thought. But there was a decided disproportion and imbalance, in favor of nonrational, mythic thought. She held all her life to mythic ideas that in a more ordinary course of development would have proved impracticable and would have been displaced by more rational assumptions about what the world was like and how her mind related to it.

A Worse Case of Stress and of Timing

Virginia's situation when she was thirteen provided just the ingredients required to transform her potential for serious emotional and mental problems into a hideous and tragic actuality. The kind and degree of stress could hardly have been worse than they proved to be. First, there was the death of her mother. At best the loss would have been exceptionally painful for Virginia; she said that it was the worst thing — "the greatest tragedy" — that could have happened.[7] Its potential for stress was compounded of course by her tenuous relationship with her mother, her unfulfilled and unresolved infantile needs for her. She said, referring to her feelings after her mother died, that she was left with the definite need for her mother and simultaneously with the awful knowledge that her need could never be met. The need was experienced as a physical reality, as a problem within her body.[8] In the words Virginia gave to Lily Briscoe in *To the Lighthouse* (pp. 265-266): "It was one's body feeling, not one's mind. . . . To want and not to have, sent all up her body a hardness, a hollowness, a strain. And then to want and not to have — to want and want — how that wrung the heart, and wrung it again and again!" But as terrible as it was, Virginia said, the pain was at least something "definite" and therefore almost welcome in the "opaque life" without reality that "blinded and choked her,"[9] the life her father forced on the Stephen children after their mother died.

The stress of her mother's dying was made worse than it might have been by Virginia's fears before Julia's death that just such a thing might occur, as for instance when she waited and watched for her mother to come home, in agony at the thought that some accident had befallen her. Even in childhood Virginia thought that the universe was rife with accidents and potential accidents for the people she loved. She believed it filled with senseless, unheeding forces that might descend at any time on them, a belief greatly exacerbated after her mother's death.[10] Virginia, like others in the family, was aware on some level that her mother's health was deteriorating well before her death and had had to watch it happen, powerless to prevent it. This unconscious knowledge had called up in Virginia a confusion of feelings about both her parents that were difficult for her to tolerate when Julia actually died. The confusion included a large measure of resentment toward her father for victimizing her mother and at least a small measure toward her mother for allowing him to do so.[11] The resentment toward her mother was increased by the fact that Julia Stephen became increasingly and understandably less patient with the children and was less often available to them in her last years.[12]

Moreover, there was Virginia's conviction that her mother, even as an extracorporeal, imaginary presence was absolutely essential to her own survival, and her fear that without her mother, Virginia's entire world would be destroyed. Sometimes Virginia went further, saying that her mother was the world.[13] Virginia's worst and most inclusive fear—that her mother's death meant the end of the world—was of course hideously realized when Julia died.[14] Virginia's father alone would have convinced her that with Julia's death the world as the family knew it had indeed been destroyed and that Virginia could not survive. His insistence that the children mourn as exaggeratedly as he and in his style, forced Virginia to lose her limited control and convinced her that she was helpless and powerless. Even worse, Leslie's mourning was a great dramatization, complete with settings, actions, and words, of the belief that neither he, nor anyone, nor anything else would ever be the same now that Julia was gone. Moreover, without intending it, Leslie did much to see that Julia was indeed gone, that no one would be able to recall her as she had been. Virginia said in her 1939-1940 memoir that Leslie's attempts to eulogize her mother had created an unrealistic, unlovable phantom that got in the way of her own ability to remember or imagine what her elusive mother had been like in life. Thus, in Virginia's experience, the equation was straightforward and its implications horrifying. Terribly afraid that she and her world could not go on without her mother, the events after Julia's death proved her right; her father's distraught condition, his words and actions, iterated that her fear had been well based and realistic.

Leslie Stephen did far more than convince Virginia that all her worst fears had come true: he exacerbated her already painful conflicts about him. Then of all times she needed some adult in her life to be stable, consistent, and uncomplicated, and her father should have tried to assume that responsibility. But, in part for reasons beyond his control, he proceeded as never before, or afterward, to be a person about whom she could only feel and think inconsistently. He portrayed both sides of his nature, alternately acting the old wretch, the self-pitying and blind tyrant Virginia hated most, and the father whom she had always loved. Moreover, a major part of his tyranny consisted in the demand that she and others love him and sympathize with him at the very times when he was doing most to provoke their resentment. He exacerbated Virginia's conflicts about him still more because his mourning included strains both of the most patent falsity and self-histrionics which could only be despised, and of the most pathetic sincerity, that called up sympathy in no way compatible with Virginia's anger and hatred for him.

There was of course nothing new in Virginia's finding that her father was complex and contradictory, that he was an old wretch who also needed and merited love, and that he could be both patently false and utterly sincere. The difference was that he carried all of these facets and manifestations of himself to new proportions when Julia died, making it impossible for Virginia not to respond to *all* of them simultaneously—hence much of her emotional confusion. And he managed to add some new elements, especially through his relationship with Stella. Although Virginia did not know fully how to interpret the relationship between her father and Stella, or whom to blame, she did not overlook the implications. She was, as she said in her 1939-1940 memoir, "terribly alive" to everything that went on around her; she was at the same time a child in her relationship with Stella and an adult in her understanding of Stella's emotions for her father.

Thus conflict in Virginia's emotions and ideas developed around Stella as well as her father. She loved Stella and sympathized with her, admired her, and was grateful to her. She was more aware of and in tune with Stella's grief than was Leslie, whose own needs, then and always, loomed so large that he could never really see or appreciate those of others. Virginia received some of Stella's attention, love and sympathy. She looked "naturally" to Stella for those, she said, and Stella responded as best she could, when Leslie and household responsibilities were not occupying her. For example, when Virginia's health was at its worst during her crisis between ages thirteen to fifteen, Stella was the person who willingly took on the responsibility of seeing that Virginia got the daily four hours outdoors prescribed by her doctor.[15] During the long mourning, when Virginia said she was unable to write or even to want to write, it was Stella who showed that she believed in Virginia's genius and Stella who found her amusing.[16] Just before Stella's death, when Virginia was sick and emotionally distraught, it was Stella who cared for her, sitting by her, stroking and soothing her.[17]

As Virginia summarized it in her 1908 and her 1939-1940 memoirs, Stella was a stable force in a largely chaotic world between 1895 and 1897. Stella sometimes "raised the shroud" and permitted some light to enter the Oriental gloom imposed by Leslie. Stella was everything wonderful, and yet — there were things that Virginia resented in Stella, half aware that her resentment was irrational. Her resentment put her in the state of strange ambivalence even about the half sister whom she loved and admired. A few sources of her resentment are indicated in Virginia's references to that period of her life. She resented the fact — fact only in Virginia's estimation, as far as one can tell — that Stella confused Leslie with her "indiscriminate" attentions to him. Probably she resented and was jealous of Stella's closeness with her father at a time when Virginia herself was not able to be close to him. She also seemed to resent what she called Stella's need for sacrifice, meaning Stella's need of sympathy after Julia's death. Quentin Bell cited (p. 56) another probable source of Virginia's resentment — simply that Stella was in a position of authority over Virginia.

Later, at the time of Stella's approaching marriage, Virginia was asked to make other sacrifices for Stella which she greatly resented, principally because they required of her things she was terribly and probably pathologically frightened to do. She resented being asked to go on vacation with Stella and Jack Hills during their engagement. As Virginia recorded the matter in her diary of 1897, a "terrible" idea had started that she and Stella would take rooms at Bognor where Jack was to go the next week. It put her into a "dreadful temper" all day and, as she said further, caused her to lead Stella and Vanessa "quite a life." When it was "almost settled" that they would go to Bognor, with Vanessa and Leslie joining the group for part of the time, Virginia pronounced the whole thing horrible. When the plan was firm that they should go, she noted that it left her in a fit of a temper all evening. Once they were in Bognor, Virginia hated it as much as she had expected. She felt even worse when another "terrible idea" was proposed that she and Stella stay on for an additional week after Vanessa and Leslie returned. She "absolutely" refused and only then Stella agreed that Virginia might return home. A fortnight after they had returned, Virginia continued to feel irritated and angry for reasons she could not understand. Then she had to face the frightening and much hated request that she and Vanessa be bridesmaids in Stella's wedding. Virginia considered this request another "sacrifice." She tried, she said in her diary, to squelch that idea, but finally had no choice. She was able to go through with her part in the wedding and called Stella's wedding half nightmare (her own) and half a pleasant dream (Stella's).[18]

Virginia's contradictory, irrational feelings for Stella were unresolved and possibly had increased by the time of Stella's fatal illness. There was something in Stella, or symbolized by her, that almost made Virginia wish her half sister dead, and Virginia didn't know whether she was relieved or angry when it seemed that Stella was recovering. She noted in her 1897 diary that the reports of Stella's improved health were satisfying, but that she herself was "unreasonable enough to be irritated." At the same time, Virginia was so upset about Stella's condition that she was made physically sick. Only after Stella had died did Virginia's resentment for her subside. But then she was faced with other problems and conflicts in reference to Stella. There was her feeling of profound loss, made worse by the fact that Stella's death came at a time of renewed promise for greater happiness in the family. The loss, coming when it did, cogently symbolized that life could and would betray. Virginia described her shock and horror and recalled saying to herself that "this impossible thing has happened, as if it were unnatural, against the law, horrible, as a treachery, and betrayal. . . ."[19] There was also a reenactment, in part, of the awful mourning to which the family had been subjected when Julia died, but fortunately with fewer of Leslie's histrionics. Finally, Virginia was left with terrible guilt for having resented Stella while she was dying and for the trouble she thought she had caused her. In her own last years, Virginia was still bothered by remnants of her guilt about Stella. She wrote in her 1939-1940 memoir that she hoped she had given Stella some amusement and some happy moments, but that her own irritability and need for care, between the time of her mother's death and Stella's, had taken hours out of Stella's short life.

Finally, the possibility of George Duckworth's indiscriminate attentions and affections, his surreptitious erotic gropings, must be mentioned in this partial cataloguing of the sources of Virginia's stress and confusion in the years after her mother died. As Bell phrased it (p. 44), George added the "final element of foulness in what was already an appalling situation." But as earlier discussions of this topic have suggested, George's conduct and intentions—whatever they actually were—may have been relatively innocent and may have been misinterpreted by Virginia.

## Gigantic Chaos Streaked with Lightning

When one as susceptible as Virginia encounters stress almost beyond measure, and when the stress is such that it attacks where one is most vulnerable, inevitably there will be turmoil and loss of control. When one is little more than a child and is already in a transitional state, and when the stress continues for more than two years, the upheaval is bound to be catastrophic and, as we have said, as inevitable as a force of nature. And so it was for Virginia. She evinced almost every known variety of "symptom,"[20] including anger and irritability; mental confusion; physical pain, racing pulse, and other physiological irregularities; delusions, illusions, and possibly hallucinations; and difficulty in keeping track of time. Having had few ways to conceive of herself and only a tenuous sense of self, she now became frighteningly aware of her own person, learned to derogate herself, to be morbidly shy and afraid to face people and to go out into the streets. According to Leonard Woolf,[21] she attempted suicide, although Quentin Bell (pp. 89-90) thought Virginia's first attempt to kill herself was made during her second attack of madness, not her first. Most important, however, the reputed suicide attempt notwithstanding, from the beginning she seems to have been determined to fight her way out of the morass of her emotions and thoughts and to find her way back to sanity.

In her fictionalized account of this period, given in the second part of *To the Lighthouse,* Virginia referred to it as a time of chaos streaked with lightning. In one sense she was correct, but mostly she was wrong. As chaotic as it must have seemed, little in her situation was random and unpatterned. Nor was she in complete turmoil, for her statements about her reactions reveal distinct patterns. For the most part, what she did, thought, and felt was not inappropriate to her situation. Other emotions than those she felt or no emotions at all would have been far less appropriate and only a lack of awareness of the events around her could have prevented her mental conflict. Thus, although distraught and out of control, Virginia was not out of touch with reality. Rather, she was too much in contact with it. As she said in her 1939-1940 memoir, her "experiencing mechanism" was very great at that time and she was painfully aware of all that went on around her and of her emotions as well. The result was that she became less able than before to know the difference between inner and outer reality.

Another aspect of the problem was that Virginia could not sort out events and her emotions, could not reconcile them with each other, and could not find meaning in them. Nor could she give up her efforts to find sense and meaning even though the sense and meaning to be found were ugly and painful. Still another difficulty was Virginia's guilt and her inability to determine whether she or the situation was most at fault. Maybe she was being vain, egotistical, and selfish to be so concerned with her own feelings; perhaps she had only herself to blame for her mental and emotional predicament.[22] Sometimes she truly blamed herself, and according to Leonard Woolf's report, it was at one of those times that she tried to kill herself by jumping from a window. At other times she would become furious and "tantrumical," blaming the situation and turning her anger toward it. She was especially angry at her father, and with good reason. Mostly, however, her anger was general and undirected, not attached to anything in particular and therefore appeared to her and to her family to be unreasonable and inexplicable.

Thus, although Virginia was in many respects in contact with reality, her condition was not improved thereby. Obviously it would have been easier for her if she had achieved greater distance from the problems around her, or if she had seen less and felt less. It would have been best, of course, if she could have consistently kept the perspective she always sought on the problems but only briefly and intermittently attained. It would have been an improvement also if Virginia had been selective in her view of reality as apparently Vanessa and Thoby were. As we have noted, Thoby was able to extricate himself from the morass, refusing to do what was demanded of the Stephen children during the mourning and advising the others to follow his lead. Vanessa was evidently able to begin simplifying and clarifying her emotions and thoughts by disdaining her father and marshalling her ideas in concert with her feelings. She disdained him even in the face of his tantrums when she was responsible for the household accounts, knowing that her silence and indifference made him angrier. Virginia said further in her 1939-1940 memoir that she felt rage not disdain for her father—a far more insistent emotion and one more difficult to reconcile with her other feelings about him. She said that she spent much of her time in her room, raging at Leslie and trying to distract herself by reading, simultaneously hating him and behaving very much like him. Vanessa found the situation easier to handle because she apparently did not love Leslie or identify with him to the extent Virginia did, and did not experience the conflicting emotions toward him that Virginia felt so strongly. Virginia's inability to follow either

Vanessa's or Thoby's lead gave rise to some of her unrealistic self-reproach. She said that when she compared herself with Vanessa, she was most inclined to blame herself for being vain, egotistical, and inordinately cross and angry.

Virginia's reactions also fell short of complete chaos because, quite predictably, her turmoil and confusion bore the marks of her individuality. Her emotions were a case in point; they varied from painful excitement and nervousness to profound depression, thus showing a continuation of the emotional pattern she recalled from her earliest years. There were even times during the worst of the mourning when she experienced rapture and elation, chiefly when Stella found time out from her care of Leslie to mother Virginia.

There was a certain pattern and rationale in Virginia's mental turmoil, evident in her illusions and possible hallucinations. Several conditions combined to produce them, and to make them understandable though nonetheless irrational. These conditions included Virginia's propensity and facility for sense imagery so vivid that it was very easy for her to mistake her images for perceptions of actual events. There was also her limited ability to distinguish the boundaries separating her mind from the objective world beyond her senses. Finally her greater ability and propensity for mythic rather than rational thought made it likely that the meaning she found in what went on around her would be relatively mystical.

Therefore it is understandable that sometimes she thought she saw and heard things that did not occur. Even so, she did maintain enough awareness of self to know that she might be "dramatizing" her imagination. For example, she saw, or perhaps didn't quite see, a man who sat on the bed beside the body of her dead mother, just as she either saw or perhaps only dreamed that she saw the ugly, animallike face over her shoulder in the mirror when she was younger. On one hand, if she had had a firmer sense of self and the limits of her ego, she

269

would have recognized these images as the products of her own mind. On the other hand, if she had had less sense of self, she would have been convinced that they were coming from the world beyond her. Perhaps she actually did believe some of them came from beyond. She herself said that during the period of mourning any hallucination was possible,[23] and according to Quentin Bell (p. 45), she heard "horrible voices" that returned at intervals later in her life.

## "Scene-Making"

Virginia's mind also saved her from complete chaos by forming dreamlike images that she did acknowledge to be coming from within herself and by transforming some external events into "pictures" or "perceptions." In writing about them in her 1939-1940 memoir, she called both kinds of experiences "scene-making." Although she knew the "scenes" were of her own making, it was as if her mind produced them automatically, without conscious bidding or control. The scene seemed to her to arrange itself into something "representative and enduring," into which a great store of meaning was condensed and telescoped, as in the case of actual dream images, in the manner described by Freud. Apparently, Virginia was not surprised or frightened by the scenes or pictures, so one may surmise that they were not a new experience for the thirteen-year-old girl, and that their content was not especially threatening. She said that scene-making came naturally, implying that she had always been able to think in that manner, and that she found it a useful device when writing. She became especially conscious of scene-making when her mother died and in other periods of tension. Some of the later occurrences were also associated with or precipitated by the death of someone close to her. In a letter to Ethel Smyth in 1934, after

Roger Fry's death, she described the pictures her mind produced uncontrollably at that time, and asked whether Ethel had similar reactions after a shock.[24] In writing to Ethel, Virginia made it evident that most of the scenes came from memory and that their content was not unpleasant.

In her 1939-1940 memoir, Virginia described and explained one such scene that seemed to form itself in her mind when she was fifteen and that illustrates the mechanism. She began automatically, without knowing why or how, to think of Jack Hills's pain and distress after Stella's death as a leafless bush, a skeleton tree in a garden, near where she and Jack sat inside a garden house. There were little buds on the tree—"chill red buds"—that represented the discomfort, misery, and quarrels that ensued at 22 Hyde Park Gate after Stella died and as Jack and Vanessa began to fall in love.

It is obvious that Virginia's tendency to think in scenes was not unlike her tendency to see or hear things in the external world for which there was no basis in reality. Therefore her scenes fell only a little short of hallucinations. Also, the spontaneously created scenes closely resembled the symbols she employed with so much beauty in her novels. And although the process seemed to her unguided and uncontrolled, her unconscious search for stability undoubtably directed it. For example, the scenes became a way to detach herself from painful realities and to reduce them to manageable proportions. Even during her first breakdown, Virginia's scene-making therefore represented an impulse toward health and a way to create sanity in a world that seemed insane and meaningless. Her scene-making was not rational, however. It was a manifestation of her mythic consciousness at work, and an example of the manner in which myth may comprehend realities the person cannot understand on a rational level.

The phenomenon that Virginia called her scene-making was central both to her madness and to her creative genius. She

271

indicated its place in her art in a passage in *To the Lighthouse* (p. 258), where Lily Briscoe is ruminating about her portrait of Mrs. Ramsay and James. Virginia Woolf's portraits were a species of her scenes. However, the novel implies a far more radical departure from "truth" and reality than was the case in either the portraits or other scenes, for Lily's credo is not identical with Virginia's. "And this, Lily thought, . . . this making up scenes about them is what we call 'knowing' people, 'thinking' of them, 'being fond' of them! Not a word of it was true; she had made it up; but it was what she knew them by, all the same."

Virginia's scene-making took her into, or very close to, madness whenever she lost her tenuous grasp on the distinction between subjective thought and objective reality. She was also close to a breakdown when her scene-making became automatic and uncontrolled, when her nonreflective, unconscious mind in effect, took over, unguided by her reflective mind. Then again, her scene-making took her toward madness when it became almost completely detached from words and language, just as she might approach madness when words became phenomena in themselves, separated from perceptions and seemingly from her mind. An example of the latter phenomenon that is often cited occurred when she was completing *The Waves.* She said then that her own voice seemed to fly ahead of her and that she could only stumble after it, trying to record what it was saying.[25] When Virginia had at least slight reflective, conscious control, and when she coordinated her scenes with language, the balance was tipped toward genius. Leonard Woolf, among others, provided descriptions of Virginia's scene-making and of how it was sometimes directly expressed in ordinary conversation.[26] But his descriptions also showed that Virginia's conscious control was very slight indeed, even in her moments of genius. "She was an unusually amusing talker in the usual way of talk and talkers, her mind being very quick and intelligent, witty and humorous, appropriately serious or frivolous as the occasion or subject demanded. But at any moment, in a general conversation with five or six people or when we were alone together, she might suddenly 'leave the ground' and give some fantastic, entrancing, amusing, dreamlike, almost lyrical description of an event, a place, or a person. It always made me think of the breaking and gushing out of the springs in autumn after the first rains. The ordinary mental processes stopped, and in their place the waters of creativeness and imagination welled up and, almost undirected, carried her and her listeners into another world.

"When she soared into one of these fantasies, one felt it to be a kind of inspiration. The thoughts and images fountained up spontaneously, not directed and consciously controlled as they were ordinarily by her in conversation and are always by most people."

Virginia's scene-making might, of course, at one time be relatively automatic and separated from words and later be worked out and expressed in language. This is true of certain scenes she made after her mother's death, when she was mad, and which were expressed much later in her novels. Therefore, unless "writing" is defined in an extremely narrow and limited way, one cannot fully agree with Virginia's belief that she neither wrote nor had any impulse to write between her mother's death and Stella's.

One scene, typical of those that evolved into Virginia's later novels, embodied the idea that the tragedy of her mother's death was shared and expressed by the physical world, especially by nature. The scene originated when she, Vanessa, and George went to Paddington Station to meet Thoby on the afternoon after their mother died and Virginia saw the sudden, great blaze of sunlight on the dark structure of the sta-

273

tion, which seemed to her to be mystical and apocalyptic. She said that it was as if her mother's death had shaded over a burning glass that formerly had magnified the light of the sun. Then came the blaze of light, signifying to her that somehow her mother still existed.[27]

Obviously, the meaning and interpretation of the event were Virginia's own, but in her mind it seemed that they were in fact being expressed by the world beyond her. Virginia's belief that the world shared and expressed her feelings did not differ in kind from the everyday experience of most persons. People commonly feel that the whole world participates in their moods, that it is literally dark and gloomy when they are sad, and brighter again when they are happy. The reverse is also commonplace; many persons are sufficiently in tune with changes of color and light to assume the feelings these phenomena seem to express, for example, to become sad when there is little light or when the colors of their surroundings are dull. Such experiences are so commonplace that even the language used in science has metaphors for them, yet are interesting enough that many poets have expressed ideas similar to Virginia's.

However, Virginia's sense that the physical world shared and expressed her feelings was extraordinarily intense and lasting. She was so much impressed by the "reality" of her experience that she tried repeatedly to explain the apparent change in the physical world, which accompanied her mother's death. In her 1908 memoir she said that when Julia died, clouds stood still and darkened the earth; winds had collected themselves; and creatures began to wander aimlessly and futilely, searching for something they would never find. Thus in 1908 she was still preoccupied with the symbolism of light and dark, but her poetic and mythic consciousness had begun to turn the original, specific scene into a universal one. Also, the original scene had begun to take on the proportions of a narrative myth, reminiscent of the world's becoming infertile and drought-stricken when Demeter mourned Persephone in the Greek myth and when Ceres mourned Proserpine in the Roman counterpart of the myth.

When Virginia wrote *To the Lighthouse,* she returned to the change that seemed to take place in the physical world after her mother's death, and light and darkness became important symbols in the novel. Also, the middle section of the book became Virginia's most elaborate statement of how the entire world appeared to express and act out the desolation and inner turmoil she experienced. It was in this section of the book that she referred to her first major episode of madness as gigantic chaos streaked with lightning, chaos tumbling and breeding (pp. 202-203), and nature creating chaos by means of its own fertility and insensibility (p. 207). She returned on later occasions to the theme that nature expresses one's feelings and made her final statement of it in her last novel, completed just before her suicide. In *Between the Acts,* inanimate objects, nature—indeed everything—have a legitimate role and a legitimate right to the stage where human beings act out history. Moreover, everything expresses some important, though ultimately incomprehensible, meaning. One may assume therefore that during Virginia's last period of madness, as in her first, nature and the entire world seemed to be expressing what was going on inside her. Even then she was not totally out of touch with reality. It was 1941; England was two years into World War II; and Virginia's personal life and writing had been greatly disturbed by the war. The world situation, viewed broadly, seemed once again much more insane than sane; seemed once again, in reality, to be acting out some of Virginia's fears.


The One Sure Thing . . . in Strife, Ruin and Chaos

From the viewpoint of art, it is impossible to regret entirely what happened to Virginia when she was thirteen. Nor did she entirely regret her madness, as she said to Ethel Smyth. She could not realize it as a terribly frightened, confused thirteen-year-old child, but her first experience of madness went far toward shaping the content of her unique personal vision. It also went far toward shaping some of her modes of thinking, such as those exemplified by what she chose to call her scene-making. Thus her first breakdown appears essential to her art as it evolved. It was, moreover, a source of important new motivation for writing. If her own determination to be a writer had not been sufficient, her first breakdown alone might have given her sufficient impetus. At a minimum, that breakdown created new, more serious reasons to write and gave her new objectives which were renewed with each successive episode of madness.

Before Virginia was thirteen, she wrote principally because she enjoyed it, found it useful in relating to others, and gained a sense of her identity from it. Most of these reasons continued unabated after her first breakdown, but she had foisted upon her new and far more compelling reasons to write. Beginning with her first period of madness but of course culminating much later, writing became the means whereby she confronted and tried to resolve the discrepancies and conflicts in her world, which in her novels were expressed as the omnipresent dialectics. It became, specifically, her way of finding or creating unity, order, and meaning in a personal world that seemed to her almost perpetually chaotic and disordered. As she stated with great understanding in the journal she kept during a trip to Italy in 1908, "As for writing—I want to express beauty too —but beauty (symmetry?) of life and the world, in action. Conflict?—is that it?"[28] In the same reference she compared writing with painting: "I attain a different kind of beauty, achieve a symmetry by means of infinite discords, showing all the traces of the mind's passage through the world; achieve in the end, some kind of whole made of shivering fragments. . . ."

She also used writing to combat the problems of death and nothingness or nonbeing and to reconcile her varying experiences of the world. Writing also became her essential means for bringing her perceptions and her scenes into the realm of language. In short, writing provided her with a means of creating sanity, of discovering her own wisdom, and of fighting off madness. As she said in *To the Lighthouse* (p. 224) art—the painter's brush—became the "one dependable thing in a world of strife, ruin and chaos. . . ."

Therefore, writing became far more necessary to Virginia than it might have been and was less likely to be sheer fun. In her later years, she found some relatively lighthearted enjoyment in certain kinds of public writing—her reviews, some of her essays, and her novel, *Flush*. Her letters to her friends and to Vanessa were the most enjoyable writing she did, judging from the whimsy and ribaldry in them. Some of her portraits were almost equally whimsical and some contain a streak of satire. But her novels were more serious, and the writing of many was perilous for her. Even when she began a novel in fun or with the intention of writing satirically, it might become serious in spite of her intentions. She was all too inclined, as she knew, to "call in all the immensities" as though her writing were beyond her control. Although she professed to have enjoyed the writing of *Night and Day,* both that novel and *Mrs. Dalloway* seem to have developed in the manner described above. *Orlando,* one of her more frolicsome books, became more than a gambol, though it was not as serious as most of her novels. Many of them seem to have been guided in part by the harsh lessons Virginia learned from her first madness. As she suggested in *To the Lighthouse* (p. 224), she could never entirely believe that art was meant to be played with, even in those instances when she was least serious in her writing.

# 11

# Matters of Love and Death:
# The Future Plain

Virginia's first major breakdown continued for more than two years, from the death of her mother until some time after the death of Stella Duckworth, and its effects lasted even longer. She implied in her 1939-1940 memoir that it continued until after her father's death in 1904. Although the years between Stella's and her father's deaths were unhappy and unsettled ones, her difficulties lessened markedly and she lived a relatively normal life from about 1897 until 1904 when her father's death brought on an acute emotional and mental illness, worse than the episode beginning when she was thirteen. Virginia was left much changed by the two painful years after her mother's death. In matters of health, the balance for Virginia had shifted radically, from external to internal forces. As a result, she was much more vulnerable, and much more susceptible to emotional and mental disorder, and therefore in the future it took less external stress to bring on disaster.

A major cause of Virginia's increased instability, Quentin Bell has noted (p. 44), was the new, terrifying and erosive way of thinking about herself that her first madness had forced upon her. She had reached the age of thirteen with few conceptions of self, but after the period of "nothingness" and of "positive death" (Bell's terms for Virginia's first breakdown), "she knew that she had been mad and might be mad again." The specter of her permanently mad half sister Laura was, of course, lurking somewhere in the back reaches of her consciousness to convince her, if she were not fully persuaded by her experience and her fears. Bell said further (p. 44), "To know that you have had cancer in your body and to know that it may return must be very horrible; but a cancer of the mind, a corruption of the spirit striking one at the age of thirteen and for the rest of one's life working away somewhere, always in suspense, a Dionysian [sic] sword above one's head—this must be almost unendurable. So unendurable that in the end, when the voices of insanity spoke to her in 1941, she took the only remedy that remained, the cure of death."

The immediate ways she found to extricate herself from the emotional and mental confusion of the two years following her mother's death also increased her chances for becoming seriously disturbed again. In addition to her scene-making, she resorted to two defenses, neither of them constructive. First, she relied more and more upon women for emotional support, increasingly associating women with security and safety, and remaining childishly dependent on them rather than relying upon herself. Consequently, she learned still another way to think of herself, that is, as a person more attracted to women than to men. Within the next decade she acknowledged this attraction and said that it was in part an erotic one. She was encouraged in this self-concept by Vanessa, who occasionally wrote to Virginia about her "Sapphist tendencies," sometimes seriously and at other times to tease her.[1] Since whatever Vanessa said carried disproportionate weight with Virginia, her opinion must have helped convince Virginia that her sexual attraction was indeed for women. Virginia's reliance on women for emotional support, and Vanessa's appraisal of the matter thus made it increasingly unlikely that Virginia's adult sexuality would be conventional. Her reliance on women also made it much less probable that she would ever resolve, on an adult level, the problems of how to love and be loved, for she

279

continued to approach the women she loved less as an equal than as a child in need of emotional nurturing and mothering. Her writing was of course an important exception. Although she was delighted when women encouraged her to write, as Violet Dickinson did, Virginia never assumed a dependent role in literary matters.

Virginia's other defense against her problems after her mother's death had far greater liability for the future. She tried to overcome the fact of her mother's death by imagining that her mother was still with her. Even though this defense may have helped take the immediate edge off Virginia's grief, ultimately it solved nothing. Instead, it prevented her from learning more rational ways to deal with death, either as a personal or theoretical problem (see chapter 12).

Both of Virginia's immediate defenses against her first mental breakdown were extensions of tendencies and habits present since infancy. The events of the next decade of her life not only encouraged her continued use of these defenses, but also firmly set the general patterns of her adult personality and, therefore, her future. For crucial and traumatic experiences were not ended with the deaths of her mother and Stella, nor with the mourning for them. Needing to overcome her fear and dislike of men and learn to love them, Virginia instead got further lessons in distrust and acquired more reasons to dread the male sex. Needing less stress to overthrow her self-control, Virginia received more and more stress, and once again the stress struck where she was most vulnerable. Therefore, if forces of her first madness were insufficient to ensure that Virginia's mental health would be permanently in jeopardy, they were amply supplemented in the next eleven years. During that time her father and her brother, Thoby, died; Virginia had her first serious postadolescent love relationship with a woman; and her second breakdown occurred, further undermining her limited stability.

Sexuality and Turning Points

The years between the ages of thirteen and fifteen were more critical for Virginia's sexual development, than they are for most people. From all reports, including her own, she reached the age of thirteen relatively ignorant about sex. In the words of Quentin Bell (p. 43), both Virginia and her sister were trained "to preserve a condition of ignorant purity" in sexual matters; or at least a social facade reflecting "purity." Also, the nature of Virginia's sexuality was far less certain than is true for most persons of her age. But she was not totally unformed sexually, and in some respects her sexuality was already an area of potential difficulty.

Therefore, whatever can be fairly charged against George Duckworth, he need not bear the entire responsibility for Virginia's sexual problems. Quentin Bell held this view. "Vanessa, Leonard and, I think, Virginia herself were inclined to blame George Duckworth," he said. "George had certainly left Virginia with a deep aversion to lust; but perhaps he did no more than inflame a deeper wound and confirm Virginia in her disposition to shrink from the crudities of sex . . . ."[2] Bell said also (p. 44), "Virginia felt that George had spoilt her life before it had fairly begun. Naturally shy in sexual matters, she was from this time on terrified back into a posture of frozen and defensive panic." The key words in his statement are "frozen" and "back into" — back into something already present. In addition to her disposition to shrink from sex, one thing already present was of course her shame about the sexual parts of her body. As we have noted, her shame was so profound it seemed to her an archetypal inheritance, as old as time. And Gerald Duckworth, not George, was responsible for initially arousing this deep sense of shame.

Nor was Virginia's sexuality as gender or self-identification wholly unformed when she became thirteen. She had already, to some extent, adopted a masculine role and the ambition to be like her father, finding her greatest sense of self in her plan to be a writer, as he was. Moreover, her first attempts to write novels show that she could assume the persona of the male as readily as that of the female. She also shared many of her father's emotional attitudes toward her mother, which reinforced her tendencies to look to women (as he did) for fulfillment of emotional needs. Correspondingly, to some extent Virginia had already rejected feminine roles. She had not accepted her mother as a model; she had learned she was different from her sister; and as we have seen, she had developed an irrational fear of stereotypically "feminine" behavior such as looking at her reflection in a mirror and being fitted for clothing. Even so, it is inaccurate to think of Virginia at thirteen or later in life as "masculine" in any conventional sense of the term. Rather, she came much closer to fulfilling a feminine stereotype and accepted many of the so-called feminine behavioral roles without question. In the final analysis, however, one must agree with her belief that she was fundamentally outside conventional sex roles and attitudes and was, as she termed it, androgynous in her feeling and thinking.[3]

Virginia's emotional needs added to potential problems with her sexuality. As I have established, long before she was thirteen, her deepest emotional attachments were to females — her mother and Vanessa — making it easier for her to look to women than to men for all kinds of love and emotional gratification. There can be no doubt of her deep attachment to her father, but more often than not her affection for him was opposed by dislike and dread, making it impossible for her to find lasting satisfaction in affection between them.

Virginia's unsatisfied, unresolved infantile love for her mother was crucial in her sexual development; to the extent that any one source of her sexual difficulties can be said to be more fundamental than another, it would be the longing for

her mother. It caused Virginia all her life to search for someone who might be to her all that her mother was and, more
important, all that she had never been to Virginia. Since Virginia usually turned to women for affection, and since these
women had their own needs and expectations of friendship,
the odds were great that eventually a sexual element would
enter one of her relationships, as it did with Vita Sackville-
West,[4] and as perhaps it did earlier, with Violet Dickinson.

Her infantile need for her mother was fundamental also because until it was resolved (and of course that time never
came), Virginia could not easily move ahead to more mature
forms of love and sexual gratification. So much has been made
of the Oedipal and Electra attachments of children for parents
of the opposite sex that it is often overlooked that the first emotional attachment and first "love affair" of both girls and boys
is with the person who mothers them, and that the first family
romance antedates by some years the Oedipal and Electra
attachments. It is often overlooked, too, that a girl needs to
resolve, as Virginia could not, the emotional attachment to the
mother in order to form an Electra attachment to the father. If
the attachment to the mother is not resolved, a likely outcome
is precisely what occurred with Virginia — the continued search
for the mother and difficulty in learning to find men attractive. Another probable outcome is a continued need for relatively infantile expressions of love, rather than mature sexual
expressions of it. Again, Virginia's history is a case in point. At
troubled times throughout her childhood and early adult
years, she needed to be held and soothed physically, as an
infant is held by its mother. She was like her father in that
regard; he called it, in his own case, being petted and comforted. For example, when Virginia was fifteen years old and
was upset and ill, Stella Duckworth sat up stroking and soothing her well into the night, even though she too was ill and was
within five days of her death.[5] Another example occurred

when Virginia and Adrian returned from a voyage to Spain and Portugal in 1905. Virginia, who was twenty-three, by her own account sat all afternoon on Vanessa's lap, in a "maudlin condition."[6] George Duckworth's alleged sexual advances may have consisted in nothing more than his attempts to comfort Virginia as Stella and Vanessa did.

Virginia's letters to Vanessa included frequent references to or requests for physical expressions of love, as did her letters to her friends, Violet Dickinson and Vita Sackville-West. Bell quotes her as saying, during her relationship with Vita, that Vita lavished on her "the maternal protection which, for some reason, is what I had always most wished from everyone. What L[eonard] gives me, and Nessa gives me and Vita, in her more clumsy external way, tries to give me."[7]

Virginia's apparent inability to outgrow infantile expressions of love did not mean that she was asexual, for of course, such manifestations of love have a sexual overtone that in her was exceptionally strong. She was very sensuous despite the fact that, as an adult, her sexuality was not localized in the usual erogenous zones of the body and she could not be gratified by conventionally "sexual" means. Her diffuse sexuality subtly pervaded many of her novels and frequently goes unrecognized by her critics.

Because Virginia's adult sexuality remained so diffuse, it is difficult, and inaccurate, to think of her in terms of familiar sexual models—homosexual, heterosexual, bisexual, and so on. She used the term "androgynous," and it applies well to her. The fact remains that she preferred the affection of women but there is little evidence that she was able to be more than generally stimulated and generally (as opposed to orgasmically) responsive, even in the known instance of a sexual affair with a woman, Vita Sackville-West.[8] Moreover, as Virginia implied, the maternal protection Vita tried to give her was more important than the erotic relationship and was inseparable from it. Virginia was also able to accept affection and love from Leonard Woolf, a mature, loving man who was generous enough to relinquish some of his own sexual needs in order to be mother and father as well as husband and friend to Virginia.

Still other conditions prevented Virginia from developing maturely and adopting a more conventional sexual orientation. As I have suggested, Virginia's limited opportunities to see men and women in happy, uncomplicated romantic involvements presented a serious problem. The complex, often tense relationship between Virginia's parents was hardly one to make love between the sexes attractive. If loving a man required of a woman the sacrifices Julia made for Leslie, and if Leslie's confused feelings about Julia typified a man's love for a woman, the idea of either loving a man or being loved by one could hardly have been enticing to someone as dependent and unsure of herself as Virginia. There were no clear and uncomplicated enactments of love relationships between the sexes in Virginia's immediate view. Quite the contrary, the situation within the Stephen family was especially confusing when it came to the portrayal of male and female roles, either separately or in relationship to each other.

Virginia's first chance to observe, at close range, a beautiful and relatively (only relatively) uncomplicated enactment of heterosexual roles in a love relationship came when she was fifteen and Stella became engaged to Jack Hills. Even that was made stressful for Virginia by her painful excitement over the engagement and the resentment she felt for Stella, as well as by her father's hostility and jealousy about the engagement. Another chance for Virginia to observe a beautiful relationship between a man and a woman came after Stella's death when Jack Hills and Vanessa began to fall in love. But her observations were confused at best; the relationship was destroyed by George Duckworth's outraged, if ironic, sense of propriety for which he had the backing of the English law which forbade men to marry sisters of their deceased wives. George made the innocent love between Jack and Vanessa seem ugly. He also managed to make the matter especially distressing for Virginia by asking her to side with him against Vanessa, which she did before realizing how her sister would view her actions. In general, George succeeded in setting members of the Stephen family against each other: Thoby sided with George; Virginia was torn; and surprisingly, Leslie sided with Vanessa and Jack, against convention and against George.[9]

Jack Hills was thus indirectly involved in what may be broadly characterized as Virginia's sexual education. According to Virginia's 1939-1940 memoir, he was more directly involved when she lived in Fitzroy Square which would mean when she was twenty-five or more. She said that she had learned about homosexuality (in her terms, sodomy) from reading Plato when she was sixteen, but that until Jack spoke to her she had known little about love between men and women. He told her about the love that a man has for a woman and how it is often specifically sexual. He told her also about the extent to which he, as a man, was preoccupied with sex. Until then, Virginia said, no man had spoken to her openly and "cleanly" about sex, and she had supposed that all men were as chaste and as faithful to one woman as her father. Or, she supposed, they vacillated from "priggishness" to "brutishness," and a lack of control and discrimination, as she claimed George Duckworth did.

## Tyranny of the Male

In a general sense, Virginia's experiences with the men in her family helped to complete her sexual education. Unfortunately, these experiences very frequently were negative and

served to amplify her dislike and fear of men in their traditional roles. An example of such an experience was the tyranny
exemplified most of all by her father and to an outrageous
extent also by George Duckworth. In her father's case the
tyranny was pervasive; it occurred in the more positive aspects
of his relationship with Virginia and in the most negative, in
both subtle and flagrant forms. He acted in almost every way
as if he believed a father's duty were to control his children's
lives, by planning their future and dominating their present,
with little regard for their talents, predilections, and interests.
Thoby, who liked mathematics, should definitely not study
that subject at Cambridge; Virginia, who had an almost end
lessly creative imagination and who had problems with empirical thought, should write history. Worse, he wanted to control
their thinking, the manner in which they viewed and concep-
tualized the world. He was of course making traditional
assumptions about the matter: he was their teacher as well as
their father, he was older and therefore must be wiser. He himself had found the one "true" way to conceive of matters; or so
he believed, and it devolved upon him to show his children the
way. Virginia suggested in *Mrs. Dalloway* that intellectual
tyranny such as her father's had colored her view of psychiatry
and psychiatrists. She thought that psychiatry was a "rape of
mind," a "forcing of the soul," an embodiment of much that
she loathed in her father — "They make life intolerable, men
like that."[10] Given that view, a psychiatric route to the solution
of her emotional and mental problems could never have been
an option for her.

In her actual relationship with her father, Virginia was not
always able to resist his influence. One part of her did not want
to resist, but wanted to yield. For several years after his death,
she sometimes wanted very much to think as he thought; in her
1908 memoir it is apparent that many of her conceptions of
her mother were shaped by the "Mausoleum Book." As late as

1928 or 1929, when Virginia wrote *A Room of One's Own,* a few of her statements were influenced by her father—paradoxically so, since the book was opposed to his kind of tyranny. For example, when she said, ". . . a man is terribly hampered and partial in his knowledge of women, as a woman in her knowledge of men" (p. 144), she was almost paraphrasing her father's statement in the "Mausoleum Book" (p. 74) that it is difficult for a woman to understand how a man regards her, and vice versa.

As we have noted, of all the manifestations of Leslie's tyranny, none was more blatant than his weekly exchange with the luckless female who at the time had responsibility for keeping the household accounts. It was then that anything approaching the loveable in Leslie was abruptly discarded, including his boyish dependency upon women and his sweet, reasonable, humble, diffident, sometimes humorous role played in public and with men. He became a veritable Mr. Hyde, raging and verbally brutalizing the women as he never would have done, Virginia believed, if they had been men. It was the occasion when he called the woman to account not only for money, but also for her success or failure (he always found it the latter) in what to Leslie was the ultimate feminine role, inclusive of all other feminine roles—that of keeping the house. In Victorian terms and to Leslie's mind, that meant keeping the sanctuary of the male. Thus, if the woman identified with the role, as Julia and Stella did, Leslie's attack was existential. In *To the Lighthouse* (pp. 62-63), Virginia Woolf indicated how well aware of this she was.

Leslie also manifested his tyranny by representing the old, the passing society, dominated by Victorian standards very much in harmony with his lifelong prudishness and narrow intellectual outlook. Aside from their alleged erotic interest in her, it seemed to Virginia that George and Gerald Duckworth were at their most offensive when they joined Leslie in representing and enforcing conventions of the past.[11] She could almost forgive her father, if only to resolve some of her conflicts about him. But she saw few reasons to forgive George or Gerald, and of course the search for any such reasons ran against her grain.

Many of her father's limitations were native to him, Virginia thought, while many were imposed by circumstances. Reviewing the situation from the vantage point of 1939-1940 and with far more detachment than she could summon in the late 1890s when she lived with him, Virginia gave reasons for his insistence on past values. She mentioned so many that one suspects she was not persuaded by the truth of her arguments. These included his predilection for rational thought rather than creativity and the arts; the "crippling" influence of his Cambridge education; nineteenth-century restrictions on him as a writer; and his social isolation by the time he was sixty-five. She said also that he was unable to face his own feelings or to understand those of others, and even these rather damaging estimates she seemed willing to forgive.

Mitigating factors notwithstanding, the sum of it was that Leslie was in control, and that as an agent of the past, he was abetted by George and Gerald. Thus "cruelly," Virginia said, she and the other Stephen children were under the tyrannical power of the past, and had to live in a model of Victorian society at 22 Hyde Park Gate in the years after her mother's death. They did not succumb to it, however, and were able to move out of it, both literally and figuratively, as soon as Leslie died in 1904. Nevertheless, it had its effect upon Virginia in her professional as well as personal life. She said that she never quite recovered from the feeling that she should be polite to men, especially to older men who were in symbolic or actual authority over her. She thought that it had marred her literary criticism, and that she tended, symbolically, to "pass the buns," as she might graciously do at tea time, when writing criticism of the work of men, especially of older men. Apparently she was doing more than a little of that when she wrote her overly polite and sentimental essay about her father on the centennial of his birth.[12] She did not think the courtesy and restraint entirely regrettable, but felt less inhibited when writing about a woman's book. In writing her novels she was not influenced one whit, she said, by what anyone might think.[13] However, that was long after the "reign" of Leslie Stephen, when Virginia, encouraged and bolstered emotionally by Leonard Woolf, felt more in control of her life.

Virginia said that her father was always an obstacle, even to friendship, and that she and Vanessa tried to keep their friends away from him. More important, in the years after her mother's and Stella's deaths, Virginia learned to escape him herself, entering a "room of her own," in body and spirit, by mounting to her room to read, write, or do Greek lessons with Janet Case. Vanessa escaped to the academy where she was studying art. As Virginia phrased it years later, both sisters escaped "in mind" to the "world" of art and literature they were to inhabit permanently in the future. But escape was only possible during a few hours in the middle of each day, when Leslie, George, and Gerald went about their individual pursuits. By 4:30 in the afternoon, Virginia and Vanessa dressed for tea with Leslie and were returned to the Victorian world in all its tyranny. Facing a social evening with George was even worse, for he often humiliated them at dances and parties, by putting them on display. His parading them made parties seem too much like vital, tribal rites, and therefore made them more frightening than they should have been. Worse still, if Virginia's charges are to be believed, was having to face George's efforts to caress them at bedtime.[14]

Sympathy of the Female

Virginia's fears and her desire to escape from men made it increasingly unlikely that she could learn to love a man fully or sexually. Correspondingly, in late adolescence Virginia began to find females even more sympathetic and began turning more than ever to them for emotional satisfaction. There can be no doubt that she was still acting primarily out of her longing for her mother. But Virginia was, after all, past puberty and thus biologically mature, even if socially and personally quite immature, especially in sexual matters. Thus her needs, motives, and expectations of women had become more complicated than when she was a child. Also, Virginia was acting out of long years of a close and, as she later acknowledged, erotic attachment to Vanessa. She also acted on the basis of skills acquired in "flirting" with Vanessa and "courting" her attentions. She had developed few skills in trying to attract men, and said she found courtship between the sexes difficult to comprehend.

She did not stop her "courtship" of Vanessa, in late adolescence or ever. But by the time Virginia was recovering from the deaths of her mother and Stella, Vanessa was looking away from Virginia and from females for fulfillment of her emotional needs and was "in love" with Jack Hills. Perhaps for that reason, when Virginia was fifteen or sixteen, she began a half-passionate attachment to Madge Vaughan (the wife of Virginia's cousin) that continued, for more than a decade.[15] She found much to attract her to Madge, especially Madge's sympathetic and motherly treatment of her. Later, after Madge's children were born, Virginia identified with them. For a time Virginia called Madge "Mama Vaughan" and "Foster Parent," and referred to herself as Madge's "infant."[16] She also paid some rather awkward, juvenile compliments to Madge. In

1907 she told Madge in a letter that she thought Madge should some day grow into a northern moor and she could climb her heights. She added: "That is meant for a compliment. I wish I could play with the children and have you treat me as a child — a very nice child."[17]

There were other reasons for Virginia's attraction. Madge was beautiful and glamorous in a way that particularly appealed to Virginia and gave her a reason to identify with her. As Trautmann has said (p. 17), Madge respected the arts, was a writer, and the daughter of a writer, but even better, "a friend of the daring writers of the period — Wilde, Swinburne, Meredith." Heretofore, "Virginia had known the more stable Victorians," writers like her father and his circle of friends.

About the time of her interest in Madge Vaughan, Emma Vaughan (Madge's sister-in-law and a cousin of Virginia's) was also an attraction, though apparently a less erotic attraction than Madge. She was the recipient of some of Virginia's personal, epistolary and literary attentions. Virginia had enough confidence in Emma to engage in some of her wilder fantasies in writing to her, and accorded Emma the tribute of an animal nickname. Since the nickname was "Toad," modified variously as "Toadkins," "Todkins," "Toadus," and "Reptile," the tribute may have seemed to Emma a little odd. Emma was the heroine in one of Virginia's early literary efforts, which she entitled, "A Terrible Tragedy in a Duckpond."[18]

It was only when Virginia came to know Violet Dickinson that she found the person who met many of her particular demands and expectations in friendship, and who, moreover, was willing to reciprocate. Julia had befriended Violet and consoled her at the time of her mother's death. Stella had been a closer friend. Like Julia, Violet was identified in Virginia's mind with charitable work and nursing, and she had been eager to mother Virginia and to bring some "light into the gloom" that predominated at 22 Hyde Park Gate.[19] She loved

Virginia, which made her seem charismatic. Violet was at least androgynous and possibly was more masculine than feminine in her identity. She was patient and indulgent with Virginia, even when Virginia vented some of her irritability on her.[20] She would tolerate, from Virginia and the other Stephen children, a great deal of teasing, and Virginia's teasing was not always kind or tactful. For example, Violet's height (more than six feet) seemed to Virginia ridiculous and funny, and she often reminded Violet of her unkind estimation.[21]

Perhaps most important of all, Violet was interested in Virginia's writing. That interest and Violet's love for her elated the young Virginia almost abnormally and had, as we noted, the "miraculous" effect that Virginia likened to bringing "fire out of ashes." Violet read and criticized some of Virginia's early essays, recognizing her talent. Sometimes she angered Virginia by showing her manuscripts to others without her permission.[22] Violet's best contribution, after her general encouragement of Virginia's writing, was introducing her to the editor of the *Women's Supplement* of the *Guardian*. Thus she assisted in bringing Virginia's first writings to publication.[23]

Violet Dickinson could not meet all of Virginia's expectations, however. She was relatively inept with language and considerably less sophisticated intellectually than Virginia would have liked her closest friend to be. Virginia teased and ridiculed Violet for both of these deficiencies. Violet's lack of sophistication and her disapproval of Virginia's plan in 1911 to set up a house at 38 Brunswick Square to be "shared" with young men (her brother Adrian, Maynard Keynes, and eventually Leonard Woolf), caused the friendship to cool.[24] Before that occurred, however, Violet had helped nurse Virginia through the breakdown after her father's death and had assisted in getting her early essays published. But Virginia saw no reason to continue the friendship on its earlier basis. Gratitude was neither extended by Virginia nor expected by Violet, who was an extremely magnanimous and generous woman.

Before Virginia's friendship with Violet Dickinson cooled, it was a very warm one indeed. After a slow and formal beginning, Virginia's shyness disappeared with Violet. She became preoccupied with her friend and was aggressive and self-confident in seeking her out and in writing to her. There were almost daily letters between them for several years. In her letters, Virginia often combined the whimsical language of a child with the language of a lover. Customarily she addressed Violet as "My Woman," "My Violet," or "My Beloved," but also playfully called her from time to time "My Child," "Aunt," and "Niece." She asked Violet for "hot" and affectionate letters.[25] Animal nicknames and other instances of intimate, private language such as that Virginia employed with Vanessa became standard in the letters. Virginia referred to herself as "Wallaby," "baby Kangaroo," and "Sparroy," and she referred to Violet as "mother Kangaroo." In fantasy, at least, Virginia was attracted to a physical relationship with Violet, and Violet tolerated and encouraged Virginia's attraction to a physical relationship. Whether or not such a relationship actually developed is not known; Virginia's letters were so playful and teasing one does now know what to interpret literally. Virginia spoke of "tender memories of a long embrace, in a bedroom,"[26] an embrace that may or may not have occurred. She once asked whether Violet would "like to feel the Wallaby snout" on her bosom. In the same letter, written when Violet was sick, Virginia said, "Goodnight, my Violet. Believe that I snuffle all over you, very soft and comforting. . . ."[27]

Whatever Virginia actually wanted and actually got from Violet Dickinson, mothering was central and fundamental. She compared her letters to Violet to a "baby's slobbering,"[28] and asked Violet to be her "mother Kangaroo," for she (Virginia) would earn her "Kangaroo nest" before she died.[29] She wanted to be stroked by Violet, saying, "Beatrice took us driving today; she brings tears to my eyes sometimes. 'I like being stroked. No one strokes me' she says simply as a child. But Violet is my woman."[30] Virginia felt that Violet belonged to her in a very special fashion, and if she was not hers exclusively (Violet had many strong friendships with women), she belonged more completely to her than to anyone else. In turn, Virginia felt committed to Violet as to no one else. She made avowals that, much sooner than she expected, she was not willing to keep: "Say come and I come—Go and I go," and "'to the ends of the Earth she followed her.'"[31]

Many years later, Virginia was reluctant even to remember her friendship with its impetuous vows and extreme expressions of affection. In 1936, Violet returned to Virginia a carefully preserved collection of Virginia's letters to her, hoping that she might get encouragement from Virginia to publish them.[32] Embarrassed, Virginia asked that the letters not be shown to anyone else and commented that she wasn't sure she entirely liked the young woman she had been when she wrote them.[33]

The women whom Virginia found appealing and sympathetic in her late adolescence and early adult years sometimes annoyed her. With perhaps the prominent exception of Violet Dickinson, most of them were oriented toward men and marriage. As a result, they urged Virginia to marry, against what she thought by that time to be her orientation toward women and what she was coming to regard as her "nature."[34] The pressure to marry resembled that exerted by Mrs. Ramsay (Julia Stephen) on Lily Briscoe (Virginia) in *To the Lighthouse* (pp. 77, 152-157, 253-262). In real life, the pressure to marry worked no better than it did in the novel. It made Virginia feel, and resent, that she was expected to prove her womanhood by eliciting marriage proposals from men and, therefore, made her more resistant to both men and marriage.[35]

*Matters of Love and Death*

## How Not to Mourn for Julia

By forming her attachments to other women, Virginia partly resolved the problem of giving up the mother she had never really had. Although not a fully satisfactory solution, it was on the whole better than the other means she had used to deal with the problem. As I have said, her other solution was to keep Julia Stephen "alive" in fantasy. To the extent that Virginia was able to do so, she may have resolved somewhat the pain of mourning, for Julia still "present" was not a Julia to be mourned at all. Julia still "present" was also an answer to the unlovable phantom Leslie tried to foist upon the children's memory, and therefore to one of the many manifestations of his tyranny. Virginia was of course using a strategy of her father's, for he had comforted himself when he was lonely by calling up memory images of his wife or his children. It is possible that she got her clues from him and was both imitating and besting him. In the "Mausoleum Book" (p. 24) he said that it still "thrilled him to the core" to call up memories of Julia, adding mournfully that alas, his memory was aging, and soon he would be unable to imagine Julia. Finally, by keeping her mother alive in fantasy, Virginia found or created one of her answers to the problem of death as an abstract and general phenomenon. It was one of an evolving series of such answers which she began to form when she was very young, according to her recollections, and continued throughout her life.

Evidently, Virginia began the fantasy of her mother soon, but not immediately, after Julia died, She continued it until she wrote *To the Lighthouse,* her final laying to rest of her mother.[36] After writing that novel, she could no longer call up her long-established fantasies of her mother, a fact Virginia thought inexplicable. Evidently Virginia kept the fantasy of her relatively secret. She referred to it obliquely in her 1908 memoir, which was shown to Vanessa, and directly in her

1939-1940 memoir, which apparently was not seen by anyone until well after her death. She intimated something of the fantasy in *To the Lighthouse* (p. 300) when Lily Briscoe "brings back" Mrs. Ramsay in order to complete her portrait of her. Virginia's correspondence with her sister after the publication of the novel indicated that she had not told Vanessa about her fantasy of Julia, and Vanessa was the person most likely to have been told. More important, in the same correspondence Virginia denied her ability to remember her mother as she actually had been in life, a denial in direct opposition to the other claim of a years-long fantasy of Julia Stephen.

In her 1939-1940 memoir, Virginia was most explicit in describing the fantasy, saying that it had obsessed her. She could see and hear her mother and could imagine what she would be doing or saying as Virginia went about her own life. Therefore, in the development of her own personality, Virginia said, she was "tugged about," "pushed," and "pulled" by this imagined mother. It was analogous, she said, to the way society moulds the person and keeps one in her place. In view of Virginia's need for her mother to love her, which dominated so much of her life, the mother she created in fantasy is significant. Instead of a loving, tender mother, she imagined the stern taskmaster Julia sometimes was in life. One must suppose that Virginia needed the security of a stern, controlling mother as much as she did that of the affectionate one.

Virginia kept more than the specific fantasy of her mother alive. She retained as many of her pleasant memories of the past as possible, especially those in which Julia seemed an extracorporeal, diffuse presence. As I have suggested previously, those memories were probably in part memories of actual infantile experience and in part memories of what Virginia imagined as a child. She retained memories of the past for their own sake, always fascinated by her ability to recover "the moment." But in her novels, at least, the past interacted with the present and the future and therefore had to be reconciled with them. In Virginia's conception, the future acted retroactively on the past, sometimes interfering with memories. Her continued imagination of her mother reflected back upon earlier memories of her and for that reason, Julia did not remain whole and complete in Virginia's memory. She was not permanently established in memory by death as Virginia said people usually were. Virginia said also that the fact of Thoby's death retroactively affected her memories of him and of the time when his death was not anticipated. She saw no way to prevent this kind of distortion[37] and was obviously fascinated by it since she developed it into the dialectic confrontation of present, past, and future expressed in her novels, especially in *The Waves* (pp. 107 ff.).

It is as easy to understand *how* Virginia was able to maintain the fantasy of her mother as it is to understand *why* she did so. The necessary skills were rooted in her extraordinary ability to form sensory images of actual, perceived events and to create such images in her own mind, independent of immediate perception. The necessary skills were also the product of years of practice, of imagining (in the literal sense of creating images) her "familiars" and other mythic creatures in her childhood stories. As in the case of the familiars, who usually were recognized as fiction and not mistaken for reality, Virginia seems to have known that her fantasy of her mother who continued "alive," was only fantasy. That is, she seems to have known that her mother was not really "out there," and was "alive" only in her own mind. Apparently the fantasy was enough to help Virginia overcome some of the utter desolation and abandonment she felt when Julia died, and to feel that the world was once again a little less threatening. However, Virginia confused her fantasy with reality at least once while she was mad; Leonard Woolf reported that she "talked to her mother" during the 1913-1915 episode.

Virginia's use of fantasy to keep her mother with her after death was not of course a true solution to any of the problems she hoped it would solve. In particular it was no solution when death struck the family again. It is not known whether or not Virginia tried to keep Stella "alive," or whether she had any fundamental impulsion to keep her "alive." She did refer to Stella's ghost, and Julia's, as presiding over some of George's and Gerald's "social antics,"[38] but perhaps she was speaking metaphorically. She very much wanted her father after he had died, but the fantasy solution apparently did not work with him, even to the extent it apparently did with her mother, and its failure accounted in part for her second psychotic breakdown. Her most profound use of such fantasy came after Thoby's death. Possibly in that instance it was more successful, but it was also unhealthy and macabre.

# 12

# The Enemies: Death and Madness

Leslie Stephen's health began to fail in 1899, and in 1902 he developed cancer.[1] He died on February 22, 1904, in the first floor bedroom at 22 Hyde Park Gate with a portrait of Julia hanging on the wall facing him.[2] He died with surprising grace, Quentin Bell noted (pp. 84 ff.), for many of his onerous traits dropped away during the long invalidism of his last years. He was in many ways a more integrated person as he died than he had managed to be earlier, perhaps because he found it easier than most to think of himself as a sick man facing death. He had believed himself frail since childhood and sick for some years before his second wife died. In a sense, he had schooled himself for the part of the invalid. More important perhaps, a man who is approaching death no longer has to plan and work for the future as he professed to dislike doing, or pretend to be more manly than he feels, or beg and play games to get sympathy and attention.

But Virginia's father did not overcome all the traits that had made him a problem to himself and his family. He continued to worry about money, though less stormily. Virginia hoped he could worry less as he became weaker.[3] He was still irritable at times. When his sister called, he found her as boring as ever and flared up at her, sending her from the sickroom in tears—a spectacle that Virginia and the other children, who shared Leslie's dislike for Caroline Emilia, found as ludicrous as it was

300

pathetic.[4] Months later, when her brother was closer to death and she called again, Leslie was kinder. He asked her to prolong her visit saying, "Don't go" (Virginia's phrase), and she said that his asking her not to go had made her visit worthwhile.[5] Anny Thackeray Ritchie managed her visits to Leslie with more aplomb, according to Anny's daughter. After several visits, when he poured "jeremiads and invectives" into her "sympathetic ear," Anny took the initiative. Coming in for her next visit, she sat down and said, " 'Well Leslie — Damn — Damn — DAMN!' which made him burst out laughing and the visit was much gayer than usual."[6] There were other reports of Anny's visits, however. Bell said (p. 85) that Anny was cruelly optimistic when visiting Leslie. Leslie himself said in a letter to Charles Norton that his "beloved Annie Ritchie," like his children and his sister, was of great comfort to him[7] — but that was very likely the public Leslie Stephen speaking.

Their father's slow dying was emotionally more difficult for the Stephen children than for himself. It was especially traumatic for Virginia who had not learned how to deal either with her father or with the fact of death. She found her father's decline far worse to bear than her mother's. During the years when Julia's health was failing, neither Virginia nor anyone else, except perhaps Stella, had confronted the fact openly. But when Leslie began to die, the situation was reversed: no one — especially not Leslie — tried to avoid the reality of his condition. Moreover, Virginia was now an adult and was expected to face up to death as adults do.

## Old and New Conflict

Virginia found her father consistently more lovable and more pathetic during his last two years. Therefore, her feelings were less conflicting than they had been when he had aroused her to hatred as well. He became "such an attractive" and "such a lovable creature."⁸ On her twenty-second birthday, he gave Virginia an emerald ring. Elated, she wrote to Violet: "Father gave me a ring—really a beautiful one, which I love, the first ring I have ever had." She said in the same letter: "It amazes me how much I get out of my Father still—and he says I am a very good daughter! He is the most delightful of people —and Lord knows how we shall ever get along alone."⁹ Like James in *To the Lighthouse,* Virginia had her "well done."

Leslie's behavior during his last years of life brought only surface relief for one of Virginia's conflicts about him. It also brought new problems, for she had to face the impending loss of the father she had come to believe she could love unequivocably. Perhaps it would have been better, she said, if he had died immediately after becoming ill, when she had had less to give up.¹⁰ There were other conflicts concerning his death: he wanted to die, and since it was terrible to watch him die, not knowing what was going to happen—why not wish him dead? Then she saw the other side, believed he wanted to live, and that if he did live there was great promise that she might work out all her problems with him. She vacillated from one position to the other, trying to prepare herself for his death and at the same time trying to postpone even thinking about it, saying there was no need yet to decide what she felt.¹¹ And she did in fact both want him to die and not to die, as perhaps she'd both wanted Stella to die and not to die. The strength that kept her father going, she concluded, was both terrible and wonderful.¹²

Virginia, her sister, and brothers managed at times to almost forget that Leslie was dying and to go sanguinely about their daily business. They talked of Thoby's career and agreed that he should prepare for the bar.¹³ Eager to break with the past, actually and symbolically, they planned new living arrangements away from 22 Hyde Park Gate with all of its somber associations. They plotted and worried about how they might separate from their Duckworth half brothers, not quite knowing whether or how to do so and not believing they could.[14] They were saved in the end when Gerald decided to go his own way[15] and when George married.[16] Daily business and planning for the future made Virginia increasingly aware of the constant juxtaposition and opposition of the forces of life and death—another theme for her later writing.[17] She said that it was right for Thoby and Adrian to celebrate the New Year as 1903 approached even though Leslie was ill. "We are the sanest family in London and talk and laugh as though nothing were happening; Adrian and Thoby are going to sing the new year in! We should never get on without this kind of thing."[18] Yet it seemed strange to her for the family to be so detached. She was bothered by their realistic planning for the future, yet recognized it to be right and necessary. She said to Violet that it was "damned pathetic" to take life so seriously.[19]

No one could forget Leslie's condition very long, for he was there to remind them. He reminded Virginia most specifically on November 14, 1903, when he decided that it was time to close the "Mausoleum Book" and symbolically to close his life. He made Virginia a principal in this rite by dictating his last entry to her. She recorded it in her best handwriting. He began by saying that he would write no more in that book. Then he reviewed the course of his illness, how he'd had surgery, made some progress, then began to grow weaker. He concluded by saying that his children had all been "as good and as tender" to him as anyone could have been during his last months and years. It comforted him to know that they were so fond of each other that when he was gone they would be better able to get on without him.[20]

Still other reminders were the nurses installed in the house and the doctors whose repeatedly inaccurate speculations increased the family's distress. Leslie would be dead within four months; then he had improved amazingly; still later, he would be dead within six months. Death and the unconsciousness that would precede death were said time and again to be imminent, while Leslie and the death watch continued for two years or more. As Virginia said bitterly in her 1939-1940 memoir, her father had found it difficult to die of cancer at the age of seventy-two, while her mother, who had made his health her fetish, had died of overwork at forty-nine.[21]

There were other reminders and other painful and annoying aspects of Leslie's long slow dying. Well before his death, relatives began their letters and calls, one presumes not very different in kind from those after Julia and Stella died.[22] Virginia was made "damned mad," she said to Violet, by their sentimentality and by their talk about death. "The precise and only thing that anyone can do is to stay away and be silent."[23]

The relatives also talked about religion, a topic few would have dared discuss with Leslie. But in the relatives' minds religion was inevitably associated with death. They took the occasion of Leslie's last illness to argue with the Stephen children whose lack of religious training appalled many of them. Virginia especially loathed the talk about religion.[24] Nevertheless, she thought over the question. She wrote to Violet that she wanted a God—quick—but not the "Christian one." She also said that she could suffice with a God who was half Katie Thynne (a friend of hers and Violet's), who reminded Virginia of a Greek goddess, and half an old Pagan god like Violet Dickinson.[25] She wrote again to Violet to say that the only reason "to believe in a God [was] that *some* life grows in one and outgrows most things. But otherwise—it seems to me he has a heavy hand."[26]

The stress of the two or more years of her father's last illness would have taxed the nerves of a much stronger person than Virginia, and the strain on her in the months before her father died was almost unendurable. It manifested itself in her ruminations about the true nature of her feelings concerning Leslie's approaching demise. The strain also showed itself in Virginia's identification with his illness and in her desire for the comforting attentions of some of the women who called on her father. By this time, in writing to Violet Dickinson, Virginia was frank about being especially attracted to women. In a half serious letter to her, Virginia said, "Father is a fraud, only an invalid for the sake of his ladies. I wish I could be an invalid and have ladies. I am so susceptible to female charms. . . ."[27] Virginia supposed her father to enjoy his callers more than he actually did. He wrote to a sister-in-law, "The amiable ladies who come to see me are not many and I fear are rather apt to bore me." But he had his ways to be rid of them, for he was still capable of playing games, even though he was dying. "One [lady] has been here just now, talking very fast till I had to look as tired as I could to get her to go."[28] Virginia identified also with Violet Dickinson's illness when she injured her back in an accident. "I wish these things would happen to me and not to you. I could carry on my existence quite well flat on my back. . . ."[29] Later she said: ". . . I wish *I* could hurt my back and have all the beautiful ladies holding up their hands and saying Darling!"[30]

Virginia's reaction to the increased strain was also evident in the vague thoughts of suicide she expressed several times in her letters to Violet Dickinson. Sometimes she expressed them as denials that she wanted to die. She said that life was horrible, but that she didn't want to "creep into her narrow bed" just yet, and she made her meaning clear by specifying that by "narrow bed" she meant "grave."[31] In September she said that a gift of violets (from Violet) reminded her of the flowers that grow in the unhallowed part of the churchyard (where suicides are buried), where she would someday lie. She added that she found September the saddest time of the year, the time that made her think of death and dying.[32]

Leslie continued to hang on to life — needlessly it seemed to Virginia. She began to admit that she now wanted him to die. As for her part, she said, she would ruin her health long before she was his age so that she would not have to die slowly as he was.[33] Avowing a preference for death rather than infirmity was not uncommon in the Stephen family. In 1893, Leslie expressed that preference when his brother was dying.[34] In 1909 Vanessa visited a "decrepit" old aunt, and commented to Virginia that she would commit suicide before letting herself reach such a state.[35] Virginia's repeated plaint was that "life" was strange and unpleasant because it forced one to go through such horrors. The "world" was like a "burned out moon."[36] The only thing that made living worthwhile was affection, specifically the affection between herself and Violet Dickinson. "My Violet, Dont [sic] think me damned sentimental but its [sic] peace and balm to talk to you, and that is the only kind of good there is in the world. What all these tragedies are made for I believe. Otherwise it seems needless torture."[37]

Other than escape into affection — or into death — dulling her emotions and living within her mind seemed to Virginia the only recourse. ". . . [T]he normal state of things now is a kind of grimness — and nothing much matters. I am sure the facts of life — the marryings and bearings and buryings are the least important — and one acts one's drama under the hat. . . ."[38]

## A Second Breakdown

Despite the terrible strain, Virginia was able to maintain control of her emotions until her father finally died and for several months thereafter. Much of the reason for her control was the quasi-maternal care and whatever else, in reality or in fantasy, Virginia gained from her friendship with Violet Dickinson. Credit must also go to Leslie, who, as he died, became much more lovable and deserving of pity and much less the old wretch, making it possible for Virginia to hope and believe that she could finally work out her differences with him. After he died her belief recoiled, for she concluded that "life" had betrayed her, as it seemed so often to betray the Stephen family. As she said in her 1908 memoir, with time and good intentions, the unhappy aspects of the relationship with her father would have worked themselves out, had not death once again intervened. Quentin Bell said (pp. 84-85), "In his present state [Leslie] could no longer be a tyrant and his tyranny might be forgotten. Between him and Virginia a special bond had been established. She loved him and he, for his part, had for some time felt a special tenderness towards her. 'Ginia,' he wrote, 'continues to be good to me and is a great comfort,' and again: 'She can be most fascinating.'"

But most of the credit for Virginia's control during Leslie's illness belongs to her, not to others. This seems especially true when one recalls that she had not entirely thrown off the effects of the disaster after her mother died and was much more vulnerable than before her first round with madness. But her means of control as Leslie died were not altogether healthy ones. She got through the long death watch by grim determination, by trying not to think, and finally by convincing herself that her father wanted to die and that therefore she wanted him to do so.[39] Her decision that she wanted him dead recoiled even more devastatingly than did her belief that she and her father were moving toward a complete resolution of the problems between them. Soon after he died, she began to be preoccupied with the idea that he had not really wanted to die but had wanted very much to live.[40] Quentin Bell said (p. 84) that before her father's death Virginia had known "that he was reluctant to die because his children had at last got to an age at which he could know them and, knowing, love them. He wanted to see what would become of them." However, Bell said (p. 86) that eventually Leslie did want to die, implying that Virginia was perhaps unrealistic. Certainly Virginia's growing belief that she had killed her father by wishing him dead was unrealistic and bizarre and was a pathetic instance of her mythic sense that internal psychological processes such as thoughts can act with physical force in the world beyond oneself. She was overwhelmed by terrible guilt for "causing" her father to die and for not having been more comfort to him in his last years. According to Quentin Bell (p. 84), Vanessa felt similar but more moderate guilt after Leslie's death, dreaming once that she had committed a murder. Guilt notwithstanding, Bell said further (p. 89), Vanessa was unabashedly "delighted" to be "delivered from the care and ill-temper of her father" and her happiness to be free added to Virginia's stress.

There was at least one poignant instance after Leslie Stephen died of Virginia's belief that the external world expressed her emotions. Her thoughts were similar to ideas she had after her mother's death, but Virginia had far less insight after her father's death than at the earlier time. Either Virginia had broken the emerald ring her father had given her, or she imagined it changed. Subsequent events suggest that she only imagined it broken. The ring was taken to be repaired, and when it was returned, it still seemed damaged to Virginia.[41] She then dreamed that she had told her father that she loved him, and the next day the ring seemed to be much improved.[42] It still appeared to Virginia as if the emerald were damaged, but she thought the general effect beautiful.[43] Years later, in 1918, apparently having entirely forgotten about the ring her father gave her, Virginia noted in her diary that she had become strangely fascinated by a broken emerald ring while shopping for a stone lost from another ring.[44]

Virginia's unrealistic guilt was not a new dimension in her personality, but in her second breakdown it was carried to radical proportions. As has been observed, she had been bothered by guilt when her mother died, not because she believed that she had killed her (at least as far as one knows), but because she was so "vain, selfish, and egotistical" as to worry about her own feelings. As noted also, she felt guilty about Stella but apparently did not blame herself for causing her to die despite having almost wished her dead. There was, therefore, a painful and ominous progression in Virginia's sense of guilt and in her tendency to lose touch with reality. There was a corresponding increase in internal pressure, to which her second breakdown can be largely attributed.

This is to say that she had no external pressures, only that the balance had tragically shifted. Her father *was* dead and she was forced to go through more of the hated mourning rituals and to submit herself once again to sympathy from irritating though well-meaning relatives and friends. She found their letters of condolence particularly excremental. "The relations have been relieving their souls in pen and ink," she wrote to Violet. The eulogies and obituaries for her father became still another source of special stress, not unlike the stress she felt when her father had tried to eulogize her mother nearly a decade earlier. Virginia complained to Violet that the newspapers took too little trouble with the obituary notices. She said that her father had always thought his own obituary notices would amuse him, but that he would not have been able to tolerate the ones she had seen. It was odd, she continued, what dull impressions people seem to have had of her father. "All this stupid writing and reading about Father seems to put him farther away...." But she concluded that there was nothing she could do about it.

Possibly Virginia tried to create a fantasy to keep her father "alive" as she had with her mother. "...I have the curious feeling of living with him every day. I often wonder as we sit talking what it is I am waiting for, and then I know I want to hear what he thinks. It was a most exquisite feeling to be with him, even to touch his hand—he was so quick, and that one finds in no one else."[45] If she did in fact try to imagine her father still present, she must have been less successful in bringing him back than her mother, since she only mentioned using the fantasy to keep her mother with her. However, she dreamed of both her father and her mother nightly, she admitted after writing *To the Lighthouse*. So in one sense her father was not laid to rest until her mother was. But he was sufficiently at rest that she could write in her own fashion as she said would have been impossible if her father had continued to live.[46]

Since she was unable or unwilling to create her father in fantasy, another recourse was to try not to think at all about his death. She said to Violet, "Much thinking would send me down to bottomless pits...."[47] She and the other Stephen children tried to divert themselves by vacationing, going first to Manorbier in Pembrokeshire. While on that trip, Virginia wrote to Violet, "I don't want to think; I feel like a cow with her nose in the grass...."[48] Being in Manorbier made her father's death seem less terrible and more natural, she said, but she continued to reproach herself for not having done enough for him in the years when he was lonely. During this trip, the Stephens began to plan another trip, to Italy, where Violet would join them. Virginia commented to Violet that she did not find the planning easy, that it all seemed dreamlike, and that "the affairs of this world" were difficult to realize.[49]

While she mourned for her father, Virginia found support from Vanessa and from her association with her brothers as well. She spoke of this to Violet, using a peculiar analogy: "You cant [sic] think how amicable we all are together—like husbands and wives, more than anything else—and the odd thing is we dont [sic] get bored at all, but go on our own ways, and meet fresh and cheerful."[50]

At times Virginia seemed to become more rational about

her father's death, but nevertheless her preoccupation with it continued. She wrote to Violet, "You mustnt [sic] think that I always feel as I do sometimes." Her father's death "had to be," and she knew she was not really at fault but was still haunted by his loneliness and her failure to help him. "I think he just knew how much I cared, and the happy time was just beginning. . . ." She believed now that her father had wanted to go on living, ". . . as a young man does," although she admitted that others did not think as she did.[51]

Virginia's second major disturbance began to reach a crisis stage during the trip to the Continent. After their visit to Italy, the Stephens returned by way of Paris from which point, clearly desperate, Virginia wrote to Violet who had returned to England ahead of the rest of the party. "Oh Lord, how cross I have been, how dull, how tempersome, — and am still. You had much to stand: I wish I could repay all the bad times with good times. . . . Oh my Violet if you could only find me a great solid bit of work to do when I get back that will make me forget my own stupidity I should be most grateful. I *must* work."[52] ("Must" was underlined three times.)

Virginia returned from the trip to Italy on May 9, 1904, and for the next several months was acutely disturbed. Dr. George Savage, a family friend, and three nurses attended her much of the time. She was also nursed by Vanessa, who had difficulty managing Virginia, and by Violet Dickinson. She spent three months of her second breakdown at Burnham Wood, Violet's home in Welwyn, and she also had scarlet fever there.[53]

The symptoms of Virginia's second breakdown were similar to but more extreme than those of her first. There was no longer any doubt that she had lost the ability to distinguish inner and outer realities or that she was hallucinatory.[54] She attempted suicide by throwing herself from a window so close to the ground that she did herself no serious harm, according to Quentin Bell (pp. 89-90). Headaches, sleeplessness, and other physical symptoms were once again present.[55] These continued after the worst of the breakdown was over and returned at intervals for the rest of Virginia's life as danger signals that serious emotional and mental problems were imminent.[56] Further, there was a new symptom, or one not mentioned in relation to her first breakdown: she began refusing to eat, thus manifesting her psychological distress, especially her morbid guilt, in the same bizarre manner as in later years when she was mad or threatened by madness. She said that she had brought her problems on herself by eating too much. Her refusal of food led to general fractiousness and angry quarrels when Vanessa insisted that she eat, and it led also to similar quarrels with Leonard Woolf and her nurses during her breakdown beginning in 1913.[57]

Virginia's own estimation of her problems was stated in a letter she wrote to Violet as she was recovering. "I think the blood has really been getting into my brain at last. It is the oddest feeling, as though a dead part of me were coming to life. I cant [sic] tell you how delightful it is — and I don't mind how much I eat to keep it going. All the voices I used to hear telling me to do all kinds of wild things have gone — and Nessa says they were always only my imagination. They used to drive me nearly mad at Welwyn, and I thought they came from overeating — but they can't, as I still stuff and they are gone."[58] Nevertheless, she continued occasionally to be resistant to eating for the next several years. It no doubt helped when she ate properly, but affection helped more. "I am so happy that people are fond of me — you can't think. . . . I do love affection!"[59]

Obituary for Father

In the fall of 1904, Virginia was beginning to recover, but Vanessa still found her difficult to manage. She spent two periods in Cambridge with her father's sister, Caroline Emilia Stephen, whom Virginia called "Nun" or "Quaker."[60] During her first visit, Virginia finally got her "great solid bit of work" when Frederic Maitland invited her to help in preparing his book, *The Life and Letters of Sir Leslie Stephen.* She also got her chance to write her version of an "obituary" for her father. Virginia's role in Maitland's biography was to read and abstract the family letters and to write a brief account of her father from the family's perspective.[61] Virginia wanted the task for reasons other than the work involved, for she was apprehensive that "Nun" would write about him from her particular biases. Virginia was "maddened," she wrote to Violet Dickinson, whenever her aunt talked about her father, and she wanted to assist Maitland in order to dispose of "Nun's" theories about him. Evidently, Virginia was confused about the matter; she had said earlier in the same letter to Violet that her aunt was admittedly reluctant and "nervous" to give Maitland her memories of Leslie because they "weren't altogether happy or characteristic."[62] In addition, Virginia learned that "Nun" considered her the right person to write about Leslie from the family viewpoint.[63] Vanessa at first agreed also, telling Virginia that she understood Leslie better than anyone else.[64]

Not everyone concurred, however. Jack Hills, who had been Stella Duckworth's husband, questioned the propriety of Virginia's assignment to abstract the family letters. He was concerned that family privacy be protected and that no "personal" facts be made public.[65] In light of Leslie Stephen's confused emotions about Stella, as well as family dissention over Stella's marriage to Jack and, later, over Vanessa's brief romance with him, perhaps his worry about the letters was not inordinate. Nevertheless, Virginia thought him unreasonable and believed that he was meddling in affairs that did not concern him. Worse, it seemed to her that he was attacking her good sense and judgment.[66] Then Vanessa changed her view and agreed with Jack as a matter of principle and perhaps because of her affection for him. She was horrified, she wrote to Virginia, that any third person, even Frederic Maitland, should read anything meant for only two or should see "intimate bits" of family letters.[67] But Virginia had Vanessa check her abstracts,[68] and as it turned out, neither Jack nor Vanessa needed to have worried. Both Virginia's comments about her father, pages 474-476 in Maitland's book, and the published abstracts of family letters were extremely circumspect and cautious. Unfortunately, her contributions did nothing to offset Maitland's rather limited perspective of Leslie Stephen.

### Recovery

Virginia made a poor and tenuous recovery from her breakdown after her father's death, as she had from her earlier period of madness. She continued to be plagued by headaches, backaches, and sleeplessness and to be bored and irritable — possibly because she was required to rest and to limit her reading, writing, and physical activity. Another source of irritation was "Nun." That Virginia found her aunt so trying was more a reflection of Virginia's problems than of her aunt's deficiencies. "Nun's" whole system of "toleration, benignity, and resignation" was one to which Virginia objected strenuously. One could only count on trivial talk from "Nun," Virginia complained, but trivial talk that was painfully well expressed and well pronounced.[69] Probably as a twist on the expression "blow one up," used in the Stephen family to mean "give one a scolding," Virginia said she would like to blow "Nun" up with gunpowder, just to see what would happen.[70] But she took her revenge, or at least vented her irritabilities, through more characteristic means by writing about "Nun." She sent a "comic" description of "Nun's" household to Vanessa which amused and perhaps alarmed her by the hostility expressed. Virginia was "somewhat rabid," Vanessa said.[71] A little later Virginia wrote one of her portraits of "Nun" and Vanessa reported to Virginia that Violet Dickinson said that it was well thought out and howlingly funny.[72]

Undoubtedly, Virginia, like Leslie, was unfair to "Nun," and occasionally Vanessa would come to "Nun's" defense, though in a rather backhanded fashion. Vanessa said, for example, that "Sows" were good beasts and had their uses, and that they had brains of sorts if one knew how to dig for them.[73] Vanessa also commented to Virginia that "Nun" could not be entirely selfish since she took such a firebrand as Virginia to her bosom.[74]

Dr. Savage continued for several years to be in charge of Virginia's treatment. He charged no fee, being proud, he said, to do what he could for Leslie Stephen's children.[75] Virginia became disillusioned and resistant, saying that his sleep medication did not induce sleep, but rather made her headaches worse.[76] She was pleased, however, to have his blessing when she took up pipe smoking.[77] Often Vanessa was the intermediary between Dr. Savage and Virginia, reporting Virginia's symptoms to him and relaying his advice, in turn, to Virginia.[78] Because Vanessa liked Dr. Savage, she argued that Virginia should follow his advice, knowing that she would almost certainly anger Virginia by agreeing with him.[79] It was her opinion, she wrote Virginia, who was then staying with "Nun" in Cambridge, that Dr. Savage understood Virginia well and that not many people did understand her. On one hand, she agreed with Dr. Savage that Virginia should lead a quiet life outside London for a time and told Virginia she believed that her boredom and irritability in Cambridge were symptoms of her illness, not "of place." On the other hand, she said, she agreed with the doctor's recommendations that Virginia should not be "forced" to do anything, but should decide for herself whether or not to come back to London.[80]

Letters from Vanessa to Virginia through 1904, 1905, 1906, and 1907 carry evidence of her concern about Virginia's slow recovery. They also reveal some of Dr. Savage's interpretations and treatments of Virginia's problems, which Vanessa accepted with few questions. The interpretations and treatments confirmed to Virginia and others that her problems were more physical than mental and emotional. Also, if Virginia had not by that time become convinced that she was like her father, Dr. Savage's appraisal of matters must have persuaded her, for his statements parallel many things that the family believed about Leslie and that Leslie believed about himself. Vanessa's concurrence with Dr. Savage, added weight to his opinions, even when it angered Virginia.[81] Apparently Dr. Savage was a proponent of the George Beard-Weir Mitchell school of thought concerning emotional and mental disturbances, a philosophy much in vogue before Freudian influence made itself widely felt.[82] Beard and Mitchell thought that mental and emotional problems came literally from "nerve weakness" due to inheritance or to fatigue, poor diet, disease, and so on. In keeping with their theory of causation, they proposed that such illnesses be treated with rich diet, relaxation, and rest. Among other dubious contributions, they helped to establish concepts such as "rest-cure," "neurasthenia," and "neurosis," all of which originally implied physical rather than psychological causes for problems such as Virginia's.

Dr. Savage, Vanessa, Virginia, and later Leonard Woolf were convinced that Virginia's problem basically derived from her physical constitution. She had a "sensitive," "very delicately made" organism, Vanessa once said to Virginia,[83] one that was easily upset by such things as poor diet, lack of sleep and rest, and too much excitement and activity. Although it is apparent now that some of the effects or symptoms of Virginia's problems were being interpreted as causes, Dr. Savage's ideas must have seemed logical enough at the time. Virginia was seriously undernourished as a consequence of her refusal to eat and her inability to sleep or rest, and, of course, she had many physiological symptoms deriving from her emotional problems.

Vanessa usually stated Dr. Savage's interpretations directly and frankly to Virginia, but sometimes she tried to cajole Virginia by putting them into the affectionate, private language that Virginia loved. She also "babied" Virginia. "Poor little monkeys" are so easily "tramped on and squashed," she said in one letter.[84] She frequently reminded Virginia to adhere to the prescribed treatment which followed the Beard-Mitchell formula closely. Rest above all: rest, sleep, and be quiet.[85] Be careful about diet; eat meat at least twice each day; eat a balanced diet;[86] take the prescribed tonic.[87] Drink chocolate at bedtime, for "want of nourishment" will keep one awake.[88] Expect more tension during menstruation, and rest more at that time.[89] Back pains come from a lack of nourishment, Vanessa cautioned Virginia, and were another indication that she needed more food. Eat. Be sensible. Don't work so much.[90]

Did Dr. Savage's prescribed treatment help? Probably not; rather, it seems to have added to Virginia's discomfort, tension, and irritability. She was not always able to follow the advice to eat and sleep, and she resented it. Even if she had been able to follow the doctor's instructions, she would have felt only superficially improved at best. Fundamentally, nothing would have changed. The advice to rest was probably harmful, for it meant giving up physical exercise, reading, and writing, leaving Virginia too much with her thoughts and with no outlet for her tension.

Although Vanessa followed Dr. Savage in emphasizing physical causes and the good to be derived from better physical care, she indicated repeatedly that she didn't think all of Virginia's problems were physical. Some of Vanessa's opinions were accurate to a fault, though they were perhaps of little value to Virginia and may have disturbed her. Virginia was peculiar.[91] Virginia could not be trusted to act sensibly about herself and someone had to tell her what to do.[92] Virginia was sensible about herself only in theory, and used poor judgment in applying her theories.[93] Virginia was forgetful and should work to overcome that fault.[94] Vanessa was correct that Virginia was forgetful, but her description was a case of the pot chiding the kettle; Vanessa frequently forgot things and several times wrote to Virginia that she had lost her luggage while traveling. Vanessa also cautioned Virginia about her dress and toilet, telling her that Lady Robert Cecil, whose portrait Vanessa was painting, had said that others worried that Virginia could not attend to her appearance properly.[95] A better piece of advice was that Virginia shouldn't bottle up her "irritations," but should let them out,[96] which Virginia was inclined to do anyway.

When Vanessa was less direct, she was perhaps more helpful, as when she tried to address Virginia's difficulties by building her self-confidence, much as Julia Stephen had tried to build Leslie's when he worried about his success in life. Vanessa praised Virginia for her "genius," and was sincerely convinced that Virginia had extraordinary talent.[97] She relayed compliments, evidently hoarding them as Julia had done for Leslie. For example, she reported that Violet called Virginia's letters "brilliant"[98] and that another friend was "struck by" Virginia's loveliness, growing independence, decreased shyness, and increased ability to "hold her own."[99] Vanessa jokingly hedged the compliment from Violet; after all, she said, Violet's taste was peculiar.[100]

In the main, Vanessa seems to have been less patient and indulgent with Virginia's foibles than either Violet Dickinson, Madge Vaughan, or "Nun," with each of whom Virginia spent periods of time during her second breakdown and recovery period. But then Vanessa was more often with Virginia and felt more responsibility to control her behavior. Moreover, Virginia more openly resisted Vanessa than she did the others. Virginia could arouse Vanessa to impatience even when they were apart as for instance, with her irrational fear about Vanessa's welfare. Virginia evidently transferred to Vanessa many of the anxieties she had had about their mother, thinking that disaster might at any time overtake her. When she was separated from Vanessa and did not receive daily letters from her, Virginia would write to her of the fears. Was Vanessa sick that she did not write? Was Vanessa dead, and were people keeping the news from Virginia? Virginia overstated her fears and anxieties, and tried to joke about them but did feel truly threatened when she was out of touch with her sister. Vanessa did not hide her annoyance: Virginia was absurd to "fidget" when she didn't hear from her;[101] Virginia was "an owl" to imagine her "with diseases" and should not be "so foolish."[102] Her letters reached Virginia erratically because of problems with the post, she insisted, and would Virginia please be assured that "dead or alive" she would write to her.[103]

In the spring of 1905, while still very unstable, Virginia made the trip to Spain and Portugal with Adrian. She began the trip poorly prepared, forgetting her sponge bag and toilet articles. Vanessa wired ahead to advise her about buying others.[104] Also, Adrian had to supervise Virginia and assist her in dressing and combing her hair.[105] As noted previously, when she returned, she was so "maudlin" that she had to sit all afternoon on Vanessa's lap.[106] However, the trip evidently gave her some of her ideas for *The Voyage Out,* her first novel. This may be inferred from her letters to Violet while on the trip. She wrote that she had conversed with a young woman who, like Rachel Vinrace in the novel, was the daughter of the owner of the shipping line, and who was taking a voyage on her father's ship.[107] Also, Virginia referred to the trip as "the voyage out."[108]

## The Enemies

### Another Betrayal

In her early twenties Virginia knew what her "enemies" were. She had lived through the deaths of three people she loved, albeit ambivalently, and the distressing rituals attendant upon death. Two of the deaths had precipitated her into madness. She had gone through other trauma and stress — far more than her share. And then came more tragedy: Thoby died in 1906, at the age of twenty-six. His death was so horrifying that she could not, and did not, face up to the reality of it. There were several reasons for this, but mainly it was because she loved her brother. Also, as was true of her mother, she had lost someone she believed she had not really known.[109]

When she wrote *Jacob's Room* (1922) and *The Waves* (1931), she tried to rediscover, eulogize, and memorialize him, but could not approach Thoby's memory directly. In *Jacob's Room,* she decided to divine Thoby by apprehending his surroundings and the world as she believed he had experienced them. Her rationale was that he had lived in the universe of the persons and objects he had experienced and therefore to apprehend them was to apprehend the personality of her brother. In *The Waves,* Thoby is the spirit of Percival who, although dead, is the center of the book and the focus of the lives of its characters. Virginia wrote about Thoby, still with difficulty, in her 1939-1940 memoir. In her notes for it she referred to his "temperamental melancholia" and his resentment of their mother's authority.[110] When she wrote the actual memoir, apparently she was unable to say much more about him. She made several efforts, then admitted that she "wafted and shirked" the task of writing about Thoby because he was too much associated with the seven unhappy years between Stella's death and her father's.

Thoby's death was on a par with Stella's in that it represented to Virginia the tragic theme of the Stephen family, the betrayal of life. He was young, and he showed great promise for the future. Also, the circumstances preceding his death bespoke promise in multifold ways. The Stephen children had succeeded in throwing off the past, actually and symbolically, by moving away from 22 Hyde Park Gate. Their father was dead, and except for Virginia's continued irrationality and involvement with his memory, he was a closed chapter in their lives. Virginia was recovering from her second madness. The despised Duckworth half brothers were out of their immediate lives. And Thoby's death came at the end of and, in a sense, was a consequence of what everyone expected to be a happy vacation in Greece.

The family, accompanied by Violet Dickinson, set off in great anticipation and returned to tragedy. They were disappointed in the trip itself, and they seemed to be attended by a malevolent spirit almost from its beginning. There was a flood on the *wagon-lit,* and some of their belongings, including Virginia's "stays," floated away in the car. Violet undertook to rescue them, and it was such a comic sight that the Stephens laughed uproariously — and for once went too far in teasing her. She spoke of the trip and their unkind laughter thirty-five years later, in a letter to Vanessa, saying that it was one of the few times she had been displeased with the young Stephens.[111] Vanessa became ill on the trip. She seemed to recover but then became worse.[112] Thoby separated from the rest of the party while Vanessa was ill, going off to join Clive Bell and other friends. Adrian was upset because Thoby seemed not to care what was happening to Vanessa, or even to know, and wrote to tell Clive of Vanessa's continued ill health and to complain of Thoby's lack of interest in the family.[113]

Thoby returned to England before the rest of the family where he developed typhoid fever. Evidently, he had contracted it in Greece. Violet became ill with typhoid before the trip ended, Vanessa was still sick, and Virginia and Adrian were faced with the responsibility of getting one invalid and one partial invalid back to England. There they found Thoby sick. Violet was taken to her home where she was seriously ill for several months. Vanessa became worse, then better, and Thoby was worst of all. The least practical of the Stephens, Virginia and Adrian, were in charge. But, as was often true in crises, Virginia was better able to manage than she expected. Neither she nor anyone else — including Thoby's doctors — understood how serious his condition was.

Thoby died on November 20, 1906. Afterward, Virginia called on her fantasy solution to the problem of death. She was encouraged or even required to resort to fantasy by Violet's condition, for she remained gravely ill at Welwyn and could not be told of Thoby's death. Rather, she had to be made to think that Thoby was still alive and was improving. Thus Virginia, who wrote Violet almost daily, kept her brother "alive" in her letters.[114] She described how he looked each day, his irritability, his appetite, what he was able to eat, and what the doctors said about him. She talked also of a trip he planned to take on his recovery.

Virginia gave a brilliant though macabre performance, and it apparently served to prevent an immediate emotional and mental collapse. It did not prevent a great deal of suffering, however. In 1929, she said that she had to fight her anguish, alone without anyone to help her.[115] As she described her anguish in her 1939-1940 memoir, she felt as if she were between two great grindstones, and as if she were in a fight with invisible giants. Life came to have for her an "extreme reality," and the challenge and opposition gave her a greater sense of her own importance, though not in respect to people. Through it all, her loneliness was paramount.[116]

Her loneliness was increased when Vanessa became engaged to Clive Bell, Thoby's friend, and the suitor whose first proposal Vanessa had rejected. The engagement occurred on

November 22, 1906, two days after Thoby died. Virginia kept the news of Vanessa's engagement from Violet, only telling her of it after Violet inadvertently learned that Thoby had died.[117] Virginia's omission of direct reference to the engagement may have indicated something of her feeling about it, for Vanessa's engagement and marriage were another source of distress for Virginia and a kind of betrayal, for they meant that she would now be physically separated from her sister. In a letter to Violet during the period immediately after Thoby's death, Virginia referred rather obliquely to Vanessa's interest in Clive whom Virginia then called Peter.[118] She also mentioned "plans" for Clive and Thoby to go on a trip together — leading one to suspect that she preferred Clive to be Thoby's friend rather than Vanessa's husband. Whatever Virginia's more self-ish feelings, she could also see that Vanessa was happy, in spite of the fact that Thoby had so recently died.[119]

Vanessa and Clive were married on February 7, 1907. After that, Virginia was on her own and would remain so until her own marriage to Leonard Woolf in 1912. It was the only period of her life when she did not live within and have the protection of a family. However, she did share a house with Adrian. They moved into 29 Fitzroy Square (coincidentally George Bernard Shaw's address in the late 1890s) so that Clive and Vanessa could live in the house at 46 Gordon Square where the Stephens had moved after their father died. Although they shared a house and sometimes traveled together, Virginia and Adrian were moving apart in other respects. Julia Stephen's youngest, and favorite, child had never been as close to his older siblings as they were to each other, and the increasing emotional distance between Virginia and Adrian seems to have been by mutual consent.[120] It was also encouraged by Vanessa.[121]

Thus with Thoby's death and Vanessa's marriage, a close family situation for Virginia was temporarily at an end and the "children's republic" was permanently over. The "Bloomsbury

Group," a new kind of "republic" for Virginia, and in many respects a substitute for the former one, was in its early stages of aggregation, and friends were already beginning to take the place of siblings.

Virginia was, of course, very unsure that she could manage life on her own, and in writing to Vanessa spoke of her longing to be reunited with her and to be made part of Vanessa's menage.[122] She expressed some of that longing, perhaps, in her flirtation with Vanessa's husband.[123] Although she did not want to be on her own, Virginia apparently managed her life and affairs quite well much of the time, with the exception of the periods in 1910 and 1912 when she was disturbed enough to enter a nursing home for brief "rest cures."

She was sustained by several things, most of all by continuing to feel close to her sister, despite separations. She wrote poignant, often passionate letters to Vanessa, to maintain a sense of their intimacy. However, there were intermittent strains between the sisters, in part because of the mutual attraction between Virginia and Clive.[124] There were also times when Virginia severely distrusted Vanessa — usually those were occasions when madness threatened.[125] Virginia was also sustained by her writing which had become a present activity and was no longer something merely anticipated for the future. She was well into journalistic writing, contributing both essays and reviews — including a review of Henry James's *The Golden Bowl* — to the *Women's Supplement* of the *Guardian* and the *Times Literary Supplement*. She had an income from her journalistic writing, no doubt a slender one, but earned by herself, and was able to repay some of the money expended during her 1904 madness.[126] She also had a small allowance from Stella's estate, granted to her by Jack Hills.[127] Her other sources of income were a legacy of £6,681 (the value in 1906) from Thoby's estate and another legacy of £2,500 from "Nun," who died in 1909. She tried to share the latter with Adrian, apparently without success.[128] She was also a lecturer at Morley College's institute for working men and women, but was an unpaid volunteer.[129]

Far more significant than her journalistic writing was the fact that she had begun her first novel. In its early stages it was called "Melymbrosia," but it was later entitled *The Voyage Out*. The actual writing covered the entire period of five and one-half years between Vanessa's marriage and her own, and much of the first year of her marriage.

Where was Virginia in her personal development? I think one may say that in most respects, though obviously not in her writing, she had reached what, in her, passed for maturity: in her own fashion she had come of age. Perhaps it is more accurate to say only that her childhood was technically at an end. Her childhood continued vividly present in her mind for the remainder of her life; its happy and tragic themes became a main focus of her fiction and her major personal preoccupation.

Therefore, by 1907, Virginia's childhood and past had effectively become her future and her destiny. She would of course change as she lived out and realized her destiny, but she was never to escape her childhood completely. She could no more want to be finished with it than she could want to be free of the persons who had dominated it.

# Abbreviations and Locations
# of Correspondence

AS/CB    Adrian Stephen to Clive Bell; Kings College, Cambridge

AS/VSB    Adrian Stephen to Vanessa Bell; Berg Collection

JJS/LS    Julia Jackson Stephen to Leslie Stephen; "Calendar of Correspondence," British Museum

JJS/VW    Julia Jackson Stephen to Virginia Woolf; Berg Collection

JKS/SDH    James Kenneth Stephen to Stella Duckworth Hills; Berg Collection

JMC/JJS    Julia Margaret Cameron to Julia Jackson Stephen; Berg Collection

JMC/MPJ    Julia Margaret Cameron to Maria Pattle Jackson; Berg Collection

LS/JJS    Leslie Stephen to Julia Jackson Stephen. Letters dated on or after March 31, 1877 are in the Berg Collection. Letters prior to that date are in "Calendar of Correspondence," British Museum.

LS/JPJ    Leslie Stephen to Maria Pattle Jackson; Berg Collection

LS/MPJ,    Leslie Stephen to Maria Pattle Jackson; "Calendar of Correspondence," British Museum

LS/SDH    Leslie Stephen to Stella Duckworth Hills; Berg Collection

LW/JWH    Leonard Woolf to John Waller Hills; Berg Collection

OW/ER    Octavia Wilberforce to Elizabeth Robins; Sussex University

SDH/JJS    Stella Duckworth Hills to Julia Jackson Stephen; Berg Collection

VD/VSB    Violet Dickinson to Vanessa Bell; Kings College, Cambridge

## Abbreviations and Locations of Correspondence

| | |
|---|---|
| VSB/CB | Vanessa Bell to Clive Bell; Kings College, Cambridge |
| VSB/LW | Vanessa Bell to Leonard Woolf; Sussex University |
| VSB/VW | Vanessa Bell to Virginia Woolf; Berg Collection |
| VW/JC | Virginia Woolf to Janet Case; Sussex University |
| VW/EMS | Virginia Woolf to Ethel Smyth; Berg Collection |
| VW/VD | Virginia Woolf to Violet Dickinson; Berg Collection |
| VW/MSV | Virginia Woolf to Madge Vaughan; Kings College, Cambridge |
| VW/VSB | Virginia Woolf to Vanessa Bell; Berg Collection |

# Notes

Chapter I: Visions and Reality

1. Quentin Bell, *Virginia Woolf: A Biography,* 2 vols. (New York, 1972); all on-line page numbers refer to Volume I.
2. VW/EMS, June 22, 1930.
3. Nigel Nicolson and Joanne Trautmann, eds., *The Letters of Virginia Woolf,* I, *1888-1912* (New York, 1975); *The Letters of Virginia Woolf,* II, *1912-1922* (New York, 1976).
4. Leonard Woolf, *Sowing* (New York, 1960); *Growing* (London, 1961); *Beginning Again* (New York, 1963); *Downhill All the Way* (New York, 1967); *The Journey Not the Arrival Matters* (New York, 1969).
5. Nigel Nicolson, *Portrait of a Marriage* (New York, 1973).
6. *Moments of Being,* ed., Jeanne Schulkind (Brighton, 1976).
7. Nicolson and Trautmann, *Letters,* I.
8. Virginia Woolf, *A Writer's Diary* (New York, 1953).
9. Located in the Berg Collection.
10. Virginia Woolf, *To the Lighthouse* (New York, 1927).
11. Virginia Woolf, *The Waves* (London, 1931).
12. *Moments of Being,* pp. 80-81.
13. Virginia Woolf, *Orlando* (London, 1928).
14. VW/VSB, July 30, 1916; Apr. 22, 1918; Jan. 2, 1920, in Nicolson and Trautmann, *Letters,* II, pp. 107-109, 231-233, 411-412; VW/JC, Nov. 19, 1919, in Nicolson and Trautmann, *Letters,* II, p. 400.
15. Virginia Woolf, *Night and Day* (London, 1919).

16. *Moments of Being,* pp. 40-53.

17. Located in the Berg Collection.

18. *To the Lighthouse,* p. 81.

19. Most of these are included in *Moments of Being.* The 1908 memoir entitled "Reminiscences," is found on pp. 28-59, and the 1939-1940 memoir entitled "A Sketch of the Past," on pp. 64-137. However, several brief sections and versions of other sections are not included.

20. VSB/VW, May 11, 1927.

21. VSB/VW, Apr. 20, 1908.

22. Both the "Mausoleum Book" (holograph) and the "Calendar of Correspondence" (holograph) are in the British Museum. The "Mausoleum Book" is being edited for publication by Alan Bell of the National Library of Scotland.

23. Located in the Berg Collection.

24. Personal correspondence from Mrs. Quentin Bell, July 13, 1974.

25. Noel Annan, *Leslie Stephen: His Thought and Character in Relation to His Time* (Cambridge, Mass., 1952).

26. VW/EMS, Feb. 27, 1930.

27. *Moments of Being,* pp. 34-36.

28. John W. Bicknell, "Virginia Woolf in Homage and Understanding," rev. of *Virginia Woolf,* by Quentin Bell, *Journal of Modern Literature,* 3, no. 1 (Feb. 1973), 108-115, see especially note, p. 112; see also second impressions of the Hogarth edition of Professor Bell's biography.


Chapter 2: That Old Wretch

1. Noel Annan, *Leslie Stephen: His Thought and Character in Relation to His Time* (Cambridge, Mass., 1952); Desmond Mac-Carthy, *Leslie Stephen* (Cambridge, London, 1937); Frederic Maitland, *The Life and Letters of Leslie Stephen* (London, 1906); David Zink, *Leslie Stephen* (New York, 1972), Quentin Bell, *Virginia Woolf: A Biography,* 2 vols. (New York, 1972), I, pp. 6-86.

2. Zink, *Leslie Stephen,* p. 110.

3. Leon Edel, ed., *Henry James Letters,* I (Cambridge, Mass., 1974), p. 91.

4. Ibid., p. 99; Zink, *Leslie Stephen,* p. 110.

5. Zink, *Leslie Stephen,* p. 32.

6. Quentin Bell, *Virginia Woolf,* I, p. 63; *Moments of Being,* p. 125.

7. VW/EMS, Nov. 29, 1930, and Nov. 13, 1932.

8. LS/JJS, Jan. 26, 1893.

9. LS/JJS, Aug. 6/7, 1877.

10. Zink, *Leslie Stephen,* p. 18.

11. "Mausoleum Book" in the British Museum, p. 4; LS/JJS, Apr. 16, 1881.

12. LS/JJS, July 20, 1885.

13. Zink, *Leslie Stephen,* pp. 27, 79.

14. Ibid., p. 28; Quentin Bell, *Virginia Woolf,* I, p. 9.

15. "Mausoleum Book," entry dated Feb. 28, 1902; Maitland, *Life and Letters,* pp. 472-473.

16. Maitland, *Life and Letters,* pp. 119-120.

17. Annan, *Leslie Stephen,* p. 57.

18. LS/JJS, Aug. 6/7, 1877.

19. Annan, *Leslie Stephen,* p. 98.

20. See also Maitland, *Life and Letters,* pp. 469-471.

21. Maitland, *Life and Letters,* pp. 10-12.

22. "Mausoleum Book," p. 69; LS/JJS, Feb. 8, 1885, Feb. 4 and Feb. 6, 1887.

23. Maitland, *Life and Letters,* pp. 10-15; Quentin Bell, *Virginia Woolf,* I, p. 6.

24. Maitland, *Life and Letters,* p. 12.

25. Annan, *Leslie Stephen,* p. 21.

26. Maitland, *Life and Letters,* pp. 8-10; Annan, *Leslie Stephen,* pp. 4-6, 116-117; Zink, *Leslie Stephen,* pp. 13-14.

27. LS/JJS, July 1, 1894.

28. Quentin Bell, *Virginia Woolf,* I, pp. 5-6; Annan, *Leslie Stephen,* p. 14.

29. Maitland, *Life and Letters,* p. 12.

30. Zink, *Leslie Stephen,* p. 14; Maitland, *Life and Letters,* pp. 9-10; Quentin Bell, *Virginia Woolf,* I, pp. 4-5.

31. Quentin Bell, *Virginia Woolf,* I, p. 7; Annan, *Leslie Stephen,* p. 21.

32. Maitland, *Life and Letters,* p. 19.

33. Ibid., p. 20.

34. AS/VSB, June 11, 1947.

35. Maitland, *Life and Letters,* p. 39.

36. "Mausoleum Book," pp. 36, 69; LS/JJS, Feb. 8, 1885; Maitland, *Life and Letters,* pp. 11-12.

37. "Mausoleum Book," p. 69; LS/JJS, Feb. 6 and Apr. 2, 1887.

38. Annan, *Leslie Stephen,* p. 97.

39. *Moments of Being,* p. 125.

40. Maitland, *Life and Letters,* pp. 23-24.

41. Annan, *Leslie Stephen,* p. 97.

42. Maitland, *Life and Letters,* pp. 23-26.

43. LS/JJS, July 1, 1894.

44. Maitland, *Life and Letters,* p. 24.

45. LS/JJS, Aug. 12, 1877.

46. LS/JJS, Aug. 15, 1877.

47. LS/JJS, Aug. 6/7, 1877.

48. LS/JJS, Jan. 25, 1891.

49. LS/JJS, Apr. 10, Aug. 6/7, and Aug. 18, 1877; Oct. 4, 1887; Jan. 25, 1891.

50. LS/JJS, Aug. 6/7, 1877; JJS/LS, Aug. 8, 1877.

51. Virginia Woolf, "Leslie Stephen," in *The Captain's Death Bed* (London, 1950), p. 68.

52. Maitland, *Life and Letters,* pp. 26-27.

53. Annan, *Leslie Stephen,* p. 12.

54. Maitland, *Life and Letters,* p. 28.

55. Leslie Stephen, *The Life of Sir James Fitzjames Stephen* (London, 1895), p. 74.

56. Ibid., pp. 74-75.

57. LS/JJS, Mar. 27, 1892.

58. Quentin Bell, *Virginia Woolf,* I, pp. 7-8; Maitland, *Life and Letters,* p. 30; Leslie Stephen, *The Life of Sir James Fitzjames Stephen,* p. 78; Annan, *Leslie Stephen,* pp. 21-22.

59. Annan, *Leslie Stephen,* p. 12; Leslie Stephen, *The Life of Sir James Fitzjames Stephen,* p. 83.

60. LS/JJS, Mar. 25, 1887.

61. Annan, *Leslie Stephen,* pp. 15-21; Maitland, *Life and Letters,* pp. 30-36.

62. Leslie Stephen, *The Life of Sir James Fitzjames Stephen,* pp. 78-80.

63. Maitland, *Life and Letters,* pp. 30-33.

64. Annan, *Leslie Stephen,* pp. 29-30; Zink, *Leslie Stephen,* p. 17.

65. Zink, *Leslie Stephen,* p. 25.

66. *Moments of Being,* p. 126.

67. Annan, *Leslie Stephen,* pp. 32-38.

68. "Leslie Stephen" in *The Captain's Death Bed,* p. 72.

69. LS/JJS, Aug. 15, 1877.

70. Zink, *Leslie Stephen,* p. 73.

71. Robert Gittings, *Young Thomas Hardy* (Boston, 1975), pp. 171-172, 187-190, 193-196.

72. Annan, *Leslie Stephen,* p. 66.

73. Ibid., p. 76.

74. VW/EMS, Dec. 22, 1932.

75. *To the Lighthouse,* p. 50.

76. LS/JJS, Oct. 15, 1886.

77. Annan, *Leslie Stephen,* p. 101.

78. Ibid., pp. 63-64; Quentin Bell, *Virginia Woolf,* I, pp. 10-11; Hester Ritchie Fuller and Violet Hammersley, *Thackeray's Daughter* (Dublin, 1951), pp. 101-110.

Chapter 3: A Large and Austere Presence

1. JJS/LS, Aug. 5, 1877.

2. Brian Hill, *Julia Margaret Cameron: A Victorian Family Portrait* (New York, 1973).

3. Leonard Woolf, *Sowing* (New York, 1960), p. 202; Hill, *Julia Margaret Cameron,* p. 192.

4. Quentin Bell, *Virginia Woolf: A Biography,* 2 vols. (New York, 1972), I, p. 19.

5. JJS/LS, Apr. 11, 1877.

6. Quentin Bell, *Virginia Woolf,* I, pp. 15-16; Hill, *Julia Margaret Cameron,* p. 58.

7. Quentin Bell, *Virginia Woolf,* I, p. 14; Hill, *Julia Margaret*

*Cameron,* pp. 27-39; Ethel Smyth, *Impressions That Remain* (New York, 1946), pp. 476-477; Julia Margaret Cameron, *Victorian Photographs of Famous Men and Fair Women* (London, 1926), introduction by Virginia Woolf, p. 1.

8. Virginia Woolf, Diary (holograph, 1918, Berg).

9. Helmut Gernsheim, *Julia Margaret Cameron* (London, 1948); Hill, *Julia Margaret Cameron,* pp. 100-124.

10. Hill, *Julia Margaret Cameron,* pp. 84-85.

11. Ibid., pp. 158-159.

12. Ibid., pp. 51-66.

13. Ibid., pp. 133-134.

14. *Moments of Being,* ed., Jeanne Schulkind (Brighton, 1976), p. 88.

15. Hill, *Julia Margaret Cameron,* pp. 58-59.

16. Ibid., pp. 57-58.

17. *Moments of Being,* pp. 86-87.

18. JJS/LS, Apr. 8, 1877.

19. Hill, *Julia Margaret Cameron,* pp. 48, 158-159.

20. *Moments of Being,* p. 85.

21. Hill, *Julia Margaret Cameron,* p. 158.

22. "Mausoleum Book" in the British Museum, pp. 54, 57.

23. Hill, *Julia Margaret Cameron,* pp. 48, 158-159.

24. "Mausoleum Book," p. 24.

25. *To the Lighthouse,* pp. 41, 64-65.

26. JJS/LS, Aug. 8, 1877.

27. Quentin Bell, *Virginia Woolf,* I, p. 71; Noel Annan, *Leslie Stephen: His Thought and Character in Relation to His Time* (Cambridge, Mass., 1952), p. 297.

28. Hill, *Julia Margaret Cameron,* p. 68.

29. *Moments of Being,* pp. 32-33; Quentin Bell, *Virginia Woolf,* I, p. 13.

30. Quentin Bell, *Virginia Woolf,* I, p. 17; "Mausoleum Book," p. 25.

31. LS/JJS, July 18, 1877.

32. JJS/LS, July 19, 1877.

33. Walter E. Houghton, *The Victorian Frame of Mind* (New Haven, 1957), p. 353; Virginia Woolf, Autobiographical fragment,

"The tea table was the centre of Victorian family life" (holograph, Berg, dated Jan. 28, 1940).

34. "Mausoleum Book," p. 28; *Moments of Being,* p. 89.
35. "Mausoleum Book," p. 30; JJS/LS, Aug. 5, 1877.
36. *Moments of Being,* p. 90.
37. "Mausoleum Book," p. 30; JJS/LS, Mar. 31 and Aug. 5, 1877.
38. JMC/MPJ, Feb. 6, 1878.
39. "Mausoleum Book," p. 30.
40. Ibid., p. 63.
41. *Moments of Being,* p. 90.
42. "Mausoleum Book," pp. 31, 49, 63-64.
43. Quentin Bell, *Virginia Woolf,* I, pp. 15-16.
44. *To the Lighthouse,* pp. 256-263; Quentin Bell, *Virginia Woolf,* I, p. 18.
45. *Moments of Being,* p. 38.
46. Quentin Bell, *Virginia Woolf,* II, pp. 201-202.
47. JJS/VW, Feb. 7, no year.


Chapter 4: Winning a Great Prize

1. Noel Annan, *Leslie Stephen: His Thought and Character in Relation to His Time* (Cambridge, Mass., 1952), p. 73.
2. Hester Ritchie Fuller and Violet Hammersley, *Thackeray's Daughter* (Dublin, 1951), p. 142.
3. Annan, *Leslie Stephen,* pp. 63-64.
4. Fuller and Hammersley, *Thackeray's Daughter,* pp. 143-144.
5. Annan, *Leslie Stephen,* pp. 63-64; Quentin Bell, *Virginia Woolf: A Biography,* 2 vols. (New York, 1972), I, p. 11.
6. "Mausoleum Book" in the British Museum, pp. 17-18.
7. LS/JJS, Mar. 31, 1877.
8. "Mausoleum Book," p. 18.
9. LS/JJS, Apr. 10, June 28, Aug. 12, Aug. 13, and Aug. 17, 1877.
10. LS/JJS, Mar. 31, 1877.
11. LS/JJS, Apr. 3, Apr. 7, Apr. 10, and Apr. 11, 1877.
12. LS/JJS, Apr. 4, 1877.
13. LS/JJS, June 29, 1877.

14. LS/JJS, Aug. 13, 1877.
15. LS/MPJ, Feb. 2, 1877, in "Calendar of Correspondence."
16. "Mausoleum Book," p. 46.
17. Ibid., p. 32.
18. Ibid., p. 36.
19. LS/MPJ, Feb. 2, 1877.
20. LS/JJS, Feb. 5, 1877, in "Calendar of Correspondence"; "Mausoleum Book," p. 37.
21. "Mausoleum Book," p. 36-37; LS/JJS, Feb. 5, 1877.
22. JJS/LS, July 20, 1877.
23. Brian Hill, *Julia Margaret Cameron: A Victorian Family Portrait* (New York, 1973), p. 189.
24. JJS/LS, ca. Feb. 6, 1877.
25. JJS/LS, Feb. 8, 1877; "Mausoleum Book," pp. 32, 36.
26. LS/JJS, Aug. 18, 1877.
27. JJS/LS, Feb. 8, 1877.
28. LS/JJS, ca. Feb. 5, 1877.
29. JJS/LS, Feb. 8, 1877.
30. JJS/LS, Apr. 11, July 19 (two letters), and Aug. 5, 1877 (two letters).
31. LS/JJS, July 19, 1877.
32. LS/JJS, Aug. 6/7, 1877.
33. LS/JJS, ca. Feb. 6, 1877.
34. JJS/LS, Apr. 6, Apr. 7, July 19, July 20, and ca. July 31, 1877.
35. JJS/LS, Apr. 6 and July 20, 1877; "Mausoleum Book," pp. 39-40.
36. JJS/LS, Mar. 31, 1877.
37. Ibid.
38. JJS/LS, Apr. 2, 1877.
39. JJS/LS, July 20, 1877.
40. JJS/LS, July 31, 1877.
41. JJS/LS, Aug. 5, 1877.
42. JJS/LS, Apr. 8, 1877.
43. JJS/LS, Apr. 2, 1877.
44. JJS/LS, July 19, 1877.
45. JJS/LS, Apr. 6, 1877.

46. JJS/LS, July 19, 1877; "Mausoleum Book," p. 31.
47. LS/JJS, July 19, 1877.
48. JJS/LS, July 20, 1877.
49. LS/JJS, Apr. 10 and June 27, 1877.
50. LS/JJS, Aug. 15, 1877.
51. LS/JJS, Aug. 16, 1877.
52. LS/JJS, Aug. 12, 1877.
53. JJS/LS, Apr. 6, 1877.
54. JJS/LS, Apr. 7, 1877.
55. LS/JJS, Apr. 9, 1877.
56. LS/JJS, Aug. 17, 1877.
57. LS/JJS, Apr. 10, 1877.
58. LS/JJS, Aug. 6/7, 1877.
59. In "Calendar of Correspondence" in the British Museum.
60. JMC/JJS, Feb. (no day), 1878.
61. LS/JJS, July 13, July 16, July 17, and July 18, 1877.
62. LS/JJS, July 25, 1877.
63. LS/JJS, Mar. 30, 1887; Jan. 28, 1891.
64. LS/JJS, July 19, 1877.
65. LS/JJS, Aug. 11, 1877.
66. LS/JJS, Aug. 16, 1877.
67. LS/JJS, Aug. 3, 1877.
68. LS/JJS, Aug. 15, 1877.
69. JJS/LS, Apr. 9, 1877.
70. LS/JJS, Aug. 18, 1877.
71. JJS/LS, Apr. 1, 1877.
72. JJS/LS, Aug. 7, 1877.
73. JJS/LS, Aug. 13, 1877.
74. JJS/LS, Mar. 31, 1877.
75. JJS/LS, July 19, 1877.
76. JJS/LS, Aug. 8, 1877.
77. JJS/LS, Aug. 11, 1877.
78. LS/JJS, Aug. 8/9, 1877.
79. JJS/LS, Aug. 7, 1877.
80. LS/MPJ, ca. Mar. 25, 1877; Frederic Maitland, *The Life and Letters of Leslie Stephen* (London, 1906), pp. 313-316.

81. LS/MPJ, ca. Mar. 25, 1877.
82. LS/MPJ, Mar. 25, 1877; Maitland, *The Life and Letters,* pp. 313-316.
83. JJS/LS, Aug. 7, 1877.
84. LS/MPJ, Jan. 9, 1879; June 27, 1880.
85. LS/MPJ, June 27, 1880.
86. "Mausoleum Book," p. 43.
87. Ibid., p. 34; JJS/LS, July 19, 1877.
88. "Mausoleum Book," p. 34; Annan, *Leslie Stephen,* p. 72.
89. Fuller and Hammersley, *Thackeray's Daughter,* p. 150.
90. Ibid., p. 151.
91. Ibid.
92. LS/JJS, Apr. 5, Apr. 7 (two letters), Apr. 9, Apr. 10, July 25, Aug. 6/7, Aug. 7/8, Aug. 8/9, Aug. 10, Aug. 13, Aug. 14, Aug. 15, and Aug. 16, 1877.
93. "Mausoleum Book," p. 35.
94. VSB/VW, Oct. 24, 1904.
95. "Mausoleum Book," p. 18.
96. Fuller and Hammersley, *Thackeray's Daughter,* p. 151.
97. Ibid., pp. 151-152.
98. LS/JJS, Aug. 3, 1877.
99. Fuller and Hammersley, *Thackeray's Daughter,* p. 152.
100. LS/JJS, Aug. 7/8 and Aug. 8/9, 1877.
101. LS/JJS, Aug. 3, 1877.
102. Annan lists the books: *The Service of the Poor* (1871); *Quaker Strongholds* (1890); *Light Arising* (1908); *Vision of Faith* (1911); see Annan, *Leslie Stephen,* p. 296.
103. "Mausoleum Book," p. 43.
104. Ibid.; Quentin Bell, *Virginia Woolf,* I, p. 13.
105. JJS/LS, Dec. 24, Dec. 25, Dec. 28, Dec. 29, and Dec. 31, 1877; "Mausoleum Book," p. 43.
106. "Mausoleum Book," p. 43.
107. Ibid.; JJS/LS, Dec. 25, 1877; Jan. 1, 1878.
108. LS/JJS, Aug. 11, 1877.
109. JJS/LS, Dec. 24, 1877.
110. JJS/LS, Dec. 25, 1877.
111. LS/JJS, Dec. 26, 1877.
112. LS/JJS, Dec. 27, 1877.

113. "Mausoleum Book," p. 44.
114. JJS/LS, Dec. 28, 1877.
115. LS/JJS, Dec. 25 and Dec. 26, 1877.
116. LS/JJS, Dec. 29, 1877.
117. "Mausoleum Book," p. 44.
118. JMC/MPJ, Feb. 6, 1878.
119. JJS/LS, Jan. 1, 1878.
120. "Mausoleum Book," p. 44.
121. JJS/LS, Jan. 15, 1878.
122. Maitland, *Life and Letters,* p. 324.
123. Ibid., pp. 310-311.
124. Ibid., p. 311.
125. Ibid., p. 312.
126. LS/JJS, Feb. 10 and Feb. 11, 1878.
127. LS/JJS, Feb. 10, 1878.
128. LS/JJS, Feb. 11, 1878.
129. LS/JJS, Feb. 11, 1878 (second letter of that date).

Chapter 5: Good Times, Bad Times

1. "Mausoleum Book" in the British Museum, p. 71.
2. Quentin Bell, *Virginia Woolf: A Biography,* 2 vols. (New York, 1972), I, pp. 30-31; LS/JJS, Apr. 6 (2 letters), Apr. 7, Apr. 8, and Apr. 9, 1882.
3. LS/JJS, Oct. 17, 1881.
4. Quentin Bell, *Virginia Woolf,* I, p. 74.
5. LS/JJS, July 12, 1886.
6. LS/JJS, Mar. 29, 1894.
7. LS/JJS, Mar. 26, 1894.
8. LS/JJS, Mar. 27, 1887.
9. LS/JJS, Apr. 12, 1877; Feb. 7, 1887.
10. *Moments of Being,* ed., Jeanne Schulkind (Brighton, 1976), pp. 35-36.
11. Noel Annan, *Leslie Stephen: His Thought and Character in Relation to His Time* (Cambridge, Mass., 1952), p. 71.
12. LS/JJS, Apr. 6, 1882.

13. *Moments of Being,* p. 125.

14. Quentin Bell, *Virginia Woolf,* I, p. 62; Annan, *Leslie Stephen,* p. 71.

15. *Moments of Being,* p. 34.

16. Virginia Woolf, Autobiographical fragment, "The tea table was the centre of Victorian family life," (holograph, Berg, dated Jan. 28, 1940).

17. *Moments of Being,* p. 160.

18. David Zink, *Leslie Stephen* (New York, 1972), pp. 75-76.

19. LS/JJS, Mar. 31, 1884.

20. JJS/LS, July 20, 1877.

21. LS/JJS, Sept. 4, 1884; "Mausoleum Book," p. 72.

22. LS/JJS, Sept. 4, 1884.

23. LS/JJS, Apr. 9, 1882.

24. *Moments of Being,* p. 39.

25. LS/JJS, Apr. 12 and Apr. 15, 1884; Oct. 3/4, 1887.

26. LS/JJS, Apr. 17, 1881; Jan. 17, 1883.

27. LS/JJS, Jan. 17, 1883.

28. LS/JJS, Oct. 23, 1884; Jan. 31, 1894.

29. LS/JJS, Apr. 11 and Sept. 5, 1884.

30. LS/JJS, July 21, 1885.

31. LS/JJS, Oct. 3/4, 1887.

32. LS/JJS, July 21, 1885.

33. LS/JJS, Aug. 16, 1877.

34. Quentin Bell, *Virginia Woolf,* I, pp. 74-75.

35. LS/JJS, Apr. 16, 1881.

36. LS/JJS, Apr. 30, 1886.

37. LS/JJS, Apr. 23, 1886.

38. LS/JJS, Sept. 5, 1884.

39. LS/JJS, Apr. 18, 1881.

40. LS/JJS, Aug. 3 and Aug. 4, 1885; Oct. 5, 1886.

41. LS/JJS, Aug. 3 and Aug. 4, 1885.

42. LS/JJS, Oct. 5, 1886.

43. LS/JJS, Mar. 31, 1884.

44. LS/JJS, Apr. 8, 1882.

45. LS/JJS, July 25, 1893.

46. AS/VSB, Oct. 1, 1945.

47. LS/JJS, July 25, 1893.

48. LS/JJS, July 29, 1893.

49. LS/JJS, July 31, 1893.

50. LS/JJS, Aug. 2, 1893.

51. LS/JJS, July 29 and Aug. 1, 1893.

52. LS/JJS, Apr. 9, 1884.

53. LS/JJS, July 29, 1893.

54. LS/JJS, Dec. 4, 1879.

55. "Mausoleum Book," p. 55.

56. LS/JJS, Jan. 29, 1894.

57. LS/JJS, Oct. 17, 1881.

58. LS/JJS, Mar. 31, 1884.

59. LS/JJS, Apr. 3, 1884.

60. LS/JJS, Mar. 22, 1887.

61. LS/JJS, Oct. 5, Oct. 6, Oct. 7, Oct. 11, and Oct. 13, 1877.

62. LS/JJS, Feb. 4, 1887.

63. LS/JJS, Feb. 6, 1887.

64. LS/JJS, Feb. 7, 1887.

65. LS/JJS, Mar. 21, 1887.

66. LS/JJS, Mar. 31, 1887.

67. LS/JJS, Apr. 1, 1887 (second letter of that date).

68. LS/JJS, Apr. 6, 1887.

69. LS/JJS, Apr. 5, 1887.

70. LS/JJS, Apr. 6, 1887.

71. LS/JJS, Apr. 7, 1887.

72. LS/JJS, Apr. 15, 1887.

73. LS/JJS, Apr. 14, 1887.

74. LS/JJS, Apr. 13, 1887.

75. LS/JJS, Apr. 17, 1882; Apr. 15, 1887.

76. LS/JJS, Apr. 17, 1887.

77. "Mausoleum Book," pp. 38, 70; *To The Lighthouse,* pp. 184-186.

78. LS/JJS, Mar. 27, 1894.

79. "Mausoleum Book," pp. 31, 49, 63-64.

80. Walter E. Houghton, *The Victorian Frame of Mind* (New Haven, 1957), pp. 352, 353.

81. LS/JJS, July 29, 1893.

82. LS/JJS, July 31, 1893.

83. LS/JJS, Jan. 27, 1894.

84. LS/JJS, July 18 and Aug. 1, 1885.

85. "Mausoleum Book," p. 62.

86. LS/JJS, Oct. 18, 1884.

87. LS/JJS, Apr. 21, 1885.

88. "Mausoleum Book," p. 68.

89. LS/JJS, Sept. 4, 1884.

90. "Mausoleum Book," p. 73.

91. LS/JJS, Feb. 5, 1893.

92. LS/JJS, Jan. 26, 1893.

93. LS/JJS, July 29, 1893.

94. LS/JJS, Jan. 2, 1895.

95. "Mausoleum Book," p. 73.

96. *Moments of Being,* p. 114.

97. "Mausoleum Book," p. 31.

98. LS/JJS, Mar. 27, 1892.

99. LS/JJS, Oct. 3/4, 1887.

100. LS/JJS, Apr. 15, 1884.

101. LS/JJS, July 7, 1887.

102. LS/JJS, July 24, 1887.

103. LS/JJS, Jan. 29, 1887.

104. LS/JJS, Dec. 29, 1884.

105. LS/JJS, Dec. 28, 1884.

106. LS/JJS, Jan. 28, 1891.

107. LS/JJS, Jan. 20, 1891.

108. LS/JJS, Dec. 21, 1884.

109. "Mausoleum Book," p. 75.

110. Quentin Bell, *Virginia Woolf,* I, p. 38.

111. Ibid., p. 41; *Moments of Being,* pp. 43-44; "Memoir," typescript, continuation of the 1939-1940 memoir entitled "A Sketch of the Past," included with Sussex documents designated MH/A 5a.

112. *Moments of Being,* p. 43.

113. Quentin Bell, *Virginia Woolf,* I, pp. 41-42.

114. LS/JJS, Apr. 16, 1895.

115. "Mausoleum Book," p. 75.

116. Ibid., p. 44.

Chapter 6: A Bad and Good Piece of Work

1. LS/JJS, Aug. 3, 1893.
2. LS/JJS, Feb. 8, 1885.
3. LS/JJS, Oct. 18, 1884.
4. "Mausoleum Book" in the British Museum, p. 65.
5. *Moments of Being,* ed., Jeanne Schulkind (Brighton, 1976), pp. 33-40.
6. LS/JJS, Apr. 4, Apr. 12, Aug. 16, and Aug. 18, 1877; Apr. 17, 1881; Jan. 17, 1883; Oct. 23, 1884; Nov. 16, 1885; Mar. 21 and Apr. 6, 1887; Mar. 27, 1892; Aug. 1, 1893; Mar. 26, 1894.
7. LS/JJS, Apr. 9, 1882.
8. VW/VSB, May 22, 1927.
9. LS/JJS, Sept. 4, 1884; Feb. 4, 1886.
10. LS/JJS, Oct. 22, 1884; Virginia Woolf, "Leslie Stephen," in *The Captain's Death Bed* (London, 1950), p. 68.
11. Leon Edel, ed., *Henry James Letters,* I (Cambridge, Mass., 1974), p. 90.
12. LS/JJS, Mar. 22, 1887.
13. LS/JJS, Jan. 28, 1886.
14. VSB/VW, Aug. 27, 1908.
15. LS/JJS, Jan. 21, Jan. 22, and Feb. 24, 1887.
16. LS/JJS, Jan. 23, 1883; Apr. 5 and Oct. 22, 1884.
17. *Moments of Being,* p. 97.
18. Virginia Woolf, Diary, 1897; Quentin Bell, *Virginia Woolf: A Biography,* 2 vols. (New York, 1972), I, p. 56.
19. "Leslie Stephen," in *The Captain's Death Bed,* p. 68.
20. LS/JJS, Oct. 18, 1881.
21. LS/JJS, July 21, 1877.
22. LS/JJS, Aug. 18, 1877.
23. LS/JJS, May 24, 1887.
24. LS/JJS, Apr. 2, 1882.
25. LS/JJS, Jan. 18, 1888.
26. LS/JJS, Aug. 6/7, 1877; "Mausoleum Book," p. 41.
27. LS/JJS, Jan. 28, 1886.
28. LS/JJS, Apr. 16, 1881.
29. LS/JJS, Jan. 28, 1894.

30. LS/JJS, July 27, 1893.

31. LS/JJS, Feb. 3, 1886.

32. LS/JJS, Feb. 6, 1887.

33. LS/JJS, Mar. 24, 1884.

34. LS/JJS, Apr. 29, 1886.

35. LS/JJS, Feb. 5-8, 1885.

36. LS/JJS, Apr. 3, 1884.

37. Vanessa Bell, *Notes on Virginia's Childhood* (New York, 1974), unpaged; Quentin Bell, *Virginia Woolf,* I, p. 23.

38. SDH/JJS, Feb. 14 and ca. Feb. 15-20, 1882.

39. LS/JJS, Oct. 18, 1884.

40. LS/JJS, July 22 and July 23, 1885.

41. LS/JJS, Sept. 2, 1884.

42. LS/JJS, Mar. 23, 1886.

43. LS/JJS, Apr. 13, 1884.

44. LS/JJS, Apr. 16, 1881.

45. LS/JJS, Nov. 16, 1885.

46. LS/JJS, Jan. 25, 1891.

47. LS/JJS, July 29, 1893.

48. LS/JJS, Jan. 29, 1894.

49. LS/JJS, Oct. 21, 1884.

50. LS/JJS, Oct. 22, 1884.

51. LS/JJS, Oct. 18, 1884.

52. LS/JJS, Mar. 26, 1894.

53. LS/JJS, Apr. 15, 1881.

54. LS/JJS, Oct. 21, 1884.

55. Ibid.

56. LS/JJS, Sept. 29, 1882.

57. Frederic Maitland, *The Life and Letters of Leslie Stephen* (London, 1906), p. 474; Quentin Bell, *Virginia Woolf,* I, p. 27.

58. LS/JJS, July 17, 1885.

59. Noel Annan, *Leslie Stephen: His Thought and Character in Relation to His Time* (Cambridge, Mass., 1952), p. 100.

60. LS/JJS, Apr. 13 and Oct. 21, 1884; July 17, 1885; Jan. 28 and Apr. 27, 1886; Oct. 27, 1891.

61. Quentin Bell, *Virginia Woolf,* I, p. 7.

62. LS/JJS, Apr. 12 and Apr. 13, 1884; July 11, 1893.

63. LS/JJS, Apr. 14, 1887.

64. LS/JJS, Sept. 2, 1884.

65. *Moments of Being,* p. 108.

66. Quentin Bell, *Virginia Woolf,* I, p. 33.

67. LS/JJS, July 17 and Aug. 5, 1877.

68. "Leslie Stephen," in *The Captain's Death Bed,* p. 71.

69. *Moments of Being,* p. 114.

70. LS/JJS, Oct. 24, 1884.

71. LS/JJS, July 20, 1885.

72. LS/JJS, Apr. 12, 1884.

73. LS/JJS, Apr. 9, 1884.

74. LS/JJS, June 1, 1887.

75. AS/VSB, June 13, 1942; Aug. 6, 1944.

76. LS/JJS, Oct. 10, 1883.

77. LS/JJS, Apr. 13, 1884.

78. LS/JJS, Oct. 20, 1884; Jan. 23, 1887; July 25, 1891.

79. LS/JJS, June 6-15, 1890.

80. LS/JJS, Apr. 5, 1884.

81. LS/JJS, Jan. 23, 1887.

82. LS/JJS, Jan. 25 and Jan. 28, 1887.

83. LS/JJS, Jan. 29, 1887.

84. LS/JJS, Jan. 25, 1891.

85. LS/JJS, Jan. 28, 1894.

86. LS/JJS, Oct. 18, 1884.

87. LS/JJS, Oct. 20 and Oct. 21, 1884.

88. Quentin Bell, *Virginia Woolf,* I, p. 68; Nicolson and Traut-mann, *Letters,* I, p. 9.

89. Ibid., p. 51.

90. LS/JJS, Aug. 3, 1893.

91. Ibid.

92. LS/JJS, July 27, 1893.

93. LS/JJS, July 22, 1885.

94. VSB/VW, Aug. 3, 1907.

95. LS/JJS, Jan. 21, Jan. 22, Jan. 24, Jan. 25, and Jan. 28, 1891.

96. LS/JJS, Jan. 26, 1894.

97. LS/JJS, Jan. 22, 1891.
98. LS/JJS, Jan. 24, 1891.
99. LS/JJS, Jan. 28 and Oct. 25, 1891.
100. LS/JJS, Oct. 25, 1891.
101. LS/JJS, July 22, 1894.
102. LS/JJS, Oct. 25, 1891.
103. LS/JJS, July 11, 1893.
104. Fuller and Hammersley, *Thackeray's Daughter* (Dublin, 1951), p. 156.
105. "Mausoleum Book," p. 71.
106. *Moments of Being,* p. 160.
107. LS/JJS, Mar. 22, 1887.
108. "Mausoleum Book," p. 71.
109. LS/JJS, Aug. 1, 1893.
110. E. Seguin, *Idiocy: and Its Treatment by the Physiological Method* (New York, 1907).
111. R. H. Haskell, "Mental Deficiency Over a Hundred Years: A Brief Historical Sketch of Trends in this Field," *American Journal of Psychiatry,* 100, pp. 107-118.
112. Emil Kraepelin, *Clinical Psychiatry: A Textbook for Students and Physicians* (New York, 1927).
113. Ephraim Rosen, et. al., *Abnormal Psychology,* 2nd ed. (Philadelphia, 1972), pp. 45-49.
114. LS/JJS, Apr. 5 and Aug. 11, 1877.
115. LS/JJS, Apr. 2, 1882.
116. LS/JJS, Apr. 9 and Sept. 29, 1882.
117. LS/JJS, Oct. 11, 1882.
118. LS/JJS, Apr. 7, 1877.
119. LS/JJS, Aug. 3, 1877.
120. LS/JJS, Apr. 29, 1881.
121. LS/JJS, Apr. 29, 1881.
122. LS/JJS, Apr. 12, 1877.
123. LS/JJS, Dec. 26, 1877.
124. LS/JJS, Aug. 11, 1877.
125. LS/JJS, Aug. 8, 1877.
126. LS/JJS, Aug. 11, 1877.
127. LS/JJS, Apr. 16, 1881.

128. LS/JJS, Oct. 22, 1884.

129. LS/JJS, Apr. 26, 1886.

130. LS/JJS, Aug. 15, 1877.

131. LS/JJS, Apr. 7, 1877.

132. LS/JJS, Apr. 11, 1883.

133. LS/JJS, Nov. 16, 1885.

134. LS/JJS, Oct. 21, 1884.

135. LS/JJS, Aug. 17, 1877.

136. LS/JJS, Oct. 19, 1884.

137. LS/JJS, Oct. 11, 1882 (two letters).

138. LS/JJS, July 28, 1881; July 17, 1885.

139. LS/JJS, Nov. 13, 1885.

140. LS/JJS, Oct. 11, 1882.

141. LS/JJS, Apr. 2, 1882; Apr. 11 and Oct. 9, 1883; Nov. 11, 1885.

142. Fuller and Hammersley, *Thackeray's Daughter,* p. 21.

143. Ibid., p. 148.

144. Ibid., p. 25.

145. Ibid., p. 142.

146. LS/JJS, Jan. 25, 1883; "Mausoleum Book," p. 71.

147. LS/JJS, Apr. 5, 1877.

148. LS/JJS, Oct. 2, 1882.

149. LS/JJS, July 17 and July 21, 1877; "Mausoleum Book," p. 42.

150. LS/JJS, Apr. 2, 1882.

151. LS/JJS, Oct. 2, 1882.

152. LS/JJS, Mar. 24, 1884.

153. LS/JJS, Oct. 19, 1884.

154. "Mausoleum Book," p. 71.

155. LS/JJS, Aug. 1, 1893.

156. *Moments of Being,* p. 78.

157. Nigel Nicholson and Joanne Trautmann, eds., *The Letters of Virginia Woolf, II, 1912-1922* (New York, 1976), p. 487.

158. Diary (holograph, Berg), Jan. 1-Feb. 15, 1915.

159. VW/VSB, May 4, 1934.

160. LS/JJS, Aug. 1, 1893.

161. "Mausoleum Book," entry dated Apr. 10, 1897; Virginia Woolf, Diary, 1897, entry dated Mar. 19, 1897.

162. VSB/VW, Aug. 9, 1909.

163. VW/VSB, Oct. 24, 1921, in Nicolson and Trautmann, *Letters,* II, pp. 486-487.

164. AS/VSB, July 10, Aug. 13, and Nov. 19, 1946; Apr. 2, 1947; Nov. 8, no year.

Chapter 7: The Duckworth Children

1. Virginia Woolf, Autobiographical fragment, "The tea table was the centre of Victorian family life," (holograph, Berg, dated Jan. 28, 1940).

2. LS/JJS, Aug. 11, 1877; "Mausoleum Book" in the British Museum, p. 50.

3. "Mausoleum Book," p. 50.

4. Ibid., p. 71.

5. *Moments of Being,* ed., Jeanne Schulkind (Brighton, 1976), p. 43.

6. Quentin Bell, *Virginia Woolf: A Biography,* 2 vols. (New York, 1972), I, p. 58.

7. *Moments of Being,* p. 96.

8. Ibid., pp. 96-98; Quentin Bell, *Virginia Woolf,* I, pp. 36-39, 41-42.

9. Quentin Bell, *Virginia Woolf,* I, pp. 36-39, 41-42; *Moments of Being,* pp. 40-44, 96-98.

10. "Mausoleum Book," p. 64.

11. Ibid., p. 45; Quentin Bell, *Virginia Woolf,* I, p. 41; *Moments of Being,* pp. 42, 96.

12. *Moments of Being,* p. 42.

13. "Mausoleum Book," pp. 45-46.

14. *Moments of Being,* p. 43.

15. Ibid., p. 96.

16. Ibid., p. 43.

17. Ibid., pp. 42-43, 96.

18. Ibid., pp. 41-42; Quentin Bell, *Virginia Woolf,* I, p. 36.

19. LS/JJS, July 28, 1881.

20. LS/JJS, July 27, 1893.

21. Virginia Woolf, "Professions for Women," in *The Death of the Moth* (New York, 1942), pp. 235 ff.

22. LS/JJS, Oct. 22, 1884.

23. LS/JJS, Oct. 20, 1884.

24. LS/JJS, Oct. 21, 1884.

25. LS/JJS, Oct. 22, 1884.

26. Ibid.

27. LS/JJS, July 21, 1885.

28. LS/JJS, July 18, 1885.

29. LS/JJS, June 1, 1887.

30. Noel Annan, *Leslie Stephen: His Thought and Character in Relation to His Time* (Cambridge, Mass., 1952), p. 101.

31. LS/JJS, June 16, 1890.

32. LS/JJS, Feb. 2, 1895.

33. LS/JJS, Mar. 30, 1887.

34. LS/JJS, Oct. 10, 1891.

35. LS/JJS, Jan. 23, 1893.

36. *Moments of Being,* p. 44.

37. "Mausoleum Book," entry of Apr. 10, 1897.

38. *Moments of Being,* p. 46.

39. Quentin Bell, *Virginia Woolf,* I, p. 40.

40. Ibid., p. 41.

41. *Moments of Being,* p. 45.

42. Ibid., p. 94.

43. Quentin Bell, *Virginia Woolf,* I, p. 41.

44. Leon Edel, ed. *The Selected Letters of Henry James* (New York, 1955), p. 149.

45. *Moments of Being,* p. 40; Quentin Bell, *Virginia Woolf,* I, p. 40.

46. *Moments of Being,* p. 95.

47. Quentin Bell, *Virginia Woolf,* I, p. 42.

48. *Moments of Being,* p. 45.

49. Ibid., pp. 40-41, 94-95; Quentin Bell, *Virginia Woolf,* I, p. 41.

50. *Moments of Being,* p. 94.

51. Stella Duckworth Hills, Diary, 1896 (holograph, Berg).

52. VSB/VW, July 24, 1910.

53. Quentin Bell, *Virginia Woolf,* I, p. 42; *Moments of Being,* p. 94.

54. LS/SDH, Apr. 13, 1897.

55. Quentin Bell, *Virginia Woolf,* I, pp. 47-48.

56. Ibid., p. 36; *Moments of Being,* p. 99; JKS/SDH, Oct. 25, 1890 (two letters), Nov. 2 and Nov. 11, 1890.

57. Quentin Bell, *Virginia Woolf,* I, pp. 45-47; LS/JJS, Aug. 2, 1893.

58. LS/JJS, Aug. 2, 1893.

59. *Moments of Being,* pp. 99-100.

60. Quentin Bell, *Virginia Woolf,* I, p. 46.

61. *Moments of Being,* pp. 48-50.

62. Ibid., p. 143.

63. Ibid., p. 105.

64. Published as Leslie Stephen, *A Bookworm's Birthday Book.*

65. "Mausoleum Book," entry of Sept. 23, 1896.

66. Ibid., p. 82; Quentin Bell, *Virginia Woolf,* I, p. 47.

67. Quentin Bell, *Virginia Woolf,* I, pp. 47-48.

68. *Moments of Being,* p. 106.

69. Quentin Bell, *Virginia Woolf,* I, pp. 53-54.

70. "Mausoleum Book," entry of Apr. 10, 1897.

71. LS/SDH, Apr. 10 and Apr. 13, 1897.

72. LS/SDH, Apr. 13, 1897.

73. VW/VSB, Aug. 24, 1909, in Nigel Nicolson and Joanne Trautmann, eds. *The Letters of Virginia Woolf, I, 1888-1912* (New York, 1975), pp. 410-411.

74. Quentin Bell, *Virginia Woolf,* I, p. 54.

75. Ibid., pp. 54-55.

76. VD/VSB, June 16, 1942.

77. VD/VSB, July 6, 1942.

78. "Mausoleum Book," entry of July 19, 1897.

79. LW/JWH, Mar. 17, 1915.

80. *Moments of Being,* p. 69; VW/EMS, Jan. 12, 1941.

81. *Moments of Being,* pp. 142-145.

82. LS/JJS, Apr. 17, 1881.

83. LS/JJS, Oct. 14, 1886.

84. *Moments of Being,* pp. 57-59.

85. LS/JJS, Apr. 10, 1893.

86. *Moments of Being,* pp. 91-94, 141.

87. "Mausoleum Book," p. 75.

88. Quentin Bell, *Virginia Woolf,* I, p. 45.

89. *Moments of Being,* p. 69; VW/EMS, Jan. 12, 1941.

90. Quentin Bell, *Virginia Woolf,* I, pp. 44, 95-96; *Moments of Being,* p. 160.

91. Quentin Bell, *Virginia Woolf,* I, p. 75.

92. Virginia Woolf, "The tea table was the centre of Victorian family life."

93. *Moments of Being,* p. 131.

94. Ibid., pp. 57-59.

95. Quentin Bell, *Virginia Woolf,* I, p. 43.

96. VSB/VW, Aug. 8, 1907.

97. Quentin Bell, *Virginia Woolf,* I, pp. 44, 95-96; *Moments of Being,* p. 160.

98. *Moments of Being,* pp. 57-58.

99. VW/VSB, July 25 (?), 1911, in Nicolson and Trautmann, *Letters,* I, pp. 471-473.

100. VW/VSB, Feb. 20, 1922.

101. The Memoir Club was organized in 1920 by the "thirteen original members of old Bloomsbury," according to Leonard Woolf (*Downhill All the Way,* pp. 114-115). Most prominent in the group werc Virginia and Leonard Woolf, Vanessa and Clive Bell, Adrian Stephen, Duncan Grant, J. M. Keynes, Saxon Sydney-Turner, Lytton Strachey, Roger Fry, E. M. Forster, and Desmond and Molly MacCarthy. The members met, dined, read, and listened to memoirs. A few of the memoirs were later published as they were read to the group, but most were less formal and remained unfinished drafts. The group continued for thirty-six years, until 1956. Its membership changed slowly over the years as original members died or left the group and new members joined. When it disbanded, only four of the original members remained. See also Quentin Bell, *Virginia Woolf,* I, p. 83.

102. "22 Hyde Park Gate," in *Moments of Being,* pp. 142-155.

103. "Old Bloomsbury," in *Moments of Being,* pp. 159-179.

104. VW/EMS, Feb. 2, 1932.

105. *Moments of Being,* p. 147.

106. Ibid., p. 155.

107. *A Writer's Diary,* p. 34; *Moments of Being,* p. 140.

108. *Moments of Being,* p. 160.

109. VSB/LW, Sept. 19, Sept. 26, Sept. 27, and Sept. 29, 1913.

110. See Suzanne Henig's review of Quentin Bell's *Virginia Woolf* in *Virginia Woolf Quarterly,* I, no. 2 (Winter 1973), 55-69.

111. VW/EMS, Aug. 8, 1930.

112. Quentin Bell, *Virginia Woolf,* I, pp. 75-80.

113. *Moments of Being,* p. 144.

114. Ibid., p. 185.

115. Brian Hill, *Julia Margaret Cameron: A Victorian Family Portrait* (New York, 1973), p. 188; Quentin Bell, *Virginia Woolf,* I, p. 73.

116. VW/VD, Aug. 1, 1924.

117. Hill, *Julia Margaret Cameron,* p. 188.

118. VW/VSB, May 4, 1934.


Chapter 8: The Past That Lay on the Future


1. LS/JJS, Oct. 10, 1883.

2. LS/JJS, Apr. 13, 1884.

3. OW/ER, Mar. 29, 1941.

4. VW/EMS, June 28, 1932.

5. SDH/JJS, ca. Feb. 16, 1882.

6. LS/JJS, Apr. 9, 1882.

7. Ibid.

8. Vanessa Bell, *Notes on Virginia's Childhood* (New York, 1974), unpaged.

9. SDH/JJS, Apr. 13, 1884.

10. AS/VSB, Sept. 29, 1944.

11. Heinz Werner and Bernard Kaplan, *Symbol Formation* (New York, 1963), pp. 40-44.

12. *Moments of Being,* ed., Jeanne Schulkind (Brighton, 1976), pp. 64, 66-67.

13. VW/EMS, Sept. 24, 1934.

14. *Moments of Being,* p. 122.

15. VW/VSB, Aug. 10, 1908, in Nicolson and Trautmann, eds., *The Letters of Virginia Woolf,* I, *1888-1912* (New York, 1975), pp. 348-349.

16. *Moments of Being,* pp. 72-73, 93.

17. Vanessa Bell, *Notes on Virginia's Childhood.*

18. LS/JJS, Apr. 15, 1887.

19. LS/JJS, Apr. 17, 1887.

20. *Moments of Being,* pp. 67, 122.

21. VW/VSB, Dec. 25, 1909, in Nicolson and Trautmann, *Letters,* I, pp. 414-415.

22. *Moments of Being,* pp. 29, 78-79.

23. Located in the Berg Collection.

24. LS/JJS, Apr. 13, 1884.

25. Vanessa Bell, *Notes on Virginia's Childhood.*

26. Jean Piaget, *Play, Dreams and Imitation in Childhood* (New York, 1962); Heinz Werner, *Comparative Psychology of Mental Development* (New York, 1964).

27. *Moments of Being,* p. 78.

28. *A Writer's Diary,* p. 100.

Chapter 9: Imagination and Language

1. Quentin Bell, *Virginia Woolf: A Biography,* 2 vols. (New York, 1972), I, p. 33.

2. Margaret Lane, *The Brontë Story* (London, 1969); F. A. Ratchford, *The Brontës' Web of Childhood* (New York, 1941).

3. Vanessa Bell, *Notes on Virginia's Childhood* (New York, 1974), unpaged.

4. Virginia Woolf, "Memoir," typescript, a continuation of the 1939-1940 memoir entitled "A Sketch of the Past," included with Sussex documents designated MH/A 5a.

5. Virginia Woolf, Diary (Berg), typescript carbon, original unlocated, Sept. 14, 1906-April 25, 1909, entry of April, 1909.

6. VW/VSB, May 22 and May 25, 1927; VSB/VW, May 11, 1927.

7. Virginia Woolf, Autobiographical fragment, "The tea table was the centre of Victorian family life," (holograph, Berg, dated Jan. 28, 1940).

8. There is a large psychological literature on these topics. See especially: Harry Stack Sullivan, *The Interpersonal Theory of Psychiatry* (New York, n.d.), pp. 110-125; Heinz Werner and Bernard Kaplan, *Symbol Formation* (New York, 1963), pp. 72 ff.; Rene A. Spitz, "Anaclitic Depression," in *Psychoanalytic Study of the Child,* II, (New York, 1946), pp. 313-342; Donald L. Burnham, et. al., *Schizophrenia and the Need-Fear Dilemma* (New York, 1969), pp. 15-66; Erik H. Erikson, *Childhood and Society* (New York, 1950); Anna Freud and Dorothy Burlingham, "War and Children" in Toby Talbot, *The World of the Child* (New York, 1968), pp. 329-348; John Bowlby, "Grief and Mourning in Infancy and Early Childhood," in *Psychoanalytic Study of the Child,* XV (New York, 1960).

9. VW/VSB, Aug. 14, 1908, in Nicolson and Trautmann, eds., *The Letters of Virginia Woolf,* I, *1888-1912* (New York, 1975), pp. 354-355; VSB/CB, June 25, 1910.

10. Quentin Bell, *Virginia Woolf,* I, pp. 25-26; *Moments of Being,* ed., Jeanne Schulkind (Brighton, 1976), p. 78.

11. Quentin Bell, *Virginia Woolf,* I, pp. 22-23.

12. LS/JJS, Apr. 14, 1884.

13. LS/JJS, Apr. 14, 1887; Oct. 10, 1891.

14. VW/VSB, Aug. 14, 1908, in Nicolson and Trautmann, *Letters,* I, pp. 354-355.

15. VW/VSB, Aug. 20, 1908, in Nicolson and Trautmann, *Letters,* I, pp. 357-358.

16. Quentin Bell, *Virginia Woolf,* I, p. 25.

17. *Moments of Being,* p. 29.

18. Vanessa Bell, *Notes on Virginia's Childhood.*

19. Quentin Bell, *Virginia Woolf,* I, p. 25; VW/VSB, Feb. 25, 1918; *Moments of Being,* pp. 78-79.

20. *Moments of Being,* p. 79.

21. VW/VSB, Feb. 25, 1918.

22. Ibid.

23. VSB/VW, Aug. 25, 1908.

24. VSB/VW, June 25, 1910; May 11 and May 19, 1927.

25. VW/VSB, Aug. 7, 1908, in Nicolson and Trautmann, *Letters,* I, pp. 342-344.

26. VW/VSB, Aug. 10, 1908, in Nicolson and Trautmann, *Letters,* I, pp. 348-349.

27. VW/VSB, Aug. 19, 1909, in Nicolson and Trautmann, *Letters,* I, pp. 408-410.

28. *Moments of Being,* p. 84.

29. VSB/VW, Aug. 21, 1908.

30. Jean O. Love, *Worlds in Consciousness* (Berkeley and Los Angeles, 1970), pp. 52-62.

31. VW/VD, Oct. 2, 1903, in Nicolson and Trautmann, *Letters,* I, pp. 97-98.

32. *To the Lighthouse,* pp. 95-100.

33. *Mrs. Dalloway,* pp. 231-232.

34. *To the Lighthouse,* pp. 223-227.

35. Virginia Woolf, "Friendships Gallery" (Berg), typescript, 1907, p. 14.

36. Virginia Woolf, *A Cockney's Farming Experiences* and *The Experiences of a Pater-familias* (San Diego, 1972).

37. *Moments of Being,* p. 95.

38. Vanessa Bell, *Notes on Virginia's Childhood.*

39. LS/JJS, Feb. 2, 1893.

40. LS/JJS, July 27, 1893.

41. LS/JJS, July 29, 1893.


Chapter 10: Matters of Health and Art

1. Leonard Woolf, *Beginning Again* (New York, 1963), p. 76.

2. LS/JJS, Nov. 16, 1885.

3. LS/JJS, Apr. 10, 1893.

4. Gordon Allport, *Pattern and Growth in Personality* (New York, 1961), pp. 110 ff.; Gardner Murphy, *Personality* (New York, 1947), pp. 479 ff.

5. See also James Naremore, *The World Without a Self* (New Haven, 1973).

6. Jean Piaget, *The Origins of Intelligence in Children* (New York,

1963), pp. 19-20; *Play, Dreams and Imitation in Childhood,* pp. 161 ff.

7. Quentin Bell, *Virginia Woolf: A Biography,* 2 vols. (New York, 1972), I, p. 40; *Moments of Being,* ed., Jeanne Schulkind (Brighton, 1976), pp. 33, 40, 91-95.

8. Quentin Bell, *Virginia Woolf,* I, pp. 44-45; Virginia Woolf, "Memoir," typescript, a continuation of the 1939-1940 memoir entitled "A Sketch of the Past," included with Sussex documents designated MH/A 5a; *Moments of Being,* p. 45.

9. *Moments of Being,* p. 45.

10. Ibid., p. 84; Quentin Bell, *Virginia Woolf,* I, p. 55.

11. *Moments of Being,* p. 34.

12. Ibid., p. 39.

13. Ibid., p. 84.

14. Ibid., pp. 84, 94-95.

15. Quentin Bell, *Virginia Woolf,* I, p. 45.

16. Virginia Woolf, "Memoir," typescript, a continuation of the 1939-1940 memoir entitled "A Sketch of the Past," included with Sussex documents designated MH/A 5a.

17. Virginia Woolf, Diary, 1897; Quentin Bell, *Virginia Woolf,* I, p. 57.

18. Virginia Woolf, Diary, 1897; Quentin Bell, *Virginia Woolf,* I, pp. 52-54.

19. Virginia Woolf, Autobiographical fragment, "The tea table was the centre of Victorian family life," (holograph, Berg, dated Jan. 28, 1940).

20. I have identified Virginia Woolf's "symptoms" during her 1895-1897 breakdown principally from her 1897 diary and her autobiographical memoirs of 1908 and 1939-1940, which contain some of her recollections of the breakdown. I have also relied on Quentin Bell's biography of Mrs. Woolf.

21. *Beginning Again,* p. 77.

22. Quentin Bell, *Virginia Woolf,* I, p. 45; Virginia Woolf, "Memoir," typescript, a continuation of the 1939-1940 memoir entitled "A Sketch of the Past," included with Sussex documents designated MH/A 5a.

23. *Moments of Being,* p. 92.

24. VW/EMS, Sep. 24, 1934.

25. Virginia Woolf, *A Writer's Diary* (New York, 1953), p. 165.

26. Clive Bell, *Old Friends* (London, 1956), pp. 92-118; Ann Stephen, in Joan Russell Noble, ed., *Recollections of Virginia Woolf* (London, 1972), pp. 15-17; Leonard Woolf, *Beginning Again,* pp. 30-31.

27. *Moments of Being,* pp. 92-93.

28. Virginia Woolf, Diary, Sept. 14, 1906-Apr. 25, 1909, entries of Sept., 1908.


Chapter 11: Matters of Love and Death

1. VSB/VW, May 16, 1909; July 5 and July 17, 1910.

2. Quentin Bell, *Virginia Woolf: A Biography,* 2 vols. (New York, 1972), II, p. 6.

3. Virginia Woolf, *A Room of One's Own* (New York, 1953), pp. 165-176.

4. Quentin Bell, *Virginia Woolf,* II, pp. 116-119; Nigel Nicolson, *Portrait of a Marriage* (New York, 1973), pp. 200-208.

5. Virginia Woolf, Diary, 1897; Quentin Bell, *Virginia Woolf,* I, p. 47.

6. VW/VD, Apr. 24, 1905, in Nicolson and Trautmann, eds., *The Letters of Virginia Woolf,* I, *1888-1912* (New York, 1975), pp. 186-188.

7. Quentin Bell, *Virginia Woolf,* II, p. 118.

8. Ibid., p. 119.

9. Quentin Bell, *Virginia Woolf,* I, pp. 70 ff.; *Moments of Being,* ed., Jeanne Schulkind (Brighton, 1976), pp. 121 ff.

10. *Mrs. Dalloway,* p. 281.

11. *Moments of Being,* pp. 127-137.

12. Virginia Woolf, "Leslie Stephen," in *The Captain's Death Bed* (London, 1950), pp. 67-73.

13. *Moments of Being,* p. 129; Quentin Bell, *Virginia Woolf,* I, p. 74.

14. *Moments of Being,* pp. 154-155; Quentin Bell, *Virginia Woolf,* I, pp. 73-78.

15. Joanne Trautmann, *The Jessamy Brides: The Friendship of Virginia Woolf and V. Sackville-West* (University Park, Pa., 1973), pp. 2, 17; Quentin Bell, *Virginia Woolf,* I, pp. 60-61.

16. VW/MV, Nov. 30 and Dec. 11, 1904, in Nicolson and Trautmann, *Letters,* I, pp. 161; 165-167.

17. VW/MV, Apr. 1907, in Nicolson and Trautmann, *Letters,* I, p. 292.

18. Manuscript dated 1904, and designated MH/A 10, Sussex University.

19. Quentin Bell, *Virginia Woolf,* I, p. 82; VD/VSB, June 16, 1942.

20. VW/VD, Feb. 1904, in Nicolson and Trautmann, *Letters,* I, p. 127.

21. Virginia Woolf, "Friendships Gallery" (Berg), typescript, 1907; VW/VD, Nov. 21, 1904 and Apr. 24, 1905, in Nicolson and Trautmann, *Letters,* I, pp. 156-158, 186-188.

22. VW/VD, June 30 (?), 1903, in Nicolson and Trautmann, *Letters,* I, pp. 82-83.

23. VW/VD, Nov. 10, Nov. 11, Nov. 14, Nov. 21, Nov. 26, and Dec. 6, 1904; May 1905, in Nicolson and Trautmann, *Letters,* I, pp. 154-158, 163-164, 189-190; Quentin Bell, *Virginia Woolf,* I, p. 194.

24. Quentin Bell, *Virginia Woolf,* I, p. 175.

25. VW/VD, Oct./Nov. 1902 and June 30 (?), 1903, in Nicolson and Trautmann, *Letters,* I, pp. 60, 82-83.

26. VW/VD, Mar. 1903, in Nicolson and Trautmann, *Letters,* I, p. 71.

27. VW/VD, late Sept. 1903, in Nicolson and Trautmann, *Letters,* I, pp. 95-96.

28. VW/VD, Oct./Nov., 1903, in Nicolson and Trautmann, *Letters,* I, pp. 101-102.

29. VW/VD, June (?) 30, 1903, in Nicolson and Trautmann, *Letters,* I, pp. 82-83.

30. VW/VD, Dec. 28, 1903, in Nicolson and Trautmann, *Letters,* I, p. 119.

31. VW/VD, late Sept., 1903, in Nicolson and Trautmann, *Letters,* I, pp. 95-96.

32. VD/VSB, June 16, 1942.

33. VW/VD, Dec. 2 and Dec. 6, 1936.

34. VW/VD, Nov. 30 (?), 1906, and Jan. 3, 1907, in Nicolson and Trautmann, *Letters,* I, pp. 254, 275-276.

35. VW/VD, Aug. 10, 1908, in Nicolson and Trautmann, *Letters,* I, pp. 348-349.

36. *A Writer's Diary,* p. 135; *Moments of Being,*. p. 81; Helen Storm Corso, "*To the Lighthouse:* Death, Mourning, and Transfiguration," *Literature and Psychology,* 21, 115-131.

37. *Moments of Being,* p. 120.

38. Ibid., p. 135.

Chapter 12: The Enemies

1. Frederic Maitland, *The Life and Letters of Leslie Stephen* (London, 1906), p. 471.

2. Virginia Woolf, Autobiographical fragment, "The tea table was the centre of Victorian family life" (holograph, Berg, dated Jan. 28, 1940).

3. VW/VD, early Oct., 1903, in Nigel Nicolson and Joanne Trautmann, eds., *The Letters of Virginia Woolf, I, 1888-1912* (New York, 1975), pp. 98-99.

4. Quentin Bell, *Virginia Woolf: A Biography,* 2 vols. (New York, 1972), I, p. 85; VW/VD, June (?) 4, 1903, in Nicolson and Trautmann, *Letters,* I, pp. 78-79.

5. VW/VD, Autumn, 1903, in Nicolson and Trautmann, *Letters,* I, p. 107.

6. Hester Ritchie Fuller and Violet Hammersley, *Thackeray's Daughter* (Dublin, 1951), p. 156.

7. Maitland, *Life and Letters,* p. 487.

8. VW/VD, Oct./Nov., 1902; Apr. 28, 1903; Feb. 1904; in Nicolson and Trautmann, *Letters,* I, pp. 61-62, 74-75, 124.

9. VW/VD, Jan. 25, 1904, in Nicolson and Trautmann, *Letters,* I, pp. 122-123.

10. VW/VD, Dec. 31, 1903, in Nicolson and Trautmann, *Letters,* I, pp. 119-120.

11. VW/VD, Autumn, 1903; Dec. 25, Dec. 31, Dec. (?), 1903; Jan., 1904, in Nicolson and Trautmann, *Letters,* I, pp. 105, 118, 119-120, 121.

12. VW/VD, Dec. (?), 1903, in Nicolson and Trautmann, *Letters,* I, p. 117.

13. VW/VD, Oct. 2, 1903, in Nicolson and Trautmann, *Letters,* I, pp. 97-98.

14. VW/VD, late Sept., 1903, in Nicolson and Trautmann, *Letters,* I, pp. 95-96; Quentin Bell, *Virginia Woolf,* I, p. 95.

15. VW/VD, end Sept., early Oct., 1903; Jan., 1904; Mar. 8, 1904, in Nicolson and Trautmann, *Letters,* I, pp. 96-97, 98-99, 120, 132.

16. Quentin Bell, *Virginia Woolf,* I, p. 96.

17. See especially *The Waves,* p. 109.

18. VW/VD, Dec. 31, 1903, in Nicolson and Trautmann, *Letters,* I, pp. 119-120.

19. VW/VD, Oct. 2, 1903, in Nicolson and Trautmann, *Letters,* I, pp. 97-98.

20. "Mausoleum Book" in the British Museum, entry dated Nov. 14, 1903; Noel Annan, *The Thought and Character of Leslie Stephen in Relation to His Time* (Cambridge, Mass., 1952), pp. 93, 297.

21. *Moments of Being,* ed., Jeanne Schulkind (Brighton, 1976), p. 114.

22. Quentin Bell, *Virginia Woolf,* I, p. 85.

23. VW/VD, June 8, 1903; see also VW/VD Oct. 2, Oct./Nov., Autumn, 1903, in Nicolson and Trautmann, *Letters,* I, pp. 79-80; see also pp. 97-98, 102, 108.

24. VW/VD, Jan. 25 and July 7 (?), 1903, in Nicolson and Trautmann, *Letters,* I, pp. 65-66, 85.

25. VW/VD, Apr. 10, 1903, in Nicolson and Trautmann, *Letters,* I, pp. 65-66, 72-73.

26. VW/VD, July 7 (?), 1903, in Nicolson and Trautmann, *Letters,* I, p. 85.

27. VW/VD, Feb., 1903, in Nicolson and Trautmann, *Letters,* I, pp. 69-70.

28. Quentin Bell, *Virginia Woolf,* I, p. 85.

29. VW/VD, June, 1903, in Nicolson and Trautmann, *Letters,* I, p. 81.

30. VW/VD, June, 1903, in Nicolson and Trautmann, *Letters,* I, pp. 81-82.

31. VW/VD, Dec. 12, 1902, in Nicolson and Trautmann, *Letters,* I, p. 62.

32. VW/VD, late Sept., 1903, in Nicolson and Trautmann, *Letters,* I, p. 95.

33. VW/VD, Feb. (?), 1904, in Nicolson and Trautmann, *Letters,* I, p. 125.

34. LS/JJS, Jan. 29, 1893.

35. VSB/VW, Aug. 11, 1909.

36. VW/VD, May 4, 1903, in Nicolson and Trautmann, *Letters,* I, pp. 75-76.

37. VW/VD, Dec., 1903, in Nicolson and Trautmann, *Letters,* I, p. 114.

38. VW/VD, June 8, 1903, in Nicolson and Trautmann, *Letters,* I, pp. 79-80.

39. VW/VD, Jan. and Feb., 1904 (four letters), in Nicolson and Trautmann, *Letters,* I, pp. 121, 123, 124, 125; Quentin Bell, *Virginia Woolf,* I, p. 85.

40. VW/VD, Mar. 31, 1904, in Nicolson and Trautmann, *Letters,* I, pp. 136-137.

41. VW/VD, Feb. 28 and Mar. 8, 1904, in Nicolson and Trautmann, *Letters,* I, pp. 130, 132.

42. VW/VD, Mar., 1904, in Nicolson and Trautmann, *Letters,* I, p. 133.

43. VW/VD, Mar., 1904, in Nicolson and Trautmann, *Letters,* I, pp. 135-136.

44. Virginia Woolf, Diary (Berg), entry dated July 13, 1918.

45. VW/VD, Mar. 4, 1904, in Nicolson and Trautmann, *Letters,* I, pp. 130-131.

46. *A Writer's Diary,* p. 135.

47. VW/VD, Mar., 1904, in Nicolson and Trautmann, *Letters,* I, p. 133.

48. VW/VD, Feb. 28, 1904, in Nicolson and Trautmann, *Letters,* I, p. 130.

49. VW/VD, Mar., 1904, in Nicolson and Trautmann, *Letters,* I, p. 133.

50. VW/VD, Mar., 1904, in Nicolson and Trautmann, *Letters,* I,

pp. 135-136.

51. VW/VD, Mar. 31, 1904, in Nicolson and Trautmann, *Letters,* I, pp. 136-137.

52. VW/VD, May 6 (?), 1904, in Nicolson and Trautmann, *Letters,* I, pp. 139-140.

53. Quentin Bell, *Virginia Woolf,* I, pp. 89-90, 193.

54. Ibid., p. 89.

55. Leonard Woolf, *Beginning Again,* pp. 148-166; VW/VD, Sept. 26, Sept. 30, Oct. 24, Oct. 30, Nov. 8, Nov. 10, and Nov. 11, 1904, in Nicolson and Trautmann, *Letters,* I, pp. 143, 144, 146, 147-148, 153, 154, 154-155.

56. Leonard Woolf, *Beginning Again,* pp. 148-166; Quentin Bell, *Virginia Woolf,* I, p. 90.

57. Leonard Woolf, *Beginning Again,* pp. 148-166.

58. VW/VD, Sept. 22 (?), 1904, in Nicolson and Trautmann, *Letters,* I, pp. 142-143.

59. VW/VD, Sept. 30, 1904, in Nicolson and Trautmann, *Letters,* I, p. 144.

60. Quentin Bell, *Virginia Woolf,* I, p. 194.

61. Ibid., p. 91.

62. VW/VD, Oct. 24, 1904, in Nicolson and Trautmann, *Letters,* I, pp. 146-147.

63. VW/VD, Nov., 1904, in Nicolson and Trautmann, *Letters,* I, pp. 151-152.

64. VSB/VW, Oct. 25, 1904.

65. VW/VD, Nov., 1904, in Nicolson and Trautmann, *Letters,* I, pp. 151-152.

66. Ibid.; Quentin Bell, *Virginia Woolf,* I, p. 91.

67. VSB/VW, Oct. 30, 1904.

68. VSB/VW, Dec. 5, 1904.

69. VW/VD, Oct. 24, 1904, in Nicolson and Trautmann, *Letters,* I, pp. 146-147.

70. VW/VD, Oct. 22, 1904, in Nicolson and Trautmann, *Letters,* I, pp. 144-145.

71. VSB/VW, Oct. 24, 1904.

72. VSB/VW, Dec. 7, 1904.

73. VSB/VW, Oct. 22, 1904.

74. VSB/VW, Oct. 24, 1904.

75. VSB/VW, Oct. 25, 1904.

76. VW/VD, Oct. 30, 1904, in Nicolson and Trautmann, *Letters,* I, pp. 147-148.

77. VW/VD, Sept. 30, 1904, in Nicolson and Trautmann, *Letters,* I, p. 144.

78. VSB/VW, Oct. 25 and Oct. 28, 1904.

79. VSB/VW, Nov. 22, 1904.

80. VSB/VW, Oct. 25, 1904.

81. Quentin Bell, *Virginia Woolf,* I, p. 91.

82. George M. Beard, *A Practical Treatise on Nervous Exhaustion* (New York, 1880); L. E. Cole, *Understanding Abnormal Behavior* (Scranton, Pa., 1970), pp. 163 ff.; VSB/VW June 23, 1909.

83. VSB/VW, Nov. 4, 1904.

84. VSB/VW, Apr. 13, 1905.

85. VSB/VW, Oct. 21, 1904 and Mar. 31, 1905.

86. VSB/VW, Apr. 13, 1906.

87. VSB/VW, Dec. 5, 1905.

88. VSB/VW, Oct. 22, 1904.

89. VSB/VW, Oct. 30, 1904.

90. VSB/VW, Dec. 5, 1904.

91. VSB/VW, Oct. 22, 1904.

92. VSB/VW, Apr. 15, 1905.

93. VSB/VW, Dec. 7, 1904.

94. VSB/VW, Mar. 31, 1905.

95. VSB/VW, Apr. 14, 1906.

96. VSB/VW, Oct. 24, 1904.

97. VSB/VW, Dec. 7, 1904; Apr. 13 and Apr. 15, 1906; Aug. 12, 1907.

98. VSB/VW, Oct. 25, 1904.

99. VSB/VW, Nov. 20, 1907.

100. VSB/VW, Oct. 25, 1904.

101. VSB/VW, Dec. 4, 1904.

102. VSB/VW, Apr. 17, 1906.

103. VSB/VW, Apr. 18/19, 1906; Feb. 13, 1907.

104. VSB/VW, Mar. 31, 1905.

105. VW/VD, Apr. 5, 1905, in Nicolson and Trautmann, *Letters,* I, pp. 183-185.

106. VW/VD, Apr. 24, 1905, in Nicolson and Trautmann,

*Letters,* I, pp. 186-188.

107. VW/VD, Apr. 5, 1905, in Nicolson and Trautmann, *Letters,* I, pp. 183-185.

108. VW/VD, Apr. 10, 1905, in Nicolson and Trautmann, *Letters,* I, pp. 185-186.

109. Quentin Bell, *Virginia Woolf,* I, pp. 112 ff.

110. (Sussex University), document designated MH/A 13a.

111. VD/VSB, May 19, 1941.

112. Quentin Bell, *Virginia Woolf,* I, p. 109; VD/VSB, June 11, 1941; AS/CB, Oct. 24, 1906.

113. AS/CB, Oct. 24, 1906.

114. VW/VD, Nov. 22, Nov. 23, Nov. 25, Nov. 26 (?), Nov. 28 (?), Nov. 29, Nov. 30, Dec. 1 (?), Dec. 2, Dec. 4 (?), Dec. 5, Dec. 8, Dec. 10, Dec. 12, Dec. 13 (?), Dec. 14 (?), Dec. 16, and Dec. 17, 1906, in Nicolson and Trautmann, pp. 249-264.

115. *A Writer's Diary,* p. 144.

116. *Moments of Being,* p. 118.

117. Nicolson and Trautmann, *Letters,* I, p. 266.

118. VW/VD, Dec. 5, Dec. 12 and Dec. 13 (?), 1906, in Nicolson and Trautmann, *Letters,* I, pp. 257-258, 260, 261.

119. VW/VD, Dec. 10 and Dec. 12, 1906, in Nicolson and Trautmann, *Letters,* I, pp. 259, 260.

120. VSB/VW, June 23, 1909.

121. VSB/VW, July 24, 1909.

122. VW/VSB, Aug. 12, 1908, in Nicolson and Trautmann, *Letters,* I, p. 352.

123. Quentin Bell, *Virginia Woolf,* I, pp. 132-140.

124. Ibid., p. 134.

125. Ibid., pp. 89-90; VSB/VW, July 29, 1910.

126. VW/VD, Nov. 11, 1904, in Nicolson and Trautmann, *Letters,* I, pp. 154-155.

127. LW/JWH, Mar. 17, 1915.

128. Quentin Bell, *Virginia Woolf,* I, p. 199; II, p. 39.

129. Ibid., pp. 105-107.

# Selected References

Allport, Gordon. *Pattern and Growth in Personality.* New York: Holt, Rinehart, and Winston, 1961.

Annan, Noel. *Leslie Stephen: His Thought and Character in Relationship to His Time.* Cambridge, Mass.: Harvard University Press, 1952.

Bartlett, H. F. C. *Remembering.* Cambridge: Cambridge University Press, 1967.

Bazin, Nancy Topping. *Virginia Woolf and the Androgynous Vision.* New Brunswick, N.J.: Rutgers University Press, 1973.

Beard, George M. *A Practical Treatise on Nervous Exhaustion.* 5th ed. New York: Treat, 1905. First published, 1880.

Bell, Clive. *Old Friends.* London: Chatto and Windus, 1956.

Bell, Quentin. *Bloomsbury.* New York: Basic Books, 1969.

Bell, Quentin. *Virginia Woolf: A Biography.* 2 vols. New York: Harcourt, Brace, Jovanovich, 1972.

Bell, Vanessa. *Notes on Virginia's Childhood.* New York: Frank Hallman, 1974.

Bicknell, John W. "Virginia Woolf in Homage and Understanding," a review of *Virginia Woolf,* by Quentin Bell. *Journal of Modern Literature,* 3, no. 1 (Feb. 1973), pp. 108-115; see note, p. 000.

Blackstone, Bernard. *Virginia Woolf: A Commentary.* New York: Harcourt, Brace, 1949.

Bowlby, John. "Grief and Mourning in Infancy and Early Childhood." In *Psychoanalytic Study of the Child,* XV. New York: International Universities Press, 1960.

Buckley, Jerome Hamilton. *The Victorian Temper,* New York: Random House, 1964.

## Selected References

Cameron, Julia Margaret. *Victorian Photographs of Famous Men and Fair Women.* London: Hogarth, 1926.

Cassirer, Ernst. *Language and Myth.* Trans. Suzanne Langer. New York: Dover, 1946.

Cassirer, Ernst. *Philosophy of Symbolic Forms.* Trans. Ralph Manheim. Vol. II: *Mythical Thought.* New Haven: Yale University Press, 1955.

Cole, L. E. *Understanding Abnormal Behavior.* Scranton, Pa.: Chandler, 1970.

Corso, Helen Storm. "To the Lighthouse: Death, Mourning and Transfiguration." *Literature and Psychology,* 21, 115-131.

Edel, Leon, ed. *Henry James Letters,* I. Cambridge, Mass.: Harvard, Belknap, 1974.

Edel, Leon, ed. *The Selected Letters of Henry James.* New York: Farrar, Straus, 1955.

Erikson, Erik. *Childhood and Society.* New York: Norton, 1950.

Forster, E. M. *Virginia Woolf.* New York: Harcourt, Brace, 1942.

Freud, Anna and Dorothy Burlingham. "War and Children." In *The World of the Child,* by Toby Talbot. New York: Doubleday, 1968.

Fuller, Hester Ritchie and Violet Hammersley. *Thackeray's Daughter.* Dublin: W. J. Pollock, 1951.

Gernsheim, Helmut. *Julia Margaret Cameron.* London: Fountain Press, 1948.

Gittings, Robert. *Young Thomas Hardy.* Boston: Little, Brown, 1975.

Haskell, R. H. "Mental Deficiency Over a Hundred Years: A Brief Historical Sketch of Trends in this Field." *American Journal of Psychiatry,* 100, pp. 107-118.

Heilbrun, Carolyn G. *Toward a Recognition of Androgyny.* New York: Harper and Row, 1974.

Henig, Suzanne. "Book Review, Quentin Bell: Virginia Woolf." *Virginia Woolf. Quarterly,* I, no. 2 (Winter, 1973), 55-69.

Hill, Brian. *Julia Margaret Cameron: A Victorian Family Portrait.* New York: St. Martin's, 1973.

Holroyd, Michael. *Lytton Strachey and the Bloomsbury Group.* London: William Heinemann, Ltd., 1968.

Holtby, Winifred. *Virginia Woolf.* London: Weshard, 1932.

Houghton, Walter E. *The Victorian Frame of Mind.* New Haven: Yale, 1957.

Johnstone, J. K. *The Bloomsbury Group.* New York: Farrar, Straus, 1963.

Kraepilin, Emil. *Clinical Psychiatry; a Textbook for Students and Physicians.* Abstracted and adapted from the 6th German ed. of author's *Lehrbuch der Psychiatrie,* by A. Ross Diefendarf. New York: MacMillan, 1927. First edition published, 1883.

Kwant, Remy. *Phenomenology of Language.* Pittsburgh: Duquesne University Press, 1965.

Lane, Margaret. *The Brontë Story.* London: Collins-Fontana, 1969.

Lee, Sidney. "Sir Leslie Stephen." Entry, *Dictionary of National Biography.* Oxford: Oxford University Press, 1912.

Love, Jean O. *Worlds in Consciousness: Mythopoetic Thought in the Novels of Virginia Woolf.* Berkeley and Los Angeles: University of California Press, 1970.

MacCarthy, Desmond. *Leslie Stephen.* Cambridge: Cambridge University Press, 1937.

Maitland, Frederic W. *The Life and Letters of Leslie Stephen.* London: Duckworth, 1906.

Marden, Herbert. *Feminism and Art: A Study of Virginia Woolf.* Chicago: University of Chicago Press, 1968.

Murphy, Gardner. *Personality: A Biosocial Approach to Origins and Structure.* New York: Basic Books, 1947.

Naremore, James. *The World Without a Self.* New Haven: Yale University Press, 1973.

Nicolson, Nigel and Joanne Trautmann, eds. *The Letters of Virginia Woolf.* Vol. I: *1888-1912* (1975); Vol. II: *1912-1922* (1976). New York: Harcourt, Brace, Jovanovich, 1975-1976.

Nicolson, Nigel. *Portrait of a Marriage.* New York: Athaneum, 1973.

Noble, Joan Russell. *Recollections of Virginia Woolf by Her Contemporaries.* London: Peter Owen, 1972.

Piaget, Jean. *The Child's Conception of the World.* Trans. Jean and Andrew Tomlinson. London: Routledge and Kegan Paul, 1929.

Piaget, Jean. *The Construction of Reality in the Child.* Trans. Margaret Cook. New York: Basic Books, 1954.

## Selected References

Piaget, Jean. *The Origins of Intelligence in Children.* New York: Norton, 1963.

Piaget, Jean. *Play, Dreams and Imitation in Childhood.* New York: Norton, 1962.

Pippett, Aileen. *The Moth and the Star.* New York: Viking, 1957.

Ratchford, F. A. *The Brontës' Web of Childhood.* New York: Columbia University Press, 1941.

Richter, Harvena. *Virginia Woolf: The Inward Voyage.* Princeton: Princeton University Press, 1970.

Roberts, R. E. "Virginia Woolf: 1882-1941." *Saturday Review of Literature,* 23 (Apr. 12, 1941), 12 f.

Rosen, Ephraim, et al. *Abnormal Psychology.* 2d ed. Philadelphia: W. B. Saunders, 1972.

Rosenbaum, S. P. *The Bloomsbury Group.* Toronto: University of Toronto Press, 1975.

Seguin, E. *Idiocy: and Its Treatment by the Physiological Method.* New York: Columbia Teachers College, 1907. First published, 1866.

Smyth, Ethel. *As Time Went On.* London: Longman, Green, 1936.

Smyth, Ethel. *Impressions That Remain.* New York: Knopf, 1946.

Spender, Stephen. *World Within a World.* London: Hamish Hamilton, 1951.

Spitz, Rene. "Anaclitic Depression." In *Psychoanalytic Study of the Child,* II. New York: International Universities Press, 1946.

Stephen, Leslie. *The Life of Sir James Fitzjames Stephen.* London: Smith, Elder, 1895.

Sullivan, Harry Stack. *The Interpersonal Theory of Psychiatry.* New York: Norton, 1953.

Szladits, Lola. "The Life, Character and Opinions of Flush, the Spaniel." *Bulletin of New York Public Library,* 74, no. 4 (April 1970), 211-218.

Trautmann, Joanne. *The Jessamy Brides: The Friendship of Virginia Woolf and V. Sackville-West.* University Park, Pa.: Pennsylvania State University Press, 1973.

Werner, Heinz. *Comparative Psychology of Mental Development.* New York: International Universities Press, 1964. First published, 1940.

Werner, Heinz and Bernard Kaplan. *Symbol Formation.* New York: Wylie, 1963.

Wilson, John Dover. *Leslie Stephen and Matthew Arnold as Critics of Wordsworth.* Cambridge: Cambridge University Press, 1939.

Woodring, Carl. *Virginia Woolf.* New York: Columbia University Press, 1966.

Woolf, Leonard. *Beginning Again: An Autobiography of the Years 1911 to 1918.* New York: Harcourt, Brace and World, 1963.

Woolf, Leonard. *Downhill All the Way: An Autobiography of the Years 1919-1939.* New York: Harcourt, Brace and World, 1967.

Woolf, Leonard. *Growing: An Autobiography of the Years 1904-1911.* London: Hogarth, 1961.

Woolf, Leonard. *Sowing: An Autobiography of the Years 1880 to 1904.* New York: Harcourt, Brace & Company, 1960.

Woolf, Leonard. *The Journey, Not the Arrival Matters: An Autobiography of the Years 1939 to 1969.* New York: Harcourt, Brace and World, 1969.

Woolf, Virginia. *A Cockney's Farming Experiences* and *The Experiences of a pater-familias.* San Diego: San Diego State University Press, 1972.

Woolf, Virginia. *A Room of One's Own.* New York: Harcourt, Brace, 1953.

Woolf, Virginia. *A Writer's Diary.* Ed. Leonard Woolf. New York: Harcourt, Brace, 1953.

Woolf, Virginia. *Between the Acts.* London: Hogarth, 1941.

Woolf, Virginia. *Contemporary Writers.* New York: Harcourt, Brace, 1965.

Woolf, Virginia. *Flush: A Biography.* London: Hogarth, 1933.

Woolf, Virginia. *Granite and Rainbow.* London: Hogarth, 1958.

Woolf, Virginia. *Jacob's Room.* London: Hogarth, 1960. First published, 1922.

Woolf, Virginia. *Kew Gardens.* London: Hogarth, 1919.

Woolf, Virginia. *Letter to a Young Poet.* London: Hogarth, 1932.

Woolf, Virginia. *Moments of Being.* Ed. Jeanne Schulkind. Brighton: Sussex University Press, 1976.

Woolf, Virginia. *Mrs. Dalloway.* New York: Harcourt, Brace, 1925.

Woolf, Virginia. *Night and Day.* London: Hogarth, 1960. First published, 1919.

Woolf, Virginia. *Orlando*. London: Hogarth, 1960. First published, 1928.

Woolf, Virginia. *Roger Fry: A Biography*. London: Hogarth, 1940.

Woolf, Virginia. *The Captain's Death Bed*. London: Hogarth, 1950.

Woolf, Virginia. *The Common Reader: First Series*. London: Hogarth, 1932.

Woolf, Virginia. *The Death of the Moth*. New York: Harcourt, Brace, 1942.

Woolf, Virginia. *The Moment*. London: Hogarth, 1952. First published, 1947.

Woolf, Virginia. *The Voyage Out*. London: Hogarth, 1957. First published, 1915.

Woolf, Virginia. *The Waves*. London: Hogarth, 1960. First published, 1931.

Woolf, Virginia. *The Years*. London: Hogarth, 1958. First published, 1937.

Woolf, Virginia. *Three Guineas*. London: Hogarth, 1938.

Woolf, Virginia. *To the Lighthouse*. New York: Harcourt, Brace, 1927.

Woolf, Virginia, and Lytton Strachey. *Letters*. New York: Harcourt, Brace, 1956.

Zink, David. *Leslie Stephen*. New York: Twayne Publishers, 1972.

# Index